Hitler's Nordic Ally?

Hitler's Nordic Ally?

*Finland and the Total War
1939–45*

Claes Johansen

Pen & Sword
MILITARY

First published in Great Britain in 2016 by
PEN AND SWORD MILITARY
an imprint of
Pen and Sword Books Ltd
47 Church Street
Barnsley
South Yorkshire S70 2AS

Copyright © Claes Johansen, 2016

ISBN 978 1 47385 314 0

The right of Claes Johansen to be identified
as the author of this work has been asserted by him
in accordance with the Copyright, Designs and Patents Act 1988.

A CIP record for this book is available from the British Library.

All rights reserved. No part of this book may be reproduced or transmitted
in any form or by any means, electronic or mechanical including
photocopying, recording or by any information storage and retrieval
system, without permission from the Publisher in writing.

Printed and bound in England by
CPI Group (UK) Ltd, Croydon, CR0 4YY

Typeset in Times by CHIC GRAPHICS

Pen & Sword Books Ltd incorporates the imprints of
Archaeology, Atlas, Aviation, Battleground, Discovery,
Family History, History, Maritime, Military, Naval, Politics,
Railways, Select, Social History, Transport, True Crime,
Claymore Press, Frontline Books, Leo Cooper, Praetorian Press,
Remember When, Seaforth Publishing and Wharncliffe.

For a complete list of Pen and Sword titles please contact
Pen and Sword Books Limited
47 Church Street, Barnsley, South Yorkshire, S70 2AS, England
E-mail: enquiries@pen-and-sword.co.uk
Website: www.pen-and-sword.co.uk

Front cover images courtesy of SA-Kuva

Contents

Introduction viii
Preface x
Pronunciation, abbreviations and important suffixes xv

PART ONE
The Winter War
30 November 1939 – 13 March 1940

I Prelude 3
II Two Armies 24
III The First Month of the War 41
IV The Second Month of the War 79
V The Third Month of the War 94
VI Endgame in March 104

PART TWO
The Interim Peace
13 March 1940 – 25 June 1941

I Little Country – What Now? 119
II Brothers in Arms 149
III The Finnish Choice 165

PART THREE
The Continuation War
25 June 1941 – 19 September 1944

I Reconquests and More 181
II Crossing the Border 211
III PoW Camps and Internment Camps for Civilians 228
IV Trench War 242
V The Volunteers 256
VI Peace Negotiations in Trouble 264
VII The Soviet Steamroller 272

PART FOUR
The Last War – And the Peace
(1944–1945)

I The Lapland War 303
II The Post War Era 306

APPENDICES

Appendix I:	Structure of a typical Soviet infantry division during the Winter War 311
Appendix II:	The deployment and tasks of the Red Army at the start of the Winter War 312
Appendix III:	Comparison between a typical Finnish and a typical Soviet infantry division at the outbreak of the Winter War 313
Appendix IV:	Order of battle for the Finnish Army at the outbreak of the Winter War 314
Appendix V:	Soviet and Finnish forces on the Karelian Isthmus on 1 February 1940 315
Appendix VI:	Soviet and Finnish forces at the Viipuri Front on 1 March 1940 316
Appendix VII:	The Soviet General Staff's operational plan for an isolated attack on Finland, made in the autumn of 1940 317
Appendix VIII:	Order of battle for the Soviet and Finnish forces along the border on 1 July 1941 (from south to north) 318
Appendix IX:	Mannerheim's Order of the Day 10 July 1941 (translated from Swedish, the language in which it was originally written) 320
Appendix X:	Order of battle for the Red Army before the offensive on the Karelian Isthmus, June 1944 321
Appendix XI:	Order of battle for the Finnish Army before the Soviet offensive in June 1944 322
Appendix XII:	President Ryti's letter to Adolf Hitler dated 26 June 1944 323

Appendix XIII:	Soviet and Finnish order of battle on the Karelian Isthmus before the fighting at Tali and Ihantala	324
Appendix XIV:	Finnish-German forces during the fighting at Tali and Ihantala	325
Appendix XV:	The Soviet Petsamo-Kirkenes offensive in October 1944	326

Notes 328
Place Names 340
Literature, Audio, Video and DVD 342
Maps 350
Index 357

Introduction

Please consider the following facts:

- Finland was the only nation with an elected and democratic government to fight on the German side in the Second World War.
- Both Churchill and Hitler anticipated that the Nordic countries would be a critical front in the Second World War due to the German war machine's dependency on iron ore from Kiruna in Sweden and nickel from Petsamo in Finland. Meanwhile, Stalin feared a German attack on Leningrad via Finnish territory.
- The Finnish Army was probably the most effective fighting force in all of the Second World War. Despite being made up of conscripts, small and poorly armed, it managed with practically no outside help to keep the mighty Red Army at bay for more than three months during the Winter War of 1939-40.
- The Finnish Front during the invasion of the Soviet Union constituted almost *one third of the length of the entire Russian Front*.
- The Finnish Army held the north-western sector during the German siege of Leningrad, but never actively attacked the city.
- Negotiations were held in Moscow at various points during these wars between Finnish politicians and Molotov and Stalin.
- Helsinki was one of only three capital cities of European belligerents that were never occupied by the enemy.
- Finland mainly fought the Russians in the Second World War, but made a separate peace with them in 1944 and subsequently fought the Germans instead.
- The devastating Soviet mass attack against the Finnish Army in the summer of 1944 involved the largest artillery assault of the entire Second World War theatre of operations up until this point. Nevertheless, the Finns eventually managed to halt the attack.
- Despite the Finnish cooperation with Nazi Germany, Finland itself remained so detached from Nazi ideology that local Jews were conscripted into the Finnish Army as regular soldiers and even had a field synagogue situated in close proximity to German camps.

Most English books on Finland in the Second World War concentrate on the brief but heroic Winter War and make very little mention of Finland's involvement in the remainder of the Second World War, fighting for more than three years alongside the Germans against the Soviet Union, and later on against Germany in the Lapland War. It is the intention of this book to portray in its entirety this extremely important, highly dramatic and often overlooked chapter of the Second World War to a broad, English-speaking audience, showing how the Finnish war effort was connected to the overall events of the era, and how a state of total war can affect a modern democratic society militarily, politically, diplomatically and on various levels of civilian life.

Preface

Though Finland is not a Scandinavian country, it *is* Nordic, and its historic and cultural connections with the other Nordic states mainly go through neighbouring Sweden. Quite simply, Finland constituted the Eastern part of Sweden until the Swedish defeat by Russia in the Finnish War 1808-9. Then followed more than a hundred years where the region was a grand duchy of Russia under the Tsar, with a high degree of self-government while maintaining Swedish legislation. It was not until December 1917 that the country declared its independence. The following year a bitter and violent civil war broke out between Red and White forces, as in Russia. However, in Finland the White side won, supported by German troops, while the Red side lost despite assistance from the new leaders in Russia.

During the following years the political conditions in Russia moved in the direction of a dictatorship, often with dire consequences for the common people. Due to the geographic proximity and the long common border, this development could be followed more closely in Finland than in most other West European countries. Meanwhile, the Finns themselves were busy trying to catch up with the hundred years of society development they had in some respects missed out on during the 'Russian Period'. The wounds from the Civil War were hard to heal, but in many ways Finland managed within a remarkably short span of time to bring their country up to a level close to that of the other Nordic states.

Economically and in welfare-related matters Finland was moving forward. Political extremism on both sides was kept in check through legislation. Even the leading victor of the Civil War, Commander-in-Chief of the White Guard Carl Gustaf Emil Mannerheim, managed to soften his reputation in some circles as 'the White Butcher' and become a more broadly appreciated figure. Many of those who had previously sympathised with the Reds had to admit to themselves that the defeat had been an unforeseeable blessing in disguise. Though the Whites had won the war, the society that was now developing was not far removed from the ideals hailed by moderates among the Reds.

But around the world weapons were rattled. Mussolini had come to power in Italy in 1922. Several East European states which, like Finland, had gained independence from Russia in the wake of the First World War were now run by Fascistoid governments who of course had a very strained relationship with the Soviet Union. The Spanish Civil War broke out and ended in a Fascist victory. Meanwhile, Hitler had become Germany's chancellor in 1933 and the following year its Führer, with ambitions to revive the super power confrontation of the First World War. The plan was to re-establish Germany's powerful position and win the seemingly inevitable gigantic clash between Nazism and Communism.

Geographic and resource-related factors caused Finland to be drawn into these events to such a degree that it resulted in no less than three wars during 1939-45. This led to big losses and tragedies, and on top of that the drama had an extra psychological dimension since Finland ended up fighting on 'the wrong side' for most of the war.

The last of the three wars, the Lapland War, was aimed at the German troops in the country, but Finland's main enemy during the Second World War was indisputably the Soviet Union. This placed the Finns in a unique and paradoxical situation for a western democracy. For a period of three years (1941-44), while Denmark and Norway were occupied by Germany, and Sweden remained neutral, the Finns found themselves involved in a military cooperation with Hitler's regime in Berlin. At the same time, the Finnish leaders tried in various ways to stay on good terms with the western powers. It was, in other words, a situation marked by complicated compromises and delicate balancing acts. That the Finns managed to come out of this nightmare as an independent nation was not down to one single factor but a whole string of circumstances, which are in practise inseparable.

As with the governments in several other small European nations during that period, the Finnish leaders were playing a double game while caught between the super powers. It was a situation that had been forced upon them, unquestionably against their will. Nevertheless, whilst trying desperately not to be crushed in the apocalyptic clash between the giants, the Finnish leaders were also cunningly trying to harvest whatever benefits might come their way in various shapes or forms (mostly territorial).

But it was even more complicated than that. Despite its close military relation with Nazi Germany, Finland by and large maintained internally its Nordic democratic form of governing. It was certainly never a Nazi puppet state. In fact, the sympathy for Nazi ideology among the broad Finnish population was practically non-existent. There was no National Socialist movement comparable even to the very small Nazi parties in the other Nordic states. Although there was a right wing extremist, Fascistoid party called the IKL (see list of abbreviation after this introduction), its size and its influence on the parliamentary processes were very limited. Likewise, anti-Semitism only existed to a very small degree, even during a period where more than 200,000 German troops were deployed in Finnish Lapland, and Finland's independence and security was thought to depend on what was described as a brotherhood-in-arms with Nazi Germany. The small

Jewish minority was treated like everyone else; for instance, its male members under a certain age were called up for military service.

Still, it cannot be denied that there existed among the Finnish upper class, particularly in business and academic circles, strong pro-German passions. Similar feelings inevitably had to be present among the higher-ranking officers, the overwhelming majority of whom had participated in the First World War on the German side in a special battalion made up of Finnish volunteers. So strong were these pro-German forces that their most significant hindrance at times was Marshal Mannerheim who, with his aristocratic, ultra-conservative views, was no admirer of the upstart Adolf Hitler, and who was not easily impressed by the German military, as he himself had fought against them as an officer in the Imperial Russian Army during the First World War.

Working in tandem with the abovementioned groups there were powerful organisations consisting of nationalist fantasists who dreamt about the creation of a Greater-Finland stretching east as far as the Urals, south into Estonia and even west a few kilometres into Sweden and Norway.

To sum it up: for those who mainly see the Second World War from the traditional Western Allied perspective, the history of Finland can seem at times a nearly unfathomable paradox, where easy solutions and explanations are few and far between.

Though the story of Finland's part in the Second World War is full of human, political and military drama, it has not been the subject of much literature outside of the country itself. This might have to do with the complexity of the aforementioned paradoxes, which may also partly explain why the first of the three Finnish conflicts during the Second World War, the Winter War, which lasted only three and a half months, is the one to which most attention has been paid internationally. This war is easier to understand politically, it fitted well into western Cold War perceptions, and it could without difficulty make for a simple and exciting heroes-and-villains narrative, a modern David and Goliath tale.

However, to investigate the issue raised by the title of this book one needs to look at what happened next. Unfortunately, a simple answer to the query of whether or not Finland was really an ally of Adolf Hitler is virtually impossible to give, if only for the fact that there is no fixed, established definition of the term 'alliance'; and even if there were, borderline cases would still exist and Finland would probably be one of them. Still, the question of what actually took place in Finland during those years, and what motivated it, remains. The purpose of this book is to familiarise the reader with the background story and then leave it up to him or her to decide which label seems appropriate for the role played by Finland at various stages during the Second World War.

Although I admire and respect the Finnish people very much, it has been important for me as an author not to fall into the trap of portraying the Finnish soldiers as super heroes or white-clad warrior angels, so often favoured by western writers dealing with this subject matter. The Finns, at the end of the day, are only human beings, too. They can get scared and run for their lives, make political mistakes, they can freeze in the winter, and some of them can act towards other humans in atrocious ways. I feel it would be wrong to hide any of this, even if it might sometimes go against the popular images that were created by western media during the Winter War, and which some people – Finns and others alike – can find it hard to release themselves from, even today. There certainly are some dark and criticisable sides to the Finnish conduct during the second of the three wars – known as the Continuation War – as you would expect in any country cooperating with Nazi Germany, whether of its own choice or of necessity in order to survive as a nation. And there are certainly instances where it is reasonable to distinguish sharply between the often secret and manipulative conduct of Finland's political leaders (whether justifiable or not) and the feelings and opinions among the broader population.

Before we start, a couple of practical circumstances need to be mentioned. First, there are the differences between place names etc., particularly in the areas along the Finnish-Russian border. Landscape features and built-up areas there often have entirely different names in Finnish, Russian, Swedish, Karelian and so on. When writing a book of this kind it is therefore necessary to select some kind of consistent approach, although it can never be completely coherent and perfect.

I have chosen to let my choice of names follow the border between Finland and Russia before the Winter War (often referred to as the 1939 border). Localities on the Finnish side of this border are called by their Finnish names, while those on the Russian side are called by the Russian names in use *at the time* (for instance Leningrad instead of St Petersburg). A list of name variations can be found in the back of the book. The exception to the rule is where localities have specific English names (sometimes taken from Swedish), primarily of course Finland for Suomi, but also place names such as the Gulf of Finland, the Kremlin etc. A few common Finnish suffixes used in connection with place names are essential to know in order to determine the kind of landscape features they are referring to. The reader can find them listed at the end of this introduction.

Second, there is my choice of an 'outside angle'. This has to do with how the surrounding world perceived the Finnish wars as they were happening. In the few existing non-Finnish books dealing with these wars, the outside angle is often either British-American or Swedish. These angles are important and are therefore dealt with in this book, too. However, I have also chosen to pay attention to the events as they were seen from Denmark. This country delivered the second largest group of volunteers in the Winter War and received the second largest group of refugees from Finland during the whole period, in both cases only exceeded by Sweden. During the Continuation War, Danish exports to Finland grew considerably, particularly when it is taken into consideration that a substantial amount of the foodstuffs that Finland received from Germany would most probably have originated from occupied Denmark. Hence, Denmark's position in the Finnish drama is at the same time both intimate and distant. The feelings among Danish people in relation to the Winter War were extremely supportive towards the Finns, yet during the Continuation War they became much more ambivalent due to the Finnish-German military cooperation. Since I am Danish born and bred I have had easy access to Danish sources dealing with this part of the story, making Denmark an obvious choice for that reason, too. Furthermore, it is my hope that by introducing this aspect into the material it will shine a light on some lesser known aspects of inter-Nordic relations and by doing so offer the reader yet another rare piece of the great historic puzzle known as the Second World War.

Finally in this preface I would like to thank the following people for the incredible and indispensable help they have given me along the way: Ole Knudsen (Gyldendal Publishers, Denmark), Lea Toivola (MA, University of Jyväskylä), Mikko Merilainen (MA, University of Eastern Finland), Henrik Grønholm, Bodil Albertsen, Nigel Hayhurst (www.alternativefinland.com), Jarkko Vihavainen (www.jaegerplatoon.net), Bair Irincheev, Bent Johansen, Tine Johansen, Cathrine A. Johansen, The Finnish Defence University, The Ministry of Defence of Finland (Photographic Centre), Mauno Jokisipilä (Doc-Soc.Sc, University of Turku), Michael Jonas (PhD, Helmut-Schmidt-University in Hamburg), Ville Kivimäki (PhD, Åbo Akademy University), Tenho Pimiä (PhD University of Jyväskylä), Paasi Tuunainen (PhD, University of Eastern Finland) and Veera Weisdorf (Finland's Embassy in Copenhagen).

And more generally for friendship, encouragement and sound advice I thank Peter Purnell (Angel Air), Bill Allerton, Philip Patterson (Marjacq), Heidi Amsinck and Mark Lucas (LAW Agency).

Also thanks to everyone at Pen & Sword Books.

Pronunciation, abbreviations and important sufffixes

Finnish is always pronounced with emphasis on the first syllable of each word and with soft consonants.

The following five suffixes are often used in relation to Finnish place names:

joki = river
järvi = lake
lahti = bay
niemi = peninsula
saari = island

Towns and villages situated near a lake are often named after the lake.

Abbreviations

AKS (Finnish) = *Akateeminen Karjala-Seura* (Academic Karelian Society)

AOK Norwegen (German) = *Armeeoberkommando Norwegen*, one of two army headquarter for the German troops in Northern Norway during the Second World War. Subordinated OKH (see below)

IKL (Finnish) = *Isänmaallinen kansanliike* (The Patriotic People's Movement) Fascistoid political party in Finland 1932–44

NKVD (Russian) = *Narodnyy Komissariat Vnutrennikh Del* (The People's Commissariat for Internal Affairs), a predecessor of the KGB etc.

OKH (German) = *Oberkommando des Heeres* (Supreme Command of the Army), was in charge of the German war effort on the Eastern Front from 1941

OKW (German) = *Oberkommando der Wehrmacht* (Supreme Command of the Wehrmacht), was in charge of the German war effort on the Western Front from 1941

OKM (German) = *Oberkommando der Marine* (Supreme Command of the Navy)

SKDL (Finnish) = *Suomen Kansan Demokraattinen Liitto* (The Finnish People's Democratic League)

SKP (Finnish) = *Suomen Kommunistinen Puolue* (The Communist Party of Finland)

SNS (Finnish) = *Suomen-Neuvostoliiton rauhan ja ystävyyden seura* (The Finland–Soviet Union Peace and Friendship Society). This organisation was launched and dissolved in 1940. In 1944 a new SNS was launched, whose full name was *Suomi-Neuvostoliitto-Seura* (Finnish-Soviet Society)

UFA (German) = *Universum Film A.G.*, Nazi Party-owned film company, which among other things produced German propaganda newsreels for cinema use during the Second World War

VALPO (Finnish) = *Valtiollinen poliisi* (State Police)

Yle (Finnish) = *Yleisradio* (The Finnish Broadcasting Company), state-owned Finnish radio and television

PART ONE

THE WINTER WAR

(30 November 1939 – 13 March 1940)

Väinö Tanner (left, 1881-1966) and Juho Paasikivi (1870-1956) on their way to negotiations in Moscow, October 1939. (SA-Kuva)

I

Prelude

A question comes up: did we have the legal and moral right to do what we did? Legally of course we did not have the right. From the moral point of view, the desire to ensure our security and reach an agreement to that effect with our neighbour was justified in our eyes.
NIKITA KHRUSHCHEV[1]

An Early Soviet Approach
On 14 April 1938, the Finnish Minister for Foreign Affairs, Rudolf Holsti, received a telephone call from a certain Boris Yartsev, who officially held a mid-level position at the Soviet Embassy in Helsinki. The caller asked for a confidential meeting, saying he had an important message from Moscow that must be handed over in person.

The approach somewhat puzzled Holsti. Normally, such requests were only made by diplomats of a much higher rank than Yartsev's. However, it turned out at the meeting that Yartsev's post at the embassy was merely a cover. He was in truth a diplomatic messenger who received his orders directly from the highest Soviet leaders. It has later been revealed that Yartsev was really Boris Rybkin, an agent for the NKVD (a predecessor to the KGB).

Yartsev suggested to Holsti the establishing of a mutual Finnish-Soviet defence and assistance pact. The reason was Soviet fear of a German invasion, he explained, an act of war that Hitler himself had mentioned in his autobiography from 1925, *My Struggle*. The southernmost part of the Finnish-Russian border ran only 30km from the western suburbs of Leningrad. The Russians feared a German attack on the city would partly be directed via Finland, and they did not expect the Finns would be able to defend themselves sufficiently against a German invasion.

In reality that was only part of the problem. Shortly before the meeting serious concerns had developed in Moscow over an apparent strengthening in Finland's relationship with Nazi Germany. In fact, Yartsev's approach came just two days after the conclusion of a visit to Helsinki by the German Major General Goltz, who had headed a delegation attending the twentieth anniversary celebration of the German intervention in the Finnish Civil War.

Rudolf Holsti rejected the Soviet offer and guaranteed instead that Finland both could and would defend its neutrality against any invading foreign power. Still, the Russian fear for Leningrad's security was deeply rooted and could not be easily ignored. It went all the way back to the founder of the city, Peter the Great, who in the early 1700s had announced: 'The women of St Petersburg cannot sleep calmly as long as the Finnish border runs so close to our capital.'

The Finnish Army was small and poorly equipped, Yartsev stressed. It could soon be overrun by the Germans. After that, the road down to Leningrad along the Karelian Isthmus – i.e. the strip of land between the Gulf of Finland and Lake Ladoga – would lie wide open (Map 1).

During a series of subsequent meetings, Yartsev tried on Moscow's behalf to reach a compromise with the Finnish leaders. However, the Finns continued to reject the idea of a pact between the two countries. They too had a nightmare scenario in the back of their minds. It gradually emerged that Moscow also wanted to deploy Soviet troops on Finnish soil in peacetime. The Finnish expectation was that once Soviet troops had been allowed into Finland, they would be hard to get rid of again. In other words, the Finnish leaders feared that their country could end up being annexed to the Soviet Union.

The negotiations between Finland and the Soviet Union continued in deepest secrecy throughout the summer of 1938, as the proposals made by the Kremlin gradually became more clearly defined. Still, the mistrust between the parties prevailed, and on 29 August the talks broke down after the Finnish leaders had declared that any acceptance of the Soviet terms would be in breach of the Finnish Constitution. Furthermore, the proposals were incompatible with Finland's established foreign policy which, in accordance with the other Nordic countries, was based on neutrality.

On 3 October Yartsev returned with a set of modified Soviet proposals, perhaps hoping that the Munich Agreement, which had meanwhile been signed, had softened the Finnish attitude. By signing this agreement, Great Britain and France had accepted Hitler's annexation of the Czech Sudetenland and thereby shown how little the smaller nations of Europe could expect in the way of outside support when threatened by one of the major dictatorships. But the Finns were as unyielding as before and by mid-November the dialogue once again stalled.

Around the same time, Holsti was forced to resign from his post as minister for foreign affairs due to a personal scandal. He was replaced by Eljas Erkko who, like Holsti, represented the National Progressive Party in the then-ruling coalition government stretching across the centre of Finnish politics. Erkko, furthermore, owned Finland's largest daily newspaper, the officially independent *Helsingin Sanomat* (*Helsinki Messages*) and was a board member of several large corporations.[2] He was a man of substantial influence and had, according to some, a bit too much trust in himself and his belief that the Soviet demands on Finland were just a bluff.

A Nordic or Baltic Country?
The negotiations with Yartsev had been conducted in deepest secrecy and involved only a few Finnish government members who, like Erkko, seemed remarkably unconcerned by the threat lurking beneath the surface of the Soviet demands.

On the whole there was a strong sense of optimism in Finland around this time. Compared with many other European nations the Finns had not been hit too hard by the financial crises of the 1930s. The beginning of the decade had seen some severe political confrontations, particularly an unsuccessful coup against the state carried out by the extremist right wing Lapua Movement, but things had moved forward from there at a steady pace. This in particular was due to a favourable world market for the paper and pulp industry and discoveries of large nickel and copper deposits in the northern districts of the country. At an international liberal conference held in Copenhagen in 1939, the Finnish Prime Minister, Aimo Cajander, described his country as 'a mature democracy in which the wounds inflicted by the Civil War have largely healed.'[3] Even the language dispute between the Finnish-speaking majority and Swedish-speaking minority had practically solved itself, he said.

As if underlining Finland's Nordic affiliations, the foundation of a Finnish-Swedish military union had been negotiated during the preceding year. In fact, secret negotiations of this kind had taken place intermittently since 1923, not only with Sweden but also with the Government of Estonia – a project that was even more worrying to the Russians than Nordic military cooperation, since a Finnish-Estonian naval blockade across the Gulf of Finland could have trapped the Soviet Baltic Fleet inside Leningrad. In short, what the Finns regarded as defensive measures the Russians saw as potential aggression aimed at them, and vice versa.

So far the Finnish-Swedish negotiations had only concerned the defence of the strategically important archipelago at the mouth of the Gulf of Bothnia, called the Åland Islands, but that was merely intended as a trial balloon. It was hoped that in the longer run the union could be expanded into a larger military alliance with participation of not just Sweden but also of Norway and Denmark.

The Åland Agreement between Finland and Sweden was signed on 5 January 1939 in Stockholm by representatives of the two countries. But before the agreement could be implemented it had to be officially accepted by a number of states with coastlines along the Sea of Bothnia. Denmark, Poland and the Baltic States complied without further ado, as did the Axis Powers (Germany and its allies). Moscow was willing to let the Finns fortify the Åland Islands as well as Hogland (an island 35km off the south coast of Finland), but only if the Finns guaranteed they would defend themselves against a German invasion, specifically, and expanded their military weaponry with Soviet arms.[4]

The Finns rejected the idea. Moscow then changed tactics once more, offering to turn a blind eye to the Finnish fortification of the Åland Islands while also proposing a trade agreement beneficial to the Finns. The Russians, furthermore, offered to hand over some territories north of Lake Ladoga, if in return the Soviet Union was allowed to lease a group of Finnish islands in the western part of the Gulf of Finland over a period of thirty years.[5] Again, the Finnish leaders turned down the proposal.

By and large, Marshal Mannerheim was the only Finnish representative at the negotiations who favoured a more cooperative approach. The marshal's former career as an officer in the Imperial Russian Army gave him unique insight into the overall objectives of Russian strategic thinking, which in fact had changed very little despite the new regime that had come into power during the 1917 Revolution. Primarily, Mannerheim understood the Russian concern with regard to Leningrad, realising that the Kremlin might go so far as to use military force against Finland. However, the marshal's influence on Finnish politics was limited during this period, and his advice and warnings were largely ignored.

The idea of a joint Finnish-Swedish defence of the Åland Islands resurfaced during the spring of 1939 during the Anglo-French-Soviet pact negotiations. Once again the Finnish leaders felt that unreasonable Soviet demands made any agreement on this impossible. On the whole, the Soviet attitude had become more aggressive, a development which increased from early May onwards, when the post as Soviet Minister of Foreign Affairs was taken over by Vyacheslav Mikhailovich Molotov, at the time best known for his role as Stalin's right hand during the political purges of the preceding years.

The alliance negotiations were conducted only half-heartedly by the Soviets. Since the Munich Agreement they had, in practise, lost all confidence in French and British willingness to take a strong line against Nazi Germany. Instead, Moscow sought to protect itself in the traditional Russian manner, by turning the countries along Russia's eastern borders into military buffer zones. This was the idea for which they had sought support during the negotiations, and it went hand in hand with the kind of imperialism that Moscow termed Internationalism, the Socialist World Revolution and so on.

The approach was at first to offer the Baltic States mutual defence and assistance treaties similar to the proposals with which the Finns had already become familiar through Yartsev. The bait was favourable trade agreements and promises of Soviet military help in case of a German attack. But the political leaders in the Baltic States feared the Soviet Union far more than they did Germany, and like Finland they wanted no cooperation of this kind with Moscow.

In the case of Finland, the disagreements soon developed into a discussion over whether the country was basically Nordic or Baltic. The issue had long been heatedly discussed within Finland and had political, linguistic, cultural and historic implications. In the current situation, however, it turned into something far more tangible and immediately pressing, namely the country's ability to maintain its independence in the face of its mighty eastern neighbour. Erkko told the British ambassador to Helsinki that Finland refused to be lumped with 'Romania, Poland and all that ... We want to be treated as a member of the Nordic group and no other.'[6] During the Anglo-French-Soviet pact negotiations this view was supported by the British and French diplomats, while the Russians insisted that Finland must be seen as a Baltic state.

The underlying problem was that Moscow respected the neutrality and borders of the Nordic states, while they saw the Baltic States as destined to become buffer zones for Russia. Of course the Soviets did not announce this publically, but the Finns were perfectly aware which label gave them more protection – Nordic or Baltic – so the Finnish leaders and negotiators did their best to convince Moscow that Finland did not harbour the same hostile feeling towards the Soviet Union as 'Romania, Poland and all that'.

Still, Molotov refused to agree. In his memoirs, Nikita Khrushchev, who later became leader of the Soviet Union and at that time was already close to the centre of political action, described the atmosphere in Moscow as follows:

> We made contact with Helsinki to come to an agreement. The question we raised was that in the event of war it was necessary to protect Leningrad, which was within range of artillery fire from the Finnish border ... Finland really did represent a threat to us, but not in and of itself. Its territory could be used against us by enemy forces from more powerful countries.[7]

Likewise, the Finns were left unconvinced by any promises from Moscow about peace and friendliness. The void of suspicion and lack of understanding continued and would only grow stronger with time.

The Anglo-French-Soviet pact negotiations could not solve these entanglements either. Besides, the talks were soon to be lost in the sands. These developments only strengthened Molotov and Stalin's belief that the right way to move ahead for the Soviet Union was the establishing of military buffer zones in the west. The only problem was that Moscow could not put sufficient pressure on the Baltic States as long as there was a risk it might lead to a war against Germany. Here was a hurdle that needed to be removed before the Soviet plan could go ahead.

The Molotov-Ribbentrop Pact
On 23 August 1939 in Moscow, Molotov and his German foreign minister colleague, Joachim von Ribbentrop, signed the Molotov-Ribbentrop Pact. Officially a non-aggression agreement, it included a secret protocol whose existence was not publically revealed until after the end of the Second World War. The protocol reached much further than the official agreement and described how the eastern parts of Europe were to be divided into so-called spheres of interest. In practice, Germany and the Soviet Union promised not to intervene in each other's affairs and activities in areas belonging to the other party's domain.

As the only Nordic country, Finland was included in the secret protocol,

Foreign Ministers Molotov and Ribbentrop, the men behind the Molotov-Ribbentrop Pact of 23 August 1939, shake hands after the German and Soviet invasions of Poland in September that same year.

where the country was placed within the Soviet sphere of interest. Khrushchev later wrote:

> Stalin ... understood that Hitler wanted to trick us but was just outfoxing himself ... Estonia, Latvia, Lithuania, Bessarabia and Finland would be allotted to us in such a way that we ourselves could decide with their government the fate of those territories.[8]

Just one week after the pact had been signed, the German Army invaded Poland from the west. Seventeen days later the Soviet Union invaded the same country from the east (Poland had been divided into a German and a Soviet sphere of interest). On 21 September the two invading armies made an agreement on how to coordinate their operations. The next day German and Soviet troops met in the Polish town of Brest-Litovsk, congratulating each other on a job well done.

On 6 October the war in Poland was over. In their respective halves of the country the occupiers immediately started suppressing the local population through political terror with widespread use of imprisonment, torture, executions and so on.

Great Britain had signed a mutual defence treaty with Poland six days before the start of the German invasion and it declared war on Germany on 3 September. However, no military intervention took place. The lack of action was underlined by London not declaring war on the Soviet Union when it launched its part of the invasion. Meanwhile, the US kept to its policy of not intervening in internal European affairs.

The smaller European countries followed the situation in Poland with a mixture of anxiety and disbelief. Previously, the dictatorial regimes in Berlin and Moscow had expressed nothing but the deepest contempt for each other. Now they were suddenly carving Eastern Europe up between them, seemingly without any animosity.

Even before the war in Poland was over, the Kremlin started expanding its activities into Estonia, Latvia and Lithuania. The small Baltic nations were individually approached with proposed defence and assistance treaties similar to those formerly presented to Finland, the true purpose of which was to let the Soviet Union establish military bases along the east coast of the Baltic Sea.

The treaties formally secured the independence of the Baltic States, but none of their governments believed the guarantees, particularly when they viewed them in the light of what was going on in Poland. However, the Soviet leaders backed their proposals up by deploying large numbers of troops along the borders of the Baltic countries, who one by one yielded to the pressure. Molotov later described the situation:

> There was no escape for them. A country somehow has to see to its security. When we laid down our demands – you have to act before it's too late – they vacillated. Of course bourgeois governments could not join a Socialist state with alacrity. But the international situation was forcing their decision ... And we needed the Baltic States.[9]

The political leaders in Helsinki kept a keen eye on the developments in Poland and the Baltic States. They feared they were next in line to receive an offer that would be hard to refuse.

A Soviet 'Invitation'
In the evening of 5 October 1939 the telephone rang at the Stockholm residency of Juho Kusti Paasikivi, the Finnish ambassador to Sweden. Paasikivi, who had gone to bed for the night, got up and answered the call, which turned out to come from the Finnish Ministry for Foreign Affairs. The ambassador was asked if he could be in Helsinki the following day and he gave a confirmatory answer. What the matter concerned he was not told.[10]

Arriving in Helsinki as agreed, Paasikivi met with Erkko who said he had received a telegram from Moscow containing an invitation. In reality, it was a demand for him to arrive in Moscow within forty-eight hours or at least to send a plenipotentiary. The subject of the meeting would be an expansion of political and trade related connections between Finland and the Soviet Union, seen in the light of the new political situation caused by the war in Poland. The question now was if Paasikivi was willing to take on the role of plenipotentiary and travel to Moscow to negotiate on Finland's behalf.

Paasikivi asked for twenty-four hours to consider the matter. Thus the very short deadline given by Molotov expired. He soon pressed Helsinki for a reply, reminding Erkko that the Soviet Union had 'other means' that could be employed if Finland refused to negotiate.[11]

The next day (9 October 1939) the Finnish Army started gradually mobilising under the guise of carrying out 'refresher training'.

The choice of Paasikivi as Finland's leading negotiator in Moscow during the following years may serve as an example of the criteria used by the Finnish leaders when selecting diplomatic representatives. It was not enough that the envoy was experienced and skilled; he also had to make himself personally liked by his counterpart. In this case it seems to have worked. Molotov said about Paasikivi:

> He spoke a bit of Russian but was understandable. He had a good library at home, he read Lenin. He realised that without an agreement with Russia, Finland would be in trouble. I sensed that he wanted to meet us halfway, but he had many opponents.[12]

Ideologically, Paasikivi was in no way sympathetic to Soviet Communism. He had a long career behind him in Finland's conservative National Coalition Party and was 69 years old when the negotiations with Moscow began. In fact, he had left active politics several years before to take up the rather convenient position of Finland's ambassador to Sweden.

One might wonder how a person such as he could get along with Stalin and Molotov. The answer is that Paasikivi belonged to the political faction known as the 'old Finns', a group of conservatives who still vividly remembered the period before Finnish independence in 1917. The ruling thesis among these people was that certain geographic facts had to be accepted in order to make things work smoothly in relation to Finland's great neighbour in the east.

Other factors also pointed to Paasikivi as the right man for the job. He had no time for the anti-Russian tendencies that had characterised vast parts of Finnish society through the 1920s and 1930s. As a young man he had studied in Leningrad (when it was named St Petersburg, as it is again today). He was a huge admirer of Russian culture, knowledgeable on its history, and as Molotov points out he spoke the language. When the talks between Paasikivi and the Soviet negotiators occasionally stalled, it was primarily because of limitations in the mandate that the Finn had been granted from his superiors back home.

First Round of Negotiations
Paasikivi arrived in Moscow by train on Wednesday, 11 October 1939. The next day at 5pm the negotiations began in Molotov's study inside the Kremlin. Paasikivi writes in his memoirs:

> Stalin participated energetically in the negotiations. Got up now and then, walked back and forth seemingly following the discussion thoroughly ...
>
> Molotov was very diligent, humble with regard to social conventions, speaks matter-of-factly, briefly, avoided clichés ... but he was difficult to deal with during negotiations.[13]

The instructions to the Finnish delegation set out that that no compliance must be shown towards Soviet demands on military bases in Finland or agreements on mutual military assistance. Only in an absolute emergency could Paasikivi accept handing over some small islands far off the southern coast of Finland. He was to emphasise the country's intentions to maintain its policy of neutrality and its willingness to defend itself militarily.

These narrow limitations were somewhat in opposition to the verbal instructions Paasikivi was also given before his departure, which said he had to prevent the negotiations from breaking down. Furthermore, Mannerheim insisted that the security interests of the Soviet Union were to be respected and allowed to form the basis of a proposed compromise.[14]

Stalin and Molotov opened the meeting by suggesting that the frontier on the Karelian Isthmus be moved north to Viipuri, then the second largest city in Finland. As compensation the Finns were offered an area in East Karelia, which was more than twice as large but consisted of wild and uncultivated landscape. Finland was also to hand over some islands in the Gulf of Finland and had to permit the establishment of Soviet Navy and aircraft bases on the Hanko peninsula (on the extreme southwest corner of the Finnish mainland), which were to be leased to the Soviet Union for thirty years. At the opposite end of the country, the Finns had to hand over their part of the Rybachy Peninsula on the Barents Sea.

Åland came up for discussion as well, as the Soviet Union wished to fortify these islands together with Sweden. The Soviet proposals also included a mutual Finnish-Soviet assistance pact, largely similar to the ones Moscow had recently signed with Estonia, Latvia and Lithuania; but heavy Finnish resistance to this led Stalin to abandon the idea early in the negotiations. The other demands he upheld and described as minimum requests.

Paasikivi's mandate did not allow him to initiate constructive negotiations on such a basis, so he telegraphed home asking for an extended degree of authorisation. This was refused. Subsequent conversations with him, Stalin and Molotov seem to have been little more than private discussions where both parties tried to convince the other of their peaceful and sympathetic intentions. It was leading nowhere, so on 14 October it was agreed that Paasikivi should go home, present the Finnish leaders with a memorandum of the Soviet demands and debate the situation with them.[15] The negotiations were then to be resumed later on in the month.

The Second Round of Negotiations
In Helsinki the situation was still not openly discussed by the government or in the parliament, the *Eduskunta*. Instead, the decisions took place among a small circle of people within the cabinet, with Mannerheim participating. Based on his knowledge of Russian strategic thinking he again suggested a more compromise-seeking course. But the rest of the group supported Erkko's dismissive attitude and were only prepared to make some smaller concessions, such as giving the Russians right of disposal over Hogland. The idea of leasing out Hanko was deemed completely unacceptable, and only some smaller border adjustments on the Karelian Isthmus could come into question.

Before Paasikivi went on his next journey to Moscow, he asked if Väinö

Tanner, Finland's foremost Social Democrat politician, could come along. The idea was willingly accepted by Foreign Minister Erkko, who in the meantime seems to have regretted choosing Paasikivi as negotiator. Since Erkko was convinced that the Soviet leaders were bluffing and had no intention of backing up their demands with military power, he regarded Paasikivi's conduct in Moscow as unnecessarily forthcoming. Tanner, on the other hand, was known as a tough negotiator.[16] It was also hoped that his presence would show the Soviet leaders that the Finnish working class agreed with the government's dismissive approach.[17]

The small Finnish concessions were very far from the so-called minimum demands that Stalin had presented at the first meeting. With such a mandate there was nothing Paasikivi and Tanner could achieve in Moscow, where the negotiations were set to begin on 23 October at 6pm. The overall atmosphere was tense and the negotiations turned out unsatisfactorily. They were rounded off with the following exchange of remarks:

> MOLOTOV: Do you wish for this to end in conflict?
> PAASIKIVI: We naturally wish to avoid conflict, but we have to take the interests of Finland into consideration.[18]

Nevertheless, an important issue was clarified at the meeting: Hanko constituted a hurdle that blocked the way for further negotiation. It was there that the Germans had landed in 1918 during the Finnish Civil War in support of the White Guard, and in Stalin's opinion it was there the Germans would land again to move east and attack Leningrad across the Karelian Isthmus.

On his arrival in Helsinki, Paasikivi advised the political leaders to offer the Russians Jussarö, an archipelago due east of Hanko, as an alternative to Hanko. The waters around these islands are important to the shipping routes through the Gulf of Finland, and a lease would give the Russians substantial strategic advances that could perhaps form the basis of a compromise. In fact, Mannerheim had previously made a similar suggestion. But any suggested solution of the kind was blankly refused by the political parties in the *Eduskunta*, where the situation was now debated and thus became known to the public.

The Third and Final Round of Negotiations

On the evening of 31 October 1939, Paasikivi and Tanner left Helsinki and headed for Moscow to take part in a new round of negotiations. Before their arrival, the Soviet Union publicly announced its demands, a worrying development for the Finnish side since it would now be very difficult for the Russians to accept compromises. Still, Stalin and Molotov had on several occasions cut back considerably on their proposals, and the inflexibility of the Finns clearly upset and frustrated them. The Finnish diplomat and journalist Max Jakobson writes: 'The astonishment and disappointment that Stalin and Molotov had expressed in the course of their talks with the Finns must have been perfectly genuine … Probably they sincerely believed they had asked Finland only what was their due, and the rejection of their demands must have seemed to them an incomprehensible, almost perverse, act of defiance; after all, even most Western observers thought the Finns were behaving in a most quixotic manner – bravely, perhaps, but quite unrealistically.'[19]

Despite this, Stalin was eventually willing to make a compromise regarding Hanko, and as an alternative he suggested some islands close to the peninsula. It seemed a breakthrough that the Russians, on their own initiative, had dropped their demand on Hanko; but the Finnish negotiators knew there was no hope that the government in Helsinki would accept this compromise. The suggested islands were too close to the mainland and included parts of Hanko's fortifications. Instead, the moment seemed ripe for bringing up Jussarö, if only the Finnish government would show less rigidity on the issue. In consequence, the negotiators telegraphed home to the government in Helsinki asking for permission to put forward Jussarö as an alternative to Stalin's latest proposal.

In his memoirs, Paasikivi mentions several reasons why Stalin would probably have accepted such an arrangement. But when the reply arrived from Helsinki on 9 November it was still a blank refusal.

With that the negotiations collapsed irrevocably. On 13 November Paasikivi wrote to Molotov that he and Tanner now intended to go home:

> … since during the negotiations with you and Mr Stalin we have had no luck in finding a basis for the planned agreement between Finland and the Soviet Union.[20]

The Spirit of 1939
Meanwhile, the overall atmosphere in Finland had developed into a state of patriotic excitement. For the first time in their short history as an independent nation the Finnish people stood united on a common cause. They had shown the mighty Russia they would not let themselves be intimidated. They had shown the world that small countries need not always bow and scrape before the major powers. The feeling among the general public was similar to Erkko's. People refused to believe there would be a war but if the Red Army should turn up anyway, Finland would stand its ground. Minister of Defence Juho Niukkanen even claimed that a Soviet

invasion could be held back for six months,[21] more than enough for foreign military assistance to arrive.

Unfortunately, it was unclear where these foreign troops were supposed to come from. Finland had no guarantees from other nations, and in any case the events in Poland two months previously had shown how little such promises counted when it really mattered. The League of Nations, officially a protector of the small neutral countries, had long ago proven powerless against the big dictatorships. Great Britain and France were sympathetic towards Finland, but only as long as it coincided with their own interests. Besides, they had enough to worry about already. Both were officially at war with Germany, a phony war that might at any time break out in full force. Likewise, there was no shortage of friendly words and supportive declarations from Scandinavia, but these countries too had more than enough to worry about when it came to their own security, which was primarily threatened by Germany, not the Soviet Union.

Finland was a young nation whose leaders had not yet learned to probe the undercurrents of international political waters, the mood swings in popular opinion and the hidden agendas. And so they let themselves be impressed and led astray by grandiose statements and Nordic brotherly spirit, moral back patting from France and Britain, and displays of sympathy from the US. Also, the same countries would willingly criticise the conduct of the Soviet Union, officially as well as directly through diplomatic channels. A more critical, well-informed and alert Finnish press could perhaps have promoted a more realistic view on the situation, but here one has to remember Erkko's powerful position as owner of the largest newspaper in the country.

Finally, there was the German stance.

The close relations between Finland and Germany are well documented. The German historian Michael Jonas describes Finland as 'one of the most Germanophile states in the Baltic Sea area for centuries … Finland could in a state of existential emergency rely upon Germany as its traditional guardian.'[22]

Another century-old thesis was that Germany would resist any expansion of Russian power in the Baltic Sea region. But there was now a non-aggression pact between Germany and the Soviet Union. Its most dangerous part, seen from a Finnish point of view, was secret, but the way the two major powers had acted during their invasions of Poland indicated that deals had been made behind the curtains which could prove fateful to the smaller states along Russia's western border.

In fact, parts of the Finnish press *had* been critical and outspoken about the German attitude lately. In August, before the invasion of Poland, some of the daily newspapers claimed that Germany had sold Finland and the

Baltic States to the Russians to make them accept the Molotov-Ribbentrop Pact. Still, this was only guesswork and was blankly denied by the German Embassy. All in all, there is hardly any doubt that Germany was seen as a potential ally of Finland, both by the general Finnish population and by the country's political leaders. In fact, this may well be the main explanation for the otherwise peculiar Finnish optimism and diplomatic inflexibility at a time when the future should have seemed dark and threatening.

This notion is confirmed by the bitterness that followed during the Winter War when German help failed to arrive. The Finnish historian Henrik Meinander even describes it as a shock for 'the rather strong Germanophile wing of the national elite'.[23] Michael Jonas writes: 'The abandonment of the small state in the face of an unprovoked and internationally condemned aggression was … the biggest surprise for both the Finnish elite and the country's population at large.'[24]

There is almost something touching about the optimism that spread all over Finland during the final few weeks leading up to the Winter War, strengthened by the feeling of finally acting as one united, unanimous people. Philosophical voices belonging to the older generation, itself safely beyond the realms of National Conscription, even claimed that a country hardly deserved to be called a real nation until it had demonstrated willingness to sacrifice life and limb to save its independence. More prosaic arguments also entered into the discussion about whether waging a war would be the right thing to do at the moment. The Finnish high command analysed the situation in Czechoslovakia over the last six months. Their conclusion was that by handing over the Sudetenland, the Czechs had ruined their own possibilities for setting up a solid defence. In consequence, they had been forced to cave in to the German threat of an invasion in March 1939 and capitulate without resistance. The Sudetenland had included the most important Czech fortifications facing west, just as the Karelian Isthmus included Finland's main defence line against the Soviet Union (later known as the Mannerheim Line). To the Finns, the negotiations in Moscow were every bit as much about security as they were to the Soviets.

Another argument to continue the unyielding attitude was that public opinion at the moment was unanimous. No one could expect that to continue forever, not in Finland at that time. It was only twenty years since the inhabitants of the country had been murdering each other in the most bestial manner, and neighbours had locked each other up in concentration camps where thousands had lost their lives under terrible conditions. A national consensus open to the idea of self-sacrifice was not a factor the political leadership could rely on for any long period of time.

One has to remember, though, that these considerations were aimed at a war which the majority did not believe would happen – at least not for a while. And perhaps this was not as naïve as it seems in hindsight. At least the Finns were not alone in thinking this way. The view was shared by most international journalists, diplomats and other observers visiting the country at that time. If nothing else, the approach of the winter season spoke against the risk of a Soviet attack happening soon.

Not even Paasikivi and Tanner thought that war was just around the corner. On leaving Moscow they had felt as if a door was still left open to another round of negotiations. So far, Molotov and Stalin had seemed eager to reach a peaceful solution. It was unlikely that they would start a war before they had tried at least once more to negotiate.

The one person not sharing all this optimism was Marshal Mannerheim, who presented the government with a gloomy account of the military situation along the border. The army's equipment was scarce and in poor condition. Anti-aircraft guns and heavy artillery were low in numbers; anti-tank guns were practically non-existent. Of the meagre sixty tanks the army possessed, half were old Renault F-17s bought just after the First World War. Mannerheim placed the responsibility for this predicament on the democratically elected leaders. For years they had refused to listen to him when he suggested that military budgets be raised, and now they allowed themselves to pursue a stubborn and deadly dangerous policy towards the mighty Russia.[25] In protest the marshal threatened to hand in his resignation. It was, however, merely a form of protest he would occasionally employ over the following years. In the end, he always remained at his post but he had at least clarified his views.

The Shelling at Mainila
The real attitude among the Soviet leaders was in direct opposition to what was imagined in Finland. When the third round of negotiations collapsed in mid-November 1939, the Kremlin concluded it was a waste of time to negotiate any further with the unyielding Finns. Instead, they started to prepare for an invasion.

The atmosphere in Helsinki remained optimistic in ignorance of the imminent Soviet threat, even on 26 November when there was a strong warning of things to come. In a note addressed to the government in Helsinki, Molotov claimed that Finnish artillery, early that same morning, had fired several rounds on Mainila Village on the Soviet side of the border on the Karelian Isthmus, 32km from Leningrad. Four Soviet soldiers had supposedly been killed and nine wounded. Molotov called the episode a provocation and an act of aggression against the Soviet Union.[26] To avoid more of the same he demanded that the Finnish troops be moved 25km back from the border.

A Finnish patrol had reported that guns had been fired *on the Soviet side of the border* at the stated point in time, but apart from that the military and government denied any knowledge of the matter. They suggested instead that Soviet artillery had released the shots by mistake and hit a target within their own territory. It was impossible that the shots could have come from the Finnish side, since Mannerheim had already pulled his artillery back out of range of the border precisely so as to avoid accusations of this kind.

To get to the bottom of the matter, the Finnish government suggested that *both* parties pull their troops back from the border and that a common investigation of the incident be conducted, in accordance with the Finnish-Soviet Non-Aggression Pact of 1932. Molotov rejected the idea on 28 November, claiming it would weaken the security of Leningrad considerably. In fact, a suggestion of this kind was in itself an act of aggression against the Soviet Union, he said, and so Moscow now regarded the non-aggression pact as violated and annulled. The following day the Soviet Union officially severed its diplomatic connections with Finland.

The story behind the shelling of Mainila remains a mystery to this day. The Soviet claims of a Finnish provocation have long been buried, but even after the opening of the Soviet archives nothing has emerged to determine with certainty who on the Russian side ordered the bombardment and what the reason might have been. The only certain thing is that Molotov and Stalin managed to milk the episode to the last drop.

On 29 November, following long discussions, the Finnish government decided to carry out a unilateral withdrawal from the border. A Finnish diplomat in Moscow was to hand the message over to Molotov. But his instructions went further than that. He was in fact to suggest that the parties returned to the negotiation table.[27]

The delivery of the note was somewhat deferred, but even without this delay it would have had no effect. The Soviet war machine on the Finnish border had already been placed in motion.

An Avoidable War?
Could the Winter War have been avoided? The answer to that would depend on definitions. If we talk about the specific war we now call the Winter War, with attached dates and so on, it would apparently have been easy to avoid. The Finnish leaders just had to accept the Soviet demands. If there had been any problems, they would have appeared on the home front, partly in relation to public opinion, partly the Finnish constitution.

Looking at things from a broader perspective, it becomes a question of whether or not a war against the Soviet Union could be avoided in the longer run. Here the fate of the Baltic States has been used as an indication of what might have happened to Finland, too, if Helsinki had yielded to the Soviet demands. During the summer of 1940 these countries were forced to accept an ultimatum that completely annexed them to the Soviet Union. Stalin and Molotov had made it clear that they viewed Finland as a Baltic state, so logic seems to suggest they had in mind a similar destiny for the Finns. The Finnish leaders would almost certainly not have yielded to an ultimatum that would have cost them their independence, and so instead of a Winter War there would have been a 'Summer War', fought from poor positions and without climatic advantages.

However, the comparison is not entirely above criticism. There is no certain proof that the Kremlin in the autumn of 1939 intended to annex the Baltic States *fully*. These annexations *might* have been a reaction to the German victories in Western Europe during the spring and summer of 1940. Likewise, Molotov's famous remark that his 'task as minister of foreign affairs was to expand the borders of our fatherland' does not divulge exactly when and how this task was defined. Furthermore, he continues: 'And it seems that Stalin and I coped with this task quite well.'[28] Since the Soviet Union never managed to annex all of Finland, only some minor territories, the quote (for whatever it is generally worth) can hardly be said to confirm that Finland was meant to be taken over completely, since in that case the task had *not* been coped with 'quite well'.

Also, it is jumping to conclusions to suggest that just because Moscow insisted on Finland being a Baltic state, the Soviet leaders were unable to differentiate between Finland and the other three countries. We know for instance that the Kremlin badly overestimated Sweden's military strength and aggressive intentions and was seriously worried about ending up in a conflict with the Swedes, which many considered a possibility if the Red Army invaded Finland (certainly the Swedish High Command had several plans made ready for such a scenario). We also know that Britain and France had made it clear to Moscow that *they* viewed Finland as a Nordic country (p. 7), which indicated that Moscow could expect reprisals in case of an invasion of Finnish territory. Furthermore, the British had economic investments in the Petsamo area in Finnish Lapland (the Inco Nickel Mine), as well as a strong strategic interest in cutting off Swedish Lapland from trade with Germany. Such an operation could be conducted on the pretext of wishing to protect the Finns against a Soviet threat (a scenario that would loom on the horizon during most of the Winter War and seems to have had a significant influence on the way the war ended).

Under no circumstances did the soviets want a war with Sweden or the Western Allies, or both, and the Soviet leaders were highly aware of the dangers hiding in that direction. If nothing else, this became clear at the start of the Winter War due to the massive Soviet land and naval forces deployed in the Petsamo area. This operation clearly had nothing to do with eliminating the two solitary Finnish companies in the region, since such a task hardly demanded the use of 44,000 troops backed by the Soviet Northern Fleet.

Both Molotov and Khrushchev claimed after the war that Stalin's plan *at the beginning* of the negotiations with Helsinki was not to annex *all* of Finland, and that this only became an issue when the Finns proved impossible to negotiate with (which is supported by other and more reliable sources known today). They did not mention the allied threat but instead pointed out that a full annexation of Finland, unlike that of the Baltic States: 'could not decide any fundamental questions of foreign policy for us'.[29] Besides, an annexed Finland could become a 'festering wound ... a pretext for anti-Soviet activity.'[30] Of course, Stalin and Molotov are hardly reliable witnesses, but there could well be some truth in these quotes since they were often surprisingly honest when speaking of their conduct against Russia's small neighbouring countries.

It cannot be denied that Stalin and Molotov, during the negotiations leading up to the war, were unexpectedly compromise-seeking. It is, of course, preferable if you can achieve what you want without having to wage costly wars, but we know that the leaders in Kremlin in the autumn of 1939 thought an invasion of Finland would be a short and easy affair, where the Finnish proletariat would rise against its White masters as soon as the first Russian boot stepped over the border. This was the impression the Kremlin received from spies and exiled Finnish Communists, and it reflects in the Soviet conduct during the first few days of the war. When you add to that the German guarantee to not intervene, as stated in the secret protocol of the Molotov-Ribbentrop Agreement, plus the fact that this agreement would probably not last very long, it seems the Russians actually had some strong reasons to invade and fully annex Finland, and the sooner the better.

So why were they holding back? Probably not because they were worried that the small and poorly armed Finnish Army would humiliate them (although perhaps they should have been). Nor is it likely that they reacted out of compassion for the Finnish people. The deciding factor was, as already mentioned, more likely a fear of how Sweden and the Allies might react. A full occupation of Finland was simply not worth the dangers it involved, and so it did not appear on the Soviet agenda until the talks broke down.

Unfortunately, we cannot dig much deeper into this question, since we still lack essential facts about the Soviet long-term plans concerning Finland. Actually, we do not even know if such plans existed at all. But at least we know that Mannerheim, until his death in 1951, felt that the Winter War could and should have been avoided. The marshal did not believe the war was avoidable in the long run, but in his opinion it would have been better to fight it at a different point in time, and so he thought the Finnish attitude should have been more compromise-orientated.

To an outsider, Mannerheim's critical opinion on the run-up to the Winter War may seem essential for an evaluation of the entire event. Yet in Finland it has not been taken seriously to any great extent. Mostly, it has been seen as one of the many well-known quirks of the marshal, such as his inability to admit mistakes and his bitterness over the subsidiary role to which he was relegated during the Moscow negotiations. All the same, Mannerheim's reputation has not exactly dwindled with time, in fact quite the opposite. In 2004 he was determined 'the Greatest Finn of all Time' by a national Finnish television show (a programme somewhat akin to the BBC's *Great Britons*). It is a truly paradoxical situation, and the paradox only grows bigger when we recall that the Winter War, whichever way you look at it, *was* the result of a political miscalculation. Foreign Minister Erkko, and those who agreed with him, never wanted to cause a war. They, however, failed to realise the immediate danger and the miniscule chance of receiving any decisive amount of outside military support if things went wrong. If they had seen what was truly coming, they would undoubtedly have opted for a different policy. But they chose to ignore insistent warnings not just from Mannerheim, but also from two of Finland's most skilful politicians: one of them later a president (Paasikivi), the other a former prime minister (Tanner), who for many hours had been sitting face to face with Stalin and Molotov in Moscow and more than anyone must be said to have had their fingers on the pulse of the whole situation.

Perhaps it would have benefitted the discussion if any of these three statesmen had described in close detail how they felt the matter could have been better solved. But in the tense political climate of post-war Finland such an act would have been highly irresponsible, and so the rest of us are left with our own guesses.

Judging from Mannerheim's views and actions in general, it seems likely he would have preferred more effort to be spent on setting up a Nordic defence treaty, followed by a marked increase in the military budgets of all four countries. As already mentioned, the marshal thought it inevitable that a war with the Soviet Union would come at some point, but in fact there seems now to be a broad consensus among historians that a Nordic military alliance could have kept not just Finland but in fact the entire region out of the Second World War.

It is a common notion that the Finnish leaders would practically have hung themselves if they had caved in to the Soviet territorial demands on the Karelian Isthmus. Mannerheim, however, did not rate the defence system on the Isthmus very highly. In fact, he said after the war that the relative success of the Finnish Army should be credited exclusively to the

Finnish soldiers; that *they* had made up the real fortification line, not a string of bunkers and trenches.

Paasikivi's views are rather more clearly documented. He simply did not feel that Stalin and Molotov at the time were aiming to annex all of Finland, and he thought an acceptable compromise could have been reached if he had been given more of a free hand. In today's Finland such an opinion is generally viewed as exceedingly naïve, and Paasikivi's views on the matter are – like Mannerheim's – put down to quirkiness and personal bitterness over not having been taken seriously enough when the events were unfolding.

Tanner was less convinced than the other two that the war could be delayed or avoided, but he fully supported Paasikivi's approach during the negotiations in Moscow.

More neutral and moderate Finnish historians have tried to solve the abovementioned paradoxes by seeing the Winter War as a kind of blessing in disguise, a diplomatic blunder that surprisingly led to the least terrible result, since Finland after all avoided the destiny of the Baltic States, i.e. decades of horrendous Soviet oppression. It has also been pointed out that Erkko's approach was supported by the Finnish population, and that the soldiers marched to the front willingly and highly motivated. However, we cannot judge if the man in the street might have had a different view if he had been more objectively and correctly informed, particularly about the limited possibilities of receiving outside military support.

Paasikivi later on scornfully described the Winter War as 'Erkko's War'. Other critical voices have called it 'a struggle over some small islands in the Gulf of Finland'. At the opposite end of the spectrum, we find the most widespread opinion in today's Finland which is that the Winter War was an unavoidable existential struggle.

Again these views and interpretations are uncertain. The notion of 'a war over some small islands' is only valid if we could prove that Stalin was truly willing to accept Jussarö as an alternative to Hanko – which we cannot. And even if we could, there would still be other problematic issues left over, particularly concerning the border adjustment on the Karelian Isthmus. With regard to the idea of an existential struggle, it is only provable if we talk about the period after 13 November 1939 (when the negotiations broke down for good). To put it another way: the existential struggle *might* have been self-inflicted due to a lack of flexibility in the negotiations with Moscow.

All in all, there are still some murky areas in this essential phase of Finland's history. Nevertheless, two basic facts remain.

First: whether diplomatically clever or not, the Finnish conduct throughout the pre-Winter War negotiations was completely legal, appropriate and correct. It was also at the time seen by many people all over the world as a welcome exception to the rule that small nations must always bow their heads to the super powers and accept the role of 'low man' in the global power struggle. Viewed in this light, the Finnish attitude looks more like steadfastness than stubbornness, and as such it became an inspiration to the later resistance movements in the Nazi occupied countries, not least in Norway and Denmark.

Second: as soon at the war broke out, the Finns could only do one thing to remain an independent nation, and that was to fight back to a point far beyond anything that is normally seen as humanly and militarily possible.

II

Two Armies

> MARSHAL MANNERHEIM: *'When working on the Finnish defence plans we have always assumed that Russia in case of a war would be engaged elsewhere. Now, however, the situation is different. Germany needs support from Russia, and England is tied up elsewhere.'*
> TANNER: *'Russia has free play now.'*
> MANNERHEIM: *'Exactly.'*
> J.K. PAASIKIVI[31]

The Red Army

The Workers' and Peasants' Red Army, normally just referred to as the Red Army (although that did not become its official name until 1943), had been founded in January 1918 after the Imperial Russian Army had been dissolved. The foundation of the new army was the Red Guard, the victor of the Russian Revolution which had taken place the year before. Enrolment in the Red Army was for a brief while voluntary. No ranks or insignia were used, and the officers were democratically elected. All this, however, was soon to change.

From May 1918 onwards, conscription was introduced along with a tough discipline, which was reputedly even harsher than it had been in the Imperial Army. In addition there was the use of commissars and 'political workers' who took care of the ideological schooling (i.e. indoctrination) and ensured that the political correctness was upheld, while criticism and discontent were severely punished. The army's governing institution was the Council of People's Commissars, who delegated tasks to a number of local commissariats in the military districts.

During the first twenty years of the Red Army's existence all recruits had to pledge allegiance to International Socialism. In February 1939 a new oath was introduced where the emphasis on political motivation swung towards patriotism, in accordance with the overall policy dictated by Stalin. The oath included the following:

I vow to study the duties of a soldier conscientiously, to safeguard Army and National property in every way possible and to be true to my people, my Soviet motherland, and the Workers' and Peasants' Government ... And if through evil intent I break this solemn oath, then let the stern punishment of the Soviet law, and the universal hatred and contempt of the working people, fall upon me.[32]

The Red Army had suffered a humiliating defeat in the Polish-Russian War of 1919-21. Generally, the Russian military was weak at this stage, partly because of the on-going Civil War in the country. This worked to the advantage of the country's western neighbours, who one after the other declared themselves independent. Thus Finland's eastern border was established in 1920 in an agreement signed in the Estonian town of Tartu.

The Red Army's General Staff was initially a somewhat disjointed affair, but this changed in 1924 when it was given a clearer and more coherent role. After that it came to dominate the operations and military planning of the Soviet state. From the next year onwards the army grew bigger both in personnel and equipment. Between 1925 and 1939 the amount of artillery pieces increased by 140 per cent, the number of armoured vehicles grew 43 times bigger, and the number of aircraft increased by a factor of 6.5.[33]

From the late 1920s and up through the following decade, Soviet military theorists, led by Field-Marshal Mikhail Tukhachevsky, founded an independent tactical doctrine particularly suited to soviet conditions. It was based on the use of infantry units of corps or army size (a Soviet corps at this time comprised three divisions, a total of approximately 36,000 men, while a Soviet Army normally consisted of two to four corps plus separate units). The basic idea was to carry out parallel attacks deep in the enemy's positions, with close coordination between infantry, aircraft and armoured vehicles.[34] The philosophy was that the dominating tactical principles of the Napoleonic wars, with their main focus placed on flanking movements, must be deemed obsolete in an era of long frontlines and trench fighting (as during the First World War). The new principles were incorporated into the manuals of the Red Army from 1936.[35]

With this the traditional respect for the enemy's leaders and their integrity became irrevocably a thing of the past. The new 'deep penetration' tactics aimed at crushing the enemy's infrastructure by attacking his military and political headquarters. Air attacks were to utilise the fact that their operational radius could be longer than that of the other weapons, and they were to be carried out in vast, tight formations.

These principles would be put into practise by use of the latest military technology, and they were increasingly granted a pivotal role in Soviet strategy and tactics, backed up by large military budgets. In 1937 the Soviet

Union had the largest mechanised army in the world, controlled by a highly modern operational system. Just to mention one indicative example: in its attack on Finland the Red Army used the world's first remote controlled tanks.

During 1938-40, however, Soviet domestic politics were dominated by huge purges, which have subsequently been seen as a result of Stalin's supposed clinical paranoia. The purges hit all of Soviet society including many leading officers, among them Tukhachevsky and his closest colleagues. The figures vary from one source to another, but undoubtedly the numbers were high: 50-90 per cent of military officers depending on the ranks of the victims. These people were branded politically unreliable and, depending on the size and nature of their postulated crimes, they were executed, imprisoned or sacked.

Though the purges set the Red Army back several years, the new military doctrine influenced the tactics used against Finland during the Winter War. As it turned out, though, they were completely ineffectual due to the unique terrain on the Finnish Front and the loss of so many experienced Soviet officers of senior rank. The Red Army was a rigid and clumsy war machine, trained to fight in open and hilly terrain using vast formations and heavy firepower. None of this worked in the almost impenetrable Finnish forests (for more details on the infrastructure of the Soviet infantry divisions see Appendix I).

The Soviet Air Force and Fleet
The Red Army's air force had been founded in 1918. Organisationally, it copied the infrastructure of the land forces, with its units named in the same manner (aviation armies, divisions, regiments etc.). After the formation of the Soviet state in 1922, strong attempts were made to improve and modernise aircraft production under the leadership of General Yakov Alksnis, who later became a victim of Stalin's purges.

During the Spanish Civil War, the Soviet Air Force was put to its first major test. The enemy was the German Luftwaffe, and the Soviet pilots did excellently. But once again Stalin's purges created problems, which in this case seriously compromised the efficiency of the air force and moved its focus away from the war in Spain.

The Red Fleet, too, had been founded in 1918 on the basis of the former Imperial Fleet. However, it was given a somewhat secondary status within the new armed forces; for instance a large part of the old fleet was sold to Germany as scrap iron. Plans for the building of a new navy, meant to become the largest in the world, were put forward in the mid-1920s. The work started picking up speed during the following decade, but the project was still in its early stages when the Second World War broke out.

The Soviet Fleet only saw limited action in the Winter War, primarily in skirmishes with Finnish coastal defence forts.

Soviet Plans

A new operational plan for a military conflict against Finland had been drawn up by the Soviet general staff in 1937 (it should be mentioned that plans of this nature are frequently and routinely made by all military staffs and cannot be taken as an indication that political intentions really exist to carry them out). The next suggested plan was put forward in June 1939, but it was dismissed by Stalin who thought it relied on the use of too many troops and on the whole was too pessimistic. Instead, he ordered the making of an alternative plan that only called for about half as many forces and built on the assumption that an invasion of Finland could be carried out in two to three weeks. This plan was accepted by the end of the month.

To put pressure on the Finns during the talks in Moscow, and arguably also to start preparing for an invasion of Finland in case the negotiations broke down, the Soviet leaders began in early October to move troops from the Baltic States north to the Finnish border. This deployment continued through the following weeks and accelerated around mid-November, when the negotiations collapsed. Meanwhile, the detailed plan for a campaign against Finland had been finished by the staff at the Leningrad Military District (it has indeed been claimed that the Soviets were not negotiating seriously but just playing for time as they made ready to invade Finland; however, if that were true it would hardly have been necessary for Stalin and Molotov to personally lead the talks). The plan was approved by Minister of Defence Kliment Voroshilov, who on 15 November issued orders about troop movements and concentrations for the coming offensive.[36]

Meanwhile, Moscow also started to prepare for the installing of a puppet government in Finland, which was to happen shortly after the Red Army had entered Finnish soil. The government would be headed by the former Finnish Social Democrat Party leader, Otto Ville Kuusinen, who had lived in exile in the Soviet Union since the defeat of the Reds in the Finnish Civil War twenty years previously. Furthermore, a massive propaganda offensive was launched all over the Soviet Union, including demonstrations, resolutions, workers meetings etc.

So far only troops from the Leningrad Military District were meant to participate in the invasion. Still, the plan was based on an assumption of Finnish military inferiority in all areas. The Finns were to be crushed in a series of battles along the entire border, after which Soviet troops would carry out a forced march towards the centre of the country. Four armies were to carry out the invasion, which would be spread all the way from the

Gulf of Finland in the south, to the shores of Lapland in the far north by the Barents Sea (for the tasks and goals of each individual Soviet Army see Appendix II).

In his book *War of the White Death* the Russian historian Bair Irincheev describes the conditions in the Soviet Army in the period leading up to the invasion: 'Soviet plans were so hastily prepared that, even before the start of the campaign, some commanders had their doubts. However, an atmosphere of self-confidence in the Red Army prevailed ... Soviet propaganda described the Red Army as "legendary and unbeatable". The Red Army was well equipped with the newest military equipment and it was the pride of the Soviet Union. However, the purges of the 1930s had left their mark on morale. Some commanders were promoted too quickly without proper experience, some disappeared, but the worst consequence of the purges was an atmosphere of distrust and fear among the commanders, who feared that their subordinates would complain to the political workers or NKVD: consequently, in some cases, commanders followed the will of their men.'[37]

The Finnish Army
The Finnish Army had been founded after the Civil War in 1918 and was based on a mixture of cadre and conscripted personnel. The cadre consisted of officers and NCOs with a long service period. Together these groups formed the standing army, a framework which in case of mobilisation could be expanded with recalled members of the reserve. This system was in the early 1930s replaced by a more efficient mobilisation procedure, where the recalled reservists were to gather at regional meeting points from which they could be sent directly to the front under the leadership of cadre officers.

The Finnish recruits, too, had to swear an oath. It included the following passages, which seem to reflect a worry concerning the conscripts' loyalty towards the established order of society:

> I (name) promise and ensure before God the Almighty and All-Knowing that I shall be to the country of Finland a faithful and reliable citizen. I will readily serve my country and to all my ability, in peace as well as war, defend my fatherland, its political system and its lawful sovereignty. If I sense or experience anything aimed at overthrowing the country's lawful sovereignty or dissolving the country's legal social organisation, I will promptly report it to the authorities. As long as I have strength in me I shall in no way deviate from the unit to which I belong and the task I have been entrusted.[38]

When looking at the history of Finland in the first half of the twentieth century, one can easily get the impression that the country was a militant society. This notion is strengthened by visual factors such as the Finnish military's use of swastikas, German Army equipment (most notably the characteristic helmets) and so on. These factors were, in fact, coincidental and had nothing to do with National Socialism. Nevertheless, militarism in Finland *was* more prevalent than in the other Nordic countries. The Finnish historian Henrik Meinander writes: 'Since the Whites had won the Civil War, the cultural field was dominated by the vision of a white and predominantly agrarian Finland, whose military preparedness and strong belief in the future were to secure national survival.'[39]

There is little doubt that the Civil War had led to a brutalising of Finnish society, as one would expect. The Danish journalist Peter de Hemmer Gudme, who participated in that war as a volunteer on the White side,[40] later wrote on this:

> And so it once happened in Finland that some men were to be selected to execute some prisoners, and most of them stepped back, that a young farmer's lad from Ostrobothnia volunteered, saying: 'Oh, never mind. I have shot three men today already; a few more or less should make no difference.'
>
> In most people I suppose a certain degree of brutalisation occurs. It was particularly nasty to see some Swedish officers [also volunteers on the White side] test their new pistols by shooting prisoners.[41]

However, Finland was not a militant country in the traditional sense. Though there had been two armies, or rather guards, fighting each other in 1918, the Civil War had been characterised by a lack of military professionalism. The Norwegian journalist Edvard Welle-Strand commented on this in a contemporary article titled *Amatørkrigen i Finland* (*The Amateur War in Finland*):

> The General Staff of the Whites is the only exception. Here you could find officers with solid education, warriors with experiences from a few campaigns ... But the young soldiers, who are sent to their death, are amateurs – both Reds and Whites ... Even the simplest, basic military concepts are unknown to the workers and peasants that are killing each other in the forests and on the fields of Finland.[42]

A real national Finnish Army did not exist at all until after the Civil War, since the country had never before been independent. Finns had been conscripted to the Swedish Army during Sweden's Great-Power Period, but in 1918 this was more than a hundred years ago, and during the years under Russian rule (1809-1917) the Finns had by and large avoided participation in the wars of the mother state. A three-year conscription period had been introduced in 1878 to be served in a kind of local Finnish Army, which patriotically orientated citizens saw as a big step ahead for their cause, though the troops were in fact serving under the Russian Empire. But Finland had been far too poor a country to maintain such a military force and, as a result, less than 10 per cent of young Finnish men actually did this military service. Others were placed in the reserve where they received one month of training each year during the three-year period, while the majority were let off completely for various reasons.[43]

During much of the 'Russian Period' there was almost an implied agreement between Russians and Finns to leave each other in peace. The impression you sometimes get is that life in an autonomous grand duchy could include both the advantages of living in a small and in a big country. But towards the end of the 1800s hostility grew between the parties, as Nicholas II's attempts to centralise his empire collided with a growing Finnish urge for independence. The situation came to a head shortly after the turn of the century, when the so-called 'Finnish' Army was abolished and Finns instead were conscripted into the Imperial Russian Army. The new law caused heavy protests in Finland. Recruits stayed away from the medical examination and protest strikes were held all over the country. In the end, the Russians changed the rules so that Finland's contribution to Russia's military from then on was only of an economic nature.

Even during the First World War conscription was not introduced in Finland. Still, two groups of Finns participated in the fighting on the Eastern Front, serving on either side. One group consisted of those who had pursued a long-lasting professional career in the Imperial Russian Army or Fleet. This was the other group that Mannerheim, for instance, belonged to. The members of the group were some 2,000 young Finnish men, who had travelled south to join the Imperial German Army. These men would later have an enormous influence on the Finnish Army's strategic and tactical thinking, particularly during the Second World War. All the same, they did not represent a national military tradition as such, and the general population's attitude towards them was not unanimously enthusiastic, as we shall see.

The Finnish volunteers in the German Army were not a homogenous group, not even politically. What they had in common was primarily a dream of complete national Finnish independence, which they believed could only be gained through a military struggle against Russia. By joining the German Army they received thorough military training and war experience that could later be used in such a struggle, while at the same time they were actively fighting against their main enemy, Russia.

These young men came predominantly (but not exclusively) from the upper middle classes, and there was a particularly high number of university students among them. Yet, surveys in later years have shown that the group was considerably more mixed than previously assumed. It included, for example, members of the working class and people with left wing sympathies.[44] The practical arrangements surrounding the recruitment and the journey through Sweden was managed by nationalistic and Germanophile groups and had to be carried out in deep secrecy, since the recruits were joining an army that was fighting against Finland's mother state.

The volunteers were put in the *Königlich Preussisches Jägerbataillon Nr. 27*, also known as the Finnish Battalion, which was brought into action in 1916 in the northern sector of the Eastern Front, as part of the 8th Prussian Army. When the Civil War broke out in Finland in early 1918, the volunteers were allowed to return home if the purpose was to join the White Guard. The vast majority of the battalion chose to do just that.

Later on the former *Jägers* would form the nucleus of the Finnish officer corps, which led to the use of a strict Prussian discipline. Thus the daily routine for conscripts in the Finnish Army of the 1920s came to include severe physical punishment 'bordering on downright torture', 'abusive name-calling', 'exercises where recruits are purposelessly exposed to the risk of catching severe diseases' and 'rotten food'. Prussian discipline became an invective among Finnish conscripts and was primarily associated with officers and NCOs who had formerly served in the German Army.[45]

Written accounts from the period also indicate that the recruits had big problems with their superiors' tendency to shout at them and with having to spend a considerable amount of time indoors. For these reasons, as well as others (such as certain health-threatening initiation rituals), there was a high number of psychological breakdowns among the recruits. On several occasions the *Eduskunta* (the Finnish parliament) reprimanded the NCO and officer classes after having received complaints from appalled and deeply worried parents of conscripted soldiers.

It seems paradoxical that the same Finnish men, who during the Winter War gained a worldwide reputation as immensely tough defenders of their country, could become so deeply distressed because of loud-mouthed NCOs and stuffy barracks rooms. The reason seems to be that the recruits mainly came from isolated and thinly populated rural districts, simply because that was what Finland mainly consisted of (in 1920 84 per cent of the population lived in rural areas, 70 per cent worked in farming or forestry).[46] They were shy and taciturn people used to being outdoors and living close to nature. In any case, by the time the Finnish troops were on the way to the front in the Winter War, there was no shouting from NCOs and officers, who also otherwise acted entirely different from how they had behaved during training.

The official demands to reduce the Prussian discipline in the army were slow in taking effect, and in some ways the military seems to have functioned as a state within the state. Nevertheless, the conditions for young army recruits started to change from the early 1930s under influence from modern military psychology, which recommended the use of 'positive motivation' instead of robot-like discipline. Since this in some ways was just another term for political and nationalistic indoctrination, it went hand in hand with the concurrent anti-Russian tendencies in the rest of Finnish society, particularly in the school system. Included in this was a view of history that portrayed the relationship between Finland and Russia as far more conflict-ridden than it had actually been. Mainly, it ignored the fact that the struggles in reality had often been wars between Sweden and Russia, where the Finns were just stuck in the middle and forced to carry out the hard work for their Nordic brothers on the other side of the Gulf of Bothnia.[47]

The atmosphere and discipline was fundamentally different in the Finnish Civil Guard. Its members were volunteers, which of course made for a higher degree of motivation. Like the regular army, the Civil Guard had its roots in the White Guard of the Civil War and had since then maintained its right wing orientation. Initially, its task was not only to secure the state against outside enemies, but just as much, if not more, to secure it inwardly against left wing revolutionaries. Officially, the Civil Guard was supposed to be politically neutral, but around 1930 its right wing views became more extreme and linked to the strongly anti-Communist Lapua Movement and its illegal conduct, which included kidnappings, acts of severe violence and even murder.[48]

It all culminated in the failed Mäntsälä Rebellion in early 1932, where the government ordered the regular army to round up the rebels. After that the rebellion petered out, allegedly under the influence of copious amounts of alcohol. Overall the event had a comic tint to it, though it did land some of the Lapua leaders in prison. Meanwhile, the movement was declared illegal and dissolved, ironically enough according to the same laws that its own leaders had previously championed in order to illegalise Finland's Communist Party.

Since then the Finnish Civil Guard had become less political, but it continued to have considerable support. In the years leading up to the Winter War, the organisation had more than 100,000 members. Through its youth organisations and magazine publishing it enforced a nationalistic and anti-Russian atmosphere in large parts of Finnish society. Suffice to say the organisation was detested by the left wing.

The female wing of the Civil Guard was the Lotta Svärd organisation, which likewise had emerged from the White side of the Civil War. This voluntary axillary corps carried out kitchen work, office work, laundry work, nursing tasks, an air defence warning service etc. At the outbreak of the Winter War it counted some 80,000 members.

In the early 1930s, the Finnish Army was exposed to budget cuts. This also happened in the other Nordic countries, but there the comparison ends. Despite the cuts, the Finnish Army was still granted sums that would make the jaw drop of a contemporary Danish, Norwegian or Swedish commander-in-chief: approximately 20 per cent of the entire national budget. When Mannerheim complained and threatened to resign, it could seem like the grumbles of a spoiled child, and indeed that was how many Finnish politicians saw it. Besides, the defence budgets rose again by the end of the decade, albeit so late that the effects could not yet be felt by the time the Winter War broke out (in fact, the delay seems in some cases to have been caused by disagreements between the high ranking officers, including Mannerheim, over which equipment should be purchased).

The Finnish Army could assemble nine infantry divisions and a few separate battalions, a total of 250,000 men. During the Winter War a further three reserve divisions were called up, which raised the number to 340,000.[49] If you added up the numbers of personnel in the army, the navy, coastal defence and the air force, the result was some 400,000 troops. Additionally, there were the Lottas, who were not combatants but who freed up more or less the same number of men for active armed service.

It has often been pointed out that the Finnish Army was small and poorly armed. Yet for a country of just 3.7 million people Finland actually had a very big army with almost half a million personnel (during the Continuation War it topped at more than 600,000). That the Red Army was much bigger can hardly come as a surprise to anyone, since the population of the Soviet Union was more than forty times larger than that of Finland, and furthermore it was a military super power with a massive, state-of-the-art weapons industry etc.

Of course, the Finnish Army could never have won a war against a major power such as the Soviet Union, even if its entire national budget had been spent on the military. But that had never been the idea behind the Finnish Army. The idea was to be able to defend oneself in a war where the enemy was engaged on a larger front against one or two other enemies, or to at least hold back an invasion long enough for outside help to arrive. If Finland ended up in a situation where it was fighting all alone, as it did in the Winter War, the task was to keep the enemy at bay while the politicians tried to solve the situation by diplomatic means.

In any case, it goes without saying that the Finnish Army was completely outnumbered by the invading Soviet force in 1939, and with regard to materiel and fuel supplies the situation was equally bleak for the Finns. According to Mannerheim, the stores only had enough petrol and lubrication oil for two months, and the same went for rifle and automatic weapons ammunition. The air force would run out of fuel within a month, while ammunition for the artillery (both field pieces and fortresses guns) could last for a maximum of three weeks.[50]

The differences in size and strength were amplified by a pronounced lack of small arms for the Finnish infantry, and even the weapons that did exist were in many cases obsolete. The Finnish-made 9mm submachine gun, nicknamed the *Suomi*, was highly effective in forested terrain, but these weapons were few and far between, as well. Furthermore, each Finnish division only had half as much artillery as its Soviet counterparts and the majority of its pieces were from the First World War, while the Soviet artillery guns were state of the art.

Some historians have made direct comparisons between the Finnish Army and the entire Red Army in 1939. It must be remembered, though, that the full force of the Red Army was not employed against Finland in the Winter War. Hence, it makes more sense to make a comparison in divisions, although it must be taken into account that there were differences in size and equipment between the Finnish and Soviet formations. A rough estimate here would be that a typical Soviet division was superior to its Finnish counterpart by a factor of 2:1 (for a more detailed comparison, see Appendix III). Since more Soviet than Finnish divisions participated in the war, the Soviet superiority at the front is generally set at 3:1, though in practice it was probably a good deal larger than that.

But there were also areas where the Finnish Army had advantages, or at least could outweigh its shortcomings by various means:

For instance, it was hugely important that most upper ranking Finnish officers had combat experience from both the First World War and the Finnish Civil War. Their conduct during training may have been unnecessarily tough on the men, but they were undoubtedly a group of intelligent, highly trained and constructively thinking professionals. Before as well as during the Winter War they were constantly seeking out anything that could give them an advantage over the enemy.

It is commonly agreed that the Finnish field artillery was superior in areas concerning theoretical and practical usage of their weapons, including fire control.

Although the guns of the Finnish coastal defences were from the 'Russian Period', they were still highly effective, partly thanks to their enormous calibres.[51]

Most members of the Finnish reserve were recalled once a year to have their training refreshed and updated by NCOs from the Civil Guard. The training often focused on operations in terrain and temperatures typical for northern latitudes, with a special emphasis on winter warfare.

The Finnish lack of anti-tank guns was, during the war itself, made up for by the use of so-called Molotov cocktails. According to the Finnish Army's own reports, it destroyed some 2,000 Soviet tanks during the war, mainly by the use of these bottles filled with inflammable liquid.[52]

It proved lucky for the Finns that they had started mobilising in early October, almost two months before the war broke out. Thereby the troops along the border had time to get to know each other, improve their positions and acquaint themselves with the future battlefields.

The lack of uniforms was not a big problem, since in most cases white camouflage was worn over whatever was underneath.

Moreover, the Finns soon captured vast amounts of war booty from defeated Soviet units and thus resupplied their own stocks, while further supplies arrived from Sweden and other countries.

Still, the biggest advantage that the Finns had lay in their knowledge of the terrain. If you look at a map, the mere thought of defending this country against a Soviet attack seems hopeless in advance. Almost 1,500km of common land frontier stretches from the Gulf of Finland in the south to the Barents Sea in the north. Add to this long stretches of coastline in the southern and western parts of the country. However, a closer investigation can radically change one's view of how these areas could be military defended.

If we look at the south and west coast first, the Finnish skerries secured the country from naval attacks and landings far better than any manmade coastal defences could ever have done. There were occasional openings, but they were generally covered by the coastal artillery. The shore defences in the eastern part of the Gulf of Finland had originally been built to prevent the British Navy from sailing in and threatening St Petersburg, as it had done during the Crimean War. Now the gigantic guns from those days served a different purpose, namely to stop a landing by the Red Army for instance at Koivisto on the western side of the Karelian Isthmus. A Soviet landing at this point was particularly dangerous since it could lead to Red Army troops moving in 20km behind the main defence line on the Isthmus, later known as the Mannerheim Line (Map 3).

As the Finns saw it, the Karelian Isthmus was like an open road into the most densely populated part of their country, including Helsinki. If there were any place that the Red Army in 1939 could utilise its formidable size, it was on the Karelian Isthmus where there were real roads and occasional open areas. But it was still a Finnish landscape, intercepted and perforated everywhere by streams and lakes. Particularly in winter, with just a few hours of daylight and temperatures way below freezing, the potential for a military attack started to look considerably less promising.

However, the Karelian Isthmus *was* like an open road compared to the landscapes north of Lake Ladoga, which was the next Soviet operational zone to the north. Here the terrain was characterised by dense, endless stretches of pine forest, lakes, streams, stony ground and swampy bogs. The few, badly maintained dirt and gravel roads ran parallel to each other at huge distances apart and were practically without connecting roads, particularly within a distance of 50km from the border. To wage war with heavy equipment and huge formations in such a terrain was bound to go wrong. In winter the ground was frozen and the lakes iced over, which could give an attacker greater mobility, but only for small groups of skilled skiers.

If this sounds like an unwelcoming landscape, it was nothing compared to the conditions further north. The unbelievably harsh winter climate in northern Finland made the operations of the Red Army there particularly problematic, while the Finnish soldiers were generally well acquainted with the locality. The dangers presented by nature here included everything from snow blindness to hypothermia, dehydration and sunburn – unless you were *so* far north that it was simply dark around the clock. The frozen ground made it practically impossible to dig trenches, and temperatures regularly dropped below minus 40 centigrade. Often, wild storms raced across the vast tundra, with a wind chill factor that strongly enhanced the risk of frostbite. Soldiers' hands could easily freeze to their weapon or to the metal of vehicles. On top of all this came the demands placed on logistics in these areas with their scarce and poorly maintained roads, a need for special lubricants, engines that had to be kept running more-or-less constantly and soldiers with an increased need for calories.[53]

Putting all these factors together, the Finnish supreme command had concluded that a Soviet attack on Finnish Lapland was not a realistic development, and therefore only a few Finnish troops had been deployed in the area during the run-up to the war. This would soon turn out to be a serious miscalculation.

The Mannerheim Line
The Finnish leaders were convinced that a Soviet attack, if it ever happened, would be concentrated on the Karelian Isthmus. Hence, a defensive position had been build there, the main line of which would be nicknamed 'the Mannerheim Line' by foreign journalists soon after the Winter War had started (Map 3). The marshal personally did not like the name and only used it rarely, perhaps because it could evoke misleading images of the impressive French Maginot Line.

Work on the Finnish fortifications had started in 1920, when the government realised that the Communist regime in the Soviet Union was not just a temporary measure. In 1924 the work was halted, but it was resumed in 1932.[54] By 1939 the position consisted of three lines situated more or less behind each other. The Mannerheim Line was the most southern one and hence the line closest to the Soviet border. Starting in the west by the Gulf of Finland, it twisted and turned its way east to end on the banks of Lake Ladoga, whose northern half at the time belonged to Finland. Along the way it utilised most of the natural terrain advantages, particularly in the eastern sector where approximately one third of it followed the northern bank of the Vuoksi River. Lieutenant General Öhquist, commander of the western sector, complained that the line in his area should have been placed quite a bit further south around the town of Summa to create 'depth in the defence line and thus make it more flexible'. This would also have moved the troops up on a ridge where there was natural cover, instead of placing them in exposed positions on swampy meadows.[55]

The terrain in front of the Mannerheim Line was strongly mined, dotted with machine-gun nests and guarded by covering troops, whose task was to delay the enemy in case of surprise attacks and thus give the main position time to prepare itself.

The two fall-back lines, named the Intermediate Line and the T-Line, were considerably weaker than the Mannerheim Line. If all three lines were overrun, it could lead to the fall of Viipuri, which would open the way into southern Finland for the Red Army. As such, the Karelian Isthmus constituted the Achilles heel in the overall Finnish defence, a fact which the Soviet leaders of course were fully aware of.

The Mannerheim Line was a 136km long chain of dug-outs, bunkers (most of them armed with machine guns), anti-tank defences and trenches. By 1939 the position needed to be strengthened, extended and updated, and during the summer of that year 60,000 volunteers had worked on these improvements. Still, the work was not finished when the war broke out, so the Finnish troops had to continue improving the position in freezing cold and snowy conditions. This was in strong opposition to the image that the Soviet propaganda tried to promote, since the 210[56] small bunkers of the Mannerheim Line had very little in common with the Maginot Line and its 5,800 bunkers.

The Finnish Air Force and Navy
Like the army and the civil guard, the Finnish air force had emerged out of the White Guard of the Civil War. By the beginning of the Winter War it consisted of 110 aircraft of various kinds, although only 75 of these were ready for action. This should be compared to the 1,000 aircraft of the Red Air Force deployed to the Finnish Front at the beginning of the war. During

the conflict, Finland tried to buy more aircraft from other countries, but the attempt was only partially successful and most of the planes that were bought had still not arrived when the war ended. Meanwhile, the number of Soviet aircraft at the front had increased to 4,000.[57]

The Finnish Navy was originally put together from ships left behind by the Russians in 1918. By the beginning of the Winter War, the fleet was still very small. Its pride was two coastal battle ships, which had absorbed a big chunk of the defence budget when they were built, but which failed to contribute much to Finland's defences. Apart from that the fleet consisted mainly of minor vessels and gunboats, submarines, minelayers and torpedo boats, a few coast guard ships and civilian boats converted for military use. Also, the navy had a handful of small vessels on Lake Ladoga. Fortunately for the Finns, maritime combat was limited during the Winter War, partly because the waters around Finland in December froze up so much that icebreaking became impossible. Hence, operations were limited to minelaying, submarine activities and a few skirmishes with Soviet warships.

The Finnish coastal defence was more active. It was manned by three coastal artillery regiments and two separate coastal artillery sections. Moreover, there were a number of minelaying units, infantry companies and anti-aircraft units etc. The jagged and hard-to-navigate skerries from the island of Utö in the west to the Karelian Isthmus in the east were by contemporary standards particularly well secured with heavy, formerly Russian artillery, which the Finns had 'inherited' when they declared their independence in 1917. The Åland Islands, however, had to be left unfortified due to international agreements, as were the outer islands in the Gulf of Finland from the Toivisto archipelago and further south.[58]

Finnish Plans and Mobilisation
Finnish operational plans for a war with Russia had existed since the Civil War. Surprisingly, they included an offensive element. The idea was not just to defend Finland's own borders but also to attack into Russian territory.

It may seem bizarre that a small country would plan that way militarily. The reason can partly be traced back to the principles which the former volunteers in the Finnish Battalion in Germany had encountered during the First World War, and which several of them later studied more closely by attending lectures at military academies in France and elsewhere. Another reason was that the Finnish Army could set up better defensive positions by moving a few kilometres into East Karelia, which would also turn the occupied area into a practical buffer zone. Furthermore, the Finnish planners envisaged a situation where their army constituted the northern flank in a broad attack on the Soviet Union, probably led by France and Great Britain with participation from a string of smaller East European states (the possibility of a German attack was not realistic until the late 1930s).

In 1939 there were basically two Finnish defence plans called VK1 and VK2, which were both updated versions of previous plans. VK1 was based on an older plan codenamed K3 (later W.K.3 and V.K.27) and was far more aggressive than VK2. In K3 the Finns would attack Leningrad (then Petrograd) via the Karelian Isthmus, while their air force bombed bridges and airports near the city. Meanwhile, other Finnish units would invade East Karelia north of Lake Ladoga, where support from the local ethnically Finnish population was expected, and from where attacks would be made against the Russian right flank. Further north, Finnish ski units would push through to the Murmansk Railway.[59] Research in recent years has shown that the plan mirrored expansive intentions among the former Finnish volunteers in the Imperial German Army, who in the mid-1920s exercised pressure on the government in this regard.[60] The plan, which in part was carried out during the initial stage of the Continuation War, had in 1934 been overhauled after the launch of a new National Defence Act that same year (the same defence act which, as previously mentioned, made the mobilisation procedures more efficient).

VK2 (along with its predecessors) was based on a much less advantageous situation, where Finland only mobilised after it had been attacked by Russia. Here the covering troops on the Karelian Isthmus were to slow down the enemy's progress while the reserves were called up. Though the plan was far less optimistic than VK1, it still assumed that the Finns, as part of an alliance, would push back the Russians. North of Lake Ladoga the attackers were to be repelled as well, leading into the launching of a Finnish counteroffensive. For the northern sector, the plan was identical to VK1.

Even VK2, which by 1939 was seen as the only realistic plan of the two, seems surprisingly optimistic for the army of a small country and employs strategic principles similar to those of a major power. Still, as subsequent events would show, the Finnish high ranking officers managed (albeit with significant exceptions) to reshape these principles and suit them to Finnish conditions.[61]

Seen from a broad perspective, the Finnish military had two main tasks. The first one belonged to the field army on the frontline, who were to hold its positions and use them as launch pads for counterattacks. The second task was given to the covering troops, who often came from the areas in which they operated and hence possessed a high degree of motivation and knowledge of the terrain. Apart from carrying out the aforementioned delaying actions they sometimes had to undertake larger military operations, and for that purpose some units included light *Jäger*[62] battalions as well as groups of cavalry and, albeit more rarely, artillery.

In August 1939 the Finnish Army held a manoeuvre on the Karelian Isthmus where all the country's foreign military attaches were present as observers. The purpose of the exercise was partly to test a number of changes that had been made to the VK2 plan. Some of the recalled reservist units, which were subsequently discharged, were recalled again as soon as September. Reservists in the navy, the coastal artillery and the air force were called up, too. Soldiers who were doing their first period of National Service, and who should have been discharged in September, had their service period extended. New units of covering troops and specialist reservist units were set up during the same month. This meant that in practise the mobilising of the Finnish Army had begun, and it continued over the following two months until the war broke out.

On the evening of 29 November, six Finnish divisions were deployed on the Karelian Isthmus. Across from them on the other side of the frontier was the Red Army's main attack force made up by nine infantry divisions supported by four tank brigades and several heavy artillery regiments. Along the entire Finnish-Soviet land border a total of eight Finnish divisions were facing a soviet invasion force of four armies consisting of twenty divisions and five tank brigades (for a more detailed description of the Finnish order of battle see Appendix IV).

In the early hours of the next day the Soviet units started crossing the border. At the same time, bombers belonging to the Red Air Force took off from airfields in Estonia, their course set for Helsinki and other Finnish cities and towns.

III

The First Month of the War

In our opinion the Russians already had plenty of land. But if they really needed more, we could always give them an area of approximately one by 2 metres, which is exactly what you need for a grave.
MARTTI HAKALA[63]

The War Breaks Out

The Soviet attack that was launched on Finland in the morning of 30 November 1939 came as a complete surprise to nearly all parts of Finnish Society. Different kinds of activities had recently been observed in several places on the Soviet side of the border, but not even the Finnish intelligence services had found this particularly worrying. In fact, when reports of massive Soviet troop movements and border violations started coming in from the frontier during the early hours, the situation was still not taken seriously in Helsinki. This changed quickly, however, when the first bombers from the Red Air Force emerged in the sky above the city at dawn, a mere three hours after Soviet ground forces had crossed the border.

The bombardment was not so serious that it prevented the gathering of the *Eduskunta* in the evening in the usual parliamentary building (only later were the politicians moved to Kauhajoki, a town in southwest Finland where the parliament remained for the rest of the war). Before that, President Kyösti Kallio had declared a state of emergency and handed over his formal position as commander-in-chief to Marshal Mannerheim. The next day a new government was appointed, with Risto Ryti from the National Progress Party as prime minister. Väinö Tanner from the Social Democrats became minister for foreign affairs and Paasikivi was appointed minister without portfolio. Niukkanen from the Agrarian League (today the Centre Party) retained his post as minister of defence. Overall, this was a broader government than the previous one, with five parties participating.

It was hoped that the new leaders would do better than their predecessors in relation to the Soviet Union and that peace negotiations could be initiated as soon as possible. However, this was a miscalculation since Moscow thought that Väinö Tanner was the main reason for the collapse of the pre-

Helsinki under Soviet Bombardment, December 1939. (SA-Kuva)

war talks. The well-known animosity between the two main left wing factions, Social Democrats and Communists, was making its presence felt.

The next day Mannerheim issued an order-of-the-day (his first during the Winter War), in which he described the current situation as 'nothing other than a continuation of the War of Liberation [the common term at the time for the Finnish Civil War] and its final act'. His choice of words has later been heavily criticised, since instead of uniting the Finnish people it might remind them of the class-related clashes of the past. The declaration is undeniably strange but perhaps not as rash as it immediately appears. In the early stages of the Winter War, the Soviet Union tried hard to promote its invasion as a means to support a new Red revolt in Finland. Through Radio Moscow the Finnish Communist Party broadcast declarations aimed at encouraging the Finnish working classes to rise and rebel again under the leadership of Kuusinen's puppet government. Mannerheim at the time had a very negative view of the Finnish Army's ability to resist the on-going attack. It might be that he initially expected a Soviet occupation of Southern Finland, followed by fighting deeper inside the country while the Finnish Army retreated north, which would be a situation similar to the one that had occurred during the Civil War.[64]

The Retreat to the Mannerheim Line
When the Red Army crossed the border on the Karelian Isthmus, the Finnish

covering troops began their delaying action, conducting a fighting withdrawal. In fact, they were more or less following the same strategy as the Russians had used themselves during the Napoleonic invasion of 1812, known as the scorched earth policy. The purpose was to deprive the enemy of any cover and force him to remain outdoors in the freezing cold as much as possible. In this way, the Soviet advance was to be slowed down while the Finnish field army prepared itself inside the Mannerheim Line.

The scheme worked well, not least because of the poor equipment of the Soviet soldiers in general during the early stage of the war. They were lacking proper winter uniforms (though many Finnish soldiers were dressed in their civilian clothes, these were warm and suitable for winter weather; also, the Finnish soldiers typically slept in either dugouts or tents equipped with wood-burning stoves). Another factor causing problems for the Russians was that the roads were too small for all the trucks and tanks crossing the border on the first day of the war. As a result, the Red Army experienced massive traffic jams, long delays, a general state of confusion and tangled-up communication lines.[65] And while they were caught in this mess on the roads, the Finns moved freely and easily through the forests and between the still unfrozen streams and lakes.

But the Finnish military had its problems, too. The idea was that the covering troops should adhere to the hit-and-run principle and avoid direct confrontations as much as possible, since the units lacked the capacity to carry out larger engagements. In this regard their personal attachment to the area in which they operated soon proved a drawback. It hurt the men too much to hand their native places over to the enemy without much real resistance. Nevertheless, they managed to delay the Red Army's advance as planned until 2 December, when the first Soviet troops reached the foremost outposts of the Mannerheim Line.

On the same day, the Finnish High Command received a faulty intelligence report, leading to an ill-fated regrouping of the troops by Lipola Village 25km south of the Mannerheim Line (Map 3). In consequence, a large piece of the terrain was handed over to the Russians without struggle and at the same time the Finns exposed their remaining positions in the area.

As the Finnish soldiers at Lipola came under heavy pressure, the Russians carried out their first major attack on 4 December. This was in the western sector, in the parish of Uusikirkko. The Finns had problems with their radio communication, which delayed calls for reinforcements from the main position. In turn this led to their line being penetrated so the troops were forced to retreat northwest to the Mannerheim Line. Here the situation was brought under control and the soldiers prepared for the next Soviet attack.

This, however, was launched 30km from Uusikirkko just west of

Soviet troops crossing a bridge into Finland.

Maisniemi, a peninsula that protrudes out into Suulajärvi (see list of Finnish suffixes in the introduction to the book). Meanwhile, the Soviet pressure on Lipola became too much for the undermanned Finnish position and the troops had to evacuate the village in favour of another position further north.

Another Soviet attack took place on the same day in the eastern sector at Kiviniemi, a peninsula that protrudes into the Vuoksi River. Under heavy fire the Russians managed to cross the river and establish a bridgehead, which brought them right up to the Mannerheim Line.

The next day (5 December) the Red Army resumed its attacks at

Maisniemi where they tried to encircle the Finns in a pincer movement north of Suulajärvi. The covering troops in the area were part of Battle Group U, to which belonged the Häme Cavalry Regiment. This was the first major Soviet infantry attack supported by tanks, and due to a lack of anti-tank weapons it caused a minor outbreak of panic among some of the Finnish troops, most of whom had never seen such vehicles before. The Häme Cavalry Regiment particularly appears to have been in a state of near panic, exacerbated by the arrival of a Finnish Landsverk 182 armoured car that was supporting Battle Group U but was misidentified as a Soviet tank.

The flight, however, did not cause any major problems for the Finns, since by now their organised fighting retreat to the main position was almost completed. Meanwhile, their worst communication problems had also been solved, and as a result their following operations were more successful. When the Soviet troops attacked the Finnish positions in the eastern sector at Kiviniemi and Koukonniemi, they were repelled and heavy casualties were inflicted.

With this the Finnish covering troops had completed their mission. Mistakes had been made along the way, but by and large the operations had gone according to plan, giving the Finnish field army enough time to prepare itself inside the main position.

For the Soviet high command the events had been far less promising. From the very beginning the dense and vast employment of troops had turned into a classic example of how to stumble over oneself militarily. Furthermore, the Finns were defending themselves with surprising efficiency. Equally surprising, their society had not collapsed due to an internal revolt, as expatriate Finnish communists in Russia had led the Kremlin leaders to believe would happen. Instead, the Finnish people stood united as never before.

Soviet Mass Attacks
There now followed a few days where part of the Red Army licked its wounds, regrouped, evaluated the situation and brought in reinforcements. Meanwhile, parts of the Seventh Army (see Appendix II) carried out the first mass attacks of the war but were unable to penetrate the Mannerheim Line. Both sides also carried out artillery bombardments and sent out patrols. The Finnish lines could still not be broken, but Soviet attempts at blowing up enemy anti-tank defences were more successful. The obstructions turned out to be placed so far from the main positions that they were hard for the Finns to defend unless they went out into the open terrain and took up fighting there.

What the Russians prepared for during these days were two large-scale attacks, one at Summa Village in the western sector and the other at the

*Finnish soldiers in a dugout (*korsu*) at Taipale on the Karelian Isthmus.* (SA-Kuva)

easternmost point of the Mannerheim Line at Taipale. The latter attack, however, was mainly a diversion. The real objective was Summa. A breakthrough here might lead to catastrophic consequences for the Finnish Army, since it could open the road to Viipuri and then onwards to Helsinki.

Over the following days, the Russians carried out several attacks on Summa, but they were only of a scouting nature and were repelled by the Finns. Then, on 14 December, a Finnish reconnaissance patrol reported that a huge attack was underway and that the Russians had brought forward yet another division with additional artillery.

Next morning at dawn, the attack on Taipale started with a powerful Soviet artillery assault, which the antiquated and numerically inferior Finnish guns had no way of matching. Instead, the Finnish troops were ordered to take cover in their trenches and wait until the Soviet tanks and infantry began their part of the attack and had moved up closer to the Mannerheim Line. As it turned out, the tactic worked. The Finns managed to fight off the Russians and cause them heavy losses. Twelve tanks were completely destroyed.

Many letters from the front, written by Soviet soldiers, were at the time confiscated by the censors and archived. Some have in recent years been released to the public, and they give an excellent insight into the situation for the Red Army conscripts during the Winter War. About the conditions on the Karelian Isthmus at the start of the war, Private Churkin wrote to his sister, Yefimova, in Moscow:

> Sister! Starting from 6 December we have been trying to drive the enemy away and failed. I had a lot of dear friends near me, now they are no more. It was a battle. I guess you heard something about hell? The same thing happens here: some men cry, some complain, others shout and beg to be finished off after being wounded. The Devil himself would not understand what is going on around here.[66]

Another Soviet private called Tarasov wrote to his father in Kursk:

> Father! We await death every moment. Three times it was very near: one time a Finnish airplane attacked and two times we were under very heavy artillery fire. Many of my comrades were killed or wounded. There were days when 600 and 700 men were killed or wounded. Trucks were evacuating the wounded day and night. By now the artillery had been firing for sixteen days, but nothing helps to drive the Finns out of there.[67]

Further Fighting at Taipale and Summa
On 15 December the Russians resumed their attack on Taipale. The Finns had no other choice than to wait again until the Soviet tanks and infantry were within a distance of 50 metres and then open fire at them with all available rifles, machine guns and anti-tank guns. Wave after wave of Soviet soldiers were ordered to advance upon the Finnish positions only to be stopped with heavy losses. Here they remained under fire, until they finally gave up and fled back.

Two days after the assault on Taipale, the Red Army launched a massive attack on Summa (some Finnish historians are of the opinion that the Taipale and Summa attacks were supposed to have happened simultaneously, but that the Summa attack was delayed). What made Summa particularly important was that in this sector both the Viipuri-Leningrad main road and

Soviet assault gun in position, December 1939.

the railway crossed the Mannerheim Line. Here the Finnish 5th Division was stretched out in a long thin line, with the 6th Division positioned on the road further back by the T-Line.

The attack on Summa also started with a huge artillery preparation that lasted until 10 am. During the mass attack that followed, the Russians aimed their artillery ahead of the infantry and rolled the fire forward in front of the advancing line. This, of course, demanded close communication between artillery observers and fire-control officers. However, frequent mistakes were made so that fire was called down on their own troops.

The Finnish artillery had other problems, primarily a lack of ammunition. During the Winter War the Soviet artillery fired on average 230,000 shells a day. The Finnish amount for *the entire war* was approximately 500,000.[68]

At Summa the Soviet infantry attacked with support from both aircraft and some eighty tanks. Again, the Finns held their fire until the enemy had come up close. Lieutenant Oiva Porra, commander of the 15th Regiment's second company, later wrote about the experience:

> In the middle of our defensive sector was Bunker Sj5, or the 'One Million Bastion', a concrete machine gun bunker and shelter combined … As the morning grew light, the offensive started. Two heavy tanks drove out of the forest in front of us, followed by three more – there were more and more tanks coming, forming an assault line. They were slowly approaching our positions, roaring their

engines ... We could see assaulting lines of infantry spreading out in front of our entire sector. In lines and groups, often following one another, the enemy marched into battle sinking knee deep in snow ...
Intense fire opened from all our positions.[69]

Then began the butchery of the Soviet soldiers, whose leaders repeatedly sent them forward into what by now had started resembling regular suicide missions. The fighting lasted until nightfall, which sets in just four hours after dawn at this time of year on the Karelian Isthmus. By then the attack had been repelled by the Finns at all points except Summa, where the Russians had managed to force their way in between the buildings. However, these troops were soon pushed back too.

But the Russians were not alone in having problems. Again, the Finnish radio equipment was unreliable and to make it worse the noise from the battlefield was infernal. There was not enough time to use codes, so where orders could be communicated at all via radio or field telephones, it was done in a mixture of Finnish and Swedish, while nicknames were used for the different units and so on.[70]

The next Soviet attack came the following day (18 December) and started with a four hour long artillery preparation. Then the infantry moved forward, this time supported by seventy tanks. The Finnish Corporal Toivo Aloha, from the third company of the 15th Regiment, wrote:

Our anti-tank team managed to neutralise several tanks in no-man's land; one tank hit a mine, but there were still plenty of them coming. The bravest crews drove over our trenches and into our rear. Other tanks started driving back and forth, levelling out the barbed wire fencing, and a third group of tanks stopped in order to clear the passages through the anti-tank obstacles. The tanks that drove into our rear were in a vulnerable position – they immediately came under attack from our tank busters. A tank has rather poor visibility and a brave man in a trench with a satchel charge or a petrol bomb is a dangerous opponent for a tank.

The fire from our automatic weapons stopped the infantry assault, which lasted for several hours. Small dark hillocks – the bodies of our opponents – littered the wide battlefield. There was a terribly high number of casualties. As darkness fell, we could hear the screaming of the wounded, and among the cries we could clearly hear: 'Comrade Medic!' Two or three enemy tanks that had broken into our rear made it back to their own lines ...

That day was quite special for me, as my job was to destroy as many living creatures of the Homo sapiens species as possible.[71]

During the attack, the Finns had to abandon part of the terrain in front of their position, but after nightfall they managed to recapture at least some of what had been lost and stabilise the front. Further counterattacks carried out in the dark were repelled by the Russians, whose artillery continued firing through the night.

On 19 December, the Russians launched their biggest attack so far. This time it was spread over a broader front but it still had Summa as its centre of gravity. Six divisions, an armoured corps and two tank battalions supported by fighters and bombers conducted an attack against a single Finnish battalion.

The situation was chaotic on the Finnish side, where the only workable tactic remained the one of taking cover, waiting until the Russians came close and then trying to separate the infantry from the tanks, since this made the tanks considerably more vulnerable. Furthermore, the Soviet tactics at that time was to use the tanks as support for the infantry and hence they were not expected to advance on their own. Soviet tanks did manage to break through the Finnish trench lines on a number of occasions, but they were rather helpless without their supporting infantry, particularly if they did not escape before sunset, since the dark nights provided excellent cover for Finnish infantry attacks. In this situation it was also easier for the Finns to use their Molotov cocktails, which had been impossible as long as the enemy was at a greater distance and the Finns were hiding in their trenches or dugouts (petrol bombs of this kind should preferably be thrown so they hit the fan grill behind the gun turret, which burned the engine out and stalled it; Soviet tanks at the time had petrol engines). However, most of the Soviet tank casualties were caused by anti-tank guns, and likewise landmines and indirect fire from the Finnish field-artillery inflicted heavy losses on the Soviet armoured units. At this time Molotov cocktails and satchel charges had only recently been introduced along with hand grenade bundles, which were used to destroy some tanks; but generally the latter was only used to finish off tanks that had already been put out of action by anti-tank guns.

The battle continued over the next two days, with one Soviet attack after another being repelled. Meanwhile, the Russians had improved the efficiency of their artillery, which so far had been inaccurate and in particular had a tendency to shoot too far. When the attacks finally waned, the Finns were still in their positions holding the line. Their struggle had resulted in a remarkable defensive victory and thanks to the many international reporters in the country, the news would soon travel around the world. Toivo Ahola wrote:

> After four hours of intensive night combat we finally recaptured the trenches. Luckily, we managed to avoid high losses. Dead Red Army

men littered the bottom of the trenches – we stumbled over them all the time. It was strange to step on human bodies that had not stiffened yet. We were ordered to clear the trenches of dead bodies. It was not a problem, as there were deep shell craters in front of our positions. The Red Army men found their last refuge here.[72]

The victory gave the commander of II Corps, Lieutenant General Harald Öhquist, some vindication after a serious reprimand he had received from Mannerheim earlier in the month, where he had ignored an order to send reinforcements to the outposts at Lipola. Öhquist, who generally had his own views on how the war should be conducted, had already during the first few days of the war worked out a plan for a counterattack launched from the Mannerheim Line. Initially, the general staff had rejected it as unnecessarily risky, but on 19 December the situation had changed and the operation was permitted to go ahead.

The counterattack started early in the morning on 23 December but it ran into problems right from the start. Again, communication was compromised between the units, causing troops to be jammed up on the roads just as it had happened to the Russians earlier on. Another problem was that the pre-battle reconnaissance of the Soviet positions had been insufficient.

Despite these drawbacks the Finns initially advanced and were met with only limited resistance. But after a while the Russians managed to set up an effective defence and when their tanks arrived on the scene, it signalled the end of the Finnish advance. It became clear that once the Finnish troops were out of their trenches and bunkers, they were for all practical purposes at the mercy of the Soviet tanks. Furthermore, they lacked support from the artillery, which could not move ahead with the attack since it was only communicating with its observers via field telephones, not radios. Also heavier weapons such as anti-tank guns, 81mm mortars and medium-sized machine guns had problems keeping up with the attacking infantry, mostly due to a lack of preparation. After eight hours of fighting, the attack was called off and the Finns retreated to the Mannerheim Line.

It seems strange that the Finnish general staff allowed this counterattack to go ahead at all. In traditional military thinking an attack from a stationary position demands a marked numerical superiority and if there was one thing the Finns did *not* have during the Winter War, it was a surplus of troops. However, as we have seen already the Finnish tactics at the time were very aggressive, even in relation to defensive combat. Also, overall numerical superiority is not necessary if one has superiority where it really matters, and in fact Öhquist had been granted a whole division (the 6th) for this task in addition to his own troops. Finally, it should be remembered that the

Russian efficiency so far had been poor and on top of that the troops were expected to be worn out and tired.

Although the attack was unsuccessful, it appears to have come as a shock to the Russians that their enemies had so much resilience left in them after the extremely tough attacks they had been exposed to during the one week of continual fighting near Summa; at least it would be a long time before the Soviets launched more large scale attempts at penetrating the Mannerheim Line.

In his report, Lieutenant General Öhquist gave the following reasons why his counterattack had been a failure:

- Communication with the artillery broke down, meaning that the most important targets were not destroyed, and our infantry received no support from the artillery.
- Unfavourable weather conditions. Against all expectations, the weather was clear. This made it possible for the enemy to direct his superior heavy artillery from observation balloons.
- A lack of fighting experience in the 6th Division. As a result, the troops panicked when the enemy's artillery and tanks started participating in the battle.
- Poor planning of the offensive on behalf of the 1st Division had postponed the attack two days.[73]

Towards the end of December there was fierce fighting at Taipale as the soviets retreated from the sector, while other skirmishes took place along the Mannerheim Line; but nothing occurred of a major or decisive nature. Some of these clashes came as a surprise to certain Finnish officers, who in a celebratory mood had emptied a few more bottles than perhaps they should have. Signals Operator Lauri Keskinen from the 29th Regiment recalled:

> It was all quiet on Christmas Eve, and then all hell broke loose on Christmas Day. I am still amazed – in the early hours of Christmas Day, at 2 or 4 am, we received a message that a Russian attack could start at any time soon. The battalion commander did not react to this message at all! At that moment the battalion commander had no control over the situation. Luckily, we managed to stop the offensive in the end.[74]

North of Ladoga

The front sector just north of Lake Ladoga, along the border of Ladoga Karelia, was approximately 100km long. At the time this was also the national border between Finland and the Soviet Union. The two Finnish divisions positioned here were very vulnerable to Soviet attacks, since they were underequipped with anti-tank guns. Facing them was the Soviet Eighth Army, whose primary task was to take up key points at Tolvajärvi and Suojärvi, and from there continue their attacks towards the towns of Ilomantsi and Sortavala. If the front collapsed at this point, a crucial part of the Finnish railway system would be under threat.

From the railway between Sortavala and the town of Joensuu a dead-end side-track ran east to a terminal station at Suvilahti by the southern point of Suvijärvi 15km from the border. Here the Soviet 56th Division launched its first attack on the outbreak of the war. On 2 December the pressure was so hard that the Finnish troops had to pull back to the next station on the line, Piisoinoja, where they started building defensive positions.

Next day the task of the Finnish troops was to recapture Suvilahti, but the pressure from the Soviet tanks was too much for them. The Finnish author Erkki Palolampi took part in the defence and described it later in his first book, *Kollaa kestää* ('*Kollaa will hold out*'). A Finnish anti-tank gun had stopped several tanks on the road, but it was still not enough to halt the Soviet advance:

Finnish soldiers at Kollaa. There was a lack of uniforms so many were just handed a cockade to be pinned to their civilian hats. (SA-Kuva)

Someone shouts that the tanks are shooting at us from behind. They have broken through! His eyes are opened wide in terror, another man is registering his anxiety, people are shouting at each other, and no one can stop them.

'The tanks are coming. They have broken through!'

People start to flee, ploughing back through the snow on skies, unable to concern themselves with anything else, ignoring the officers' shouting and cursing.

Panic is spreading, one company breaks away from the others, an artillery battery receives erroneous orders and starts fleeing, too, but then returns to its positions.

At 4:15 pm the enemy penetrates our position between the railway and the road. Our side is still trying to get its troops in order.[75]

The Finnish retreat continued to the next station on the railway line, Kollaanjoki (named after the nearby river), where the troops took up new positions and were attacked again. But this time the attack was repelled and the Finns managed to stabilise the situation. The Kollaa Front has been described as one of the most difficult and important sectors for the Finnish Army during the Winter War. The troops' ability to hold their positions here was decisive for all of IV Corps' operations in the entire region and presented a constant worry to the corps commander, Major General Woldemar Hägglund (see Appendix IV).

As we have seen, the Finnish general staff's original plan supposed that only a limited Soviet attack would be launched north of the Karelian Isthmus. When this turned out to be wrong, reinforcements were sent to Ladoga Karelia from Oulu and Viipuri. Mannerheim then decided to divide IV Corps into two groups and appointed Colonel Paavo Talvela commander of the northern group. Talvela was known as a headstrong and at times even pig-headed character, but he was also a highly skilled officer, particularly good at leading offensive operations, which was exactly what the Finns needed in this area.

Hägglund remained commander of the southern group. Its task was to fight a delaying action along the east bank of Lake Ladoga, and then stop at Kitelä to launch a counterattack. The retreat went as planned and included a number of delaying skirmishes, until the Russians reached the Finnish positions north and west of the village. However, the planned Finnish attack was threatened by Soviet advances on Suvilahti (which was the main reason why the Finnish general staff on 6 December had ordered the village recaptured).

Hägglund's task seemed hopeless. Not only was his force of three battalions numerically inferior to the Soviet division that fronted it, but his men were also exhausted after the fighting and there was no sign of reinforcements, apart from one reserve battalion that had already arrived. It appeared that something drastic and unorthodox had to be done, or the situation could end in catastrophe. Hägglund's solution was to send a reinforced battalion under Lieutenant Colonel Aaro Pajari on a mission deep behind Soviet lines, where an attack was carried out during the night of 7 December. The operation led to heavy losses for the Soviet troops and paralysed their movements over the next couple of days.

In the meantime around Ilomantsi, 60km north of Tolvajärvi, the Finns had stopped their retreat to a take up new defensive positions. Soon after, reinforcements had arrived in the form of Detachment A, which at the time consisted of just two infantry companies and was subordinated to Battle Group Talvela. On 9 December the battle group's Separate Battalion 11 attacked a Soviet column about 10km from Möhkö village, causing the Soviets losses of some 200 men.

On 11 December the Soviets managed to outflank the northern sector of the Finnish position at Tolvajärvi Village, more exactly by the northern point of Hirvasjärvi, after which they launched an attack on a Finnish supply column. By coincidence, Lieutenant Colonel Pajari was in the area and took control of the situation. The supply troops, augmented with a couple of regular infantry reserve companies, fought off the Russians and sent them running. This episode also helped to strengthen morale considerably, and the next day the Finnish troops repelled a larger Soviet attack.

Pajari had now managed to turn the situation around so much that a counterattack could be considered. His plan was to carry out a large pincer movement to encircle the Russians and cut off their supply lines, but the Russians had a similar plan in mind and the two operations came up against each other. Though the progress of the Finns was halted, they still managed to capture an island in the ice-covered Tolvajärvi. The two attacks were then stuck for a while, until Pajari decided to make a direct charge on the Soviet forces inland in the area north of the lake.

In the war diary of the Finnish 16th Regiment there is a detailed description of the fighting. It is worth quoting in its entirety as a first-hand example of the intensity of the combat that took place not just at Tolvajärvi but in all of Ladoga Karelia:

> When the battalion was ready at the jumping-off positions, the battalion commander issued an order to begin the assault at 0950 hours. The assault began on time. Our machine guns carried out extremely effective supressing fire before the assault.
>
> The enemy manned good positions on the other side of Hevossalmi Bridge. They had had time to dig in and set machine guns in good positions in order to fire at the bridge and the ice field.

The companies stopped for a second to catch their breath on the western bank at Hevossalmi and then simultaneously charged across the ice with the support of machine guns. The enemy carried out a powerful counter-barrage with artillery and automatic weapons.

The Russkies opened a hurricane of fire from their machine guns, but it was poorly aimed. Nothing helped them, as our machine guns were also firing and aiming well. Soon our first men ran up to the opposite bank and destroyed the first machine gun nests. The Russkies had to retreat to the sand quarries, where they had up to fifteen machine guns in position. They fought for every inch of land, but due to pressure and heavy casualties they had to continue their retreat to the hotel, leaving the machine guns behind. Enemy tanks arrived on the battlefield but were quickly destroyed one by one by our anti-tank platoon. At that moment our men were already exhausted because of lack of sleep and heavy fighting, so the companies stopped to catch their breath at the quarries before continuing the assault. The enemy retreated to the area of the hotel and the hills in front of it.

All the companies got mixed up during the battle; officers had to attack together with the men, cheering them on. The commander of the fourth company was wounded but remained in the ranks. Second Lieutenant Leppänen, a platoon leader from the same fourth company, was killed. Lieutenant Nokkala was wounded.

The most furious battle of the day started at around 1430 hours. The enemy had superb positions on a high hill, from which they fired non-stop at our men below. The Russkies had a lot of automatic weapons on a narrow isthmus between the lakes, which also fired non-stop. Despite this, our men threw themselves at the enemy and reached the foot of the hill, but had to fall back. The enemy's deadly fire was too much for us. Then our machine guns opened fire at the defences on the hill and on the left bank of the lake. The fifth company immediately started the assault along the right bank of the isthmus and took a position for flanking fire at the enemy. The sixth company and the machine gun company managed to supress the enemy's weapons on the left flank, and when we charged again, the enemy's fire was much weaker, our men charged fearlessly against a numerically superior enemy, paying no attention to incoming fire. Nothing could stop us any more, especially when our third battalion joined the battle. The enemy had to retreat to the hotel. They had to leave some ten to fifteen machine guns, two tanks, two anti-tank guns and innumerable dead on the battlefield. Our losses were also serious. The enemy had some HQ in the hotel that did not withdraw in time. The enemy defended the area of the hotel desperately, fighting back tooth and nail. We also fought the best we could, in order to finish the whole gang. We used submachine guns, rifles, hand grenades, but the Russkies just held on. Lieutenant Heinivavo was wounded in this ferocious fight, and Second Lieutenant Lehtinen was killed in a hand-to-hand fight.

Our men on the left flank did not waste any time. They hit the enemy's flank simultaneously with us, across Myllyjärvi. A company-strong force attacked towards the hotel. Our fire drove the enemy away from the ridge and this was how we outflanked them. It was an impressive manoeuvre. We were assaulting the hotel from two sides. The Russkies fought back as best they could from the hotel, firing from windows, doors and every possible place. The most ferocious fight raged at the hotel for an hour. We assaulted their lines again and again, but time after time the Russkies repelled our assaults. Finally, our men managed to bypass the enemy on the right as well. When the Russkies saw this, they realised that there was no point in holding their ground at the hotel. They abandoned their positions and their officers, left behind their heavy weapons and fled the battlefield. The HQ that remained in the hotel fought bravely, but was suppressed by our hand grenades rather quickly.

Most of our units marched by the hotel in twilight, when the hotel was still in enemy hands and posed a certain danger for our flank. The sixth company received an order to assault and capture the hotel. The enemy defended their positions with desperation, using small arms and hand grenades, but finally our hand grenades finished the job. The brand new hotel, quite badly damaged by the uninvited guests, was again in our hands. We took some thirty to forty prisoners; most of them were wounded.

When the hotel was captured, the resistance of Russkies abated. They retreated without returning fire.[76]

The heavily battered Soviet 139th Division, commanded by General Nikolai Beliaev, tried to take up positions in Änglajärvi Village between Tolvajärvi and the border. The 75th Division was sent in as a rescue unit, but it was pushed back and sent running by the Finns along with the remnants of the 139th Division, which in the meantime had been chased out of Änglajärvi. Major Gladyshev, commander of the Soviet 75th Regiment (of the 75th Division), related:

When my regiment was on the way to the front, the units of the 139th Division were leaving the frontline in panic. There was an endless flow of men of the 139th Rifles coming against us on the road. They were telling us all sorts of horror stories about their defeat. My men and commanders did not believe them. My unit had very high morale and fought stubbornly and bravely for over twenty-four hours. We had to retreat some 500 metres only due to the high casualties of commanders, lack of artillery support, and the panic among the 139th Rifles. My 3rd Battalion, without its ninth company, arrived in the afternoon. The reason for our defeat was that units were thrown into battle piecemeal. Units were split up and I had to command not a regiment, but a battalion, and the battalion commanders had to lead companies. Not all units of the regiment took part in the battle; it was chopped into smaller units. We lacked proper artillery support.[77]

The on-going Finnish assaults forced the fleeing Russians back towards the border until they reached Aittojoki, where they set up defensive positions and held their ground. This signalled the end of the Battle of Tolvajärvi, where 4,000 Finnish troops defeated a Soviet invasion force five times bigger. The battle became the first great Finnish victory of the Winter War and cost the Red Army considerable losses: more than 1,000 dead Soviet soldiers were later found on the battlegrounds, to which must be added an unknown number of men who disappeared into the forests and presumably froze to death. The material losses included hundreds of rifles, more than sixty machine guns, two artillery batteries, some anti-tank guns and twenty tanks. The Finnish losses were 100-150 dead and approximately twice as many wounded (the uncertainty in these numbers reflects inconsistencies between the sources).

Further north, at Ilomantsi, the Finns also held control of the situation, while they kept the Soviet units encircled and waited for them to either freeze or starve to death. At Kollaa and Kitelä, the Finns held their positions, too. At Kitelä they even managed to launch several attacks against the Red Army's 168th Division, which by the end of the month found itself in a seriously weakened position.

The situation in this area is described by an unnamed Russian, seemingly a commissar, in his diary:

24 DECEMBER 1939. I am behind the frontlines of the 18th Division. The front is c. 8km from here. Terrible front. It is 22 centigrade below around here. There are no buildings. Forest, fields, fox holes. I am shivering. I would to like to write much more, but it makes no sense.

27 DECEMBER 1939. Behind the frontline of the 18th Division. I have been here four days already without being given any task. Chaos and confusion. Everywhere our troops are on the defensive, however

strange it may sound. It looks like they are preparing themselves for a fight. There is no activity at division headquarters. Everyone seems dead already. People come back from the front with terrible stories, for instance about men dying from self-inflicted wounds. Anxiety, despondency, and indifference hang in the air, even at division headquarters.[78]

Kuhmo
We will now go back to the start of the war and take a step further north to look at the situation around the middle of the border. The landscape here is so thinly populated that even today there are rarely more than a couple of inhabitants per square kilometre. Furthermore, the terrain is highly impenetrable as soon as you leave the roads, and the temperatures during the winter months are exceedingly low. These factors meant that the Finns in their operational plans had practically excluded the possibility of Soviet attacks along the northern half of the border, so only a few smaller units made up of border guards and Civil Guard members patrolled the area at the beginning of the war. Nevertheless, Soviet troops had for a while been building roads leading towards Finnish territory from their own side of the border and preparing themselves to attack.

The inhabitants on the Finnish side had for some time been aware of the road constructions and the troop concentrations. Still, they believed that peace would prevail, and so the evacuation of the civilian population only started when the war in fact broke out. In consequence, families had to pack their household belongings in great haste, collect their children from school and hurry west.

During the first two days of the war, the Red Army's 54th Division moved towards the town of Kuhmo along two roads. The few Finnish troops in the area pulled back while carrying out delaying flank attacks, until the high command on 5 December ordered reinforcements sent in from Oulu. The heaviest weapons these units had were machine guns, rendering the Finnish troops in the area almost defenceless against Soviet tanks.

Immediately after their arrival on 8 December the reserves were thrust into the struggle to halt the Soviet advance. The counterattack was successful, as was a Finnish attempt to split the southern Soviet attack column into a string of small pockets along the road between Kuhmo and the town of Reboly, on the Soviet side of the border. During the next few days, however, the Finns failed to neutralise these pockets, partly because they generally lacked radio communication between their units. Instead, they kept the situation under control, hoping that the freezing cold and the lack of supplies would put an end to the encircled Soviet troops.

The northern attack column was gradually slowed down by the Finns and finally stopped completely some 10km east of Kuhmo.

Suomussalmi
Seventy-five kilometres further north, Suomussalmi Village had meanwhile been the target of the advancing Ukrainian 163rd Division (Map 2). This Soviet formation, too, had reached the border along new roads built on the Soviet side during the run-up to the war. Like the 54th Division at Kuhmo the formation advanced along two routes, of which the most southern one was called the Raate Road. It started at Raate (a small Finnish village and border station) and continued west towards Suomussalmi. The rest of the division followed a more northern route. The aim of the whole operation was to cut Finland in two horizontally along a line reaching from Raate to Oulu. The first road junction the Soviets needed to gain control over was at Suomussalmi.

The Finnish covering troops, totalling a battalion, initially carried out a fighting retreat in front of the Soviet advance and reached Suomussalmi on 6 December. The village had by then been evacuated by its civilian inhabitants. The Finnish soldiers set fire to the houses and then retreated west across Kiantajärvi (north of Suomussalmi), which was still not frozen enough to carry tanks.

Meanwhile, Colonel Hjalmar Siilasvuo had been appointed commander of the Suomussalmi sector, which he was approaching by train along with a regiment of reinforcements from Oulu. The transport was delayed one day because of an accident on the line, but on 9 December it reached its destination. Two days later the counterattacks began.

The first Finnish attack came from the northwest and was aimed at the Soviet outposts by the scorched village. The Russians pulled back quickly and took up positions among the remnants of the buildings. Since the Finnish force was not strong enough to attack the village itself, Siilasvuo ordered his men to bypass the enemy and cut off his supply lines. In fact, this was a conscious attempt to create a string of isolated pockets so the numerically superior Soviet force could be kept in check until further Finnish reinforcements arrived and a real neutralisation could begin.

The Finnish attack force moved east along Haukiperä, an oblong, frozen lake south of the road. Just before the lake expands and changes its name to Kuivasjärvi, the troops turned north towards the main road (Map 2/1). Here they came under heavy fire from Soviet units occupying the road to the east. In answer to this, the Finnish force was split into two groups of uneven size. The smaller group remained on the road and took up positions against the Soviet attack, while the larger group turned west in the direction of Suomussalmi.

Heaps of frozen Russian corpses lying by the roadside after the Battle of Suomussalmi. The Finnish Army found 5,000 dead Russians on the battlefield after the fighting. Furthermore, an unknown number froze or starved to death after having escaped into the surrounding landscape. The Finnish losses were c. 1,000 killed, wounded and missing in action. (SA-Kuva)

The Russians in the village did not expect an attack from this direction, so they had only deployed a small force on the road east of the village. It was soon neutralised by the Finnish group, who then continued ahead towards Suomussalmi. The troops did not stop until sunset, at which point they were 2km from the road junction southeast of the village. The Finns had now gained control over some 5km of the main road.

Meanwhile, another Finnish attack had taken place on the road leading north out of Suomussalmi. This advance managed to disturb the Soviet communication lines, but after a failed attempt to gain control over the road the Finnish force had to pull back.

The next day (12 December) the Finns southeast of the village continued their advance. It was now so cold that they had to leave behind the trucks they had previously used and continue on foot. Still, the advance went ahead and the group managed to capture a small hill overlooking the road.

On 13 December the Russians used tanks for the first time in the area. This caused some panic among the Finns, but they calmed down again when they discovered that the tanks could not shoot when they were in among the trees. The Finns then marched to the road junction south of Suomussalmi, where fighting broke out over another hill overlooking the landscape. However, by nightfall the Russians abandoned the hill voluntarily and the Finnish force could occupy it without further struggle.

More than 10km of the main road was now under Finnish control and everything was going according to plan. Step by step the Russians were encapsulated in little pockets along the road, inside Suomussalmi, on the peninsula facing the village and by the junction southeast of it.

As we have seen, the tactic of splitting enemy formations into smaller, isolated pockets was something that grew out of necessity, as the Finnish troops lacked the means to neutralise the vast Soviet formations directly. It became perhaps the most significant and unique tactical feature used by the Finnish Army during the Winter War and was given its own name: a *motti*. (The word has several meanings in Finnish, but the reason for its use in this regard remains uncertain.)

The same day (13 December) Finnish troops launched an attack against the scorched village, this time from the southeast. By sunset they had pushed the Soviet outposts back and found themselves on the outskirts of Suomussalmi.

On 14 December the Finnish attack continued, albeit unsuccessfully. The Soviet positions were very strong. The soldiers had installed themselves in basements, ruins and foxholes, and along the perimeter of the village they had positioned tanks. The Finnish attack force was numerically inferior and had no anti-tank guns. Furthermore, the troops had started showing signs of exhaustion after the last few days of hard fighting.

Meanwhile, another Finnish force had launched an attack from the north against the Soviet positions on Hulkonniemi Peninsula, but tough resistance forced them to pull back again on 18 December.

On the same day Colonel Siilasvuo was forced to call off the attack on Suomussalmi, since the losses were too large and the enemy too strong. Instead, the Finns concentrated on keeping the situation under control while they waited for reinforcements that could help them neutralise the Soviet mottis.

These reinforcements finally arrived on 20 December in the shape of two artillery batteries and two anti-tank guns. However, by then a new Soviet column had been observed on the eastern part of Raate Road moving west to the rescue of the 163rd Division, whose encapsulated units were preparing for a major, coordinated attempt at breaking away. Such preparations were possible because the mottis could communicate internally via the radios in the tanks.

The Finns launched new attacks on the same day, but they still found it impossible to break Soviet resistance. Eventually, the operation was called off and the Finns returned to maintaining the status quo; yet it was a question how long this situation could go on.

On 21 and 22 December Siilasvuo sent some minor forces east to halt the Soviet relief force, which by now had reached a point between Kuomasjärvi and Kuivasjärvi, two lakes on either side of the Raate Road. The operation failed, as it started to dawn on the Finns what they were truly up against.

The Soviet relief force was the Red Army's 44th Division, an elite unit arriving directly from Moscow. The Finns were forced to retreat and take up positions behind a roadblock, as they awaited reinforcements from Suomussalmi. But Siilasvuo would not send out any more troops from the area around the village until all Soviet resistance there had been defeated.

In the meantime, the position on the Raate Road had to be held by just two companies, who were under pressure from not only the arriving Soviet 44th Division but also the nearest motti of the 163rd Division on the western side of the roadblock. However, the Soviet commander would not let his men leave the road to conduct outflanking manoeuvres, since he knew they would just make themselves easy targets for the Finnish ski patrols. Hence, the Soviets could only attack the Finnish roadblock with a limited number of troops at one time.

New Finnish attacks on Suomussalmi and Hulkonniemi were planned to start on 25 December, but before they could be launched the Soviets made an attempt at breaking out of the *mottis* on the Raate Road. Though they were supported by fighter planes and bombers, the Finns managed to stop the sortie. Still, the Finnish troops were so exhausted afterwards that their own attacks had to be postponed until the 27th. When they were finally launched, the fighting stretched over two days of constant attacks and counterattacks. Gradually, the Finns gained the upper hand, and in the end the remaining Soviet force was squeezed together within a small area inside the village. At the same time, the Soviet line on Hulkonniemi was penetrated. As the Red Army soldiers fled over the ice-covered lake north of the peninsula, they were chased by Finnish aircraft and ski troops. The following day the same destiny befell the remaining Soviets inside the village. On 30 December the only Finnish air sortie was flown: two Bristol Blenheims bombed and strafed a Soviet column on the ice of Kiantajärvi.

During the initial stages of these attacks, reports had come in from the roadblock on the Raate Road. The Russians were preparing a major attack and the Finnish soldiers were requesting support. When the Soviet attack was launched the next day, a battalion from Suomussalmi had reached the roadblock, where the two Finnish companies, altogether hardly more than 400 men, for a week had held their positions against the elite Soviet division. Strengthened now by the arriving reinforcements, the Finnish troops just about managed to keep the 44th Division east of the roadblock separated from the encircled units west of the position.

In reality, the Soviet 163rd Division was on its last legs. Most of its troops had by now either frozen or starved to death, been killed or captured by the Finns, or been chased out into the merciless Finnish winter landscape. Skirmishes kept occurring during the final few days of the year, while the Finns chased and defeated the escaped troops of the division. But the Battle of Suomussalmi itself was over. It had from start to finish been one long humiliation for the Red Army, and it had cost its Eighth Army considerable losses in human lives and equipment. The exact numbers are unknown, but the Finns later found some 5,000 of their enemies dead on the battlegrounds. No one knows how many Soviet soldiers lost their way in the woods and froze or starved to death.

The Finnish Army reported its war booty to consist of 635 rifles, 33 light machine guns, 19 heavy machine guns, 12 anti-tank guns, 27 anti-aircraft guns and field guns, 26 tanks, 2 armoured cars, 2 anti-aircraft machine guns, 350 horses, 181 trucks, two saloon cars, 11 tractors, 26 field kitchens, 800,000 rounds of rifle ammunition, 9,000 artillery shells, a bakery, an almost complete field hospital plus a vast amount of skis, snow suits and various hand weapons.

The Finnish losses were 350 men killed, 600 wounded and 70 men missing in action.

Lapland
Even further north, in the Petsamo and Salla areas, the Finnish units were more thinly spread than anywhere else along the border. As already mentioned, the leaders in Helsinki had not expected any kind of major Soviet attack in this deserted and relatively impassable terrain. Still, the area was important for several reasons. The Petsamo area was rich in nickel, an important metal in ammunition production. Moreover, it was relatively close to the Swedish iron ore mines, on which the German war machine strongly depended. In short, it was a region that could be of benefit to the Soviet Union.

The Danish news reporter and writer Peter de Hemmer Gudme visited Lapland during the first phase of the war. Because he had been a volunteer on the White side in the Finnish Civil War (p. 29) he enjoyed a privileged status during his journalistic visits to the country. According to Matti Julkunen in *Talvisotdan Kuva*, a book about the foreign journalists in Finland during the Winter War, Gudme visited Lapland from 12 to 19 December 1939. He described his visit as follows:

> A further journey of 500km through the Arctic darkness takes me from Rovaniemi and the railway all the way up to the most northern front in the world and a war that never sees sunlight. For a few hours around noon you can see in a southern direction a sometimes red, sometimes yellow gleam of a sunset, engulfing the wilderness in the strangest of colours; the snow changes from yellow to blue, then to green, but you never see the sun. The hours around midday are only as bright as a Finnish or Swedish summer night, and the two Finnish camera men and the Swedish newspaper photographer traveling with me suddenly get busy. Otherwise, darkness shrouds you around the clock, making its mark on the fighting up here near the Arctic Ocean. Only very occasionally the northern sky is lit by a sheen of aurora borealis.[79]

Initially, the Finnish military force in the huge Petsamo area was limited to just two companies, one of which was led by Major General Martti Wallenius, a mercurial gentleman whose extremist right wing views and former association with the Lapua Movement had led to both imprisonment and expulsion from the Finnsh Army after the Mäntsälä revolt in 1932 (p. 32). When the Winter War broke out he had been in Germany working as a war correspondent, but he had immediately returned to Finland, where Mannerheim forgave him for past sins and errors and gave him the aforementioned post. There were few friendly feelings between the two men, but Wallenius was undisputedly a skilful officer, at least as long as he stayed sober. Besides, he was well acquainted with the conditions in the Petsamo region where, in the wake of the Civil War in 1918, he had led a failed, semi-private war (the Viena Expedition) into Russia with the aim of joining the northern part of East Karelia to the newly founded Finnish state. He had furthermore commanded the Finnish Frontier Guard in Lapland during 1918-21 and was therefore familiar with the terrain and other local features. Moreover, for a while during the 1930s he had worked in a civilian position for one of the big fishing concerns in the area.

Petsamo is in the far north on the Barents Sea, southwest of the Rybachi Peninsula, the western half of which at the time belonged to Finland while

Finnish reindeer patrol from Detachment Pennanen in the Petsamo area. (SA-Kuva)

the eastern half belonged to the Soviet Union. Some 200km to the southeast from here is the ice-free Russian seaport of Murmansk, where three Soviet divisions, constituting the Fourteenth Army (44,000 men), stood ready to attack the aforementioned two Finnish companies (c. 400 men). In order to prevent a British landing, the Soviet high command had decided that the formations should operate alongside the Soviet Arctic Fleet. The goal was to occupy the Finnish part of the Rybachi Peninsula and from there push on to the Norwegian border, which Moscow had issued strong orders not to cross. At the same time the 104th Division was to turn south along the Arctic Ocean Road to Rovaniemi, the capital of Lapland. Here it was to link up with the Soviet Ninth Army, which had crossed the border further south in the Salla region.

On the second day of the war, the 104th Division crossed the border and occupied the Rybachi peninsula as planned, supported by the Arctic Fleet. On the next day the 242nd Regiment reached Petsamo Village, which the Finnish troops in the meantime had scorched and abandoned. The Soviets immediately prepared the village to resist a landing of British troops in support of the Finns.

Meanwhile, the Finnish troops withdrew south, blowing up bridges, sabotaging roads and burning down anything that might give the Russians warmth and shelter in the Arctic winter.

The 104th Division marched on, frequently delayed by the sabotage, while the Finnish units roamed the terrain, carrying out guerrilla-style hit-and-run attacks. These groups were mainly border guards and members of the Civil Guard, who knew the area and the special demands it made on survival skills, and who in many cases were highly skilled marksmen. Along the Arctic Road, nineteen such units were in operation, each comprising some twenty men. On 18 December they managed to halt the Soviet division, which in the meantime had encountered significant supply problems. The Russians dug in and took up positions behind their tanks at Nautsi Village, where they stayed until the end of the war.

During his visit to the region, Peter de Hemmer Gudme interviewed some wounded Finnish soldiers in a military hospital:

> Most of them came from the Petsamo Front and their wounds had worsened since it had been necessary to transport them 500 kilometres to get them to the field hospital. Many of their wounds were bad enough in the first place. Often an arm had almost been torn off by a bullet, because the constant night meant that the opponents got very close to each other before they could start shooting. One man, who looked to be in a really bad way, had been shot in the lung so that air was mixed into his blood, making his face swell up as though it were about to explode. Another had been hit by a grenade that had crushed his left knee and arm.
>
> There was a boy who had belonged to a group of seven soldiers, who had been separated from each other; still, they all came back. A grenade splinter had robbed him of his right eye and given him an open sore at his temple. At first he was unconscious but when he came to, he started walking alone without a compass through the wilderness. He walked for seven days. Only once did he find a small peasant's hut where he was given some flour, which he mixed with water and ate. Apart from that he walked for seven days with his open wound and no food or drink in minus 10-12 centigrade, and only when he had returned to his own side did he run out of strength.
>
> There was a sergeant who had been guarding the nickel mines when he heard someone approaching and went out to see who it was. It turned out to be the Russians. One of them attacked him with his bayonet, another crushed his lower arm with a bullet, but he still managed to order his men to move forward and fend off the attack. The Finns captured several machine guns and rifles, though they were just 50 men against 800-1,000 Russians.[80]

While the fighting went on in the north of the region, the Soviet 112th Division had crossed the border into Lapland further south and continued in the direction of the small town of Salla. Here two Finnish battalions had been deployed, but on 8 December they scorched the town and abandoned the area.

After arriving at Salla, the 112th Division was split into two forces. The first one marched south in the direction of the town of Kemijärvi with the intent of capturing it. Subsequently, it was to continue towards Rovaniemi and join the 104th Division there. Together the two divisions would then attack Tornio (the Finnish-Swedish border town whose name on the Swedish side is Happaranda), which was an important railway junction. Here the invasion was supposed to stop, since the Soviet troops had strict orders not to violate Swedish territory.

The other half of the 112th Division marched northwest towards Pelkosenniemi Village. Here, on 17 December, it was attacked by Wallenius' troops, who in the meantime had been reinforced from the south. The outcome was a Finnish victory in what was now becoming the established style, with the Russians fleeing and leaving behind them enormous amounts of weapons and equipment. Wallenius then sent his troops south to Kemijärvi to support the defence there and prevent the southern half of the 112th Division from capturing the town. After some heavy fighting, which also saw the participation of the Red Army's 88th Division, the Soviets were fended off. They pulled back to Märkäjärvi Lake 20km southwest of Salla, where they took up positions and remained for the rest of the war.

The Political Situation
During the early days of the war, the aforementioned Soviet puppet government was installed as planned in the small town of Terijoki on the south coast of the Karelian Isthmus, after the area had been occupied by the Red Army. The leaders in Moscow refused to communicate with anyone other than this 'democratic government' consisting of exiled Finnish Reds, whose first act was to request the Red Army for assistance in their 'struggle for the freedom of the Finnish people'. Around this farce the Soviet propaganda machine built a campaign of promises supposed to appeal to the Finnish people. However, they only managed to reveal how little they truly knew about modern living conditions in Finland, since what they offered had already been implemented in the country years ago, and more.

So for the moment the Finnish leaders were cut off from negotiating directly with Moscow, and likewise an appeal they had handed in to the League of Nations was leading nowhere. Supported by a group of South American states, a decision was made to exclude the Soviet Union from the assembly, which was exactly what the Finns did *not* wish to see, since what they wanted was dialogue. Behind it all lurked a political game that had nothing to do with Finland, and which in fact eventually caused the termination of the league. But at least the member states were encouraged to send war material and humanitarian aid to Finland.

Focus on Finland
During the Winter War, international support for Finland came from both far and near, but in particular from Sweden and Norway. In Denmark the government was initially more hesitant, yet public pressure meant that Danish politicians after a while decided to join the other two Scandinavian countries in supporting Finland in various ways.

The First World War had caused a strengthening of inter-Scandinavian relations, and during the inter-war period this manifested itself in a number of initiatives. The Nordic Association had been founded in 1919 by the three Scandinavian countries, with parallel initiatives in Iceland and Finland in 1922 and 1924, respectively. Nordic cooperation within the business community also became more prevalent. In 1918 the import organisation Scandinavian Co-operative Wholesale Society had been founded with Finnish participation. The following year the Helsinki Business Bank changed its name to the Nordic Business Bank.

These are but a few examples of how Finland from the very beginning of its time as an independent state had been moving back into the Nordic realm. Still, it should be mentioned that the notion of Nordic values differed somewhat between Finland and Scandinavia. The historian Lars Westerlund relates as a symptomatic example that while the publishing company Nordisk Familjebok (*Nordic Family Book*) in Stockholm used logos of beautiful young people and thoughtful owls, Finnish companies with the word *Pohjolan* (the North) in their names used images of watchful bears and teeth-grinding cavemen.[81]

Nonetheless, the support for Finland was substantial in all of Scandinavia from the autumn of 1939 onwards. In late October, the three Scandinavian kings met in Stockholm in what constituted a kind of public display, while their foreign ministers took care of practical matters in the backroom, as they had done twenty-five years previously on the outbreak of the First World War. However, now a fourth state leader was there as well – the Finnish President Kallio. He stood on the balcony and was applauded by the crowd, while the Nordic flags were raised and people prayed for Finland's future in churches all over Scandinavia.

After the Winter War had started, the pro-Finnish feelings in Denmark became more pronounced, with student demonstrations, windows-smashing at the Soviet Embassy, public protest meetings, pilots from the Danish air force who practically deserted so they could travel to Finland and join up under the blue-white flag, recruitment offices for other Danish citizens who wanted to volunteer for military service or labour service in Finland (by the beginning of February 1940 a total of 10,000 Danes had volunteered to go to Finland and work), money collections, the public burning of books by the Communist novelist Martin Andersen Nexø (who had described Finland as 'semi-Nazi') and a field hospital that left for Finland via Sweden, while a crowd of Copenhageners stood on the key waving their hats and calling out: 'Long live Finland.'

What Finland *really* needed, though, were alliance partners. Again an approach was made to Sweden concerning the Åland Islands, but the Swedish Prime Minister Per Albin Hansson now blankly refused the suggestion. Sweden had no wish to become directly involved in Finland's war, which was perhaps reasonable enough since the Swedes had not participated in the pre-war negotiations, or even been asked for their opinion. Nevertheless, Sweden supported Finland indirectly throughout the Winter War by its export of weapons, foodstuffs, propellants etc.

Support also came from Great Britain on in the shape of fighter aircraft: thirty semi-obsolete Gladiators (ten donated and twenty sold), twenty-two Blenheims, twenty-two Gloster Gauntlets and eight Hurricanes. And a couple of weeks later, when it became clear that the Finnish Army was a lot harder to defeat than most people had expected, the Allied (i.e. Anglo-French) leaders offered Finland all the assistance it was possible to give, including fighting troops.

As already mentioned, the real purpose behind this proposed Allied aid was to give British and French troops a foothold in Lapland in order to sever the German import of Swedish iron ore. Realising this, the Finnish leaders saw a new and frightening situation emerge on the horizon – a war between the major powers fought partly on Finnish soil. Suffice to say that by the end of the year Helsinki started looking for other nations that might be willing to act as mediators between them and Moscow.

The Volunteers
As explained in the introduction, one of the aims of this book is to use Denmark as an example of how the Winter War was seen and experienced from an outside point of view.

The biggest group of foreign volunteers in the Finnish Army during the Winter War consisted of 9,500 Swedes. A considerable number of them saw action before the war ended, which was not the norm. Denmark delivered the second largest contingent, some 1,000 soldiers, of whom only a handful became directly involved in the fighting.

The Danes who saw action were primarily pilots. The retired Finnish Colonel K.W. Janarmo portrayed this group in the magazine *Ilmailu*

Danish volunteers enjoying a cup of coffee at Oulu. Later, during the Nazi occupation of Denmark (April 1940–May 1945), the former Winter War volunteers partly split into two markedly opposite groups: those who joined the Danish Legion in the Waffen-SS and those who became active in the Resistance Movement. (SA-Kuva)

(*Aviation*), Vol. 8 1964: 'The Danish contingent was the most impressive, not because of its size, but because of its capabilities. These young, highly skilled pilots went to Finland early on, without winter equipment or official permission, with only the intention of getting to the front and joining the fight as soon as possible. Most of them would fly fighter planes, and they all displayed the same enthusiasm and untiring willingness to fight as their Finnish comrades. Four of them gave their lives for our cause … two were seriously wounded in dog fights.'

The Danish pilot Jörn Ulrich later published a book about his experiences in Finland. The following quote reflects well the horrors of war seen from a fighter pilot's perspective:

> We cruised so low over the tree tops that the Russians could not see where the attack would come from until we were right above them. We flew in the planned formation, and one after the other our planes swept through the air, passing over the entire marching column from back to front. Such an attack coming from the rear is the most

loathsome butchery of humans imaginable. From our 9x4 machine guns we sent a rain of lead into the rows of marching men.

Of course the marching column dissolved immediately. The poor devils jumped off the road on both sides. I honestly considered if I really could be made to participate in such a mass murder of fellow beings, knowing these people were someone's fathers and brothers and sons that were now mowed down. But I had to do it, of course, though it almost made me throw up.

After the first attack, we made a quick turn and came back from the opposite direction. On the road there were piles of wounded and dead soldiers, the ditches were full of men, and in between the trees you could see them pressing themselves against the trees, covering their eyes like little children afraid of receiving punishment. Once more we turned around and swept down over the poor people, with our skis almost touching the tree tops, machine guns firing.

It was deeply disgusting. An upsetting shock, the first of its kind the war had given me ... a revolting experience.[82]

Later on in his book Ulrich writes:

It almost became a habit for us to dive down over the marching columns, and of course we became more fearless when we discovered that we could do exactly as we pleased without anyone shooting back at us.[83]

The story of the Danish volunteers on the ground is considerably less dramatic, although it was not for any lack of willingness to fight. Twelve days after the war had started, five hundred Danes had already approached the Finnish embassy in Copenhagen asking to join the Finnish Army. The volunteers initially arrived in Tornio and were later sent south to Oulu to receive training there. The unit was named Dansk Finlandskorps (*Danish Finland Corps*) and included a distinctive group of Danish Nazis, among them the later commandant of the Danish Legion in the SS, C.F. von Schalburg.

The Danish author, Ole Juul, was twenty-one at the time and had travelled to Finland as a news reporter. His meeting with the Danish volunteer group was not an entirely warm experience judging from his description in his book *Den røde Sne* (*The Red Snow*):

Though the majority were sound, idealistic young men who had joined the fight against the Russians, there were also some who had travelled to Finland for considerably less sympathetic reasons. These adventurers and charlatans inevitably made their mark on the

Danish volunteer pilot during the Winter War (name unknown, possibly Flight Lieutenant Jörn Ulrich). Unlike the Danish volunteers on the ground the pilot group became highly involved in the fighting. (SA-Kuva)

garrison. Among this dubious group were several who had left Denmark to avoid paying alimony, to evade prison sentences or punishment for having deserted from the Danish Army. Also, there were some who had gone to Finland just for the thrill or because they were trigger-happy.[84]

Before any of these troops reached the front, the war was over. In fact, this was a typical experience for most of the foreign volunteers in Finland, but at least the Swedish group saw some action in the Lapland area (more of that later on).

Altogether the losses among the Danish volunteers during the Winter War were six men killed.

The Home Front
For the general Finnish public the issue was simple. The Winter War was a struggle to preserve Finland's independence. The Terijoki Government was seen as certain proof of what the Russians had intended all along. No one knew, of course, that the Soviet preparations to set up a puppet government had not started until the negotiations in Moscow had collapsed in mid-November. The same goes for many other details that have only become public knowledge at a much later date.

And perhaps it was better that way. Finland needed its national unity now that there was fighting all the way up and down the border. It was a unity of the kind that people naturally sense when they are being attacked from the outside as a collective group. But the unity was also connected to the fact that Finland since 1939 had been ruled by a coalition government, which meant that the working classes felt co-responsible for the policies in force. At the same time, the Molotov-Ribbentrop Pact and the subsequent Soviet demands on the Baltic States had given many on the political left a growing mistrust of the leadership in Moscow.

This unity was strengthened when the first reports of defensive victories appeared. Optimism on the Home Front grew, which rubbed off on the soldiers at the front. Finland was a democracy put to the test, and there was a pronounced preparedness to manage the situation with all available means, including intellectual ones. Poems were written, songs were composed and patriotic speeches were held.

Still, the Finnish leaders remained determinedly matter-of-fact. The Winter War could not be won on the battlefield. The fighting at the front was primarily aimed at holding out and achieving the best possible positions before the peace negotiations, which would hopefully soon become reality.

The support that the Home Front gave the fighting men was not just of a moral nature. The army lacked clothes to withstand the biting cold, and

Evacuation of Finnish rural families prior to the breakout of the Winter War. (SA-Kuva)

so in private homes all over the Finland a huge amount of knitting and sewing went on. Box wagons brim full of sweaters, mittens and socks left for the front on a daily basis.

Before the war, civilians had in some instances been evacuated from towns and potential combat zones. The biggest group of evacuees consisted of some 130,000 people together with large numbers of cattle and other household animals from the area between the Mannerheim Line and the Soviet border. The Swedish historian Claes-Göran Isacson describes the situation in his book *Ärans vinter* (*The Winter of Honour*): 'The suffering these people had to endure was considerable. The majority of inhabitants in the border areas were forced to set fire to their homes, which might have been in the hands of their families for generations, and to their barns and their harvests of the year. Attempts were made to take horses and cows along, together with any possessions that could be useful to the enemy ... When the desperate villagers turned around for the final time, all they saw were blackened chimney pipes and a heavy smoke spiralling upwards. Their life's work lay in ruins. Most of the people who were now leaving Karelia would never return to their scorched villages."[85]

The majority of the refugees were housed around Turku and Pori on the southwest coast of Finland. Many of their possessions (foodstuffs, pharmaceuticals etc.) were confiscated by the military along with tools and machinery that could be used for production of military equipment.

Some of the civilian population in the major cities was evacuated, too, mostly women and children. They were often accommodated by people in the countryside. Many of them returned to the cities in the second half of November 1939, when there emerged a general belief that peace would prevail. When the war nevertheless broke out, they had to be evacuated again. The general atmosphere during the first couple of weeks thereafter was deeply worried and depressed for three reasons: people had not yet grown used to the new conditions caused by the war, most of the news from the front was dealing with military retreats and many were frightened by the number of civilian losses caused by the air raids.

The Danish author Ole Juul describes in his book about the Winter War several such air attacks which he personally experienced, in the following case a Soviet attack on a civilian railway transport:

> When a plane penetrates the balloon barrages at low height, it can come upon its target with unbelievable precision. You cannot hear it before it is right above you and before you have time to think, it will have started firing at you with its machine guns, or it might have dropped its bomb load. These low-flying machines … are the most dangerous ones …
>
> The deepest fear of death you can only see in women as they try to protect their children. They have a glint in the eye, an indescribable expression you will never find in men.[86]

Judged from a modern perspective the Finnish losses during the Soviet air attacks were small, but the perception was different in an era that had not yet experienced the Blitz or the Allied bombing raids on German cities that would take place towards the end of the Second World War. Hence, the psychological atmosphere in Finland during the first days of the war was as gloomy as the December darkness in which it all took place. Still, this only lasted until the news of the Finnish defensive victory at Tolvajärvi was announced on the radio. This victory brushed aside the worry, and people in general started smiling at one another as they passed on the latest news from the front.[87]

Meanwhile, the press did its best to strengthen the country's fighting spirit. The Russians were portrayed as the arch enemy that had once again attacked the peace-loving Finns, who for some reason had become an annoyance to them. Such attitudes had previously been widespread among the middle and upper classes and owner-farmers. The new thing was that

Social Democrats and even some Communists were now also showing patriotic passion.[88]

The Soviet attempts to influence Finnish public opinion and turn the people against their government failed completely. The propaganda was primitive, talked down to people and divulged a deep ignorance about the true social conditions in Finland. When the Terijoki government tried to tempt people with promises of an eight-hour working day and basic education for everyone, the Finns just shook their heads. Such social improvements had been introduced in Finland several years previously.

The Finnish Home Front remained true to its political leaders throughout the Winter War. There was a strong feeling of having right on your side and of fighting a purely defensive war against a large, dictatorial attacker. Still, the question was how a small country could maintain its strength and motivation under such difficult and tragic conditions.

Here the church undoubtedly played an important role. The Lutheran belief was still deep-rooted in the Finnish people and its position was only strengthened by the war. Other factors played a part, too, such as the status that society granted fallen soldiers. Where it was at all possible the dead bodies were transported to their home districts and buried in a special sector of the local graveyard, officers and privates side by side. The Finnish historian Ilona Kemppainen, who has conducted profound research into the relationship between the Finnish people and their fallen soldiers during the Second World War, points out that the mothers of the deceased (and to a certain extent also the wives) were included in the honour surrounding soldiers who had died for their country. Hence, mothers who were willing to sacrifice their sons for the nation achieved a particularly privileged status in the national myth making.[89]

Finland was also home to a variety of sectarian religious movements, some of a rather bizarre nature. In one of the villages near Suomussalmi there was a religious-political sect, whose members believed that the Civil Guard represented the beast in the Book of Revelation. Moreover, the sect thought that only Communists went to heaven. As a result, its members had no qualms about collaborating with the Red Army when their village was occupied in the early days of the war. Twenty-seven of them were later sent to prison for treason.[90]

Other residents in the border areas were kidnapped by Soviet troops and taken into Soviet territory, where they were exposed to political indoctrination, threats against their families etc. Later, they were smuggled back into Finland to operate as spies.[91] For that reason people who returned to Finland after having been in Soviet captivity of one form or another were often looked upon as pariahs.[92]

During the second half of the 1930s, the Finnish state had made plans for how civilian society should be organised in case of a major European war. Though the plans had not primarily been aimed at a situation in which Finland was involved militarily, some of the measures were introduced during the Winter War. Rationing of coffee and sugar had already been implemented before the war and was administered by the Ministry for Supplies. No further rationing came into force during the Winter War itself, but shortly after it had ended sales of cereals, milk, butter, meat and eggs were regulated. Other foodstuffs disappeared completely from the shop shelves, so people had to make do with surrogates. All in all, the situation in Finland in this regard was not much different from that of many other European countries during the Second World War.

Families where the father had been called up naturally experienced a serious decrease in income. Only during the final few weeks of the war did the Finnish state start handing out daily allowances to the soldiers, with an added sum for married men. The size of the benefit also depended on the number of family members and the soldier's rank. A kind of widow's pension was likewise introduced. These arrangements later became a platform for the founding of the Finnish welfare state in the years after the Second World War.[93]

During the Winter War vulnerable Finnish citizens were evacuated to the other Nordic countries. Sweden was the main receiver of such refugees, who were mostly young children. Also some mothers and elderly people were evacuated, again mainly to Sweden. The total number of evacuees during the Winter War was around 10,000, of which the majority came from the Karelian Isthmus. This led to many tearful parting scenes between parents and children, as described here by one of those who experienced it as a young boy:

> We started by leaving Helsinki by train. And when the train started moving, many mothers stood outside and wept terribly. It was all very painful because the small children inside the train became terribly wound up. They started screaming and crying.[94]

The number of evacuated Finnish children escalated substantially during the Interim Peace and the Continuation War, so the issue shall be returned to later on in this book.

IV

The Second Month of the War

> *It is interesting to see how the Finnish soldier in the midst of battle becomes still keener, yet at the same time maintains his ingenuity and determination.*
> FINNISH BATTALION COMMANDER[95]

All Quiet on the Karelian Isthmus
After the intense combat on the Karelian Isthmus in December, the situation calmed down around New Year and changed into a positional war that lasted throughout January. Still, the Soviet attacks continued and both sides kept sending out patrols, often to operate behind enemy lines, particularly in the early days of the month.

Though this period has been named 'the Trench Phase', it would be wrong to envisage long parallel frontlines opposite one another as on the European battlefields of the First World War. The highly varied terrain on the Karelian Isthmus simply did not allow for that. The many lakes and other natural obstructions ensured that the distance between the trenches constantly altered, resulting in an uneven no man's land well suited to patrol activities.

Peter de Hemmer Gudme's privileged position among the international journalists in Finland meant that he could move closer to the front than his colleagues in general. He visited the Finnish positions on the Karelian Isthmus in January 1940 and was given rich opportunities to interview the soldiers and build up an impression of the atmosphere and the situation. The following is yet another quote from his book about the Winter War:

> For many of them the war there was pure hell but they carried on with remarkable calm. Ever since the beginning of the war a soldier from Ostrobothnia had been stationed in the Taipale sector in the easternmost part of the Isthmus, in the fixed positions behind the frozen river [Vuoksi]. The troops were suffering badly from the cold and constantly struggling to avoid getting frostbites. Every evening when they came back to the *korsu* [Finnish word for a dugout in or behind a trench] their feet were yellowy white, and they often had to massage them with snow for several hours before the blood

Finnish ski unit following forest combat in Ladoga Karelia. (SA-Kuva)

circulation was normal again. In many cases someone neglected to report a frostbite before it was too late and he would end up in the infirmary, which was under attack throughout the war.

The worst thing the soldier from Ostrobothnia had experienced was when the Russians – one evening after more than a week of artillery preparations and numerous attempts to land troops across the frozen Lake Ladoga – launched a major attack. The shelling had been so bad it was impossible to get food out to the troops in the frontline, so they had to make do with their cold one-man ration packs. They had started running low on ammunition, too, so it was important not to start firing too soon. Following their normal style, the Russians did not bend forward as they attacked across the ice but marched ahead with their backs straight, rifles held at the hip. The Finns calmly let them come up close before they started firing, and then they mowed them down like corn. But new Russian formations kept pouring forward, so you had to be quick on the trigger … six times in close succession the Russians attacked. Their bodies were piling up on the ice so the soldiers further back had to jump over their dead comrades to get ahead. Panic was spreading among them, but the Finns just calmly swept across their ranks with their machine guns. It was terrible! He was not the only machine gunner who had to step aside and vomit when it was over.

It was even worse when their ammunition started to run out. Now they had to hold their fire until the Russians were just 20 metres from their position, which took a lot of nerve. Only then did they fire, and afterwards they had to fight the enemy off in hand-to-hand combat.

It worried the Russians that they were not met with a barrage of bullets this time. Hence, they marched more and more nervously, and only at a distance of some 20 metres did they receive an intense volley of shots. This shook them considerably, and at the same time the Finns stormed forward, singing and clenching their knives in their hands. The Finnish *pukko* [traditional Finnish knife] is a formidable weapon. They can be as long as a bayonet, with a long groove to pick up the blood. The soldier from Ostrobothnia, who told me this, said he felt as if he was blinded during the fight. He heard a crunching noise the first time he stabbed someone, and in a flash he saw the soldier he had stabbed stare straight at him with a look in his eye like a calf being butchered. Another Russian tried stopping him by clinging on to his clothes, but he just continued. He only regained his senses when he suddenly saw one of his comrades in front of him. By then he had no idea what had happened, except that he had been in a mad fight. His only thought had been that this was a situation of either kill or be killed. When he got away from there, he was shaking all over and when he finally managed to fall asleep, he was dreaming about the terrible butchery, as he saw again the dead man staring at him and heard the screaming and groaning of the Russian soldiers.[96]

The minor but constant Soviet infantry and artillery attacks during January were primarily a preparation for a coming grand-scale offensive against the Mannerheim Line. The Finns were to be tenderised first and then crushed. The prestige of the Soviet Union as a military power could probably not be re-established in the short run; in fact, the situation was only worsened by the increasing numbers of troops and equipment that were thrust into attacks, which were fended off by the Finns; but that was less important as long as the war was won in the end.

It was now high time to bring home the victory, but so far experience had shown that some serious changes had to be made in order to succeed. On 28 December an instruction had been given to stop the massive offensive operations in order to avoid further Finnish encirclements and secure the Red Army's own positions. The tactic of 'deep' operations had to be modified[97] and it was found necessary to spend far more time on preparations than previously anticipated.

Finnish artillery observers in a trench at Kiviniemi in the eastern sector of the Mannerheim Line. (SA-Kuva)

Accordingly, large amounts of war materiel and ammunition were brought to the frontline, as extra divisions were transported to the Karelian Isthmus and placed in reserve. The men were trained harder than before and more explicitly in carrying out precisely the kind of attack that was soon to take place. All was clearly better organised than previously. Reconnaissance patrols were sent out and returned back with important information, observation balloons were used to map the Finnish defence and artillery positions. The results could already be measured, as throughout January the Soviet artillery hammered the Finnish positions and their accuracy was vastly improving.

The previous failures also had consequences for the military leadership. At the top, Field-Marshal Kliment Voroshilov was replaced by General Semyon Timoshenko. One of his first decisions was to divide the Seventh Army on the Isthmus into two formations, of which one kept the old name, while the other became the Thirteenth Army. Both formations then received large reinforcements. Meanwhile, the units north of Ladoga were merged together into one single Army Group.

The Finnish troops on the Mannerheim Line suffered huge losses during January. The fighting was particularly hard on the 6th Division, which so far mainly had been in reserve but was now placed on the frontlines. Meanwhile, the 5th Division was pulled back to become the main reserve. This division had, incidentally, changed its name to 3rd Division, since the Finnish divisional numbering had shifted as part of a general attempt to confuse Soviet intelligence.

For the Finns, the Soviet probing and weakening attacks were felt as one long, murderous and unreal experience, where the ground shook and bounced up and down so the men could hardly stand on their feet, while the air filled with shell splinters, and wounded soldiers were carried back screaming through the snow to the field hospitals at the rear. Troop movements and improvements of the positions could only take place during the night, while in the daytime the soldiers huddled in their dugouts trying to catch a few hours of sleep. But even when it came, sleep was constantly interrupted by new Soviet attacks, or the men were kept awake by the insanely cold temperatures. The weather in the area was particularly harsh from 17 January onwards, with temperatures as low as minus 49 centigrade.

By the end of January, the Mannerheim Line was reduced to a shadow of its former self. Bunkers and machine gun nests had been blown apart, trenches had caved in everywhere, telephone lines had been cut by shell splinters, mended and cut again endlessly, until it became impossible for the repair teams to keep up with the all-prevailing destruction, and communication between the units in practice ceased to exist.

Kitelä and Kollaa

In the last chapter we left the Soviet 168th Division by the northern bank of Lake Ladoga, where it had been stopped by the Finns at Kitelä Village. Forty kilometres east of there was another village, Uomaa, where the Finns had stopped the Soviet 18th Division. The Finnish troops had established a long, curved defence line north of the two villages. On 13 and 17 December they had tried to eliminate the Soviet force, but the attempt had failed although the Finnish grip on Uomaa had tightened.

After redeploying his forces, the commander of IV Corps, Major General Hägglund, felt the time was ready for using *motti* tactics against the two Soviet divisions. Hence, on 5 January Finnish troops stole south through the largely roadless terrain towards the Soviet positions. The next day the attack began. The Russians, instead of counterattacking, almost willingly let themselves be split into *mottis*, as Hägglund had planned. Subsequently, the 168th Division was encircled in a big pocket inside Kitelä, while the 18th Division was split into eight smaller *mottis*. Five of these were to be found on the road leading east towards Uomaa, two in a northern direction on the road towards Syskyjärvi, and one was situated were the two roads met in a fork.

From here on the situation became more static, as the Finns found it impossible to eliminate the *mottis*. The Soviets had established themselves behind tanks they had dug into the ground around the perimeter of each pocket and placed their artillery in the centre of their positions. The Finnish units lacked anti-tank guns and other medium-sized weapons, and moreover IV Corps was under heavy pressure from other Soviet formations to the north. All they could do was try and starve the Russians out of their positions, or at least weaken them so much that the pockets could be destroyed one by one using light weapons.

This procedure continued through January along the entire road between Uomaa and Kitelä and a short stretch north along the road to Syskyjärvi. The commander of the Soviet 18th Division, General Grigorii Kondrashev, wrote in his daily reports:

18 JANUARY 1940
All units of the division are in an extremely difficult situation. A lot of deaths from starvation. Men have stomach cramps and night blindness. We are waiting for your help every day.

29 JANUARY 1940
We have been encircled for sixteen days. We have 500 wounded. No ammo left, no bread. Around 600 men are sick. Hunger, sickness, death are here.[98]

The front at Kollaa north of Lake Ladoga. (SA-Kuva)

Despite the harsh weather conditions, the tough fighting and the sporadic Finnish hit-and-run assaults, most of the surviving Soviet soldiers held at least part of their positions until the end of the war. Meanwhile, General Kondrashev managed to escape and return to Russia. But on 3 March he was arrested, sentenced to death and executed.[99] Both privates and officers in the Red Army were often punished harshly for poor performances on the battlefield or for having been taken prisoner.

Sixty kilometres northeast of Kitelä the Finnish troops had, as previously described, been forced back to Kollaanjoki. Here they had established a 5km wide front behind which a single Finnish division was fending off no less than four Soviet divisions. The Finnish troops received only few reinforcements and had practically no rest at all. Still, they managed to hold their positions until the end of the war.

The Raate Road
The Finnish destruction of the Soviet 163rd Division at Suomussalmi in late December 1939 had only just been completed when the exhausted Finnish troops were ordered to carry on with the next operation in the area. The Soviet 44th Division had long been in a static position on the eastern part of the Raate Road (Map 2/2). The division was an elite unit, but its speciality was motorised warfare. The soldiers were mostly very young, and their only

ski training consisted of some instruction manuals they had been handed. Part of their equipment was Polish (presumably Soviet war booty from the campaign in September the previous year) and so comprehensive and heavy it compromised their mobility.

To move on foot out into the snow-covered forest terrain was a suicidal act, for there the Finnish ski patrols reigned supreme. Hence, the Russians were prevented from carrying out flanking manoeuvres, just as they were unable to establish a broader frontline but had to remain as a column stretching up to the Finnish roadblock. In the meantime, troops were clearing the forest on both sides of the road and digging trenches.

Day and night the 44th Division tried to eliminate the Finnish unit holding the roadblock. Unfortunately for the Russians they had still not managed to do so by the time the Finnish troops at Suomussalmi captured the scorched village and dispersed the Soviet 163rd Division to the four winds. After that the original task of the rescue column was no longer pertinent, but there was still the possibility that it could reach Suomussalmi, which, as already mentioned, constituted a strategic key point.

Once again the Finns used an oblong, frozen lake south of the main road as their transport route. That way they could move troops from Suomussalmi eastwards and then turn north through the forest to launch attacks on the Soviet column.

In fact, one such attack had already taken place on 31 December, when Suomussalmi was still being cleansed of the remaining Russians. It was a scouting operation meant to clarify the possibilities of cutting off and isolating the front part of the Soviet column. This purpose was achieved on 2 January, when Suomussalmi finally was free of enemies and the Finnish troops in the area could be moved east to participate in the attack on the Soviet 44th Division.

The main attack took place on 5 January when the Finnish units drove wedges into the column at several points, took up positions and mined the terrain in front of them. Some Soviet tanks tried to break out but were captured by the Finns, who quickly integrated them into their own defences. By sunset the 30km long Soviet column had been split into seven smaller, isolated *mottis*.

Neither side was interested in stalling the situation, so when new Finnish attacks were launched the following day, the Russians proved surprisingly easy to drive out of their positions and into the forest. They were immediately chased by Finnish units on ski. Next day the entire column on the Raate Road was either dissolved or defeated. The official final day of the Battle of the Raate Road is 7 January 1940, a month after the 163rd Division had initially captured Suomussalmi and taken up positions in the village.

The Raate Road after the destruction of the Russian column. The Finnish war booty was enormous. (SA-Kuva)

Frozen Soviet soldier after the Battle of the Raate Road. (SA-Kuva)

The losses during the battle are still to this day a mystery. The Finns announced a figure of 402 dead but said nothing of the numbers of soldiers wounded and missing in action. The Soviet losses are quoted as anything between 900 killed (the official contemporary Soviet figure) to 17,000 (the official Finnish figure). The truth seems to lie about halfway between these numbers. The total number of troops in the 44th Division also varies depending on which source you look at. To confuse these issues even further, many accounts of the Battle of Suomussalmi and the Battle of the Raate Road add up the losses related to both events.

The losses of Soviet war materiel are more certain. They were in the region of 4,000 rifles, 100 machine guns, 225 light machine guns, 60 artillery pieces, 30 anti-tank guns, 15 anti-tank rifles and 40 tanks. The Finnish accounts also mention 10 armoured cars, 260 trucks, 2 saloon cars and 1,170 horses.

The Motti at Kuhmo
The news of the Finnish victories over the New Year filled the world with astonishment and admiration. But Colonel Siilasvuo and his men had no time to rest on their laurels. Some 100km to the south, by the town of Kuhmo, the situation had been at a deadlock since 20 December. Siilasvuo's troops were now transferred to this area to participate in the fighting against the Soviet invaders.

The Soviets had positioned themselves along the main road from Kuhmo going southeast to the Soviet border. They were efficiently keeping the Finns at bay, so Siilasvuo ordered part of his division to march east along a parallel route north of the main road, just as his men had previously marched on the frozen lake south of the main road at Suomussalmi. About 25km east of Kuhmo the troops stopped and started improving a road that went south towards the Soviet force on the main road. The work was carried out at night to avoid causing a commotion and included the setting-up of depots, field hospitals, field kitchens and the like in preparation for the coming battle.

Meanwhile, the Soviet division had come dangerously close to penetrating a Finnish barricade on the road going north to Kuhmo, so a smaller Finnish attack from the northwest had been launched at this part of the column. The skirmish ended indecisively, but next day the Finns launched an attack along the improved road further east, while other units attacked from the south. As a result, the Soviet column was split into one big *motti* to the west and a string of smaller pockets to the east. Though the Finns now had anti-tank guns and other heavier weapons they had captured at Suomussalmi and the Raate Road, the Soviet positions were too strong to penetrate. It would demand the use of real artillery, which the Finns still

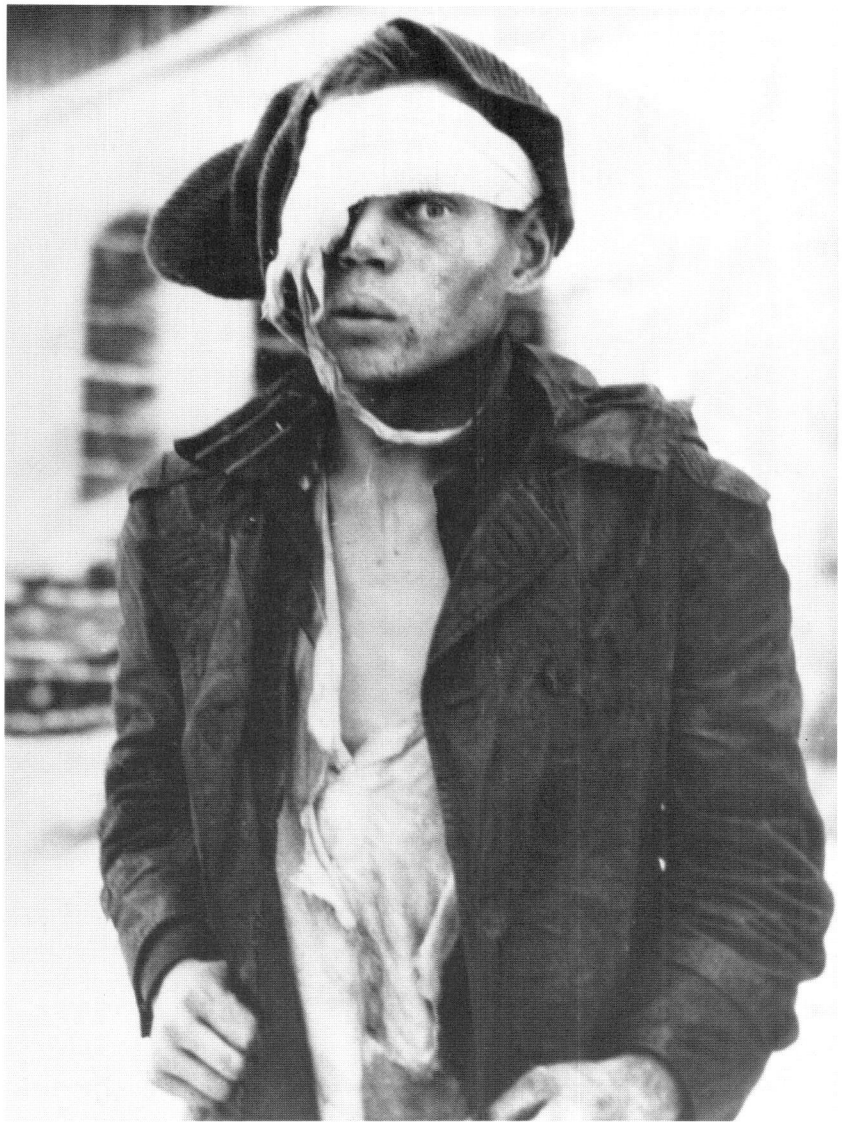

Wounded and visibly traumatised Soviet officer in Finnish captivity. (SA-Kuva)

did not have. So the attack ended in the by now well-known situation where the Russians had to be starved or frozen out, a gridlock scenario that continued through the next month.

Though the Finns saw some progress here in late February, they never managed to completely eliminate the Russians at this location. Hence, the *motti* at Kuhmo never became the same success for the Finnish Army as the former defensive victories at Suomussalmi and the Raate Road. Instead, they had become stuck in a situation more akin to the one further south at

Kitelä. Part of the problem was that the Soviets by now had learned several important lessons. They had become better at supplying their encapsulated units from the air, and they managed to continually bring reinforcements from their 23rd Division into the *mottis* at Kuhmo, supported by tanks and artillery.

Hopes and Negotiations
A few days into the New Year, Väinö Tanner suggested that the German ambassador to Finland, Wipert von Blücher, should ask the political leaders in Berlin if they had any 'advice to give Finland'. Blücher passed on the query and added his own opinion on how Germany ought to act in relation to the Finnish-Soviet war. The best thing, he wrote, would be if Berlin took on the role of intermediary. Of course, von Ribbentrop could not reply that such an act was impossible because he had made a secret agreement with the Soviet Union, which gave the latter a free hand in matters related to Finland. So he just turned down the request, commenting that there seemed to be no solution to the Finnish-Soviet conflict at the moment.

Germany itself was at war with France and Great Britain, at this point merely a *phony war* but it could break out for real at any moment. One of Hitler's basic principles was that Germany should never again end up in a war on two fronts with the Western Allies on one side and Russia on the other, as it had during the First World War. Hence, the guarantees made in the Molotov-Ribbentrop Pact had to be kept until the situation in the west had been solved.

Berlin was in other words determined not to step on any Russian toes, at least not openly. Before the war, the Finnish government had made a secret deal with Germany concerning some anti-tank guns that would be delivered through Sweden. The Swedish press got wind of the affair and brought it out into the open, the end result being that the Germans held back the weapons. Likewise, some shipments of war materiel that the Finns had bought from Italy and Hungary were stopped on their way through Germany and were not released until the Winter War was over.

The Finnish leaders also asked America for help, but again they found themselves banging on a locked door. There was an overwhelming public sympathy for Finland in the predominantly anti-Communist USA, strengthened by the occasionally rather high-flown press coverage of the war. A vast amount of humanitarian aid was sent off, but the so-called isolationists were riding high at this time, and furthermore there were various judicial complications. Instead, Washington in late January offered itself as intermediary between Helsinki and Moscow. Molotov, however, strongly rejected the idea.

German and American diplomats in the Soviet Union passed on the impression that the leaders in Moscow were not interested in ending the war. In fact, the problem was probably rather that the Soviets wanted to avoid western interference of any kind. In January 1940 the Soviet Union seriously needed to end the costly and, for them, humiliating war in Finland, but it had to be done without adding insult to injury. The Red Army was staggering around in the snow-clad forests of Finland like a helpless elephant, while the world looked on and rubbed its hands. The Soviet propaganda machine tried to reduce the moral damage internally by portraying the Mannerheim Line as an impregnable string of fortresses whilst minimizing the Soviet defeats. But the mere fact that the war was dragging on showed there was something terribly wrong with the Red Army's operations in this war.

Internally in Finland, January brought some serious changes of a political kind, showing how the nation was constantly becoming more homogenous. Most importantly, the workers and employers organisations acknowledged each other as negotiating parties and in an important act of internal reconciliation, members of the Social Democrat Party could now join the Civil Guard or the Lotta Svärd organisation, and vice versa.

Female Intervention

Documents that have emerged after the opening of the Soviet archives show that the Kremlin probably abandoned the idea of the Terijoki puppet government in late January 1940, or at least decided to put it aside for a while. Instead, the Soviet leaders wished to return to the negotiating table and try for a peace agreement based on the demands they had presented to Paasikivi and Tanner in the pre-war negotiations. This meant that the plan of taking over all of Finland was effectively abandoned, at least temporarily. Still, in order to have the strongest possible stance at such talks, the Soviets wanted to first carry out their planned grand-scale advance on the Karelian Isthmus.

But other forces wished for a more rapid ending to the war, among them the Finnish writer Hella Wuolijoki, known for her strong left-wing sympathies and feminist views. She approached Foreign Minister Tanner with an offer: with the government's permission she would travel to Stockholm and contact her old friend, Alexandra Kollontai, who was the Soviet ambassador to Sweden. The purpose would be to re-establish contacts between the Finnish and Soviet leaders.

Alexandra Kollontai likewise was a known feminist and an advocate for sexual liberation. She had participated actively in the Russian Revolution and had subsequently become the world's first female government minister. Kollontai had managed to survive the political purges of the 1930s and had even kept her position and status as one of the Soviet Union's most experienced diplomats.

Wuolijoki received permission from the Finnish government to embark on her mission, and so the two women met in Stockholm on 14 January 1940. Wuolijoki asked the ambassador if there was basis for new secret negotiations, and Kollontai promised to send a telegram to Moscow to enquire. The reply arrived on 30 January and was positive overall.

Meanwhile, the Swedish Foreign Minister Christian Günther also met with Kollontai. The Swedish government was worried about the possibility of Anglo-French support to Finland. Since Petsamo was under Soviet control, the transport of Allied troops would have to go through northern Norway and Sweden. If the two countries permitted foreign troops access to their territories, their neutrality would be violated and they too would be in danger of ending up at war with the Soviet Union. Also, the iron ore transports from northern Sweden to Nazi Germany would be severed, which the Germans would probably not accept.

Alexandra Kollontai (1872-1952).

As already mentioned, these factors were not just regrettable side effects of an Anglo-French intervention in the Winter War. They were the real but hidden agenda behind the Allied offer of help to Finland, a fact that the Norwegian, Swedish and Finnish leaders were fully aware of. The aim was to turn northern Scandinavia into a gigantic battleground, by which the British and particularly the French hoped to keep their expected future clash with Germany as far away from their own territories as possible. Sweden and Norway could of course deny access to the Allied troops, but they themselves would then be in danger of being invaded by these forces instead.

In short, Sweden had a pressing interest in seeing an end to the Winter War as soon as possible. Hence, Foreign Secretary Günther offered Kollontai his assistance and was shortly after to act as intermediary between her and the Finnish government.

In this way communication was re-established. The Finns replied to Moscow that they, too, were interested in negotiating, but that the Soviet territorial demands were too comprehensive. Again, Hanko turned out to be the sore point. When the Russians threatened to pull out of the talks, Tanner went to Stockholm to meet with Kollontai in person. Together they worked out a proposal that included, as an alternative to Hanko, the handing over of an island at the mouth of the Gulf of Finland. Tanner knew that the leaders in Helsinki would reject the proposal, but he desperately needed something that could break the gridlock in the negotiations, which were meanwhile taking place in Moscow, so a telegram was send to the Soviet leaders presenting the offer.[100] However, the proposal was refused, and so the situation had become stuck at approximately the same point as during the pre-war negotiations.

One may wonder what the Finnish leaders had expected to gain by re-opening negotiations if they were still unwilling to change their minds on practically the same issues as had proved to be sticking points before the war. The answer is that there was a big difference between the situation in early December, where the Finns had striven ardently to negotiate, and eight or nine weeks later when it finally became possible. The news of the Finnish victories and the wild enthusiasm of the world press over Finish military successes had created an unrealistic view of the overall situation, not only in the Finnish people but also among many members of parliament. Paasikivi writes in his memoires:[101]

> It is my personal impression that Stalin did not want Finland to go under entirely but would have preferred to see a solution to the conflict. On our side the situation had not yet matured. We still held our positions on the Isthmus Front, and the fortunes of war were with us in January. The general population was not yet prepared to make any larger concessions.[102]

Since the Second World War there have been several major public discussions in Finland about the handling of the pre-Winter War negotiations, and criticism has been made about the lack of pragmatism exercised by the government, parliament, press and general population. A similar discussion about the situation in late January 1940 has only emerged very recently due to the release of new Soviet documents. So far, it seems to contradict Paasikivi's rather positive view of Stalin's and Molotov's true motives. Still, it cannot be ignored that even a full Finnish acceptance of all Soviet demands at this point would have resulted in a peace agreement far less painful than the one that Finland was eventually forced to accept. The territorial concessions would have been smaller, and particularly the Finns would have kept Viipuri, their second largest city. In consequence, the numbers of refugees would have been smaller too, while the future military position would have been much stronger. But above all else Finland might have been spared the great losses in human lives and war materiel that would occur over the final six weeks of the war. A period where the Finnish resistance was no less fierce and admirable than previously – perhaps even more so – but also a period without the defensive victories of December 1939 and January 1940.

V

The Third Month of the War

*The whole world had its eyes on us and the prestige
of the Red Army was the guarantee of the
Soviet Union's security.*
JOSEF STALIN[103]

Preparing for Battle
For the Red Army, January on the Karelian Isthmus had primarily been one long period of preparation for the new large-scale offensive that was to be launched the following month over a broad front, with its centres of gravity at Summa and the Vuoksi River. Through artillery bombardments and frequent infantry and tank attacks the Soviets had tenderised the Mannerheim Line and its defenders, while the Red Army reorganised its troops under a new leadership, named 'the North-West Front Command'.

Reinforcements had arrived so that by the turn of the month the two Soviet armies (the Seventh and the Thirteenth) on the Karelian Isthmus totalled some 600,000 men, 2,000 tanks and more than 3,000 artillery guns (of which about a third were of heavy calibre).[104] The fresh new troops came from all parts of the Soviet Union, including areas such as the Urals and Siberia where people were used to harsh winters and where military training included the use of skis and white camouflage. The emphasis, however, was still on the use of tanks and artillery, and there was no shortage of vehicles or ammunition.

Against this massive war machine the Finns deployed seven divisions (one placed in reserve), two cavalry regiments and a few separate units (for a more detailed description of both forces and their equipment and organisation see Appendix V). Most of the Finnish troops had for weeks been exposed to exhaustive fighting and massive artillery bombardments, temperatures down to minus 40 centigrade and all the terrible sights and sufferings of modern warfare. They fought a struggle they had no chance of winning, with dwindling reserves and ammunition stores, and frequently failing food supplies.

Soviet soldiers resting near Kämärä on the Karelian Isthmus.

The February Offensive

General Timoshenko described the goal of the operation as 'to encircle and destroy the main enemy group acting on the Karelian Isthmus'.[105] After a nightlong artillery bombardment the Soviet attack on the Mannerheim Line was launched on 1 February, aimed at the western sector. Nearest to the coast stood the Finnish 4th Division opposite the Red Army's 43rd, 113th and 70th Divisions. As in most of December the Soviets placed their centre of gravity further northeast at Summa Village (now reduced to a blackened ruin), where the Finnish 3rd Division was facing the Soviet 123rd, 138th, 100th and 90th Divisions. In both places the Finns repelled the attacks. The fighting was, however, only a mild foretaste of what was in store.

While the Finns repelled limited attacks on 3 and 4 February, the Soviet 62nd Division was moved forward to the eastern sector of the front. Mikhail Lukinov, who served with the division's artillery, remembered:

> The first thing we noticed was the frozen corpses of our soldiers and officers, lying there, already powdered with snow. They were lying where death had found them, in various positions. We were used to treating our dead with respect. A coffin, a funeral service, the farewell celebration, everyone whispering, covering mirrors, stopping their watches. But this place was dominated by a hatred belonging to the dead. As if they were saying to us who were moving forward that

death was an ordinary occurrence in his place. They had been killed, so just let them be, nothing special has happened. There was a war going on here, and everything was different from civilian life. You had to get used to it.[106]

A Soviet artillery attack on the night of 4 February was followed by a new attack with its focus on Summa. Again, the Finns held their positions.

7 February marks a turning point in the history of the Winter War, since on this day the big Soviet offensive on the Karelian Isthmus began in earnest. The attack now stretched along the entire Finnish defence line. Again, the Russians placed their centre of gravity at Summa, but they still failed to push the Finns back. Hence, after a further three days of fighting, the focus was moved to the area around Lähde Village. At the same time Soviet infantry went out on the ice west of the Isthmus and on to Lake Ladoga by the eastern flank of the fortifications, with the intention of rolling up the Mannerheim Line from both ends. The Finns came under heavy pressure but still managed to repel the attacks long enough for their reserves to be thrown into combat, after which any lost terrain was recaptured.

The pivotal point of the Finnish defence was the One Million Bastion, so called because it had been a huge investment for the Finnish state. The legends about how the bunker was captured are both plentiful and contradictory. Still, it seems certain that the attacking force was the Red

Soviet troops advancing on the Karelian Isthmus.

Army's 255th Regiment and the defenders were the Finnish 9th Regiment's second battalion, a Swedish-speaking unit under Lieutenant M.G. Ericsson. Finnish Private Rafael Forth later described the event:

> The Russians did not shoot so much at the bunker itself, but aimed their attack to the right of the bunker at the so-called Finger Hill. Our fourth company tried to cleanse the trenches with hand grenades and submachine gun fire, but it was all in vain. The Russians held a tight grip on the hill as they moved closer and closer to the bunker through the trenches ... They climbed up on the roof of the bunker and took up defensive positions.[107]

This is supposed to have happened on 11 February at 2:30pm. The same incident is described from the Soviet point of view by the commander of the attack group, Second Lieutenant Lekanov:

> It was severely cold, but we were all covered with sweat. Finally, we reached the nearest trench. Together with the infantry we tried to inspect the bunker, but the White Finns[108] emerged at that moment and threw several hand grenades at us. A short burst of a machine gun and the enemy was destroyed.
>
> The White Finns locked themselves in their underground fortress. We crawled on to the roof of the bunker with our boxes of explosives.[109]

However, Lekanov felt he needed more explosives to destroy the bunker, so he set up some small demolitions charges that blocked the doors. Then he and his group returned to their own position to collect more explosives. Meanwhile, the Soviet infantry encircled the bunker and kept it covered. Lekanov's group returned, and according to the group leader they blew up the bunker at the following morning.

> A tremendous explosion. A huge flame shot into the sky. We were all covered with soil. Ears were ringing, our heads were spinning.[110]

Rafael Forth and a group of his comrades had already abandoned the bunker the previous evening before the first explosion. The second explosion killed three soldiers inside the bunker, but others survived and were taken prisoner as they crawled from the ruin.

Also on the night of 11 February, Soviet infantry supported by tanks managed to penetrate the Mannerheim Line at some of its weaker points, particularly near Lähde. Neither side was strong enough to keep fighting at full force, so a temporary status quo evolved over the next twenty-four hours. Then on 14 February the Soviets managed to expand a breach they had made in the Lähde sector, after which the Finnish commanding officers were ordered to pull their men back in order to avoid the line being rolled up in the direction of Summa.

Around the same time Mannerheim arrived at the HQ of II Corps, where he followed the development of the situation and had discussions with Öhquist, trying to find any available reserves that could be transferred to the area. In the afternoon of the same day he returned to Mikkeli by car.

On the morning of 15 February Soviet vanguards broke through the improvised Finnish defences on the road from Summa to Kämärä village. Once this had happened, Mannerheim decided to pull all of II Corps back to the Intermediate Line. In his memoirs he states that there were not enough reserves to make any other option viable, and that Öhquist agreed with this view. However, the Intermediate Line was weak and lacking in both bunkers and machine gun nests.

By now the Finns had thrown all their reserves on the Isthmus into the fighting, but an infantry regiment arrived on the western flank from the eastern sector after a twenty-four hour delay due to air attacks. Two Battalions and some smaller units formed by personnel from the navy also arrived,[111] and a so-called defence corps consisting of young boys was sent by cars from Viipuri. The 23rd Division, which had recently been sent north to reinforce the front at Kollaa, was ordered to stop and return to the Karelian Isthmus.

The withdrawal was carried out as planned between 15 and 18 February. Only the Koivisto Coastal Fortress was still manned in order to secure the retreat. There were initially no Soviet attacks, but on 17 February severe clashes occurred on the western flank of the Intermediate Line and even harder fighting took place at the centre of the position.

On 18 February the retreat to the Intermediate Line had just been completed when the Finnish 4th Division was attacked. The Russians managed to create a small breach in the Finnish line and capture a few houses in Ylä-Sommee Village 10km south of Viipuri. A Finnish counterattack was repelled, and at the same time the Russians started attacking and capturing several key points in the Finnish defence along the coast. Despite hard resistance the Finnish troops were forced back. The commanding officers at the Intermediate Line sent Mannerheim a message requesting permission to abandon this fortification line, too. The marshal, however, refused and instead gave the order that the line must be held at all costs. This led to some indignation among the officers, who were unaware of the reason behind Mannerheim's rejection: there were signs that new

Soviet flamethrower tank captured by Finnish troops. (SA-Kuva)

negotiations with Moscow would go ahead so it was important to remain as strong on the battlefield as possible.

The Soviet attack on the Intermediate Line at Ylä-Somme continued over 19-21 February, growing more forceful all the time. After two days under constant fire from infantry, tanks and artillery, the Finnish regiment in the sector was so reduced and battered it had to be relieved. A replacement regiment arrived, but it soon suffered similar losses. At one point the Russians penetrated the line east of the village, but a Finnish counterattack soon pushed them back.

On 22 February the artillery on the island of Koivisto used up its final ammunition. The troops demolished as much of the materiel as they could and then started out on a more than 30km long march across the frozen Viipuri Bay in a heavy snow storm. They arrived on the mainland the next morning. On the same day (23 February) Soviet troops stormed the nearby island of Lasisaari. A Finnish attempt to recapture the island failed, which seriously compromised the entire Finnish western flank. Further east the Soviets increased their pressure on the centre of the Intermediate Line.

This pressure continued on 24 February. The Finnish bunkers at the centre of the position were few and far between, with no communication via field telephones or trenches. Furthermore, there were no anti-tank guns, which placed the Finnish troops at the mercy of the Soviet tanks. During this stage of the fighting a Finnish machine gun platoon and a half-platoon of standard infantry were attacked by Soviet flamethrower tanks. The commandant of the Red Army's 85th Tank Battalion later described the situation:

> The tank crew was given the signal to fire at the gun ports and then immediately cease fire. They did exactly so. In a second, we were at the gun ports and stuffing them with two boxes of explosives each. Then we lit the fuses. When the explosion took place, the gun ports were torn wide open. The flame-thrower tank started to pour burning liquid into these holes without stopping. Men stood at the door with machine guns and hand grenades ready. The Finns had nowhere to run.
>
> After some time we ceased fire from the tank and threw four boxes of explosives into the bunker. We advised the tank crew to drive away. A powerful explosion shook the bunker. The turret was blown off, as well as the door. There was a dead silence in the bunker. Then we could report to the commanders that the bunker was neutralised.
>
> There were fifteen dead Finns in the bunker.[112]

The same episode is described from the Finnish side by Lieutenant Kauko Tiili of the 2nd Artillery Regiment:

> All of a sudden, the sky turned red in the direction of the bunker and a huge pillar of smoke shot into the air. Helpless hatred filled our hearts. We could do nothing to help the men inside the bunker. Then a blackened, wet and petrol-smelling man ran into our bunker: 'I am the man who has just made it from there.'
>
> From the voice of the man we could hear that he had just been through a great shock. He told us how a flame-thrower tank drove up to the bunker and poured burning oil inside …
>
> An officer later went to have a look at the fateful bunker. 'We should set a sentry at the door, so that no one can see what is inside,' he said quietly.[113]

On the same morning (24 February) the Red Army had thrown more tanks into the combat, and on 25 February they penetrated the Finnish positions and moved as far as the town of Honkaniemi (on the railway line from Viipuri).

The next day the Finns carried out their first and final tank attack during the Winter War. Their infantry was surprised to hear for the first time ever the sound of tanks coming from behind them, and for a moment the men became seriously worried. In every respect the attack was a failure. The seven light tanks that carried out the counterattack were practically defenceless against their much more heavily armed and armoured Soviet counterparts, which included T-26 and T-28 tanks.[114] When five of the Finnish tanks had been put out of action, the operation was called off.

The same day the motorised Soviet 278th Regiment was pulled back from the front after it had lost a considerable part of its initial strength. Anatoly Derevenets, a signals operator at the regiment's third battalion, recalled:

> We only had one battalion commander left in the regiment – commander of the first battalion, Captain Vysotski. Finnish snipers hunted down our commanders with great stubbornness and success. Vysotski realised this. He walked with great stubbornness around in a greatcoat of a private, without any commander's gear, armed with a rifle. I guess this was the reason he was still alive out of all our commanders. He is a good leader and losses in his battalion are not as high as in the others.[115]

During the final days of February, the Finnish high command realised that the Intermediate Line could not be maintained and that an attempt to hold on further would inevitably lead to catastrophe. In consequence, Mannerheim had to abandon his intentions to hold the terrain between the two fall-back lines until the beginning of the peace negotiations. The men had been driven to their ultimate limit.

> We almost lost our minds from lack of sleep and exhaustion. We knew that we could not last long; a physical collapse was approaching us with lightning speed. But we fought on, gritting our teeth. A week passed like this, or it could be two weeks. We lost all count of time; we did not know which day of the week it was, which date, if it was still February or already March. We only knew one thing: day came after night and we were still living creatures on this earth. The earth was shaking and groaning, the war went on, and the closer its end was, the more merciless it was becoming.[116]

The new withdrawal started on 27 February and took place covered by delaying skirmishes until the Finns reached the T-Line (Map 3).

On 29 February the first exchanges of fire took place at the new position, more precisely in the sector south of Viipuri. The final chapter of the Winter War had started.

Diplomacy

As previously mentioned, a positive turn in the diplomatic situation might have been possible at the end of January, only both parties stood firm on their demands and refused to compromise. The French and British leaders took this as a sign that there was still some hope for an Allied military intervention in the conflict, and on 5 February they decided to plan for such an operation. The Anglo-French force was supposed to consist of 100,000 British troops and a smaller number of French troops. Initially, the plan was to launch the operation in mid-April.

The idea of an allied intervention was originally born out of the mood among the general public in France and Great Britain. The politicians had at first been against the intervention, and though they made it look as if they eventually yielded to public pressure, they in fact did all they could to turn the project in a somewhat different direction. A closer analysis of the plan reveals its true purpose. An occupation of the Gällivare area and the town of Luleå in northern Sweden had very little to do with the war that Finland was fighting – and that was just the scaled down version of the Allied plan. Again, it was mainly about cutting Germany off from Swedish ore iron. Just 15,000 of the Allied troops were allocated to reach Finland, where they would only operate in the northern part of the country. Practical explanations were given, but the writing was on the wall. By accepting the Allied plan, Finland might turn the Nordic countries into a major theatre of war, and the further the Winter War was prolonged, the bigger the risk of such a development.

The preliminary work on a German plan for an invasion of Norway had started on 14 December 1939, and the motivation behind it was strengthened when Berlin became aware of Allied intentions to send troops to Finland. On 21 February General Nikolaus von Falkenhorst, who in 1918 had been in Finland with the German auxiliary corps, was appointed chief of Operation Weserübung, the assault on Norway and Denmark.

Meanwhile, Väinö Tanner had considered how to reopen the negotiations with Moscow. This became particularly pressing from 7 February onwards, when the Soviet offensive on the Karelian Isthmus accelerated drastically. At a meeting in the Finnish Foreign Ministry on 12 February, Tanner reported the result of a conversation he'd had two days previously with Prime Minister Ryti and Marshal Mannerheim. The three men had agreed that serious concessions had to be made to the Soviets. The most important thing was to settle on a peace agreement as soon as possible, so it was now high time to offer Moscow Jussarö as an alternative to Hanko, as Mannerheim and Paasikivi had already suggested back in November the year before.

But the suggestion still met with opposition from several government ministers. Besides, the Finnish leaders remained under severe pressure from public opinion, which the overoptimistic press coverage had influenced to believe that Finland was practically on the brink of winning the war. Mannerheim was not personally affected by public opinion; he was not elected and by and large not a subscriber to democratic governance. For the politicians it was of course a different matter. In any case, it was decided to turn the diplomatic efforts back in the direction of an attempt to attain international military assistance.

Since the offer of Anglo-French assistance smelled of a hidden agenda, the leaders once again turned to Sweden and asked for direct military aid in the form of troops and artillery guns. Mannerheim, in particular, saw this as the only plausible military solution, since the procedures related to the use of international volunteers had proven long-drawn and associated with a wealth of problems.

The swedes were not unwilling to help Finland. The public mood was warmly sympathetic to the Finnish struggle, and Sweden continued throughout the war to send weapons, humanitarian aid and thousands of volunteers to the country (this was possible because Sweden had not declared itself neutral in relation to the Finnish-Soviet War, as it had with the rest of the world, only 'non-belligerent').

The Swedes were also willing to work as intermediates between Moscow and Helsinki. That, however, was as far as their helpfulness stretched. The Swedes had no wish to end up at war with the Soviet Union. So their advice to the Finnish leaders was to face reality and end the war as soon as possible by making a compromise with Moscow.

Prime Minister Per Albin Hansson made this clear to Väinö Tanner when the Finn arrived in Stockholm, and to a certain extent Tanner agreed. He went on to meet his colleague in the Swedish government, Foreign Minister Günther, asking him to act once again as intermediary. Günther immediately agreed and asked the Swedish ambassador to Moscow, Vilhelm Assarsson, to make contact with Molotov.

At meetings on 20 and 21 February it became clear that the Soviets had increased their demands to include both Viipuri and Sortavala, a relatively large town on the northern bank of Lake Ladoga.

The Finns now faced a very difficult choice. They could either accept a form of Allied assistance that was completely insufficient and based on a dangerous hidden agenda, or they could accept the Soviet wishes. If they chose the latter, it would have to be announced very soon, since the demands clearly had a tendency to increase with time.

VI

Endgame in March

Not one Thermopylae, but Thermopylae every day.
HAROLD MCMILLAN[117]

The Situation around Viipuri
After the Finnish retreat to the T-Line in late February, the fighting primarily continued around Viipuri. Measured in a straight line, the Viipuri Front stretched some 30km west of the city along the shore of Viipuri Bay and some 40km east of the city to the Vuoksi River.

The winter of 1939-40 was considerably colder than those of the preceding years. So far the cold had been to the advantage of the Finns, but that was no longer the case. The ice on the Viipuri Bay was frozen so hard that even the heavy Soviet tanks could move safely across it, as were the lakes and rivers further inland. Under normal conditions spring would have been on its way in the Karelian Isthmus, but instead the winter continued far into March.

The Finnish defence of Viipuri had in the meantime been reorganised. Looking at it from east to west it now consisted of I Corps, II Corps and the so-called Coast Group (for a more detailed description see Appendix VI). To make for a clear understanding of the progression of the fighting in March, we shall look at the events as they happened day by day. Action involving the two corps and the Coast Group will be described individually, as will the situation of the 23rd Division, since it operated more or less as a separate unit although it formally belonged under II Corps.

The Soviet Seventh Army continued to be the main attacking force in this sector and it was still vastly superior in numbers to the Finnish force. The Coast Group and the two Finnish corps each found themselves facing four Soviet divisions strengthened by numerous separate units.

The Fighting Around Viipuri
1 March
I Corps. The corps is holding a curved position just north-east of Vuoksi River and on parts of the Äyräpää Ridge on the south-westerly bank of the river. The sector includes the island of Vasikkasaari and a position on the

west bank of the river, manned by 23rd Regiment supported by four artillery guns. There is fighting throughout the day but no Soviet penetration of the Finnish lines.

2 March
I Corps. A Soviet attack penetrates the Finnish line on the east bank of the Vuoksi River. A group of Finnish soldiers are caught in a pocket and have to call down artillery fire over their own positions, as they take cover. This forces the Soviets out of the area so the Finnish group can escape in the direction of Vuosalmi.

II Corps. The Soviet 138th Division drives a wedge into the corps' positions at Huhtila, an area just south of Viipuri.

Coast Group. The Soviet 43rd Division makes several attacks on Tuppurasaari, an island in Viipuri Bay, but is pushed back every time by the Finns. Eventually, the Russians encircle the island and bomb it from the air. Their infantry attacks are supported by tanks that are firing at the island from all angles to trap the Finnish garrison. Other islands in the bay are also attacked and in some cases the Finns have to flee across the ice to the mainland. One such island is Teikarinsaari, which is particularly important to the defence of Viipuri. The Finns make two attempts at recapturing it, but the Soviets retain their grip on the island and turn it into a base for further attacks.

3 March
23rd Division. The first fighting between this Finnish formation and the Soviet 84th Division takes place in the area around Tali Village.

II Corps. The Soviet 100th Division forces the outposts of the Finnish 5th Division back to the T-Line. The Finns, however, maintain control over a small hill by Tammisuo Village.

Coast Group. After the loss of Teikarinsaari, Mannerheim sacks Major General Wallenius as leader of the Coast Group. The relationship between Wallenius and the marshal has been tense for a while, and there are rumours that the major general has been dead drunk for days. The chief of the general staff, Lieutenant General Oesch, takes over his command. Meanwhile, the encircled Finnish unit at Tuppurasaari escapes through the Soviet lines and marches across the ice to the mainland, where several Soviet landing attempts have been repelled during the night. The attackers gain a foothold on the coast by the mouth of Viipuri Bay but are soon driven back on to the ice.

4 March
I Corps. Soviet troops penetrate the Finnish lines on the west bank of the Vuoksi River and drive the Finns out on to Vasikkasaari. Two Finnish counterattacks fail, though one of them is reinforced by troops from the 8th Division. The Finnish artillery is running out of ammunition.

23rd Division. A new Soviet attack is repelled in the southwest part of the Tali area.

II Corps. Throughout the day the corps repels attacks along its entire defence line, which stretches from the boggy area of Kerämäen Bay south of Viipuri and northeast to Tammisuo. The 3rd Division, however, is weakened after having to hand over the 9th Regiment to reinforce the Coast Group's defence of Vilaniemi. In the evening, the line starts to crumble at the peninsula and a regiment from the 5th Division is moved to the area as reinforcements.

Coast Group. All the outer islands in the Viipuri Bay have now been abandoned by the Finns, who in many cases are so exhausted by the fighting that they have to be sent to the rear to rest. Meanwhile, the Soviet landing operations continue with renewed strength. Two divisions march inland from the mouth of Viipuri Bay but are pushed back during the night by the Finnish 9th Regiment (of II Corps) who, as mentioned in the above, have been moved to the area as reinforcements. All the reserves of the Coast Group have now been thrown into the fighting. In this sector, too, the Finnish artillery is running low on ammunition.

5 March
I Corps. Soviet pressure continues to increase, forcing the corps to abandon Vasikkasaari. The situation for the few remaining Finnish troops on the west bank of Vuoksi River is uncertain.

II Corps. Soviet units penetrate the Finnish defence line southwest of Tali. Two tank attacks on the Finnish positions by Tammisuo are repelled.

Coast Group. After the failed landing operations on 2 and 3 March, the Soviets are learning 'on-the-job' how to use tanks when invading the jagged Finnish coast line. They drive the tanks up on either side of a peninsula and place the Finnish positions under crossfire. When the Finns are sufficiently weakened, the Red Army infantry starts attacking. Using this method, the Soviets last night occupied the east coast of Vilaniemi by the mouth of Viipuri Bay. During the day they also capture Kilpisaari, an island just 3km from Viipuri. A Finnish attempt to stop the enemy by cutting up the ice around the island fails because the openings immediately freeze over again. Behind the front, the supply situation is desperate. The roads are full of civilian refugees and there are frequent Soviet air attacks.

6 March
I Corps. A Finnish attempt to recapture Vasikkasaari fails. The Russians maintain their positions on the island and expose the Finnish troops on the east bank of the Vuoksi River to a fierce artillery attack.

23rd Division. The Soviets manage to penetrate the Finnish line. To stop them the Finns flood the area, which turns out to be a bad idea. The water quickly freezes over and floods up over the tank defences, making them easier to overrun. The situation is worsened for the Finnish division when one of its battalions has to be handed over to reinforce the Coast Group.

II Corps. Soviet artillery attacks on the corps' positions continue. A minor Soviet infantry attack is repelled.

Coast Group. Soviet attacks on the coastline by the mouth of Viipuri Bay continue. Meanwhile, the smaller islands deeper inside the bay are captured one at a time by the Red Army.

7 March
I Corps. A Soviet night attack including an attempt to cross the Vuoksi River is repelled.

II Corps. The Soviet 138th Division makes a small breach in the Finnish line at Huhtila, the area immediately south of Viipuri where the same division drove a wedge into the Finnish positions on 2 March.

Coast Group. Soviet troops push further inland from Vilaniemi and cut off the main road along the coast. The Finnish supply lines northwest of Viipuri are now under threat.

8 March
In general. From this day until the end of the war, the Soviet artillery is constantly hammering the Finnish positions, accompanied by air bombardment. The only interruptions occur when their infantry attacks with tank support.

I Corps. A Soviet attack penetrates the Finnish line in thirteen places. Finnish counterattacks after sunset are repelled. The Finnish 21st Division

Soviet anti-aircraft gun in position on the Karelian Isthmus, March 1940.

arrives as reinforcements, and the exhausted 1st Division is sent back behind the front to rest. Reserve units are sent west to reinforce II Corps.

23rd Division. The division's command post is moved back since it is wrongly assumed that the situation at Tali has been stabilised.

II Corps. Practically all the corps' reserves have now been thrown into the combat, even engineer and supply units. At sunset the replacement troops from I Corps' reserve have not yet arrived. In the dark a huge number of fresh Soviet troops are thrust into the fighting west of Tali, and panic breaks out among the Finnish units. Rumours are circulating that enemy tanks have penetrated the lines, and an entire Finnish battalion flees its positions. The panic spreads to other units but dies down again when it turns out that the rumour is false, whereupon the men return to their positions.

Coast Group. Nearly all the islands in the Viipuri Bay are now occupied by Soviet troops, and the fighting is mainly along the coast and further inland. There is still fierce fighting in the area by the mouth of the bay.

9 March
I Corps. A Soviet penetration of the Finnish positions at Vuosalmi is driven back. The few remaining Finnish troops on the west bank of the Vuoksi

River still manage to hold the Soviets back, though they now have three divisions in the area.

23rd Division. The retreat of the divisional command post yesterday has created a near catastrophe. An elite Soviet company has crossed the flooded terrain by Perojoki, marching in ice cold water up to the waist. These troops now attack the Finnish line and create a large breach in it. The telephone line back to the command post is out of order, but the Finns still manage to organise a counterattack, which closes the breach and stabilises the front. Their biggest problem is that the Red Army can now bring tanks into the area.

Coast Group. The massive Soviet attack in the coastal area by the mouth of Viipuri Bay continues. Moreover, a new threat is spotted: a more than 10km long column of Soviet troops including tanks are approaching from the southeast across the ice. The commander of the Finnish 4th Division gives the order to abandon an island off the coast approximately halfway up the bay. This happens in the evening and gives the Russians the opportunity to drive a wedge between the Coast Group and the Finnish 3rd Division. Still, a regiment of reinforcements augmented by a further battalion manages to rectify the situation, saving the Coast Group from being encircled.

10 March

I Corps. A massive Soviet artillery bombardment signals a coming infantry attack in the Vuosalmi sector.

23rd Division. The Soviet advance continues, and in this sector too there are signs that they are building up for a new mass attack.

II Corps. The Finnish high command on the Karelian Isthmus decides to pull back the defence line south of Viipuri, but at the last moment the order is suspended. The heavy Soviet pressure on the Finnish positions continues but fails to make for any breakthroughs.

Coast Group. The Soviets attack the last few Finnish-manned islands in the Viipuri Bay. Units from the Finnish 4th Division counterattack and advance at first but are then pushed back. Further west along the coast, in the area by the mouth of the bay, hard fighting continues. The fresh Soviet troops fail to push forward as far as expected, and their attempt to penetrate the Finnish lines and attack the enemy from the rear also fails. Nevertheless, the Finnish situation is so critical now that a single successful Soviet breakthrough can cause a disaster.

11 March
I Corps. A massive new Soviet attack is launched on Vuosalmi, and during the day the Finnish troops are pushed back almost 1km. In the evening Finnish reinforcements arrive, and the Soviet advance is halted. Meanwhile, the last Finnish positions on the southwest bank of the Vuoksi River are abandoned.

23rd Division. A Soviet tank attack pushes back the lines of the division, and at sunset the front is penetrated in three places. The Finnish commander requests support but is only allocated a single under-strength battalion from I Corps.

II Corps. After the Russians have penetrated the lines of the 3rd Division in two places, the Finnish high command on the Isthmus again orders the corps to pull back to the outskirts of Viipuri. However, Mannerheim issues a counter-order demanding that the troops remain where they are and fight on. His motives are related to the on-going peace negotiations. These are unknown to the officers at the front, who are astonished by the marshal's decision. After sunset the Soviets penetrate the Finnish line at a point between II Corps and the Coast Group, which are now again in danger of being cut off from one another.

Coast Group. The right flank still holds despite violent pressure from three Soviet divisions. The breach between II Corps and the Coast Group is closed when Mannerheim sends in an extra battalion as support.

12 March
I Corps. The fighting around Vuosalmi continues with undiminished force throughout the day. By sunset the Finnish situation is hopeless, and a retreat is considered though there is no better position which the Finns can fall back on.

23rd Division. There is calm in the division's sector, but the Russians are preparing new attacks.

II Corps. Massive Soviet attacks rage throughout the day, penetrating the corps' positions in several places. A particularly difficult situation occurs at Tammisuo Village where the entire 3rd Division is in danger of being encircled. Lieutenant General Öhquist requests permission to pull his troops in close to Viipuri, but he is only allowed to carry out a partial retreat. The retiring troops are immediately pursued by the enemy so they have to set fire to the southern outskirts of the city in order to make their escape.

Meanwhile, the 5th Division manages to separate the Soviet tanks and infantry and stabilise the situation around Tammisuo.

Coast Group. A new Soviet attack reopens the breach between the group and II Corps, and the Finns pull back. A catastrophe is drawing nearer with giant strides.

13 March
In General. The situation along the entire Viipuri Front on this day is roughly the same: massive Soviet artillery and air bombardments start in the early hours of the morning, making the sky and the earth merge into one churning mass.

The colossal inferno continues until precisely 11am when the attacks suddenly stop and a deadly silence takes over. No one in the Finnish trenches knows what is happening until an officer from the staff arrives and matter-of-factly proclaims: 'Peace has been declared.'

Other Significant Events in March
Though the Soviet effort in March was primarily on the Karelian Isthmus, no part of the front was passive. At Märkäjärvi Village in the Salla sector, where the Swedish volunteer group kept the Soviets at bay, nine men were killed when their company was encircled and had to fight its way out. The Soviet casualties were 200. There was tough fighting in the Kollaa area, and parts of the *mottis* in Ladoga Karelia and at the town of Kuhmo were destroyed. Several larger towns were bombed from the air, among them Tampere and Lahti. Mikkeli, where the Finnish general staff had its headquarters, was severely bombed on 5 March, and the day after some islands in Lake Ladoga were subjected to heavy artillery bombardments followed by attempted landing operations. At Nautsi in Petsamo the Soviets overran the Finnish positions on 7 March, and a few days later the situation looked equally bleak for the Finns at Kollaa.

The Soviet Baltic Fleet had previously occupied some islands in the eastern part of the Gulf of Finland. From these they started on 4 March to send troops over the ice towards the south coast of Finland. The Finnish coastal artillery, however, kept the attackers back. The shells blew large holes in the ice in which many of the Soviet soldiers drowned. Others became panic-stricken and fled to safety. Though these attacks were repelled, they caused considerable anxiety in Finland, and a battalion of older men and young boys were sent out to reinforce the coastal fortresses.

On 13 March at mid-morning, as the Soviet artillery attacks on both sides of Viipuri were setting new records, the Red Army also tried to make a break-through at Taipale near the west bank of Lake Ladoga, where there had been tough fighting too all through the period. This attack, however, was stopped by the cease fire.

The Moscow Peace Treaty
In early March 1940 the Anglo-French planning for an intervention on the Finnish side in the Winter War had reached a point where an approach was made to the governments of Norway and Sweden, asking for permission to send Allied troops through their northern districts to the Finnish Lapland Front. An acceptance of this was preferable, since a real invasion, of course, was politically undesirable. It was expected that the Finns would give not just their permission but also send an official invitation.

Norway and Sweden blankly refused, while the Finns found it difficult to make up their minds. Meanwhile, the Allied leaders became worried that Helsinki would soon enter into a peace agreement with Moscow and thus sink the Anglo-French plan. Hence, the French Prime Minster Daladier promised the Finns several forms of assistance. On a closer look, though, the promises were so loosely worded and unrealistic that the Finnish leaders could put no faith in them. Furthermore, there were disagreements within the Allied camp. Paris was eager to move a future conflict with Germany as far away from their own territory as possible. London was worried at the thought of a confrontation between British and Soviet troops. Such a conflict did not sit well with the notion that the war against Germany could in all likelihood only be won with the Soviet Union becoming an Allied nation.

The leaders in Berlin just wanted the Winter War to be over as soon as possible. Hermann Göring advised the Finnish leaders to accept the Soviet demands if they wanted to keep their independence (anything else would of course constitute a setback for Germany). He also more than hinted that Finland would later be given the possibility to win back the lost territories. Göring is furthermore supposed to have said confidentially to the Finnish ambassador to Berlin, Toivo Kivimäki, that a war would soon break out between Germany and the Soviet Union.[118] The Finnish professor of history Henrik Meinander writes: 'This advice was used to persuade reluctant members of the Finnish government to accept the Moscow Peace Treaty in March 1940. Some Finnish scholars have even claimed that the acceptance of the peace conditions was the first conscious step towards the [later] military alliance with Germany.'[119]

The day after the Finns had decided to accept the Soviet demands, a delegation was sent to Moscow. The group was led by Prime Minister Ryti and included Paasikivi and Major General Walden, who was the representative of the Finnish high command (i.e. Mannerheim) in the state council. At the negotiations Molotov once again represented the Soviet Union, in this case along with two fellow negotiators.

As it turned out, the Russians had increased their territorial demands since the last round of negotiations so they now included the Karelian Isthmus, Ladoga Karelia, Hanko and parts of the Kuusamo and Salla regions in north-east Finland. Furthermore, Finland had to hand over its part of the Rybachi Peninsula. This was an old demand that had been dropped before the war, but was now reintroduced.

The increased demands came as a shock to the Finnish negotiators, who had arrived with hopes of the opposite. But Molotov was unyielding. He said the territories in Northern Finland were necessary for the Soviet Union to secure the Murmansk Railway, and he claimed it was the Finns' own fault that it had all come to this, since there had been plenty of chances earlier on for them to achieve a better deal.

The new Soviet demands were sent by telegram to the government in Helsinki, who were no less horrified, and during the following week the diplomatic game continued. The French joined in, doing their best to encourage the Finns to keep up the fighting, while the peace attempts were supported by the USA though its ambassador to Moscow, Laurence Steinhardt. His efforts brought, among other things, a promise from Molotov that Finland could retain its free elections.

Many historians have wondered why Moscow at this point, when it was so close to having beaten the Finnish Army, bothered to negotiate at all. The answer most probably lies in the Soviet leaders' fear of an Allied intervention, which even appears to have been deliberately amplified by the Finnish intelligence services leaking false information to create a misconception that the intervention was much closer to becoming a reality than it actually was.[120] But other factors probably played their part too, for instance that the war had shown Finland to be a very difficult territory to control.

The peace treaty in Moscow was signed early in the morning on 13 March 1940, and by the news was broadcast over the radio to the Finnish people by Foreign Secretary Tanner, first in Finnish and then in Swedish.

> Finland has been at war for three and a half months. We had no part in causing this war ...
>
> It was not our fault that the democratic nations did not or could not help us in this uneven struggle. Our only fault was that we were too small a country. Despite some great victories won by our military, we cannot see this fight through to a victorious ending ...
>
> Peace has been restored, but what kind of a peace it is! Our country is from now on a mutilated nation.[121]

During the war, the Hotel Kämp in Helsinki had been a centre for the international press, who had now turned up to hear the news. In the crowd were the two Danish journalists we have already met several times, Peter de Hemmer Gudme and Ole Juul. The latter describes the situation in his book *Den røde Sne* (*The Red Snow*):

> Just as the reading in Swedish of this historical speech had rung out, an elderly, white-haired man stood up on a chair in the press room and shouted in a shivering voice to the gathering of journalists: 'If there are any representatives of the other Nordic countries present, I hope they are deeply ashamed of themselves – damn you lot!"
>
> No one protested. What could we say? We all had – all we representatives of Denmark, Norway and Sweden – a bad taste in the mouth, but it wasn't just our fault.
>
> I looked over at Gudme ... He suddenly bent forward and hid his face behind his elbow. He was weeping like a small child.[122]

The Finnish public was stunned. Until the very end, the media had chosen an attitude that was undoubtedly good for the Home Front morale, but which had very little to do with the actual situation for the soldiers at the front. Juul describes the atmosphere in Helsinki as follows:

> It was as if the whole city stood by the open graves while the funeral ceremony took place. Miserable, surprised, disbelieving people walked the streets slowly, as if everything suddenly appeared strange to them – like children searching in vain for their parents ... everyone's eyes were edged with red from crying. It all seemed so eerie, so inconsolable, so lost.[123]

According to the peace agreement, the Finnish Army immediately had to pull back 1km to create a demilitarised zone. From there on the retreat to the new border had to be carried out in stages. Only in the Petsamo area and immediately south of it was the Red Army to pull back.

Practically the entire population in the ceded territories now started in the direction of Finland. More than 400,000 civilians, around half of them from the Karelian Isthmus, had to be evacuated within two weeks. Since the evacuation had to take place as the army was retreating, a total of 350,000 people were on the move within the rather limited territory of the Isthmus. Travel was coordinated so that military movements occurred on certain days while civilian refugees moved on others. Nevertheless, railways and roads were often crammed with people, their household animals and other belongings.

Casualties

The casualties of the Finnish Army during the Winter War were, according to military historian Pasi Tuunainen, 27,000 killed or missing in action, while 44,000 were wounded.[124] Civilian casualties due to bombings were 892 killed, 540 badly wounded and 1,316 lightly wounded. Sixty-five men working for the merchant navy were killed.[125]

The Soviet casualty figures have been the subject of much discussion. An old and inadequate (in places perhaps even consciously misleading) translation of Khrushchev's memoirs quotes him for a casualty number of one million men. This has been corrected in the latest English translation from 2004, which also shows that the quote relates to something else (what the loss of Soviet prestige in the eyes of the rest of the world might have cost the country militarily in the longer run; in fact Khrushchev speaks not of *a* million but of *millions* of lives).[126]

Tuunainen concludes it is impossible to come up with a certain figure for the Soviet losses but nevertheless quotes the book *Soviet Casualties and Combat Losses in the Twentieth Century* (G.F. Krivosheev (ed.), London 1997, p. 79), which puts the Soviet figures at 130,000 killed and 270,000 wounded.[127]

PART TWO

THE INTERIM PEACE

(13 March 1940 – 25 June 1941)

Risto Ryti (1889-1956) with his wife, Gerda Paula Ryti (b. Serlachius, 1886-1984). (SA-Kuva)

I

Little Country – What Now?

*Finland has now taken a decisive step, which perhaps
will be misunderstood from the Swedish side. But Finland
has no alternative after the experiences they have had
with the peace agreement they made with
the Russians.*
LIEUTENANT GENERAL HEINRICHS[128]

Conclusions in Moscow
With the signing of the Moscow Peace Treaty, practically all the demands the Soviet leaders had made on Finland before the Winter War had been met, as Molotov pointed out in a speech he made in the Supreme Soviet on 29 March 1940. This in itself was enough, he claimed, to justify the Red Army's losses during the war. Apart from that the speech was primarily an attempt to explain away why the Soviet military had encountered so much trouble in its attempt to crush little Finland under its heel:

> It was not merely Finnish troops that our troops encountered, but the combined forces of the imperialists of a number of countries, including British, French and others, who assisted the Finnish bourgeoisie with every form of weapon, especially artillery and aircraft, as well as with their men in the guise of 'volunteers'.[129]

Moreover, Molotov claimed that Finland had had an army of 600,000 men, of which the Soviet forces had defeated about half. He also made accusations about the alleged brutality of the Finnish soldiers, or rather of 'the White Guard'. The Mannerheim Line he called '*a place d'armes* ready for an attack by third powers on the Soviet Union, for an attack on Leningrad', and described it as a formidable string of fortresses in the style of the Maginot Line and the Siegfried Line, constructed under the guidance of western experts.

All in all Molotov felt that the war goals of the Soviet Union had been fulfilled, in so far as the safety of Leningrad had been considerably strengthened by the signing of the Moscow Peace Treaty. The speech was followed by huge applause.

Two weeks later the central committee of the Soviet Communist Party was called in for a four-day meeting to evaluate the Red Army's performance in the Winter War, and here the tone was considerably different. One of the first speakers, referred to only as Semyonov (possibly Vladimir Semonovich Semyonov, a Soviet plenipotentiary representative in Estonia at the time), said:

> ... there were such facts as desertion, stampede, abandonment of weapons and panic ... Political education should be strengthened in peacetime ... The authority of the commander must be much higher ... Judging by the experiences of this war, we must strengthen discipline ... Combat experience shows that the work of raising senior commanders was likewise insufficient. Regiments and divisions were sometimes given to incompetent, inexperienced and poorly trained people who failed at the slightest difficulty in battle ... We paid dear for such drawbacks, we paid in blood.[130]

Both Stalin and Molotov were present during this verbal flogging and their comments show that they were well informed about conditions during the war. Stalin presented some harsh criticism, called the procedures of the Red Army obsolete and talked of officers who had not moved with the times since the revolution. He was aware that some methods had been updated along the way, but his general conclusion was that the Soviet Union had to become better at waging war in the modern way, with massive use of aircraft, tanks and artillery.

Fear and Frustrations
The Winter War had made the entire western world rejoice in the ability of the Finnish Army to repel the enormous Soviet invasion forces; but in Finland there was little to rejoice in now that the war had ended. A total loss of more than 70,000 killed and injured soldiers and civilians was a terrible blow to a people of only 3.7 million.

Every parish had been hit. In a country where the physical strength of the male population was still a decisive factor for the size of the gross domestic product, a considerable part of the workforce had perished or been mutilated. Moreover, the 400,000 refugees from the ceded areas created colossal problems with rehousing, the clearing of new farmland (more than half of them came from an agricultural background) and with integrating them into the Finnish labour market, the education system etc.

In addition to the human tragedies came economic and other practical problems. The ceded areas had constituted 10 per cent of Finland's total territory. But the loss was in fact worse than indicated by the numbers, since the Karelian Isthmus had considerably more industry and cultivated farmland than Finland in general. In a sense it was Finland's pantry that the Russians had laid their hands on. Furthermore, they had cut the country off from its most important foreign trade transport routes. Before the Winter War more than 15 per cent of Finnish exports had been shipped out from either Viipuri or Hanko.

Overall, the situation in Finland by April 1940 was highly critical, and during the following year it only grew worse. After the Nazi occupation of Denmark on 9 April, Berlin could control the considerable Danish grain export, which made Finland strongly dependent on German good-will. Though Finnish agriculture before the war had reached a stage where it could nearly meet the country's own demands for grain, it needed a high amount of fertilizers, which the Finns could now also be prevented from importing. To make matters worse, there was a drought during the summer of 1940, which ruined a large part of the Finnish harvest. Trade connections with Sweden were still open, but the Swedes needed all the grain they could produce for themselves. Besides, the Finns were already heavily in debt to Sweden due to all the weapons they had bought from their Nordic neighbour during the Winter War. It was possible to get some grain from the Soviet Union, but that would just be granting Moscow further means of exerting pressure on the government in Helsinki.

Though the fighting on the Finnish-Russian Front had stopped on 13 March 1940, it felt as if peace had not quite arrived in Finland internally. This was partly because the 'state of war' (a kind of state of emergency) was upheld. Also, the Finnish military now played a much bigger role in Finnish society than it had done before the war. Defence budgets grew until they constituted almost 45 per cent of the entire state budget. The number of troops deployed at the border was larger than normal in peacetime.

The veterans from the Winter War were sent home and replaced by younger classes of conscripts. The novelist Väinö Linna, who was one of the newcomers, described the situation in his classic novel about the Continuation War, *Tuntematon sotilas* (*Unknown Soldiers*):

> There they stood, bumbling into lines with a bit of difficulty: Mother Finland's chosen sacrifice to world history. Farmers in coarse, sturdy clothes – day-laborers in flimsy jackets, ties sticking out from underneath their cheap, milled collars – and even some clueless city slicker with a wool 'ulster' on, who had 'like, no idea what happened on the trip out here. Like, seriously, none.'[131]

The willingness to defend one's country manifested itself in many ways. Volunteers poured in to work on the Salpa Line (*Suomen Salpa* = Finland's

Bolt), a gigantic, 1,200km long defence line immediately behind the new border. Along this line there were bunkers, far stronger than those of the former Mannerheim Line. Northern Lapland continued to be the weakest point in the Finnish defence so bunkers were built there, too, mostly by important thoroughfares and bridges.

Still, none of it was enough to compensate for the weakening of the Finnish defence caused by the Moscow Peace Treaty. The border on the Karelian Isthmus was now considerably closer to Helsinki, and the protection offered by the Mannerheim Line was gone. The Soviet base at Hanko constituted a 'gun aimed at the heart of Finland', as Ryti later described it in a radio speech. And the Soviet border adjustment in the Salla area gave the Red Army a potential launch pad for new attacks on important Finnish roads and railway lines.

Uncertain Sources
While Finland's many practical problems during the period after the Winter War have never been a secret, a deeper understanding of the political events at the time has been obstructed by a deliberate cover-up campaign, which produced a smoke screen for many years after the Second World War and partly still does. This goes particularly for the country's tentative approaches to Nazi Germany, which in time would develop into a military cooperation over the invasion of the Soviet Union.

The smokescreen included an avoidance of taking down minutes during a vast number of important political meetings. Even private diaries and notebooks belonging to the parties involved have in some cases clearly been exposed to self-censorship even as they were written and therefore have often caused disappointment in later years when they have been publicised. Furthermore, seemingly significant archive material has disappeared without trace.

One of the few first-hand sources to the thoughts and feelings of the Finnish leaders, in relation to the far-reaching decision they took on behalf of their people, is *Finland's Blue-White Book II*, an anonymous government publication from 1941, which was made available in Finnish, Swedish and English shortly after the launch of the invasion of the Soviet Union in June 1941. Although words such as 'Germany' and 'Nazi' are carefully excluded, they are clearly at the core of the matter: the reader is given the understanding that pressure from the Soviet Union forced Finland over on to the German side, not sympathy for Hitler's political ideas.

There is undoubtedly a large degree of truth in this, but on the whole the book is undeniably a manipulative propaganda publication. One of the first international researchers in this area, the American Professor Peter Krosby, writes: '… some of the documents in the Blue-White Book had been edited to remove embarrassing references to Finnish-German relations whose publication would not have been opportune in 1941.'[132]

The structure of the book is in itself misleading, with conclusions presented in its first half and written in an evocative style, while the dry evidence is placed towards the end without any kind of critical discussion. For a great many years this book was the only source the Finnish people had as to the motivation behind the war they had been led into alongside the Nazis. In consequence, it has had a tremendous influence in its homeland and seemingly also in Sweden (but probably not so much in the English-speaking world, at least not directly).

Another source to the motives of the Finnish leaders could be their personal statements made after the war, but again the truthfulness is questionable on several points. Some of this material has been published as memoirs during the Cold War, where Finland's situation continued to be very difficult and even the general public were extremely careful about what they said or wrote among themselves. Other material was presented during the so-called War-Responsibility Trials in Helsinki 1945-46, a period where Finland's national destiny depended on how the surrounding world perceived the country's activities during the war, so there were good reasons not to reveal circumstances that would undoubtedly have looked compromising in the eyes of the victors.[133]

It was not until the 1970s that young Finnish historians started digging deeper into the so-called Interim Peace Period, i.e. the fifteen months between the end of the Winter War and the start of the Continuation War. Arguably the most important scholar in this field was Professor Mauno Jokipii, who took the scattered Finnish source material which *did* exist, compared it with archive material from other countries (particularly Germany and Sweden) and arrived at some interesting conclusions. The result was his ground-breaking essay in Swedish '*Finlands väg til forsättningskriget*' ('Finland's Road to the Continuation War') and later a more comprehensive work in Finnish on the phase leading up to the Continuation War with its Finnish-German cooperation, *Jatkosodan synty* (*The Birth of the Continuation War*), which unfortunately has not been translated into any other language.

In his writings, Jokipii uncovered basic discrepancies between the images that Finnish politicians and historians had promoted over the years and what must have really happened. This work is still evolving to this very day, carried on by new generations of historians, and it forms a large part of the foundation for this current account.

A Change of Government
The first few weeks after the Winter War saw some major changes internally

in Finnish politics. Two ministerial posts became vacant, as Minister for Foreign Affairs Tanner and Minister of Defence Niukkanen both chose to step down. This added to the feeling that the time had come to form a whole new government, albeit still with Ryti as prime minister. To create the broadest possible backing behind future decisions it became a coalition government with participation from all the parties in the *Eduskunta*, including the Fascistoid IKL (see list of abbreviations after the introduction to this book).

The position as defence minister was without any disagreement taken over by Major General Rudolf Walden. He was born in 1878 and was, like Mannerheim, a former officer in the Imperial Russian Army, although he had been dismissed in 1902 during the so-called National Service Crises (p. 30). During the Finnish Civil War, Walden had held several prominent posts in the White Guard, and for a year after the war he was Minister of Defence. He was without party affiliations but strongly right-wing. During the 1920s and 1930s Walden had primarily concentrated on his career in the paper and pulp industry, but he had been called up three days into the Winter War and been a cabinet member throughout the war. As previously mentioned, he participated in the final negotiations over the Moscow Peace Treaty.

Finding a new Minister for Foreign Affairs proved more complicated. Ryti and Mannerheim (whose political influence had grown considerably since the start of the Winter War) first approached G.A. Gripenberg, who was Finland's ambassador to Great Britain. This suited the government's policy, which at the time was aimed at Britain as a potential trade and alliance partner. Gripenberg, however, seems to have had a premonition of what lay ahead, for he turned down the offer stating his relationship with Berlin was too compromising.

Using the process of elimination, Ryti and his advisers then landed on the 60-year-old professor Rolf Witting. He had been a member of the *Eduskunta* from the mid-1920s onwards for ten years, and during 1933-36 he was deputy minister for foreign affairs. Witting represented the Swedish People's Party of Finland but was nevertheless very negative about Finnish-Scandinavian cooperation and felt that Sweden was developing in a far too Socialist direction. He was strongly Germanophile, perhaps more than it was realised at the time of his appointment. Admiration of Germany, however, was a general feature among Finnish scientists at the time and was borne out of a tradition for cooperation between German and Finnish universities. Witting was also managing director for the Bank of Helsinki (*Helsingin Osakepankki*).

Finnish historians have invented the term 'Ryti's inner circle' to describe the principal political faction surrounding Ryti at the time. The group consisted of Marshal Mannerheim, Minister for Foreign Affairs Rolf Witting, Minister of Defence Rudolf Walden, Minister for Supplies Väinö Tanner and, from 1941 onwards, the new Prime Minister Johan Wilhelm Rangell. When military issues were discussed, Major General Heinrichs (from 15 May 1940 chief of the general staff) was normally also present.

During the Interim Peace, political discussions about many important issues, which would normally be debated openly, took place behind closed doors within this narrow circle of people. The members of the group have since stated that these precautions were necessary, since public debate on sensitive foreign policy issues could have threatened national security. It was also claimed that their decisions were based on qualified presumptions of the views among the general public. Only after a decision had been made by Ryti's inner circle could the members of the *Eduskunta* vote on whether or not they had confidence in the choice that had been made.

The national security aspect, of course, constituted a real problem, but that does not necessarily mean the involved parties employed this method of governing entirely against their will. Mannerheim had never been a subscriber to democracy, although he had gradually learned to accept its existence, and Walden was the marshal's sworn follower. Ryti and Witting had also been known to wish for the abolishment of the parliamentary system in Finland,[134] as had already partly happened with the abovementioned arrangement, described by the American Ambassador to Helsinki, Arthur Shoenfeld, as 'a constitutional democratic dictatorship'.[135] Viewed as a political figure, Rangell was no more than a grey shadow; he was without even party political affiliations, a rather peculiar feature for a Nordic prime minister to say the least. This leaves only Väinö Tanner, but his influence was seriously diminished from August 1940 onwards, when Soviet pressure forced him to hand in his ministerial resignation and generally lower his profile.

The political line chosen by Ryti's inner circle was strongly backed by state censorship, which blocked out public criticism of the major powers (p. 176). These conditions could only exist because Finland was still officially in a 'state of war', and because the *Eduskunta*, largely without anyone protesting, accepted the situation, seemingly from the point of view that extraordinary circumstances demand extraordinary measures.

One of the new government's first tasks was to revive the attempts to set up some form of Nordic military union. In fact, a loosely worded plan of that kind had been laid out by the Swedish Prime Minister Per Albin Hansson in cooperation with Väinö Tanner (both leading Social Democrat figures) already by the end of the Winter War. Ryti's newly formed cabinet now reshaped the plan into a more specific proposition that could be extended to also include Danish and Norwegian participation. The offer was ready for parliamentary deliberation on 15 March, a mere two days after the end of the war. The enthusiasm for a Nordic military union expressed by the Finnish high command was hardly due to the rather limited help that Finland could expect from the very weak armies of the Scandinavian countries. Perhaps they partly saw an alliance as a means to make it harder for Norway and Sweden to block British and French assistance to Finland in the future, as it had happened during the Winter War.[136]

Denmark soon detached itself from the talks for fear of anything that might remotely aggravate its relations with Berlin. The Finns carried on negotiating with Norway and Sweden, but the dialogue soon bogged down. It did not help when Molotov, on 29 March, announced that Moscow saw a Nordic military union as being in opposition to the Moscow Peace Treaty. This was in reality the same as threatening Finland with war if it tried to join up militarily with Scandinavia.

Discussions between Finland, Sweden and Norway continued in secrecy for some time.[137] Meanwhile, the Finnish government also negotiated with Great Britain about a war trade agreement, according to which the British were supposed to protect Finnish shipping, while Finland would limit its trade with Germany. It has been suggested that such an agreement would effectively have placed Finland in the Allied camp.[138] On the whole, the Finns were clearly orientated towards Scandinavia and Great Britain during the first few weeks after the implementation of the Moscow Peace Treaty. Nothing was expected to be gained from Berlin due to the way the Germans had acted during the Winter War.

All this changed, however, with the German invasion of Denmark and Norway on 9 April 1940. Nine days later, Great Britain officially closed its trade with Finland via Norway 'for the duration of the war'. It was in the light of this new situation that Germanophile circles in Finland, headed by Foreign Minister Witting and with strong financial backing, started pushing Finland in a completely different direction. So obvious was this development that the German ambassador Blücher on several occasions had to warn Witting to be more careful in order not to cause suspicion in Moscow.[139]

The First Approaches to Germany
The historic ties between Germany and Finland are often seen in the light of the so-called *Jäger*-movement, i.e. the Finns who volunteered for German army service during the First World War and later formed the nucleus of the Finnish officer corps. But there were other bonds of friendship which went back several hundred years and were related mainly to the business fraternity and groups of scientists and other highly-educated people, often from a Swedish-speaking background.[140]

National Socialism as an ideology and a party political movement never caught on in Finland, which might have something to do with the fact that the Nazi racial theories categorised Finns as non-Aryan. However, among Finland's Germanophile fraternities there was a lack of either will or ability to differentiate between traditional German culture and character, and 'the New Germany' which Nazism represented.[141]

The Germanophile circles in Finland were both economically and politically powerful, and they soon started exercising influence on the country's leading politicians. This was strongly downplayed in post-war Finland, where there was a general tendency to deemphasize the country's relations with Germany during the Interim Peace. Some younger historians, however, have had a different view on these matters. Even a researcher such as Ohto Manninen, who for a number of years was attached to the Finnish Defence University, describes the conditions as follows: 'Circles, who were traditionally Germanophile, put pressure on the cabinet to make new approaches to Germany. They started a propaganda campaign in the summer of 1940 to end the negative Finnish view of Germany and to make the Germans realise that Finland should be regarded as belonging to the Germanic Zone. Also on a more directly political level this was seen as a suitable approach. Ryti and Mannerheim were rightly regarded as Anglophiles, but both are known to have made decisions during the summer of 1940 which were directly aimed at improving relations between Finland and Germany.'[142]

Meanwhile, the world war raged on in Continental Europe. During May and June 1940 the German Army overran Belgium, Holland and France. At the very last moment the British expeditionary corps escaped from the continent via Dunkirk. At high diplomatic levels there were rumours of London being about to enter into a peace agreement with Berlin. Many factors seemed to suggest that Germany would win the war.

An example of the approaches mentioned in the above took place in early May during a visit to Finland by the German diplomat Karl Schnurre. Among those he met were Prime Minister Ryti, who probed the possibilities of a trade agreement that would give Finland weapons from Germany in return for Finnish raw materials.[143] Schnurre was sympathetic to the idea, but it was rejected by Hitler.[144]

The Finnish attempts to woo Berlin were strengthened considerably during the summer of 1940, partly though sports arrangements, scientific exchange visits and the establishing of contacts between businessmen and officers. The Fenno-Swedish historian Frans Jernström writes: 'Keen-eyed observers noticed ... as early as the spring of 1940 a reawakening of German-orientated activities in Helsinki with, for instance, cultural and business related events as well as visits by industrial leaders and society delegations, among them representatives of the KdF [*Kraft durch Freude*, 'Strength through Joy', a Nazi leisure organisation]. The fact is that by 1940 Germany had replaced Britain as Finland's most important trade partner and received more and more of Finnish exports.'[145]

One of the military exchange visits included a group of Finnish officers led by Major General Viljo Tuomo, who received a guided tour of the newly occupied France and Belgium during 10-17 September 1940. The trip included the Maginot Line, Mets, Verdun, Paris and Ypres, after which the visitors were returned to Berlin via the forts at Eben-Emael.[146]

The Soviet Annexation of the Baltic States

On 14 June 1940, the same day as German troops marched into Paris, a civilian Finnish passenger and transport aircraft on its way from the Estonian capital of Tallinn to Helsinki was shot down by two bombers from the Red Air Force. All on board were killed. The tragedy was perceived by many Finns as part of a gradual process which would culminate in a new Soviet invasion of their country.

That was probably not the case, however. The passengers were mainly international diplomats, a couple of them in the process of smuggling documents out of Estonia, which at this time was under Soviet blockade.[147] But the plane and its two pilots were Finnish, so if nothing else the episode can be seen as an example of the careless attitude with which the Russians treated Finnish citizens and property at this time.

Over the following two days the governments of Estonia, Latvia and Lithuania each received an ultimatum from Moscow. For almost a year the countries had been forced to give Soviet troops access to their territory; now they were fully invaded and occupied. New governments were installed, and a general Bolshevisation of the established order commenced.[148] Eastern and northern Romania (i.e. Bessarabia and North-Bukovina, which both had been under Romanian rule since the First World War) were annexed by Moscow, too, during the summer of 1940.

Many Finns saw these events as a warning of what would happen to them in the near future, as well. The suspicion was understandable, but as the Finnish historian Olli Vehviläinen points out: 'Of course, it was not possible to treat Finland like the defenceless Baltic countries. Moscow knew that, however desperate the situation, it [Finland] would fight for its independence. A military campaign against it would be no walkover this time either.'[149]

New Soviet Demands

Finland's problems were not made any lighter when, in April, Moscow started making further demands on the country through Paasikivi, who in the meantime had moved to Moscow as Finland's permanent envoy.[150] This signalled the beginning of a diplomatic game that was to continue through the rest of 1940 and even for a short while into 1941.

The Soviet demands concerned the following issues, which we shall delve into individually:

1) The exact drawing of the new border and the right to materiel in the ceded territories
2) Soviet influence on the running of the nickel mines at Petsamo
3) Soviet influence on the strategic situation around the Åland Islands
4) Soviet influence on internal political decisions in Finland
5) Demands in relation to the Soviet troop transports to and from Hanko
6) The construction of a Finnish railway line in the Salla area

Regarding 1): The disagreements over the drawing of the border primarily concerned the industrial district of Enso 30km north of Viipuri. The drawing of the border here had been made with a very thick pen!

It says in Article 2 of the peace treaty:

> The state frontier between the Republic of Finland and the USSR shall run along a new line in such fashion that there shall be included in the territory of the USSR the entire Karelian Isthmus.[151]

Enso was situated on the outermost edge of the Karelian Isthmus, but nevertheless belonged to it. Still, the Finns claimed that during the peace negotiations they had been given the impression that Enso should continue to belong to them. In any case the discussion ended with the Finnish negotiators being forced to cave in.

Moreover, Moscow demanded that the Finns hand over a vast amount of materiel that they that taken with them as they abandoned Karelia. On this issue, too, Soviet pressure became so hard that the Finns had to yield. Much of the materiel was industrial machinery and railway equipment which could no longer be traced, so as compensation the Finns were forced to hand over other kinds of materiel taken from Finnish factories and railways, among them 75 locomotives and 2,000 railway carriages.

Furthermore, Moscow proved unyielding in regard to the distribution of fishing rights and access to waterways etc., and so the Finns were forced to yield on these points as well.

Regarding 2): The discussions about Soviet influence in Petsamo primarily concerned the nickel mines in this far north region. As already mentioned, nickel was an essential ingredient in the production of ammunition. Finland was the biggest producer in Europe of this metal. The Soviet Union produced less, but still enough to cover its own needs. Germany, though, had to import nickel to keep its war machine running. Hence, in case of a future German attack on the Soviet Union it would be to the advantage of the latter to hold control over Petsamo, which was why the Soviets tried to get a foot in the door of the administration of the mines.

The demand was outside of the peace agreement. In other respects, too, the Finns stood stronger on this issue, since both Great Britain and Germany had financial interests in the area and were opposed to the Soviet demands. These demands were initially presented to Paasikivi in Moscow on 23 June. Still, the Finns managed to drag things out so much that the issue remained unresolved a full year later when the Continuation War broke out.

Regarding 3): The Soviet demands to have influence on the strategic situation around the Åland Islands were a result of the fortifications build by the Finns during and after the Winter War. At a meeting on 27 June the Soviet negotiators demanded that the fortifications be removed and that the area be put under Soviet observation. The Finns managed to delay the procedures until their approaches to Germany made Moscow sharpen their tone in late August. The Finns then had to yield and remove their troops and bunkers, though it created a strategic vacuum which the Finnish high command found particularly worrying.

A new agreement concerning the demilitarised Åland was signed on 11 October 1940. The remaining mines and forts had to be removed no later than December. A rather big Soviet consulate was installed in the capital of the archipelago, Mariehamn, and the area was placed under Soviet surveillance.

Regarding 4): The Soviet demands to have influence on internal Finnish affairs were, among other things, related to the press censorship in the country. To summarise, it was demanded that all anti-Soviet agitation be stopped and pro-German expressions dampened.

Moscow also complained about the attitude of the Finnish authorities towards the Finnish-Soviet Society for Peace and Friendship, also known as the SNS. This society had been founded in late May 1940 by people from the left-wing fringe of the Social Democrat Party and followers of the prohibited Communist Party. Many of them had fought in the Winter War and felt that the social improvements introduced since then had been too few.

The SNS was a nationwide organisation, whose membership rose to more than 35,000 during the summer of 1940. The movement demanded improvements in the relationship between Finland and the Soviet Union, and better living conditions for the lower classes. Despite some members' affiliation with the Social Democrat Party, the SNS saw this party as its main enemy. The organisation arranged big and sometimes violent demonstrations around August 1940, which was generally a critical period.

The government saw a connection between these activities and the developments that had started in the Baltic States around mid-June. The Soviet occupation of the Baltic States had been staged to look as though Moscow was merely reacting to requests made by local left-wing groups who were eager to get rid of their Fascistoid governments.[152] To put it another way: the Finnish leaders feared that Moscow would use the SNS as a Trojan horse in connection with a similar procedure in Finland. To counteract this they set up *Aseveljien liitto*, 'the Brothers-in-Arms Association', which aimed at uniting patriotic forces across the political spectrum. Its chairman was Major General Talvela (who had been promoted from colonel in December 1939), while the vice-chairman was the director of the Finnish trade unions. Other important political initiatives were launched at the same time aimed at maintaining the unity that had emerged during the Winter War.

However, the fear of ending up in the same situation as the Baltic states increased when Molotov on 24 July, through Paasikivi, accused the Finnish government of persecuting SNS members and portrayed the organisation as aimed at 'strengthening the peace between neighbouring states'.[153] Once again Molotov pointed to Väinö Tanner as being the main culprit and demanded he be removed as Minister of Supplies. Tanner chose to go voluntarily on 15 August and thus withdrew in part from parliamentary work.

Through the newly appointed Soviet ambassador to Helsinki, Ivan Zotov, Moscow also demanded that both Minister of Social Affairs Karl-August Fagerholm and Minister of the Interior Ernst von Born step down, since both had taken initiatives to obstruct SNS activities. This, however, was prevented at the last moment when Ryti in a radio speech guaranteed Finland's peaceful intentions towards the Soviet Union.

During the autumn Moscow seemed to lose its interest in the SNS, and the activities of the society diminished considerably along with its influence.

Regarding 5): The demands in relation to the Soviet troop transports by train to and from Hanko were first presented on 8 July at a meeting in the Kremlin between Molotov and Paasikivi. Again the Soviets were asking for something beyond the framework of the peace agreement. The demands were very likely inspired by a similar concurrent agreement between Sweden and Nazi Germany.

The Finnish leaders were already deeply worried about the Soviet presence at Hanko and they feared a serious worsening of the situation if

Red Army troops were now to travel by train through southern Finland between the border and the peninsula. It would mean that an attack on Helsinki could be aimed from three directions: Viipuri, Hanko and now also from a variety of troop trains. Furthermore, the attack could be combined with landing operations along the coast. Because of the effective Finnish coastal batteries it would probably only work in conjunction with support from Finnish fifth-columnists, but then that was exactly what the government suspected the SNS of being.[154]

An agreement concerning the troop transports was signed on 6 September 1940, but only after Moscow had toned down its demands on several points. For example, only three trains were allowed to travel along the route at the same time.

Moscow demanded that the agreement be signed without ratification by the Finnish parliament. That formally made it invalid and illegal according to the Finnish constitution, but the Finnish leaders had to feign ignorance of these factors.

Regarding 6): The demand on the Finns to build a railway through the Salla area was based on the peace agreement. It said in Article 7 that a rail line was to be built from Finland's most northern town, Kemijärvi, going some 90km east through the Salla area to the new border, where the line was to join the Soviet railway network. Since there was a rail line from Kemijärvi going west to Sweden, this would create a direct connection from the Finnish-Swedish border to the White Sea, with its terminus at the Soviet town of Kandalaksha.

Officially, this was meant to improve trade and friendship between the Soviet Union and Finland. But the Finns feared that the railway in reality was meant to play a role in a new military attempt to cut their country in two. Unsurprisingly, they were less than eager to build this section of line, and despite Soviet pressure they managed to delay the proceedings so long that the work was still not finished when the Continuation War broke out.

The abovementioned Soviet demands have been seen by many as proof that Moscow was trying to exhaust the Finnish leaders with a war of nerves, which was meant to culminate in an occupation similar to that which actually happened in the Baltic States, Bessarabia and Northern Bukovina. Meanwhile, the Finnish public was to be turned against its own government through left wing activities. According to this theory, the Russians realised sometime during August 1940 that their strategy would not work. The Finnish leaders were too tough and the people too smart to succumb to such tactics. Hence, Moscow cut down on its support to the SNS and instead started developing new plans for a traditional military invasion of Finland.

The timeframe makes sense, but that of course is no proof in itself. It must be remembered that the leaders in the Kremlin had far bigger things on their agenda in 1940 than carrying out another invasion of Finland and perhaps even ending up with another moral and military humiliation. If analysed objectively, the various forms of pressure that Moscow put on Finland can all be seen as Soviet attempts to protect their country – and in particularly Leningrad – from the gigantic German offensive against them that was looming on the horizon. If that is true, the already threadbare Finnish-Soviet relationship was hardly improved by the obvious pro-German line that was allowed to flourish in Finland from the summer of 1940 onwards, warmly supported by leading circles.

The theory that a new Soviet invasion was inevitably underway must be viewed critically, simply because it too conveniently grants the Finnish leaders an excuse for their later military cooperation with Nazi Germany. However, it seems beyond doubt that the Soviet demands were truly *perceived* as a prelude to a new invasion and that the Finnish leaders honestly felt they had no other option than to seek assistance from Germany.

Turning Points
The most ground-breaking event that took place at the highest level in European politics during the summer of 1940, albeit secretly, was Hitler's decision in late July to invade the Soviet Union.

The poor performance of the Red Army in the Winter War seems to have been one of the factors that whetted the appetite of both the Führer and parts of his general staff, although the Battle of Britain was going on at the same time. The German Army was riding on a wave of success and there was a feeling of having to strike while the iron was hot. Hitler even raved about making the army ready for the task within a couple of months, but this was categorically rejected by his general staff. A 'Russian campaign' could not be launched before the summer of 1941, they said.

The planning then started and the attention soon turned to Finland, the obvious place to establish the northern flank of the invasion. To secure his navigation to and from the Leningrad area, Hitler had to have control over the south coast of Finland. Also, the German Army needed free movement from Norway through Lapland to the Finnish-Soviet border. Suddenly, Finland had risen to be high on the German agenda.

Since Finland had recently lost a war against the Soviet Union, it was felt in Berlin that there might be a basis for some form of Finnish-German cooperation. For a start it was hoped that agreements could be made on German troop transports and permissions to build military depots and air fields on Finnish territory. Time would show if there was scope for more than that, but military cooperation seemed an obvious possibility, particular if it could help Finland win back the territories it had lost in the Winter War.

There were also some fundamental problems. Most immediately, the plans for the coming invasion of the Soviet Union had to be kept an absolute secret in order to retain the element of surprise. This was an issue internally in Finland, too, since certain people on the left wing of the Social Democrat Party were suspected of wanting to pass information on to Moscow.

Other specific problems in relation to a Finnish-German partnership meant that the profile had to be kept extra low. Finland could not enter into an official alliance with Germany – i.e. become an Axis partner – since it would demand a parliamentary decision that was probably unachievable. For Berlin, the problem was that an alliance with Finland would go against the secret protocol of the Molotov-Ribbentrop Pact. Out of these purely practical circumstances grew the idea to promote the Finnish participation in the invasion of the Soviet Union as a conflict isolated from the Nazi German war of conquest – as a 'separate war'.

However, the thinking and planning had not yet reached this stage when in late July 1940 the next careful step was taken in the direction of Finnish-German co-belligerency. At this time a German envoy by the name of Ludwig Weissauer appeared in Helsinki. Officially a representative of the German foreign office, he was in fact an agent for the German intelligence department RSHA (*Reichsicherheitshauptamt*). During a meeting with Prime Minister Ryti and Marshal Mannerheim he asked about Finland's ability to resist a new Soviet attack. Mannerheim is supposed to have replied that the Finnish Army at most could hold out for a few weeks, and that the problem in particular was a lack of weapons and ammunition.

The Finnish-German Transit Agreement
On 8 August the Finnish cabinet held a crisis meeting after having received intelligence information about Soviet troop concentrations along the border. Mannerheim was present and remarked that if the development continued at the same speed, the Soviet Union would, within a week, have gathered twenty-three divisions and a large amount of tanks in the area. Hence, he demanded that the army be partly mobilised. This, however, was rejected by the cabinet who felt it would worsen the relationship with the Soviet Union and enhance the risk of an invasion.

By the end of the week it had become clear that the cabinet was right in its decision. The intelligence reports had exaggerated the situation, which had now been normalised.

Based on the same erroneous reports, which arrived not only from Finnish sources but also from German intelligence, Berlin began to take military precautions from the late summer of 1940 onwards. Hitler's constant priority was to secure his iron ore imports from northern Sweden and nickel imports from Petsamo, and so during the first two weeks of August Berlin lifted the embargo it had placed on Finland during the Winter War. Around the same time (13 August), Hitler gave the order for the 2nd Mountain Division in Norway to relocate from Trondheim to the Kirkenes area by the Finnish-Norwegian border. The German General Dietl, under whose command the division belonged, was then told to work out a plan for a swift German occupation of the Petsamo region. The plan was to be codenamed Operation Renntier.

It seems likely that the Finnish high command in Lapland was informed of the plan, if only to avoid fighting between Finnish and German forces during such an occupation. We know that there was contact between the parties. SS Battalion Commander Wilhelm Reitz had already in late July been ordered by Heinrich Himmler to 'strike up a friendship with the Finns', and on 5 August he had, in the town Ivalo on the Finnish side of the border, met with Hjalmar Siilasvuo,[155] the victor from the Battle of Suomussalmi, who in the meantime had been promoted to major general.

New negotiations about a Finnish-Swedish defence union commenced in August on Swedish initiative; but the question is how interested the Finns really were in such a project at this point. It goes without saying that Sweden alone could not guarantee Finland's security against the Soviet Union to the same extent as Germany could. Sweden's possibilities for exporting foodstuffs to Finland were also limited (the Swedes hardly had enough to feed themselves), which was the other big problem. A lack of foodstuffs had started to make itself apparent in Finland over the summer, and rationing had been tightened – a sign of things to come. Also, the Swedes demanded a guarantee that Finland would refrain from starting a war of revenge.

On 18 August a new meeting took place in Helsinki between a German representative and Marshal Mannerheim. The guest this time was Lieutenant General Joseph Veltjens, an arms dealer who also acted as personal representative for Hermann Göring.[156] On behalf of the leaders in Berlin, Veltjens requested permission to transport troops through western Finland through to northern Norway, a route which in some cases was more practical than the existing one through Sweden. Veltjens also asked about the possibilities of transporting nickel from Petsamo to Germany. If Finland showed a cooperative attitude in these matters, Germany would in return supply the country with weapons.

Mannerheim claims in his memoires that he made no reply to these questions but told the German instead to look up Minister of Defence Rudolf Walden. Veltjens replied that he had strict orders only to negotiate with Mannerheim, not with politicians. Mannerheim then personally presented Ryti with the query, adding that he found the offer of German weapons worth considering.[157] Ryti agreed and told Mannerheim to give Veltjens a confirming answer.

Ryti and the members of his inner circle all claimed after the war that they had been kept in the dark about the German arms deliveries up until German soldiers suddenly landed in Vaasa. If that is true, it would be safe to say that the military leadership had bypassed Finland's democratic rules. It has, nonetheless, been made pretty clear that Ryti did discuss Veltjens' offer with his closest advisers, whereupon Mannerheim was told to hand the German a positive reply.

On the other hand, it has never been completely clarified if President Kallio was informed of the matter before he suffered a stroke on 27 August. If he was not informed, the transit agreement was invalid. Still, Kallio's role in such matters was purely formal, so the question is only relevant if seen from a strictly judicial angle. In any case, the president was so weakened afterwards that Ryti had to take over his post while still also continuing as prime minister.

The Soviet troop transport movements to Hanko started on 6 September. Just two weeks later the first German troops landed in Vaasa. A very brief Finnish-German transit agreement was signed on 22 September following a debate in the *Eduskunta*. There was pronounced dissatisfaction particularly on the left side of the hall, where the members felt they had been lured into a fait accompli.

There were now both German and Soviet soldiers on Finnish soil, in both cases due to agreements signed without parliamentary consent. The foreign troops were at either end of the country, far from each other, but the situation can still be used as an image of the incredibly tense situation that now existed in Finland.

The German troop transports were in themselves rather small. Some 30,000 soldiers were transported to and from Norway via Finland during the following months through to May 1941. But there was a larger aspect behind the transit agreement which makes it an important turning point in the history of the Finnish-German cooperation in the Second World War. The agreement led to an expansion in military connections between the two countries, and it was the first step in a development that would eventually make it possible to move German troops from Norway all the way across Finnish Lapland to the Soviet border in the summer of 1941. The agreement also meant that the Germans could set up supply depots in Finland, which they did to a far greater extent than that which would have been justifiable based on the transports alone.

The practical arrangements related to the German troop transports were taken care of by the Finnish general staff. The rather large amount of weapons the Finns received in return for their hospitality arrived at Finnish ports during the following months. Most of it was German war booty captured from the Allied armies during the summer of that same year.

The civilian Finnish population is often claimed to have received the German troops with a welcoming air and a sigh of relief. They finally felt they were not alone against the mighty Soviet Union, or so the story goes. While there is undoubtedly a certain amount of truth in this, it must also be remembered that more than 40 per cent of the Finnish population voted Social Democrat at the national elections. This quite considerable part of the Finnish people – along with those who were even further out on the left wing – can hardly have experienced many positive feeling at the sight of German troops landing in Finland, just as in 1918.

In any case, there was no doubt that an important turning point had been reached in Finland. The same week as the transports began, a big athletics competition was held in Helsinki between Germany, Sweden and Finland. At the opening parade the German athletes greeted a group of invalid veterans from the Winter War with the well-known 'Hitler salute'.[158]

The German-Soviet Axis Negotiations
In November 1940 a meeting took place between Molotov and Hitler in Berlin, following an initiative by Stalin the month before. Officially, Stalin wanted a discussion about the relationship between the Soviet Union and Germany, which had worsened considerably over the previous summer.

By that time Berlin was well into the planning of the invasion of the Soviet Union. Nevertheless, von Ribbentrop wrote back to Stalin and told him what Hitler felt should be the crucial issue to be discussed at the meeting. In the Führer's opinion, Russia, Italy, Japan and Germany should seek to agree on a long-lasting common strategy at a global level. To put it another way, the aim was to create a kind of extended version of the Molotov-Ribbentrop Pact, with a more comprehensive division of the world map into respective spheres of interest, so once again both an official agreement and a secret protocol was to be drawn up.

This, however, was not what happened at the meeting. Instead, Hitler and Molotov both mainly concentrated on probing the future plans of the other party. It was on one such occasion during the second day of the negotiations – on 13 November 1940 – that Molotov made a remark in which many have seen a careless unveiling of Soviet intentions to invade Finland again and annex the country. However, the opening of the Soviet archives in later years has hung a big question mark over this interpretation, and even more so since we now also know the instructions that Molotov received from the Soviet politburo before his departure from Moscow.

Starting with the latter, the instructions (which are dated 9 November

1940), have two main points. The first one is relatively brief and primarily tells Molotov to probe the *true* intentions of Germany, Japan and Italy in relations to the proposed new agreement. Finland then appears under item 2a, where it says that Molotov must demand a clarification of where Finland is to be placed within the framework of the Molotov-Ribbentrop Pact, i.e. whether Finland is within the Soviet or the German sphere of interest. Through Finland was unambiguously within the Soviet sphere of interest according to the pact, the demand for clarification was relevant due to the presence of German soldiers in Finland (and perhaps also because the Molotov-Ribbentrop Pact included no definition of the term 'sphere of interest'). The instructions also told Molotov to demand that Berlin put a stop to anti-Soviet propaganda in Finland.[159]

The Molotov-Ribbentrop Pact was brought into the discussion at the end of the first day of the meeting. It says in the Russian memorandum:

> The Russians think that Germany has fulfilled its obligations according to this agreement, except in one area – Finland. In relation to this, Molotov wishes to know the German government's view regarding the existing agreement.[160]

Molotov and von Ribbentrop at Berlin Central Railway Station, November 1940. (Bundesarchiv, Bild 183-1984-1206-523, photographer unknown)

The Russian memorandum was made public in 1998; until then only the German memorandum had been available. On the same issue as above it says (here quoted from the most common English translation):

> The German-Russian agreement of last year could therefore be regarded as fulfilled, except for one point, namely, Finland. The Finnish question was still unsolved, and he [Molotov] asked the Führer to tell him whether the German-Russian agreement, as far as it concerned Finland, was still in force.[161]

Though the wording is dissimilar, there seems to be no major differences in the meaning. But if you read the German memorandum on its own, and you don't know Molotov's instructions, you can get the impression that it is not Germany but the Soviet Union who still needs to fulfil the pact, i.e. that the Soviet Union is obliged to annex Finland according to last year's treaty but cannot do so because of the German military presence in the country. Or to put it in another way: Molotov demands that the German troops be removed from Finland so the Soviet Union can fulfil last year's treaty by invading and annexing Finland.

That seems to be the way it was understood by Hitler at the meeting, and it is certainly how it was subsequently understood in Finland and in the rest of the western word throughout the Cold War. More surprisingly, it is still pretty much the ruling perception, though the Russian sources now tell us a different story. In fact, the old interpretation is illogical even if we look at the German memorandum. Nothing in the Molotov-Ribbentrop Pact *demands* that the parties invade the areas within their respective spheres of interest. The pact just makes it possible for them to do so without interference from the other party (in fact, not just Finland but also several territories within the German domain were still independent states, contrary to what Hitler claims according to the German memorandum).[162]

Another kind of misunderstanding has been caused by the way the German officials at the meeting understood the term 'the Finnish question'. We shall return to that in a moment, but first it should be pointed out that Molotov's statements in the Russian memorandum are of course written down pretty much 'from the horse's mouth', while the quotes featured in the German memorandum have been through a language interpreter. This gives the Russian memorandum more authority with regard to what Molotov actually said, and judged on that basis it is very clear what the 'Finnish question' represented for the Russians, namely an uncertainty in regard to Finland's position within the framework of the Molotov-Ribbentrop Pact (as already mentioned).

On the first day of the meeting, Hitler did not comment specifically on

Molotov's query, but the issue was brought up again as soon as the second day of the negotiations opened. Here Molotov mentioned the German troop transports through Finland and also the anti-Soviet agitation, which he claimed ruined the possibilities of creating a positive atmosphere between Finns and Russians.

Hitler replied that Germany had no influence on the agitation in Finland. In relation to the troop transports he played down the issue, promising it was only a temporary and purely practical arrangement. Then he added that Germany depended on its imports of nickel and wood from Finland, and hence could not accept a war breaking out in the Baltic Sea area.

In other words, Hitler interpreted (or at least pretended to interpret) Molotov's 'Finnish question' as the result of a Soviet wish to invade and annex Finland. The Russian memorandum continues:

> Molotov says that we are not talking about war in the Baltic Sea Area, but about the Finnish question, which must be clarified on the basis of last year's agreement.
> Hitler remarks that this agreement makes it clear that Finland belongs within Russian sphere of interest.
> Molotov asks: 'In the same manner as Estonia and Bessarabia?'[163]

In the German memorandum it says:

> Molotov replied that it was not a matter of war in the Baltic, but of the question of Finland and its settlement within the framework of the agreement of last year. In reply to a question of the Führer, he declared that he imagined this settlement on the same scale as in Bessarabia and in the adjacent countries [*den Randstaten* = the Baltic States], and he requested the Führer to give his opinion on that.[164]

The crucial question here is *why* Molotov draws a parallel between Finland on the one hand and Bessarabia and Estonia (in the German memorandum all three Baltic States) on the other. In the Russian memorandum it appears that he is simply casting doubt over Hitler's previous statement, saying: *If* you truly followed the agreement of last year, *then* the situation in Finland would be comparable to that of Estonia and Bessarabia, where a presence of German troops would obviously be unacceptable and in breach of the treaty. Since there *are* German troops in Finland, you are obviously breaking the agreement.

The German memorandum gives a different impression. Here it seems Molotov is indirectly telling Hitler that the Soviet Union intends to do to Finland what it has already done to the Baltic States and Bessarabia, i.e. annex it.

It is, of course, impossible to draw any firm conclusions on the basis of source material such as the German memorandum, and it should also be said that the official English translation is open to further misinterpretations (the translation was carried out and publicised at the beginning of the Cold War, in 1948).[165] The Russian sources seem a much better option, but you could also try to look at the matter as part of the larger overall picture. Even if the leaders in Moscow did have the intention to annex all of Finland, it would hardly have been at the top of their agenda at this point, particularly not when you consider the problems they would have to expect in the form of Finnish resistance. But why was Finland then so important to Moscow that it became a pivotal issue at the meeting?

Let us look at it logically. Molotov's instructions were to probe the real intentions of Hitler. Finding an alternative to the Finnish-German transit agreement could hardly have been a big practical problem for Berlin, since the transports were rather small and easy to redirect through Sweden. If Molotov demanded them stopped, and Hitler stubbornly refused, it would probably be a sign that there was a much larger project being prepared than the Germans formally admitted, and that project could hardly be anything else than an invasion of the USSR. Molotov himself described the situation many years later:

> For our part, we had to probe deeply as much as it was possible to speak seriously with them. We had agreed to observe the treaty – they were not doing so. We saw they didn't want to observe it. We had to draw our own conclusions, and they of course drew theirs.[166]

The next question must be how the Germans got the impression that Finland was in imminent danger of being invaded by the USSR. Part of the problem here seems to have been that they understood Molotov's 'Finnish question' according to Nazi terminology and placed it in the same category as their own 'Jewish question', 'Polish question' and so on. In fact, practically all Finnish books on this issue present it as an undisputable fact that Molotov straight-out 'told Hitler that the Soviet Union wanted to *liquidate* Finland'.

The German interpretation of the 'Finnish question' is also reflected in General Halder's diary[167] as well as several other writings by German officials who were present at the meeting. All these documents began to emerge in the post-war years, about half a century before the opening of the Soviet archives, which explains their enduring influence on the western view of the occasion.

The German perception, however, is not supported by the Russian memorandum and particularly not in Molotov's instructions from the

Politburo. He is, of course, neither ordered nor allowed to tell Hitler about any secret Soviet military or political intentions in relation to Finland.

As a counterargument it has been claimed that Molotov's remark could have been a slip of the tongue, or that Hitler simply out-foxed him. But that seems equally unlikely, since Molotov was known as a very shrewd and cunning negotiator. Rather the Germans simply misunderstood him in a way that mirrored not just their own expectations and their frame of mind, but also their search for an argument that could pull Finland further into the Nazi camp.

The same lack of reliability characterises a number of almost anecdotal stories and entangled conclusions, which over the years have been used as proclaimed proof in this matter. Instead of wasting time on hearsay and the like, the next sub-chapter in this book will go straight to the core of the matter by investigating the planning initiatives made by the Soviet general staff in regard to Finland during the Interim Peace.

There had been considerable anxiety in Finland over the meeting between Molotov and Hitler. The Finns feared they might be 'sold to the Russians', as some felt had happened the year before. But after the negotiations, the German headquarters sent a comforting message to Helsinki. It claimed Molotov had told Hitler straight out that the Soviet Union intended to invade and annex Finland, but the German Führer had made it clear that the Russians had better stay away or else there would be war. According to the exact words of the message, Hitler had 'spread his umbrella over Finland'[168], whose harassed people from now on could 'sleep calmly at night'.[169] This image of Hitler as a merciful protector has still to this day not vanished completely in Finland, though it is probably more realistic to see the 'reassuring' message from Berlin as a glaring example of how the Germans manipulated the Finnish leaders (and, in this case, even themselves).

What the Germans refrained from telling the Finnish leaders was that Molotov in a telegram dated 26 November guaranteed Berlin that the Soviet Union would *not* wage war on Finland, if only the German troops left the country. In fact, Molotov had already pointed this out during the negotiations (according to the German memorandum) and also in a conversation on the same day with the German ambassador to Moscow, von der Schulenburg (according to a Russian document).[170] It should be mentioned, however, that the telegram also included several other Soviet demands related to the proposed agreement between Berlin and Moscow.

The Germans never replied to the telegram, and with that ended the German-Soviet negotiations talks in November 1940.

New Soviet Plans
After the Winter War, Moscow estimated that the danger of an Anglo-French

attack on the Soviet Union via Finland had become negligible, but that did not entirely exclude the possibility of a conflict between the parties. An allied attack could be aimed at the Soviet Union from Turkey or Iran, so several Red Army divisions were moved to the Caucasus from the area east of the Finnish border. Some of them participated in the occupations of Bessarabia and Northern Bukovina late in June 1940, a couple of weeks after similar operations had been carried out in the Baltic States. It was a period where Moscow could largely do as it pleased, since Germany was busy with its campaigns in the west. Even in the case of Bukovina, Berlin only made a few protests, although the territory had not been directly mentioned in the Molotov-Ribbentrop Pact as included in the Soviet sphere of interest.

The territorial expansions of the Soviet Union in Eastern Europe triggered a demand for new military planning, so during the summer of 1940 the general staff under Field Marshal Boris Shaposhnikov was ordered to draw up plans for a major war on two fronts, against Japan in the east and against the Axis powers and Finland in the west. The front in the west was given the highest priority of the two.

A draft plan was sketched out and handed in during July, but Minister of Defence Semyon Timoshenko was strongly disappointed and demanded it revised. Subsequent work was carried out under the newly appointed chief of the general staff, Kirill Meretskov (Shaposhnikov had stepped down temporarily in August), who during the Winter War had been responsible for the penetration of the Finnish lines on the Karelian Isthmus. The new plan was ready on 18 August, and on the same day separate plans for isolated campaigns against Finland, Romania and Turkey were also handed in. The centre of gravity was placed on the southwest theatre, since Stalin was convinced that the Germans would attack there to capture trade and industry centres in the area.

Though operational plans in principle are not concerned with which party starts the war, this plan (the big plan) on the whole had an aggressive character.[171] Still, Finland's role in the overall scheme of things was limited, and here the Russians expected only to play a defensive role. It says in the Soviet considerations:

Troop deployment by our north-western borders
No matter how our troops are deployed in the west, the task at our north-western border must primarily be subordinated to Leningrad, the protection of the Murmansk Railway and the maintaining of full control over the Gulf of Finland. Our main task in the north is to carry out a reliable protection of Leningrad. In all probability Finland and Germany will participate simultaneously in the war.

Because of the size of the forces mentioned in the above our task in the northwest shall be limited to an active defence of our borders.[172]

Seen from a Scandinavian point of view there is an interesting detail in a contemporary directive from the Council of People's Commissars to the Soviet Baltic Fleet. It mentions the possibility that a Finnish-Swedish military alliance might attack the Soviet Union *by order from Germany* (an obvious example of how removed from reality the Soviet view of the surrounding word could be at times). The naval plans comprised a blockade of Swedish seaports and the Göta Canal, an occupation of the Åland Islands and an expansion of the Soviet presence on Hanko.[173]

As mentioned, the general staff also worked on a plan for an isolated attack on Finland. Goals and methods were in crucial areas the same as during the Winter War (for a more detailed description of the plan see Appendix VII). However, the finished detailed version of the plan appears to have never been handed in. The reason is hard to determine, but probably the general political development in the meantime had made the Soviet leaders decide to concentrate their efforts elsewhere.

To sum things up: judged from the available Soviet archive material, there was during the Interim Peace no *immediate* danger of a Soviet attack on Finland, but to a certain extent Moscow made sure that the possibility was kept open until a point where the issue simply lost its meaning (presumably around January 1941). Ohto Manninen presents his view on the matter in the following way: 'After the Winter War, Finland took a background position in Stalin's great policy, although it was still taken into consideration in military planning as a likely enemy state.'[174]

Of course, the lack of Soviet intentions to invade Finland *might* have been a result of the meeting between Molotov and Hitler in November 1940, where Hitler, if nothing else, made it clear that Germany would not tolerate a war in the Baltic Sea area. Certain details in the course of events point in that direction, but that is not the same as saying we know the true circumstances.

That appears to be all we can deduce with certainty from the currently available sources about the existence of genuine Soviet intentions to attack Finland during the Interim Peace. There is little doubt that the Finnish leaders truly felt that cooperation with Germany was necessary to save Finland's independence, and the Soviet policy towards Finland was far from inspiring an atmosphere of confidence and trust. But the sad fact is that we simply do not know if the Finnish leaders assessed the situation correctly, since the development never seems to have reached a point where a Soviet invasion and annexation of Finland was seriously on the agenda in Moscow. Still, it must be remembered that the Finns had other worries too that moved them towards Berlin, primarily in regard to the foodstuffs situation.

A Change of President

Kyösti Kallio never recovered from the stroke he had suffered in August, and by the end of November he had to step down as Finland's president. Over the years Finnish presidents have had fundamentally different perceptions of their role as national leaders, particularly how much they should intervene in the political decision-making. Kallio had chosen a role not much different from what is expected of an aging king in a limited monarchy.

Unsurprisingly, the issue of finding his replacement immediately led to intervention from Moscow. Molotov called Paasikivi in for a meeting and told him there were a handful of prominent men whom the Soviet Union under no circumstances would accept as president of Finland. Väinö Tanner, of course, was at the top of the list. The others were ambassador to Berlin and former Prime Minister Toivo Kivimäki, former President Pehr Evin Svinhufvud and Marshal Mannerheim. If any of these men were elected as the new Finnish president, the Kremlin would view it as a violation of the Moscow Peace Treaty.

Once more the Finns yielded, but this time it was less painful since none of the people on Moscow's hate list were particularly eager to take over the post anyway, in fact quite the contrary. Prime Minister Ryti had already filled the post from the time of Kallio's stroke, and it was now decided that he was to take it over permanently. Ryti had already in the 1920s been a presidential candidate, but he had lost the election. Now it was for all intents and purposes given to him without him being particularly interested. It took some persuasion before he finally accepted.

The situation demanded that Ryti step down as prime minister, and once again it was decided to select a whole new government. As the new prime minister, Ryti chose Johan Wilhelm Rangell, a lawyer with a career background in Finland's national bank and practically no political experience. It was Ryti's declared policy to surround himself with people who could make clear and objective decisions and not be affected by political idealism, so there was a strikingly high degree of financial experts and people with no party political affiliations etc. among his advisers and ministers. Rangell's most important qualification seems to have been his long-lasting friendship with the new president.

On the whole, Ryti chose people who were unlikely to contradict him (except for Mannerheim and Tanner), and the role he took on as president was practically the opposite of Kallio's. Ryti almost acted as if he was still prime minister, and in matters of foreign politics he also granted himself a larger degree of power than any previous Finnish president.

Mannerheim's influence on Finnish politics had risen to new heights after the remarkable performance of the Finnish Army during the Winter

War, which to a large degree was attributed to him personally. There was a widespread feeling that the country would be lost without him, a fact he utilised on a few occasions when he wanted to put weight behind his views. The ultimate pressure he employed was to hand in his resignation and then withdraw it a few days later when he had either had his way or was forced to accept that the game was lost.

The marshal also had his faithful supporters among Ryti's inner circle, so the political power during the Interim Peace was centred on these two men. The most important influence from the numerically strong left wing (85 members of parliament out of 200 at the 1939 election) should have been channelled through Väinö Tanner, but he only re-joined the government after the Continuation War had begun.

Talvela in Berlin
In December 1939, following the Battle of Tolvajärvi, Colonel Paavo Talvela had been promoted major general. After the Winter War he had returned to civilian life where he held a high position in the paper and pulp industry. Nevertheless, he was sent to Berlin four times during the autumn of 1940 as contact person between the Finnish and the German military. Not only the transit agreement but other issues were discussed also, among them the aforementioned attempts to set up a Finnish-Swedish military union.

The German reaction to the latter was completely dismissive. This was made clear to Talvela on 16 December by General Franz Halder, chief of the OKH general staff, who then turned the conversation towards an entirely different issue. Halder asked Talvela how fast and discreetly the Finnish Army could be mobilised. Talvela felt this was outside his field of competence and said he would have to pass the questions on to his superiors when he got back to Helsinki.

As mentioned earlier, the entire Interim Peace period is insufficiently covered by sources; however, the content of this particular conversation can be found in the diaries of both parties. First the notes of General Halder:

Finnish General Talvela with attaché Horn:

Outlined the political situation in his country – Finland threatened by Communist propaganda.

Summary of the military situation: Aaland – Petsamo – Salla; no long-range guns and planes.

Sweden's attitude depends on that of Germany.

Sweden can make available five Divs. to aid Finland.
Personal union Sweden – Finland: we are asked to help.

I want to know – how much time would be needed to make quiet preparations for an offensive to the Southeast.[175]

Among Talvela's notes can be found the following:

… touched upon the subject, on which General Halder refused to write anything down, and which can only be answered after consultation with the Finnish headquarter.[176]

The conversation may at a glance seem insignificant, but in fact a high-ranking officer would never ask such a question except under the most confidential circumstances. In other words: Halder must have had absolute confidence in Talvela and the Finnish general staff, particularly since the question is clearly related to top secret plans of an invasion of the Soviet

Marshal Carl Gustaf Emil Mannerheim (1867-1951) in conversation with Major General Paavo Talvela (1897-1973), while Lieutenant General Axel Erik Heinrichs (1890-1965) is listening. The fully visible officer standing behind Mannerheim is Artillery General Vilho Petter Nenonen (1883-1960). (SA-Kuva)

Union.[177] Likewise the Finns must have been confident that Berlin would not pass sensitive information about the Finnish military on to the Soviet Union (with whom Germany after all had a kind of alliance). Altogether, these are strong indications that during the autumn of 1940 a close relationship of trust had developed between the German and Finnish high commands.

Berlin's resistance to the Finnish-Swedish defence union was highly predictable. The American-Norwegian military historian Henrik O. Lunde writes: '… a Finnish-Swedish union would also alleviate Finland's isolation and undermine German efforts to secure Finnish participation in the attack on the Soviet Union.'[178]

The Germans were not the only ones who rejected the Finnish-Swedish plans of a union. The leaders in Moscow did the same and in this they were supported by Great Britain.

II

Brothers in Arms

From announcements made by leading Finns, articles in Finnish newspapers and many other signs coming from English, American and Russian sources, there are daily examples of how Finland has now given up its neutral position.
VILHELM ASSARSSON[179]

Heinrichs in Berlin
Lieutenant General Erik Heinrichs was a considerably more trustworthy and cautious person than his colleague, Paavo Talvela, which was probably one of the reasons why Mannerheim let Heinrichs take over the negotiations with Berlin from January 1941 onwards. Still, it was remarkable that the choice fell on Heinrichs. Mannerheim often described him as his right hand, a man he simply could not do without. January 1941 was yet another crisis month in the history of the Interim Peace. The fact that Mannerheim ordered Heinrichs to leave Finland during such a tense situation underlines the importance of the task awaiting the lieutenant general on his arrival in Berlin.

This was later denied by Mannerheim, both during the War-Responsibility Trials and in his memoirs (which, incidentally, were to a large degree written by a group of high-ranking officers, among them Heinrichs, and later merely approved by the marshal[180]). Officially, Heinrichs' task was to give a lecture to a group of German officers about Finnish strategy during the Winter War. And so he did, but he also did much more. We know that partly from Jokipii's analysis, partly from the publicised diary of Major Gerhard Engel, who at the time was liaison officer between the German Army and Adolf Hitler.

When Heinrichs arrived in Berlin, he was shown the legendary Directive 21, the overall version of Operation Barbarossa, i.e. the plan for the German invasion of the Soviet Union. Finland figured in Item II of the plan:

II. Probable Allies and Their Tasks

1. On the flanks of our operations we can count on the active support of *Romania* and *Finland* in the war against Soviet Russia.

The High Command of the Armed Forces will decide and lay down in due time the manner in which the forces of these two countries will be brought under German command.

2. It will be the task of *Romania* to support the attack of the German southern flank, at least at the outset, with its best troops; to hold down the enemy where German forces are not engaged; and to provide auxiliary services in the rear areas.

3. *Finland* will cover the advance of the *Northern Group* of German forces moving from Norway (detachments of Group XXI) and will operate in conjunction with them. Finland will also be responsible for eliminating Hanko.

4. It is possible that *Swedish* railways and roads may be available for the movement of the German Northern Group, by the beginning of the operation at the latest.[181]

The Barbarossa Directive is rather short, so it seems natural that it only mentions Finland briefly. Nevertheless, it is remarkable that the tasks of Romania are far greater in scope and described in more detail than the 'probable' Finnish involvement.

This is a tendency we know from other sources too, even at much later stages. Jokipii writes: 'In the beginning, the Germans asked only a little from Finland. On 25 May 1941, in Salzburg, Jodl[182] stated that "one should not put too many burdens on the shoulders of the Finns." Though the Germans in practise asked for quite a lot later on, this remained their general attitude. For instance, Lieutenant Colonel (later General) Hermann Hölter ... said to General Talvela on 5 July that Finland had already done its bit, since by mobilising the Finnish Army they had drawn some ten Soviet divisions away from the areas of decisive fighting.'[183]

It appears that the Finnish leaders from the very start and for quite a long while into the cooperation gave the Germans more than they were asked for and expected to give, but we don't know if this was because they miscalculated the situation, or if they simply acted out of an eagerness to jump on to the German bandwagon. Again, the lack of trustworthy sources makes such essential factors hard to judge, but in this case at least we have Gerhard Engel's diary notes from 30 January 1940:

> The chief of the Finnish general staff, General Heinrichs, visited OKH where he had a look at our preliminary Barbarossa Plan. Everyone was amazed to see his determination and willingness to accept all our plans. The Führer was very impressed and thinks we have found a good brother-in-arms. He made some general observations about Finland and the politics of the country. It can be a difficult partnership, since the Finns wish to remain alliance-free and under no circumstances break off their relations with the USA, if possible not with Great Britain either. The Führer has no worries about that. The Finns were a brave people, and in them he would at least have good protection of his flank. Besides, it was good to have a brother-in-arms who was eager to take revenge, something he had noticed. Politically we had to be careful. The Finns were sensitive and he could not frighten them as we had done with the Slavs. General Heinrichs' biggest worry was probably the question of supplies and to keep the ports open. Here we could offer guarantees. For us, Finnish nickel was as important as oil and cereals were for Finland. The Führer gave OKW a free hand in their negotiations with the Finns, but they had to be concluded within three months.[184]

There is another German source to the meeting, a note in General Halder's diary referring to a conversation he and Heinrichs had on the same day:

> Conference with General Heinrichs: Army, in war strength, on the border on ninth day. Mobilization will be discreet but cannot go unnoticed. Thrust on both sides of Lake Ladoga; five Divs. south, three Divs. north of Lake Ladoga.[185]

Furthermore Helmuth Greiner, who kept the diary for the OKW, mentions that General Halder recounted this conversation to Hitler on 3 February, adding that the Finnish Army, according to Heinrichs, expected to use two divisions for the attack on Hanko.

It has been suggested that Heinrichs already at this meeting told the Germans that Finland would not participate in an attack on Leningrad.[186] However, several factors indicate that the Germans in fact had the opposite impression. For instance, they were very surprised when the Finns held back instead of attacking the city in August and September. Greiner's diary note also indicates that General Halder understood the Finnish attack on the Karelian Isthmus as really being aimed at Leningrad. In a later German propaganda film, the Finnish attacks on both sides of Lake Ladoga are described in the same manner.[187]

At the same meeting, Lieutenant General Heinrichs is supposed to have suggested that if the attack on the Soviet Union went ahead, Germany should occupy the Åland Islands. This would provide Finland with a pretext to mobilise, since it could be made to look as a precaution against a *German* attack on the Finnish mainland, while the army was really preparing to attack the Soviet Union. From Åland the Luftwaffe could later support the Finnish operations on Hanko.

The Crises in January
By early 1941 the negotiations over Petsamo had still not been concluded, although the Finns had yielded to a string of Soviet demands during the preceding autumn. They had unilaterally annulled their contracts with the British-Canadian company Inco which had interests in the area, and they had refrained from signing a planned deal with the German company I.G. Farben.

On 14 January Moscow offered the Finnish negotiators a compromise which gave the Soviet Union 75 per cent of the exploitation rights for the mines in Petsamo. At the same time they put pressure on Finland by halting Russian grain exports to the country. After a diplomatic tug-of-war lasting several days, Moscow gave the Finnish leaders a deadline of two days to hand in their reply.

The case was now presented to the Finnish parliament, where it caused an atmosphere of pronounced insecurity and disagreement. Several Social Democrat ministers were in favour of yielding to the Soviet demands, but the right wing felt this could lead to a very dangerous situation. Berlin strongly advised the Finns to stand their ground.[188]

Meanwhile, Finland's Germanophile circles launched new, albeit discrete propaganda campaigns to strengthen sympathy for Nazi Germany among the general population and promote the notion that Finland stood under German protection.[189]

When the short deadline ran out, Helsinki had still not replied. A few days later the Finnish intelligence services reported that troop movements had been observed on the Soviet side of the border in Lapland. Other worrying signals came from the Germans in northern Norway, mainly concerning the situation in Murmansk. Here the Russians were gathering a large fleet of fishing boats, some 500 vessels in total, enough to transport an entire division. Hitler reacted by giving Army Norway's chief-of-staff, Erich Buschenhagen, orders to keep his troops in the northernmost region on full alert. If Soviet forces approached Petsamo, the area was to be occupied in accordance with Operation Renntier (p. 135).

The reaction in Finland was roughly the same as last time there had been a similar situation. Mannerheim wanted a partial mobilisation, but Ryti and Prime Minister Rangell rejected the idea, pointing out that Moscow might see it as a provocation. The marshal then handed in his resignation in protest over attitudes that 'made it impossible to defend the country'. Whether this was aimed at Ryti and Rangell, or at Paasikivi who had recently claimed he was about to reach an agreement with the Kremlin, is anyone's guess.

Ryti now sent a telegram to Paasikivi in Moscow, stating that Finland would accept a fifty-fifty arrangement in regard to the exploitation of the mines. This was in reality a rejection of both the Russian proposal and Paasikivi's compromise. Ryti's proposal suited Mannerheim so well that he withdrew his resignation, but it was rejected by Moscow on 18 February and with that the negotiations collapsed.

Paasikivi's reaction was the opposite of Mannerheim's. He handed in his resignation and returned to Helsinki, oozing with anger over what he saw as the government's stubborn and destructive attitude. In fact, he had reasons to be considerably more angry, since he had been kept completely in the dark about the courtship that was going on in Berlin between the Finnish and German high commands. It had never been the intention that Paasikivi should reach an agreement in Moscow, rather that he should only delay the proceedings. Ryti's inner circle had decided once and for all where Finland would be directing its efforts in the future.

The Cooperation is Expanded
The next stage in the developing Finnish-German cooperation unfolded in February when the chief of the Luftwaffe's division for supply and administration, Lieutenant General Hans-Georg von Seidel, went to Finland to meet Mannerheim. Afterwards he went 'bear hunting' in the Salla region where he met Major General Siilasvuo. On the way Seidel picked up important logistic information, visited the airfields at Kemijärvi and Rovaniemi and acquainted himself with the weather conditions in the region.[190]

The next high-ranking German officer to visit Finland was Colonel Erich Buschenhagen, who at the time was German liaison officer to the Finnish general staff. His accounts of the events were made at a later time when he was a PoW in the Soviet Union (his witness statements were put forward on the fifty-seventh day of the Nuremberg trials). Buschenhagen, who was released from prison in 1955 and died in 1994, was interviewed by Mauno Jokipii in the 1970s. He appeared forthcoming and sympathetic towards Finland and had very clear memories of even small and intricate details which could be verified. If he had felt the need to withdraw his original statements, he would in all likelihood have done so; hence his accounts are regarded as completely reliable.[191] Buschenhagen, who had been present at the German military headquarters during Heinrichs' visit in Berlin, recalled from his first visit in Finland during the following month:

> I received the order to travel to Helsinki and to get in touch there, personally, with the Finnish general staff and to discuss with them these operations from middle and northern Finland.
>
> On 18 February 1941 I reached Helsinki and on the two following days I had conferences with the chief of the Finnish general staff, General Heinrichs, his deputy, General Airo, and the Chief of the operations detachment of the Finnish general staff, Colonel Tapola. At these conferences we discussed the possibilities for launching operations from middle and northern Finland, especially from the area around Kuusamo and Rovaniemi; also from the area of Petsamo. These conferences led to an agreement of the different opinions.
>
> After these conferences I travelled, together with the chief of the operation detachment of the Finnish general staff, Colonel Tapola, to middle and northern Finland in order to study the ... terrain, the possibilities for deployment and billeting, and for operations from that sector. At these reconnaissance trips the local Finnish commanders were present. The trip ended on 28 February in Tornio, on the Finnish-Swedish border. In a final conference it was determined that an operation from the area of Kuusamo ... and an operation from the area east of Rovaniemi ... would prove successful; that, on the other hand, the operations from Petsamo towards Rovaniemi would have considerable difficulty with the terrain. That was the end of my first series of conferences with the Finnish general staff.
>
> As a result of these discussions the German high command of Norway worked out a plan for an operation from the Finnish areas. The operational study was presented to the OKW and found its approval. It was then by the High Command of Norway named BLAUFUCHS.[192]

Lieutenant General Heinrichs was in Germany again at the end of May, this time as leader of a delegation of high-ranking Finnish officers.

The delegation first met with the leader of the OKW and its chief of general staff, Lieutenant General Alfred Jodl, in Salzburg on 25 May. From there the Finns continued to Berlin where they had conversations with the different services of the German Army. Altogether the meetings lasted for three days while the parties informed each other about their wishes and ambitions.

Throughout these proceedings it became clear to the Finnish delegation that the Germans intended to capture the Baltic States and then continue towards Leningrad. During the advance it was expected that the Red Army's defence of the area would collapse.

Further north, on the other side of the Gulf of Finland, the Finnish Army was to tie down Russian forces around Lake Ladoga. From there the Finnish Front was to stretch up to the Salla Region.

The remainder of the front north to the Barents Sea would be manned by the Germans. From here attacks would be aimed at Kandalaksha by the White Sea and more generally at the Murmansk Railway.

Later on this railway would have great importance for the war effort of the Allies as a transport line for American and British aid to the Soviet Union. But that was hardly an issue for the Germans in the summer of 1941, since Hitler expected a short campaign where the Soviet Union would be forced to capitulate within a few months. Rather the problem was that the nickel mines at Petsamo would be threatened by Soviet forces who received their supplies along the Murmansk Railway. Therefore the line had to be cut. To meet that end it was requested that the German force attacking from the Salla region be supported by a Finnish unit.

The Finnish main attack was to be launched on both sides of Lake Ladoga under Mannerheim's command. So far the Germans had expected to give the marshal command of all forces on the Finnish Front, including German units.[193] But he refused and instead the command of the northern sector was given to General Nikolaus von Falkenhorst. This was as far as the discussion could go, since the Finnish delegation had no mandate to enter into binding agreements; but Heinrichs promised to present the Finnish leaders with a string of requests from the German high command.

The talks ended with the parties agreeing to meet and continue the negotiations in Helsinki on 3 July.

Soviet Softening and Finnish Germanifying
After having followed a sharp and unrelenting strategy towards Finland for a year, Moscow changed course in the spring of 1941. Suddenly, the Soviet leaders were no longer so negative towards the plans of a Finnish-Swedish military union. The Soviet ambassador, Zotov, who had been highly unpopular in Finland, was recalled to Moscow and replaced with Pavel Orlov, who would turn out to be more approachable. As a 'personal gift' to Paasikivi, Stalin gave Finland 20,000 tons of grain.

It seemed the Russians had finally understood that Finland was moving into the German camp, basically due to the Soviet Union's own policies towards the country, and now they were attempting to reverse the development by bestowing on the Finns various kinds of goodwill. It was far too late. Vilhelm Assarsson, a Swedish diplomat working as his country's envoy in Moscow, wrote home to Stockholm that he had met the Finnish diplomat Paavo Hynninen (later Finland's ambassador to Denmark in 1946-53), who had given him a description of the atmosphere in Finland. According to Hynninen, the government was about to put all their money on one horse, presumably under heavy influence from the Finnish ambassador in Berlin, Kivimäki. It was generally believed that Germany would soon invade the Soviet Union, and that Finland would receive 'compensations for the injustices it had suffered'. No one bothered to listen to Paasikivi any more. Assarsson continued:

> According to what Hynninen told me under strict confidentiality, he [Paasikivi] had had a raging quarrel with, among others, his old friends Mannerheim and Walden, who wanted no compliance shown towards Moscow. The Soviet Union was now regarded to be of insignificant importance, and Paasikivi's lectures about showing a forthcoming attitude in the nickel question were ignored.[194]

Paasikivi also felt that the government's pro-German line was strongly influenced by Kivimäki's reports from Berlin. Still, it is hardly fair to give a single person the whole responsibility. Many influential forces tried in those days to push Finland in the direction of Nazi Germany, with full backing from the top of the Finnish leadership. Meinander writes: 'In April 1940 a German industrial exhibition was arranged in Helsinki, where German swastikas waved side by side with the Finnish flag in many places in the centre of town. The most enthusiastic promoters of this development were naturally groups of Finnish Fascists and members of other Nationalist organisations. They could hardly resist the temptation to announce in public their visions of a so-called Greater Finland, the old Nationalist dream of expanding Finnish territory eastwards into the Russian part of Karelia. The Finnish leaders themselves were no strangers to such daydreaming.'[195]

One of the initiatives meant to impress Berlin concerned the idea of setting up a Finnish *Jäger* battalion within the German Wehrmacht as an attempt to 'revive the *Jäger* traditions from the 1915-18 period.'[196] The Germans suggested instead a battalion placed under the Waffen-SS, which was already operating with such 'national' units. Though the SS corps had not yet achieved quite the horrendous reputation it would gain later on, its image was worrying enough to make the Finnish leaders hesitate. Still, the Finnish parliament approved the idea in the end and the unit was officially born in March 1941. It was later claimed that the real reason allowing this unit to be formed was a fear that Germany would lose sympathy for Finland and leave the country to its own devices if such expressions of goodwill were not made, and hence the unit was nicknamed 'the Pawn Battalion'.

A bizarre situation appeared in relation to the recruitment for the battalion. Since, according to Nazi racial theories, the Finnish people were not pure Aryans, Berlin preferred candidates from a Swedish-speaking background. The Finnish recruitment officers seem to have paid little attention to this, since the number of Finno-Swedes among the recruits was only marginally higher than the national average.[197]

The Finns also set conditions for the founding of the battalion: the unit was only to be deployed on the Eastern Front, it had to be led by Finnish officers, the official language had to be Finnish and the period of service must not exceed two years.

The first recruits were sent to Germany for training in May 1941. A further description of the battalion's history is outside of the framework of this book. Suffice to say it was sent into combat in January 1942 and fought in different sectors of the Eastern Front until it was dissolved and its men returned to Finland in the summer of 1943.

A German Request

When Lieutenant General Heinrichs returned to Helsinki from Germany on 28 May, he brought with him the aforementioned German requests related to the invasion plan. The most pressing queries were partly in relation to the time frame of the Finnish mobilisation, partly in regard to the transport of a German division through Finnish Lapland to the Soviet border where it was to be deployed in attack formation.

Some historians have seen the latter query as an underhand German method to make the Finns reveal whether or not they were truly interested in participating in the invasion. However, that seems highly unlikely. At this stage of the proceedings the Germans must have viewed the Finns as fully committed to the undertaking. It was no small process that had been started, and the invasion was only a few weeks in the future, though there was still no fixed date attached to it. The idea that the Finns could just say no thanks if they felt like staying at home is bordering on the absurd. At the most they could present well-argued changes on single issues.

Again, the whole situation is terribly blurred and even characterised by misunderstandings between the parties, not least because the Germans still would not divulge even to their closest partners that the invasion was actually going to take place. Instead, they claimed it was merely something that *could* become real *if* some postulated on-going negotiations between Berlin and Moscow broke down. As we shall see, the Finnish *military* leaders appear to have seen through this bluff, while the *political* leaders were seriously worried that Berlin would enter into an agreement with Moscow and leave Finland in the lurch.

President Ryti's most acute problem was that he did not personally have the authority to grant the German requests. On such matters, the Finnish parliamentary rules demanded approval from both the government and the Foreign Policy Committee. In both instances it was highly doubtful that Ryti could have achieved the necessary support and even if he did, subsequent resistance in the *Eduskunta* was potentially so large as to result in a vote of no confidence.

Only a very narrow circle of people knew anything about the lengthy period of preliminary military planning between Berlin and Helsinki, so to anyone else the German requests would look as if they came completely out of the blue. No wonder that Ryti feared a negative reaction. To let a German division march through Lapland and deploy on the Russian border would seem to the uninitiated a rather bizarre decision at a time when Moscow was finally softening up and showing friendliness and compliancy towards Finland. But the implications were even more far-reaching than that, since part of the German request involved real coordination between German and Finnish military operations.

It was these factors, when taken together, that made Mauno Jokipii describe the German requests as a 'kind of' military agreement. In doing so he threatened one of the basic elements in the traditional perception of the Finnish-German cooperation during the Interim Peace, a perception which claims that there was no such agreement at all. It could be called a struggle over definitions, but at least we know for certain that the Germans saw it the same way. For example, General Waldemar Erfurth wrote in his diary on 14 June, when the Finnish leaders finally decided to let the transports go ahead:

> Heinrichs informed me of the result of the government's meeting today in the afternoon. The president of the republic had been staunch and approved the German-Finnish military agreement.[198]

It is worth paying attention to the dates here. Heinrichs had returned from Berlin on 28 May and immediately handed on the German queries to Mannerheim and Walden. The next day he had informed Ryti, too. From then on more than a week passed by before the president informed the entire government, and what he put to them was not a question – it was simply the fact that *the German troop transports through Lapland to the Soviet border had already started*.

Those in the government who were ignorant of the cooperation with Berlin were naturally surprised, and a few of them strongly dismayed, too. Someone at the very top of the Finnish political and military leadership had singlehandedly launched a process which demanded approval from several parliamentary offices, if the rules were to be observed. But that was just the formal side of things. The real problem was the momentous and irrevocable nature of the matter.

Based on the events we *do* know about from Finnish archive material and German sources, Jokipii concluded that the permission for the transports to go ahead was given no later than 5 June by the War Cabinet, which consisted of President Ryti, Prime Minister Rangell, Foreign Minister Witting, Minister for Defence Walden and Marshal Mannerheim.[199] Ohto Manninen's view on the matter is that: 'In accordance with his instructions Mannerheim gave a positive answer to the German query on coordination through his representatives in Helsinki and Kiel on 3-6 June and added some remarks.'[200]

These remarks included some practical features related to the Finnish mobilisation. Also, Mannerheim stated that Finnish troops would not attack across the border into the Soviet Union unless a Soviet attack had taken place first. The Germans saw this as a pure formality, so they accepted the Finnish conditions and went ahead with the operation.

Since the Finnish government was not informed until several days after the transports had started, it had no other choice than to accept the decision that the War Cabinet had already made. Anything else would undoubtedly have led to disaster of one kind or another. There was of course no way to turn back the German war machine. It is therefore safe to say that Ryti had set up a fait accompli to ensure that everything went his way.

The same pattern was repeated in the Foreign Policy Committee. In the *Eduskunta* there seems to have been a majority for a vote of no confidence, but the opportunity was lost when Väinö Tanner put pressure on the Social Democrat group and forced it to accept the agreement.

The Last Pieces Fall into Place
In accordance with the time schedule, the German military delegation arrived in Helsinki on 3 June, after which the mutual work on the Finnish parts of the Barbarossa Plan continued.

The Germans had already asked for support for the right flank in their attack on Kandalaksha, and the Finns now handed the task to III Corps under Major General Siilasvuo. Furthermore, three Finnish infantry companies and an artillery battery were handed over to support the German attack further north, starting from the Petsamo area.

The Finnish main offensive was still meant to take place on both sides of Lake Ladoga, but it had not been decided which of these directions should constitute the main attack, so the Germans were asked to give their opinion. They replied that the attack east of the lake offered the most potential military advantages, since the Finns could move all the way down to the River Svir and meet up there with the Germans coming from the south, after which the two forces together could annihilate Leningrad.

Colonel Buschenhagen, whose time as German liaison officer at the Finnish general staff was about to run out, later documented his recollections of the negotiations:

> At these conferences, which again took place between General Heinrichs, General Halder, and Colonel Tapola, the details of this collaboration were worked out, such as the timetable, the schedule, measures of secrecy as to the Finnish mobilization ... There was complete agreement on all these questions and also there were details discussed about exchange of information, about the use of Finnish means of transportation and by representatives of the air force about joint questions of air warfare and about the use of Finnish airports by the German air force ...
>
> All agreements between the OKW and the Finnish general staff had as their sole purpose from the very beginning the participation of the Finnish Army and the German troops on Finnish territory in the aggressive war against the Soviet Union. There was no doubt about that. If the Finnish general staff, to the outside world, always pointed out that all these measures had only the character of defence measures, that was just camouflage. There was – from the very beginning – no doubt among the Finnish general staff that all these preparations would serve only in the attack against the Soviet Union, for all the preparations that we made pointed in that same direction, namely, the plans for mobilization; above all, the objectives for the attack.[201]

The subject of common Finnish-German naval operations had only been touched upon briefly during Heinrichs' visit to Germany in May, so at the following meetings in Finland separate negotiations took place between the representative of the Finnish Navy, Commander Svante Sundman, and the German *Oberkommando der Marine* (OKM). Sundman then travelled to Kiel on 6 June as leader of a Finnish delegation. At the following meeting a framework was set for the naval cooperation, tasks were defined and the parties solved various questions regarding the use of bases and materiel.[202]

The Finns still maintained they would not cross the border unless the Russians attacked them first. General Waldemar Erfurth, an old acquaintance of Mannerheim who on 14 June had taken over from Buschenhagen as liaison officer to the Finnish general staff, wrote in his report to the OKW:

The Finns want to create the impression among their own people and people's representatives of being drawn in by the course of events.²⁰³

The wording is almost shockingly precise. What was really an aggressive military act, planned through more than four months in consultation with Berlin, was to be presented as a Finnish reaction to a Soviet assault. Only in that way could the necessary public and parliamentary support for the war be secured. Also, for the Finns, this was about staying friends with the western democracies for as long as possible, since they might after all win the war in the end.

What the Finnish leaders would have done if the Russians had *not* attacked is hard to say. There seems to have been no emergency plan for that, and Berlin would hardly have accepted it if the Finnish Army had remained behind the border, as the Germans marched into the Soviet Union. Remarkably, the problem seems not to have worried Mannerheim, who was otherwise known for his pronounced pessimism. Ryti wrote in his diary:

> On 14 June 1941 Marshal Mannerheim, Prime Minister Rangell, Ministers Walden and Witting and General Heinrichs visited me to each report on the situation within their individual fields. Mannerheim was almost certain that the Russians would attack us immediately, at least from the air, but possibly also on land and at sea.²⁰⁴

Mannerheim's attitude is also reflected in a conversation that the Finnish ambassador to London, G.A. Gripenberg, had with him shortly after the outbreak of the war:

> 'Our participation in the war was a result of the Soviet attacks,' Mannerheim said. However, he admitted that he was very pleased when the Russians attacked, since it made it possible for us to take up arms without being accused of having attacked Russia.²⁰⁵

Based on interviews and German sources, Mauno Jokipii has presented intricate but nevertheless convincing evidence of how the Finnish leaders on 15 June had confirmation from Berlin that Operation Barbarossa was really going to happen.²⁰⁶ With that, the last traces of Finnish neutrality evaporated, since the cooperation between Helsinki and Berlin had now fully taken on the character of a military agreement.

The news came after a Finnish request for certain German military and trade related guarantees in case the invasion was cancelled. The uncertainty on this issue was pronounced among some of the Finnish leaders, though probably only the politicians. It sounds unlikely that the high-ranking officers, who had been working in tandem with Berlin for so long, could be ignorant of what was really happing. This view is supported by a message Lieutenant General Heinrichs had handed the visiting German planners twelve days previously:

> The Commander-in-Chief [Mannerheim] wishes to take this opportunity to say that the interest called forth by these discussions is in no way purely operational or military-technical in nature.
> The idea which forms the basis of the propositions communicated to him by the highest echelons of the German leadership must arouse joy in the Finnish soldier's heart and is regarded here as a historic sign of a great future.[207]

If this document fails to make it clear that the Finnish High Command had understood what was going on, Heinrichs' verbal comment should leave no doubt:

> For the first and probably the last time in Finland's thousand-year history the great moment has come in which the Finnish people can free itself for all time from the pressure of its hereditary enemy.[208]

This is the earliest known proof that the Finnish military leaders had fully understood the character of the situation. However, the realisation might have occurred much earlier, perhaps as early as during Talvela's visit to Berlin in December 1940 or Heinrichs' enthusiastic performance before the German high command the following month. It must be assumed that these two intelligent and experienced generals, with their profound first-hand knowledge of the German military and the German language, could distinguish the difference between a routine operational meeting and the planning of the biggest land invasion in the history of mankind.

Nevertheless, until a week before the war broke out the *civilian* Finnish leaders were still uncertain as to whether Operation Barbarossa would ever take place. In other words, it seems that the military leaders deliberately failed to inform the politicians of the true circumstances, or at least failed to do so convincingly. It has often been claimed that the insecurity surrounding the invasion (i.e. whether it was to go ahead or not) was the key factor that made the Finnish leaders throw themselves into cooperation with Berlin more eagerly than perhaps necessary, and so it would appear that the military clique committed a sin of omission in order to increase the Finnish engagement.

In any case, the confirmatory German reply meant that the Finns could now be rather more direct in their approach. Already on 16 July Heinrichs wrote to Erfurth suggesting that the Finnish Front remain passive for two to three days after the main German attack had started.[209] The motivation was twofold. First, the Finns were worried that they could not complete their mobilisation in time. Second, the few extra days would mean that the Red Army had more time to attack and thereby give the Finns the much-needed *cause belli* to launch their part of the invasion.

As soon as the German attack had started over a broad front across the breath of Eastern Europe, it was expected that the Russians would start carrying out preventive attacks on Finnish territory, due to the German presence in the country. This way it would appear that the Soviet Union was the aggressor and Finland the innocent victim of a new invasion. Viewed superficially, that is exactly what happened. However, a closer look reveals that Finnish acts of war had been taking place in deep secrecy from several days before the Soviet air attacks on the country that started on 25 June. The list could be made longer, but it should suffice to mention a few of the more significant episodes.

On 20 June, two days before the German assault on the Soviet Union and five days before Finland officially entered the war, the German Naval High Command requested permission from the Finnish leaders to lay mines in Estonian waters in the Gulf of Finland. On instruction from Ryti and Mannerheim (relayed without any paper trail), the chiefs of the Finnish Navy and the coastal defence ordered three Finnish submarines to carry out the operation the following morning. When the commander of the submarines asked to have the order confirmed in writing, the request was denied. Nevertheless, he carried out the order. The next day the German attack on the Soviet Union was a fact, and over the following days three Soviet vessels were stricken by Finnish mines. One of them, a submarine, immediately sank.[210]

Lightly armed long-distance Finnish Army patrols in plain clothing had frequently moved into Soviet territory since the summer of 1940.[211] Most closely connected to Operation Barbarossa was a sixteen man patrol under Patrol Department Marttina, who on 22 June following a German request were flown in a Heinkel amphibious aircraft with German crew deep into Soviet territory behind the White Sea Canal. The plan was to blow up one of the lock gates between Lake Onega and Lake Vygozero. The canal, however, was too strongly guarded so the operation had to be abandoned and the group found its way back to Finland.[212]

The Finnish air force also prepared itself actively for the coming war several days before Operation Barbarossa officially began. On 17 June Finnish officers gave two plain-clothed liaison officers from the Luftwaffe a guided tour of the airfields in southern Finland. The Germans made various demands, which were promptly met. The next day German air traffic controllers took up quarters on the airfield near Utti, a village in the southeast of Finland 100km from Viipuri. On the same day the wing tips on all aircraft belonging to the Finnish air force were painted yellow, and a yellow band was painted around the fuselage. This was the mark used to identify aircraft operating on the German side of the Eastern Front. Three days later, on the evening of 21 June, the first German planes landed outside Utti. They were followed by several other Luftwaffe aircraft the next day.[213]

The German historian Michael Jonas sums up the situation as follows: '... the German-Finnish attack against the Soviet Union was at the very least a military joint venture with the shared purpose of conducting a war of aggression ... If anything, Stalin's preparations for war against Nazi Germany or his plans for a renewed invasion of Finland were so little developed and unconcrete that the German-Finnish invasion of late June 1941 does not seem to bear the central characteristics of a preventive war.'[214]

One should keep in mind that the Winter War had also constituted an illegal attack, albeit launched by the Soviet Union, which means that the Moscow Peace Treaty with its demands on Finnish territory to be handed over to the Soviet Union must be seen as void. Viewed from that angle a war waged by the Finns aimed only at taking back territories that rightfully belonged to them is in both a modern judicial sense and a classic moral sense defensible. Any problems in this regard would only emerge if the 1939 border was crossed; but of course these issues cannot realistically be separated from the overall Finnish contribution to the Nazi war effort.

III

The Finnish Choice

*The psychologists have known for a long time
that people rarely act on the basis of one single motive.
On the contrary, both individuals and groups in
practice collect information from many different
events and use them as a foundation for their decisions.
Hence, it is better to speak of 'sets of motives'.
This expression is well suited to the choice that was
made in Finland in 1941.*
MAUNO JOKIPII[215]

Alliance or Separate Wars?
During the summer of 1940 the Finnish leaders were facing two very tangible problems: how to prevent a famine from breaking out, and how to protect their country against what was perceived as the acute danger of a new Soviet invasion. On top of that there was the possibility of being invaded by Nazi Germany, whose occupation of Denmark and Norway had shown how important it was for the German war machine to secure its iron ore imports from northern Sweden, and who had been in no way helpful towards Finland during the Winter War. In the worst of cases, it might all happen at once: two invasions by the great totalitarian powers at the same time, coming from either side, could lead to Finland being divided, as had happened in Poland.

Moscow offered Finland help with foodstuffs and military protection against Germany, but such a plan had already been rejected by the Finnish leaders before the Winter War. Since then the war itself and the subsequent full Soviet annexation of the Baltic States had only increased Finnish suspicions towards the Kremlin. Furthermore, the persecution of Finno-Ugric people in East Karelia and Ingria (p. 258) was already well known to the Finns from refugees fleeing across the border into Finland. Seen in the light of these circumstances a Finnish-Soviet trade and defence agreement was completely unrealistic.

More broadly viewed, the question was if Finland should maintain its neutrality and try to tackle the problems as they presented themselves, or if the country should move into the German camp. If neutrality was chosen, the two abovementioned main problems would remain unsolved, which was seen as in practice unbearable and potentially as a catastrophic situation. In contrast to this, cooperation with Germany would solve both problems and it also held other advantages.

The Finnish leaders, like many others at that time, were almost convinced that a war between Germany and the Soviet Union would break out, and that Germany would end up winning it. If Finland was on good terms with Berlin, this situation would open the possibility of winning back the territories that had been lost in the Winter War – plus more (an aspect we shall return to). But cooperation with Germany would also include a string of secondary problems and risks. Somewhat schematically the choice could be presented as follows:

Advantages of Cooperating with Germany
- Would solve the food supply problem
- Give protection against the Soviet Union
- Could bring back the lost territories
- Open for further conquests of Soviet territory
- Make it possible to take the war into enemy territory and thereby protect one's own civilian population

Disadvantages of Cooperating with Germany
- Could alienate Finland from the other Nordic countries
- A loss of American and British sympathy
- Moral implications
- Loss of national unity
- A risk of ending up as a Nazi puppet state
- A risk of ending up on the losing side

In fact, the Finnish leaders had already decided by the end of the Winter War that their previous policy of neutrality was too dangerous, so in a way the road ahead was chosen as soon as the talks over a union with Sweden stranded in late 1940. Some form of cooperation with Germany seemed unavoidable, although the attached drawbacks still had to be taken into consideration. Here the magical solution seemed to be the idea that Finland was not really an ally of Germany but waging a separate war, which was to be presented purely as a reaction to a Soviet attack. As already described (p. 134) this idea had from the start been a practical necessity for both parties, but it soon turned out to be a handy propaganda tool, as well. The Finnish historian Ville Kivimäki remarks: '... the idea of a "separate" Finnish war against the Soviet Union comes close to absurdity. Had the

German *Blitzkrieg* of 1941 succeeded in defeating the Soviet Union, the Finns would have been ready to conform to the "New Order" in the east and in the whole of Europe.'[216]

Attached to the separate war phenomenon was also the name chosen for the Finnish war effort. The term 'the Continuation War' more than suggests that the new war was nothing other than an extension of the Winter War, with all it included of national unity and international good-will towards a Finnish Army and government fighting all alone against a mighty, dictatorial superpower.

Still, the separate war thesis could not put a damper on *all* the problems created by the cooperation with Berlin. The danger of seeing Finland run by a Nazi puppet government had to be tackled differently, which was why Mannerheim (through Heinrichs) warned the Germans that all Finnish-German military cooperation would cease immediately if the Germans tried to install a regime of that kind in Finland.[217] Thus the marshal had also made it clear to Berlin that he would reject any offer to become head of state in such a government himself.

Mannerheim's warning seems to have had a certain *delaying* effect, at least judging from a statement Hitler made a few days later, on 16 June, during a conference at his headquarters. The purpose of the meeting was the planning of the future administration of the so-called *Reichskommissariat Ostland*, i.e. the German administration of the three Baltic States and surrounding areas. The German Führer said during the meeting:

> The annexation of Finland as a federated state should be prepared with caution.[218]

The quote is interesting for another reason, too. While we lack any proof of imminent Soviet aims to annex Finland during the Interim Peace, it shows that such intentions were actually held by the power that the Finns had chosen as their belligerent partner. There is something sadly ironic in this (or perhaps it is more illustrative of the extreme pressure Finland was under), but at least Mannerheim's warning shows that the Finnish leaders were not completely naïve when it came to the true intentions of Nazi Germany. And so a simple question presents itself: what kind of acceptable outcome did the Finnish leaders hope for in relation to the military cooperation they had entered into? It seems a blatant contradiction in terms to secure Finland's democratic freedom and independence by linking the country to a massive military power whose declared goal was to make Nazi Germany the all-domineering political force of Europe.

The answer seems to be that the Finnish leaders chose 'the devil that they knew' and which also gave them the most advantages, particularly a weakening of the main enemy and the possibility of recapturing the lost territories.

A Question of Degree
Let us for a moment go back to the German requests that Heinrichs brought home with him from Berlin in late May 1941. Mauno Jokipii explains in *Jatkosodan Synty* (*The Birth of the Continuation* War) why a rejection of these requirements was probably not an appealing option for Ryti's inner circle: 'Such unfriendliness could result in a sudden German stop to all Finnish foreign trade, which would immediately have caused a lack of raw material in the industry ... Neutrality could have given advantages in foreign policy matters in relation to the western powers and the Soviet Union if there had been enough belief in their victory. But in all probability these advantages would only have borne fruit after several years of unpleasant occupation.' And Jokipii rounds off: 'Hence the neutral alternative looked highly unfavourable compared to teaming up with the expected winner of the war.'[219]

The fact that such a statement could be put forward so casually four decades after the war reveals some fundamental differences in the view on Nazism between Finland and most other European countries even in modern times. But the statement is also interesting because it draws our attention to what might be the pivotal issue in the Finnish set of motives: the belief in German victory.

Without this conviction the Finnish leaders would undoubtedly have chosen a different policy. Whether it would have led to better or worse results is impossible to say because there are way too many factors involved. But one thing is certain: though we know now that the Finns in the long run achieved what they wanted by cooperating with Germany – in so far as Finland, or at least most of the country, came out of the Second World War as an independent state – the cooperation was indisputably based on a miscalculation that could hardly have been more fundamental. Perhaps we are dealing with another blessing in disguise, as some historians have called the Finnish policies before and during the Winter War. Or perhaps, as others would say, the Continuation War was a serious political mistake that the Finnish soldiers had to make up for in blood.

As mentioned, Jokipii has little time for the neutral alternative. That is probably a valid conclusion. The prospect of facing a famine and a comprehensive collapse of Finnish society has to be added to the fact that a German or Soviet occupation of Finland would probably have turned into a nightmare even worse than what actually happened. Most likely, Finland would have become a battlefield between the major powers, while this in turn could well have rekindled the old internal confrontations from the Civil

The Finnish Choice 169

War of 1918. All in all, cooperation with Berlin does indeed seem like the least horrible solution for the Finns from December 1940 onwards. But that still leaves the question of whether the cooperation had to be *so* forthcoming and comprehensive.

'There was originally no demand for Finland to lead a major offensive into the adversary's territory,' Jokipii writes. 'It would have been enough to give the Germans access to the thoroughfares and bases they needed, and by mobilising their army the Finns would tie down a vast number of troops along the border ... The procedure was similar to the one recently seen in Bulgaria, whose military without active participation had let German troops march through their country towards southern Yugoslavia. Or the Finns could have waited until the German attack had sorted things out and then participated in a light occupation of their own former territory, as Hungary had done recently in Yugoslavia.'[220]

This kind of comparative analysis is reminiscent of the debate that has gone on in some of the European countries that were occupied by Germany during the Second World War and cooperated with the Nazis. In Finland such discussions rarely see the light of day; normally the dialogue is reduced to an either-or debate. One of the reasons lies in the way the Finnish leaders at the time carefully wiped nearly all tracks of their discussions and personal considerations, and later lied about their actions (whether justifiably or not). Another difference lies in the circumstances under which the cooperation with Berlin was launched in each individual case. Most Nazi-occupied European countries had simply been invaded and taken over, and after that the need for some kind of cooperation with the occupiers was clear to the majority of people. Therefore the post-war discussions would not tend to deal with the issue of cooperation as such, but instead with the more detailed characteristics of cooperation due to necessity versus active collaboration. In Finland, there was no occupation and the initiative to cooperate with Berlin came from the national leaders themselves without anyone outside of a very small circle of people having the faintest idea what was going on, and hence *that* becomes the main issue. Still, perhaps the time has now finally come for the Finns to put this part of the discussion to rest and instead take a closer look at the various models for a cooperation that the Finnish leaders could have considered but apparently did not.

Goals and Ambitions

Over the years there has been much discussion and guesswork regarding the real political aims behind the Finnish war effort during the Continuation War. The American military historian Earl M. Ziemke writes: 'Their announced war aims were limited to recovery of the lost territories; that they expected to take a good deal more is certain. Bellicose utterances by

Mannerheim and others, particularly during the early months of the war, are not hard to find.'[221]

The following quote contains one such utterance, made by Minister for Foreign Affairs Rolf Witting to the Finnish parliament shortly after the new war had started:

> This struggle is our defence against an attack from our neighbouring country in the east and its conscious and continuous policy of aggrandisement … but at the same time this fight is the fight of mankind against Bolshevism and its attempts to destroy and terrorise.[222]

Since Witting said this in his capacity as representative of the government we must assume that the Finnish war effort was not just aimed at defending the country and winning back the ceded territories, but also thought of as a contribution to the Nazi struggle against Soviet communism. This should be seen in the light of the German objectives, here formulated by Henrik O. Lunde on the basis of the *Barbarossa* directive: '*… to destroy the military and economic potential of the Soviet Union by conquering and occupying permanently vast regions of that country, including some areas that were to be given to Germany's allies.*'[223]

Like some other modern historians Lunde thinks that Finland should be counted among Germany's allies. That raises the question of which territories were to be handed over to Finland in the event of the expected German victory.

It goes without saying that the ceded territories were to be recaptured. But Mannerheim and those around him felt it would be both beneficial and justifiable to cross the 1939 border and continue into Soviet territory proper, particularly in East Karelia, to take up more advantageous defence positions (often forming a line across the terrain between two lakes). But the plans went further than that, even among the civilian leaders. Meinander writes: 'When optimism ran high, Finland's political leaders dreamt about territorial expansions into East Karelia and the Kola Peninsula.'[224]

At least some parts of Leningrad were also included in this 'dreaming'. In order to communicate such wishes in a discrete manner to the leaders in Berlin, President Ryti had already in 1940 hired two of Finland's leading scientists, geographer Väinö Auer and historian Eino Jutikkala, to carry out a project meant to argue in favour of a new border between Finland and Russia. The result, which was worked out under Ryti's on-going supervision, was a book published in Germany the following year titled *Finnlands Lebensraum*.[225]

In mid-May 1941 Berlin requested a more direct reply to the question of where the Finnish leaders wanted to draw their future border. This was at the time when the Germans still claimed they were negotiating with the Russians, and that Operation Barbarossa would only be realised if these talks broke down. If the Finns would clarify their wishes, Berlin would present them to the Russians as demands, it was said.

In actual fact, this was probably a German attempt to probe the level of ambition in Helsinki. Still, the Finnish leaders avoided making a clear reply. Instead, Ryti once again hired a prominent scientist for the task, Professor of History and Philosophy Jalmari Jaakkola, who was an influential figure among the small but highly active group of Nazis within Finland's academic circles. The result was a report, once again written in German and officially published in Germany.

Taking his cue from the title, *Die Ostfrage des Finnlands* (*Finland's Eastern Question*), Jaakkola argued for his country's new frontier on the basis of ethnographic factors. Starting from the Gulf of Finland, he let the border follow the River Neva through Leningrad to Lake Ladoga. Continuing east, Jaakkola drew the border along Lake Ladoga's southern bank, through the terrain south of the Svir River to Lake Onega and around its southern bank, after which it swung north and ended by the White Sea.

The Germans also asked to see a proposed new border based on strategic considerations. Again the Finns managed to circle round the issue. Instead of drawing up a single map to answer the question, the leading strategic planner of the general staff, Lieutenant General Airo, was ordered to work out no less than five suggestions; then the Germans could make their own choice and the Finns could avoid the risk of being either too greedy or too humble. The least ambitious of the plans was quite simply a redrawing of the 1939 border, while the most ambitious one ran east from Lake Ladoga, followed Lake Onega's western bank along the 'ethnic line' and ended by the White Sea (an attached map has disappeared).[226]

It was originally the intention that the Kola Peninsula with its huge mineral deposits should belong to Germany, but this changed after a revision in November-December 1941 so the area instead was deemed to be given to the Finns. With that the territory of Finland would be almost doubled. Airo avoided defining the border on the Karelian Isthmus, since it would be next to German territory and in any case would be dictated by Berlin, but in his comments the lieutenant general recommended a border along the River Neva, with Kotlin Island (home of the fortified town of Kronstadt) under Finnish domain.[227]

It seems beyond doubt that the Finnish leaders preferred the most expansive of the five plans, and that Ryti in particular was drawn to the idea of including the Kola Peninsula in the projected Greater Finland. In a conversation in 1961 with the historian Arvi Korhonen, General Heinrichs claimed that Mannerheim had been dismissive about the idea of including the Kola Peninsula in the plans, and that the marshal had strong doubts about whether East Karelia could remain in Finnish hands in the long run.[228] This statement, however, should probably be taken with a pinch of salt, since Heinrichs was not exactly a man who liked to put his former superior in a bad light.

In any case, the minutes from the Ostland Conference in mid-June 1941(p. 167) show that Hitler by then already had the impression that the Finns were interested in the Kola Peninsula, though he had no intention at that point to let them have it (as mentioned earlier, that only came about at the end of the year and was possibly meant as an incitement to encourage the Finns to re-launch their offensive, which at the time had been halted):

> The Finns wanted East Karelia, but the Kola Peninsula will be taken by Germany because of the large nickel mines there.[229]

The strategic alternatives were all built on expert views and only meant as information for the political leaders. Likewise, the contemporary plans for the administration of a Finnish military regime in East Karelia were merely suggestions. Nevertheless, these considerations reflected the opinions of the military and political leaders.[230] It is, therefore, reasonable to see the plans not only as an expression of Finland's purely military goals, but also of its overall political aims during the final phase of the Interim Peace.[231] Once that is established, the otherwise undefined Finnish war aims (at this early stage) begin to emerge from the carefully laid smoke screen: it was all about creating a Finnish mini empire with the highest possible degree of autonomy but still inevitably subordinated to the New Europe – *Neuropa* – which the Finnish leaders were convinced would come true under Nazi German rule.

With regard to Leningrad it is also interesting to see how the Finnish ambitions were interpreted at the Führer's headquarters in Berlin, not least because it might divulge aspects that are absent from the Finnish archives and later witness statements. Here we have some excellent sources, first and foremost the minutes of Martin Bormann, Hitler's private secretary, from the Ostland Conference where he recounted the Führer's view as follows:

> The area around Leningrad is wanted by the Finns; the Führer will raze Leningrad to the ground and then hand it over to the Finns.[232]

The same observation is reflected in Major Gerhard Engel's diary on 6 August, where Hitler is quoted as saying it is necessary to join the German and Finnish forces in the area southwest of the Svir if Leningrad is to be conquered. And the Führer felt certain that the Finns would be in on the idea because:

> ... Marshal Mannerheim had let him know that Leningrad was his goal, too, and the town must later be put to the plough.[233]

It is possible that Hitler misunderstood the ambitions of the Finns, who by no means had a clear and unambiguous way of presenting their views. Still, it is striking that these two crucial and easily obtainable sources are practically absent from all Finnish research in the field. Instead, attention had been focused on a speech that President Ryti made to the government on 9 June 1941 (i.e. at the meeting where he also announced that the German troop transports from Kirkenes to the Salla region had started):

> If war breaks out between Germany and Russia now, it can benefit the whole world. At the moment Germany is the only state that can defeat or at least weaken Russia, and it would probably not be bad for the world if Germany too is weakened in the process. But the greatest possible weakening of Russia is a condition for our salvation. If Russia wins the war, then our situation will be difficult, perhaps even hopeless. If Russia rules the world as victors, then no one can help us. But at the moment Russia is very strong. If peace is maintained for another year, while the other major powers are fighting each other, then neither Germany nor any other state will be able to defeat it. So we must, however terrible it may sound, almost hope that war breaks out between Germany and Russia, while hoping, of course, that we will be able to stay out of it.[234]

The speech, which is only known from a pro memoria inserted in Ryti's diary, has been granted huge importance and is often interpreted as an expression of the Finnish leaders' true hopes for the course of the war. The confrontations between Germany and the Soviet Union were wished to end in a Soviet defeat, but in the process Germany was to be crucially weakened. The latter has been seen as Ryti hoping that Great Britain in a 'second round' of the war, perhaps supported by the USA, would win over Germany or at least be able to achieve a compromise peace.

It is likely that Ryti actually hoped for something of this nature; like most Finnish businessmen and bankers at the time he was undoubtedly an Anglophile (in the sense that he was an admirer of British economic liberalism and the British Empire). But was it also what he expected? Probably not, because if so there would have been more indications of it.

There are not many signs that the Finnish leaders were preparing for or advancing a development reminiscent of the one described in Ryti's speech. Had that been the case, they would probably not have crossed the 1939 border and occupied East Karelia, since this action was bound to have a negative effect on the western powers. Furthermore, Mauno Jokipii warns his readers against putting too much into Ryti's speech at this governmental meeting: 'Because of the situation in which it was made, the speech should primarily be seen as an attempt to calm the left-wing faction of the government, who could easily be expected to go against the extended transit agreement as well as the mobilisation that had already started.'[235]

One-sided Inner Circle
The Finnish leaders seem to have had no other choice than to enter into a partnership with Berlin, but that is not to say that each and every one of them felt deeply uncomfortable about the situation. To put it perhaps a bit cryptically: you can be forced by circumstance to do something you actually want to do.

To understand this better we shall take a closer look at Ryti's inner circle and its closest advisers and representatives. The group consisted partly of professional soldiers (Mannerheim, Walden, occasionally Heinrichs and Talvela), partly pro-German politicians (Minister for Foreign Affairs Witting, Berlin ambassador and former Prime Minister Kivimäki etc.) and partly a group of people from the higher echelons of the financial world (Rangell, Ryti himself and others). Several belonged to more than one category. There were also some more loosely connected, distinctive and influential figures such as the strongly right-wing ship owner, business tycoon, lieutenant general in the army and fanatical supporter of the Greater Finland idea, Ragner Nordström.

Several of these people had experienced very serious if not traumatic confrontations with the Red Guard during the Civil War. To take but one example, Ryti had not personally participated in the conflict, but he had witnessed it at a short distance when his close friend, Alfred Kordelin (known as 'the richest man in Finland'), was shot by a Russian Bolshevik in 1917, after which Ryti himself had escaped along with his wife, Gerda. In the 1930s, Ryti was still known for his strong opposition to giving amnesty to former Red Guard members.[236]

Politically, ideologically and personally these influential men all had strong reasons to fear and hate Soviet Communism, probably more than the average Finnish person. Also, some of them had private financial interests of various kinds that could easily be incorporated into the coming military campaign. Several members of the clique held positions at the highest level in the paper and pulp industry, and East Karelia was full of forests ('our green gold' as the saying goes in Finland). The bankers and businessmen in the group were probably not entirely ignorant of the substantial nickel deposits on the Kola Peninsula. But there were other financial interests involved, too, such as those of Defence Minister Walden, who was hired by the Finnish state as an entrepreneur to build a prison camp for Soviet PoWs (the Valkeakoski Camp), which he did on such a tight budget that many of the prisoners froze to death, while the survivors were used as forced labourers at the minister's own nearby factory.

Even if we keep the political and moral aspects out of the discussion, it is striking that so many in the group had a special interest in seeing a German victory over the Soviet Union and must have found it either reasonable or advantageous (or both) if Finland participated actively. The only distinctive outsider was Väinö Tanner, but his case was critical in a different way, since Stalin and Molotov had more or less proclaimed him Moscow's Enemy No. 1 among the Finnish people. Besides, Tanner's political power was strongly reduced between August 1940 and the outbreak of the Continuation War (though he was still asked to participate in discussions on crucial issues),[237] and even after that his influence was limited, as we shall see later on, particularly in relation to the invasion of East Karelia.

To sum it all up: if against all expectation an alternative solution to the partnership with Berlin existed somewhere, or at least a scaled down version of it, then the members of Ryti's inner circle were hardly the people most prone to stumble across it. The tight security situation in Finland would have hampered the use of an alternative group, but arguably not so much that it was completely impossible. At least something of that kind should probably have been tried in order to diminish the violence and tragedy that would now inevitably befall the Finnish people, whose future unbeknownst to themselves had been firmly tied to that of Nazi Germany.

However, after December 1940 Ryti seems to have been convinced that Finland's only option was to fight a total war in a coalition with Adolf Hitler, and alternatives were not worth spending any time and energy on. In fact, the most obvious candidate for a leader of an alternative group, Paasikivi, was sent far away to a masquerade of negotiations in Moscow, while at home it was full speed ahead for the coming invasion in close cooperation with Berlin.

The Finnish Man in the Street
It was not the Finnish people who made the decision to enter into a partnership with Nazi Germany. According to the way the story was presented to the public, the Soviet Union had once again attacked Finland out of the blue by bombing several Finnish towns on 25 June 1941, although

Finland by the beginning of Operation Barbarossa, three days previously, had declared itself neutral in the war between the superpowers. This is worth bearing in mind no matter what one feels about the policies of the Finnish leaders during the Interim Peace.

For more than a year Finnish society had been under a heavy censorship which, among other things, blocked out criticism of Nazi Germany. The same should in principle have applied to the Soviet Union, but not only were such utterances allowed to slip through the censorship filter; they were in fact fabricated and distributed through various projects launched by the National Information Office.

This office had been set up in the summer of 1940 under Captain Kalle Lehmus and put out decidedly indoctrinating propaganda, often under false names and through publishing houses set up and secretly run by the office. As staff, some of Finland's leading authors were called up for this kind of 'National Intelligence Service'. Some of the inspiration for Lehmus' projects came from his visits to Joseph Goebbels's Ministry of Propaganda in Berlin.[238]

Meanwhile, the Germanophile circles in Finland had been able to freely organise and carry out comprehensive pro-Nazi campaigns. Those who understood Swedish or English, and who listened to foreign radio stations, had access to other news sources. But they were a minority, particularly outside of the upper classes.

This is a different discussion to the one about whether or not Ryti's inner circle acted appropriately. The important thing here is only to understand that the Finnish people had no idea as to what was really going on. Justifiably or not, their leaders managed to smuggle a disguised war in through the back door of the average citizen. In short, the dubious aspects of the chosen policy were kept hidden from the public, while the positive sides were praised.

Probably what enthused people most was the prospect of winning back the ceded areas. Not only would it be a well-deserved vindication for the Finns, it would also solve a string of otherwise almost impossible problems caused by the Moscow Treaty, such as ensuring that the massive numbers of refugees could return to their rightful homes. Furthermore, the Karelian Isthmus with its fertile land could make a serious contribution to the strained foodstuffs situation.

Over the years, both Finnish and non-Finnish historians have had problems coming to grips with the political and moral dilemmas presented by the Continuation War. Even in areas where the source-related smoke screen is less dense, images are often distorted by a confusion of emotional and practical features. Such a traumatic predicament on a national level is rarely solved through scientific work alone; rather it calls for high quality artistic interpretation. Even among professional academic historians in Finland there is a broad consensus that Väinö Linna's novel *Unknown Soldiers* is essential reading for anyone with even the smallest of interest in this part of Finnish history. The book does not present any cheap and easy solutions. Instead, it portrays the Continuation War as emotionally and politically complex as it really was, for example in the following scene that takes place a few days before the war begins:

> The situation was so out of the ordinary that the first section leader ventured a question that was actually rather out of line. The assignment they'd received hadn't been accompanied by any indication of why it was to be carried out, so Corporal Hietanen, boldly assuming a 'just between us' sort of air, asked, 'So, uh, where are we headed? The depths of hell, I guess?'
>
> Koskela glanced at the horizon and answered, 'I don't know. Those were the orders. I've got to get moving. You'd better hurry, too.'
>
> So that was all the men were to know of their fate. That being the case, they can be held only so responsible for it. But, anyway, they were very excited.[239]

PART THREE

THE CONTINUATION WAR

(25 June 1941 – 19 September 1944)

Finnish women carrying out field work during the height of summer 1941 shortly after the beginning of the Continuation War. (SA-Kuva)

I

Reconquests and More

For more than a year, a great proportion of the Finnish people had been quietly awaiting their moment of revenge, fists clenched in their pockets. There was real force behind the attack.
VÄINÖ LINNA[240]

Barbarossa Begins
On the night of 21 June 1941 an army of German and German-affiliated troops was deployed along the western side of an almost 3,000km long front stretching all the way through Eastern Europe, from the Black Sea in the south to the Barents Sea in the north. The force totalled some 4.3 million soldiers, 4,400 aircraft and 600,000 motorised vehicles.[241]

The middle sector of the formation consisted of the German main force, whose right flank had as its preliminary goal driving a wedge into the Soviet formations in the Ukraine. In the centre, the attack was aimed at Moscow. The task of the left flank was to push the Red Army out of the Baltic States and then attack Leningrad.

South of the German main force, Romanian troops stood ready to recapture Bessarabia. The northern sector was primarily covered by the Finnish Army, though its left flank, near the Arctic Ocean, consisted mainly of a German force.

In the early hours of the new day the attack started with a barrage from 6,000 artillery pieces. However, along the Finnish-Soviet border there was calm. The government in Helsinki even issued a statement announcing that Finland maintained its neutrality.

At 5:30 am local German time Minister of Propaganda, Joseph Goebbels, read over German radio Hitler's so-called *Barbarossa Proclamation*, in which the words 'Finland' and 'Finnish' appeared no less that thirteen times. The country was in particular mentioned towards the end of the proclamation:

German people! At this moment a deployment of forces is taking place that, in its extent and scope, is the greatest the world hitherto has seen. United with their Finnish comrades, the fighters of the victory of Narvik are standing in the Northern Arctic. German divisions commanded by the conqueror of Norway [General Dietl], together with the heroes of Finnish freedom under their marshal [Mannerheim], are protecting Finnish soil.[242]

The proclamation caused a minor panic among the Finnish leaders, who had worked so hard at toning down Finland's role in the overall scenario. Through the German ambassador Blücher they immediately made contact with Berlin and reminded the Germans of the agreement: Finland was not *yet* to be treated as a German ally (*Bundesgenosse*) in the war against Russia.[243] The text of the speech was then altered so it said instead that Finland was standing 'shoulder to shoulder with Germany and Romania in a united anti-Communist front.'[244] However, since the speech had already been broadcast that could hardly have made much difference.

Meanwhile, reports were coming in about Soviet air attacks on Finnish ships in the Finnish skerries and on one of the coastal fortresses. Foreign Minister Witting handed the Soviet ambassador to Helsinki a note in which the Finnish government protested against the attacks and reminded Moscow that Finland was upholding its neutrality. The Soviet ambassador justified the attacks by claiming that fourteen German planes launched from Finnish airfields had bombed Viipuri.

This was incorrect. But on the afternoon of the same day four German aircraft bombed the Soviet barracks camp at Hanko. Due to poor weather conditions the planes had been redirected from an operation towards Leningrad. When their bomb loads prevented them from landing, they had to jettison the bombs and decided it made sense to do so over Hanko. Also on the same day German aircraft mined the waters outside of Leningrad, and on their return they refuelled at the airfield at Utti. On board one of the planes was a Finnish liaison officer. Despite its repeatedly declared neutrality, Finland had in fact already actively joined the war on the German side.

The newly mobilised Finnish Army had so far been deployed in a defensive manner. Now the units were moved forward from camps and defence lines to the Russian border. Meanwhile, the Finnish high command relocated to Mikkeli, where Mannerheim on 25 June reinstalled himself in the headquarters he had also used during the Winter War.

It was now three days since the start of the German invasion of the Soviet Union, and in the afternoon comprehensive Soviet aerial bombings of targets on Finnish soil were carried out. Documents which have become public since the fall of the Soviet Union show that the targets were limited to airfields.[245] The main objectives were the airfields near Turku and

Joroinen, while smaller attacks were aimed at Malmi and Salänpää. But for various reasons the Soviet bombers failed to spot the Finnish airfields and decided instead to drop their bomb loads over nearby residential neighbourhoods.[246]

According to Soviet reports, forty-one enemy aircraft were destroyed during these raids while there were no Soviet losses. The Finnish war diaries (which are generally considered trustworthy) report that twenty-five to twenty-eight Soviet planes were shot down, while the Finns lost two aircraft.[247]

In the evening, the *Eduskunta* was summoned in Helsinki and it was announced that Finland due to Soviet attacks once again found itself at war with the Soviet Union.

Plans and Deployments

As soon as the war had become a fact, the Finnish Army started sending out patrols along the border and soon discovered that the enemy was doing the same. But so far both parties avoided confrontations and there were no signs of Soviet ground attacks being prepared. In fact, Red Army units were moved away from Karelia to participate in the fighting against the German invasion further south.

On 27 June Mannerheim assembled his general staff and presented it with his plans for the coming operations. It caused some surprise among the officers that the first attack was to be launched east of Lake Ladoga. They had expected an offensive on the Karelian Isthmus, directed first at Viipuri and then moving further south. But Mannerheim felt that the Soviet defence on the Isthmus was too strong at the moment. Also, it has been suggested that he was worried about carrying out operations that could be interpreted as direct Finnish participation in the German attack on Leningrad, since it could cause strong opposition internally in Finland and also damage the country's relations with the Western Allies.

The coming attacks needed to be tightly coordinated so on 29 June the marshal set up 'The Karelian Army', which gathered under one command IV and VII Corps along with the so-called Group O (consisting of a *Jäger* brigade and a cavalry brigade). Lieutenant General Heinrichs was appointed chief commander of the formation. On the same day the deployment of the Finnish Army was largely completed (for a more detailed description of the Finnish and Soviet deployments along the border see Appendix VIII).

The Finnish Army was considerably larger now than it had been during the Winter War, comprising some 475,000 men and 100,000 Lottas. Likewise, the high military budgets during the Interim Peace and the aid from Germany had expanded the striking power of the Finnish military considerably. The firepower of the infantry had tripled since the Winter War, while the artillery too had become considerably more effective and was supplied with huge amounts of ammunition. Tanks and other motorised vehicles remained somewhat of a rarity, but at that time it was still common to use horses and bicycles even in the German Army.

Another factor that had strengthened the Finnish Army's position considerably was that it no longer needed to worry about the Lapland area. This sector was now mainly covered by the German Army of Norway (*AOK Norwegen*) under General Nikolaus von Falkenhorst, the man behind the invasion of Denmark and Norway on 9 April 1940.

The Red Army too had been strengthened since the Winter War. Its General Staff had studied the German victories in Western Europe and had reorganised its own forces accordingly. Perhaps even more important was the technological development in weapons that had taken place, particularly in relation to tanks and aircraft.

The biggest new advantage for the Finns was of course that they no longer had to fight alone against the Soviet Union. The Russians were heavily involved in trying to repel the German main attack in Eastern and Central Europe and hence had only limited forces to use against Finland. During the following clashes the Finns therefore regularly managed to achieve numerical superiority at strategically important points, as exemplified by Olli Vehviläinen in his description of the Finnish offensive east of Lake Ladoga: 'In the main area of operations, the Finns had a four-to-one superiority in infantry and a nine-to-one superiority in artillery. They also had the advantage of being mobile in roadless terrain, which allowed them to penetrate deep behind enemy lines and attack from the rear.'[248] Even heavy weapons could be transported through roadless terrain and used to set up roadblocks that severed Soviet supply lines.

The Fighting in the Northernmost Areas

The German attack from Petsamo towards Murmansk was to be carried out by Mountain Corps Norway (*Gebirgskorps Norwegen*) under General Eduard Dietl. Further south in the Salla area was the German XXXVI Corps under General Hans Feige. This formation was to attack towards Kandalaksha and on the way sever the Murmansk Railway.

Between the two German corps was a 120km wide area covered by the Finnish Detachment Pennanen, which had been formed around a unit of professional border guards with their headquarters in the town of Ivalo. The unit was subordinated to Mountain Corps Norway and was referred to by the Germans as *Battalion Ivalo*.

The attack in the most northern sector started on 29 June but immediately ran into heavy resistance from the Soviets. The Germans had clearly underestimated the terrain-related problems and their preparatory work had been altogether insufficient. The planners had used poor and obsolete maps, misinterpreted telephone lines as roads etc. Dietl had warned Hitler in advance that the conditions in Lapland were not as the German General Staff seemed to think, but the Führer believed that Dietl ('the Conqueror from Norway') was a miracle man and hence he had ignored the warnings.

As Dietl started to realise that the situation was far worse than even he had feared, the Russians counterattacked directly and also carried out a landing operation behind the German lines. Mountain Corps Norway was forced to retreat. On 8 July its situation was so threatened that it had to request support from the Finns. Mannerheim then sent an infantry division to the area, a unit otherwise allocated to the defence of the Åland Islands. This stopped the German retreat, but even with Finnish support it proved impossible for the Germans to carry through any new attacks. Several attempts to penetrate the Soviet line along the River Litsa failed with heavy losses, and on 22 July the offensive had to be halted.

Later in the autumn, the Germans were forced to realise that the entire operation had been a failure, so they dug in and thus commenced a trench war that would continue all the way through to 1944. Ziemke concludes: 'In a two and one-half months' campaign, at a cost of 10,290 casualties, the Mountain Corps Norway had advanced about 15 miles. With respect to the attainment of its objective, Murmansk, it was not appreciably better off at the end of the campaign than it had been at the beginning.'[249]

Meanwhile further south, the attack towards Kandalaksha had started on 1 July, with the Finnish III Corps covering the right flank. However, the corps was not complete, as the 6th Division had been handed over to the German XXXVI Corps. The rest of the corps, which consisted of the 3rd Division and an attached German tank company, became directly subordinated to Army Norway from September onwards, so it is safe to say that the Finnish and German chains of command were tightly interwoven in the northern sector.

The attack on Kandalaksha started at midnight on 1 July, when the Finnish 6th Division crossed the border. It soon became clear, however, that one of the German units, *SS-Infanterie Kampfgruppe Nord*, was a weak link in the operation. The group was originally a police unit partly recruited from among concentration camp guards; the average age was high and the men had practically no combat training. Before long the unit was struck by panic and started running back through the corps' artillery positions.

The German 169th Division performed better, but the Soviets had positioned themselves very effectively around the small town of Salla. It took some heavy German artillery and air attacks before they abandoned the town on 8 July.

The Finnish 6th Division advanced faster than the German units, but it too was halted on 10 June by a Soviet counterattack and forced to retreat with heavy losses. General Feige then decided to strengthen the Finnish division with German troops, but the tough terrain prevented a new attack from being launched before 19 July. After that there was some progress. As the troops went forward they crossed the 1939 border, and on 31 August the formation's right flank was only 50km from Kandalaksha. The road ahead, however, was blocked by the so-called Verma Line, which turned out to be impenetrable and so the front became static here, too.

The commander of the Finnish III Corps, Major General Siilasvuo, was one of the most talented officers in the Finnish Army and his men were well acquainted with the Salla region. He now split his force into two groups and named them Group J and Group F. They both made an attack on the Soviet 54th Division and were considerably more successful than the units further north in the mainly German sector. The troops advanced quickly through the difficult terrain with its many lakes and after heavy fighting Group J captured, on 8 August, Kestenga Village some 75km east of the 1939 border. At this point the Red Army's 88th Division was brought in as reinforcement. It managed to halt Group J as well as Group F, which at the time was attacking Ukhta Village (today Kalevala) somewhat to the southeast.

The inadequate *SS-Infanteri Kampfgruppe Nord* was now added as reinforcement for Group J and new attacks were attempted, albeit unsuccessfully. Instead, the German High Command decided to move the centre of gravity to Group F for the next attack. This was launched on 30 October, when the Finns managed to encircle a Soviet regiment. The German High Command wanted Siilasvuo to continue his advance in the direction of the town of Loukhi, but he refused, claiming it was better to destroy the encircled Soviet regiment first.

This situation continued for the next few days until 13 November. Then, to the astonishment of both the German High Command and his own subordinate officers, Siilasvuo called off the rest of the planned attack. The decision seemed a mystery at the time, but it would later be revealed that he had received a secret order from Mannerheim. The marshal had recently been under heavy political pressure from the American government, who were angry that their aid to the Soviet Union via the Murmansk Railway was being interrupted (we shall return to this issue later on).

This has merely been a summarised description of the fighting in the northern sector of the Finnish Front. Is it impossible here to scrutinise all the battles and skirmishes of the Continuation War with the same degree of accuracy as we have used in relation to the Winter War. Only the early fighting in the areas north and east of Lake Ladoga, the Finnish 14th

Division's attack east via Reboly and the recapturing of the Karelian Isthmus will be described in more detail as examples of how much the style of combat had changed from the Winter War. The subsequent fighting and the abandonment by the Russians of Hanko will then be briefly described, following which we reach the final stage of the war in 1944, when once more it becomes necessary to delve into details. This approach is also reasonable considering that most of the in-between period comprised a relatively uneventful trench war.

The Fighting North and East of Lake Ladoga
On 29 June the first real fighting took place between Finnish and Soviet forces north of Lake Ladoga. The next day, the Finnish 2nd Division under Colonel Aarne Blick made an attack from the right flank and pushed the Soviet forces back. During the following days Finnish troops crossed the 1940 border at other points while preparing for the real offensive.

The instructions for the massive attack of 'The Karelian Army' were received by Lieutenant General Heinrichs on 9 July. The offensive was to begin the following morning. Its temporary goal was to drive a wedge into the Soviet forces north of Lake Ladoga and push forward to the town of Sortavala by the banks of the lake (Map 4).

VII Corps under Major General Woldemar Hägglund (the most southern corps of 'The Karelian Army', c.f. Appendix VIII) attacked straight ahead in the direction of Sortavala. The army's left flank was covered by Group Oinonen, whose main task was to secure the operation against attacks from the north. The centre of gravity was placed at VI Corps under Major General Talvela, with the army reserve right behind it.

Talvela received the order for the attack from Heinrichs in the evening of 9 July. Instead of waiting until the next day as prescribed in the instructions, Talvela ordered the commander of the 5th Division, Colonel Eino Koskimies, to get his men ready and launch an isolated attack. Koskimies started his men advancing, but in Talvela's opinion their progress was too slow so he dismissed the colonel and had him replaced. By doing that he disobeyed another of Mannerheim's orders, which stated that corps commanders could not sack their divisional commanders on their own initiative.

Once the main attack had started on the next day, the Finnish troops quickly captured the area around Tolvajärvi, famous for the fighting that had taken place there during the Winter War, and continued towards the north bank of Lake Ladoga. Together with the 11th Division, which attacked from the northwest under Colonel Kaarlo Heiskanen, the 5th Division trapped the entire Soviet 168th Division on the banks of Lake Ladoga, from where the Russians had to be evacuated by the Soviet Ladoga Fleet.

188 *Hitler's Nordic Ally?*

The Finns then continued their advance south along the east bank of Lake Ladoga, where a string of small towns and defensive positions were captured in quick succession. But the Soviet resistance was getting tougher all the time, as reinforcements were sent forward to the Seventh Army (the formation responsible for defending the area). A similar but even more difficult situation unfolded further north, where the left flank of the Finnish VI Corps became stuck and had to request reinforcements. These arrived but they were not enough, and meanwhile the advance along the lake continued, so there appeared a serious risk of creating an opening in the northern flank.

It was in this situation that Heinrichs decided to bring forward the German 163rd Division under Lieutenant General Erwin Engelbrecht, a formation belonging to the reserve. Engelbrecht was also given command of the Finnish forces in the area, i.e. VI Corps and Group Oinonen. The German general ordered the Finnish units to attack in three directions, but the Finns ran into severe Soviet resistance and their casualties soon became so high that Heinrichs stopped the operation, calling Engelbrecht's performance a 'scandal' and making it no secret that he was downright shocked over the German troop's inability to fight in forest terrain.

New reserves were sent forward to the centre of the formation, and a

A Group of Soviet PoWs, Sortavala 1941. (SA Kuva)

small advance took place helped by a flanking manoeuvre. Shortly after that the attack became stuck again, but in the meantime the deadlock on the northern flank had been broken and the Finns managed to capture a string of Soviet positions in the wilderness, until they stopped their advance on 20 July and dug in.

Engelbrecht's attempt at forest fighting had been so hopeless that Heinrichs decided to replace him. The new commander, the Finnish Colonel Heiskanen, launched a string of attacks on 21 July, one of which was supported by a cavalry brigade and resulted in the encirclement of a large group of enemy units. The Russians broke through the Finnish lines and most of them managed to escape, but still the Finnish troops along with the German 163rd Division had managed to take control over the area between Säämäjärvi and Sotjärvi, two lakes situated more than 100km east of the 1940 border.

After receiving further reinforcements, the Soviet Seventh Army launched a counterattack on 23 July. Though it was repelled, the Finns could not progress any further along the east bank of Lake Ladoga due to the danger of attacks on their northern flank at Tolvajärvi. Once more it proved impossible to control the rebellious Major General Talvela, who launched one attack after the other on Vitele, led from the front by himself. Even when he finally stopped on the other side of the town, it was only to request permission to continue. The Germans supported the idea, but Mannerheim said no. He was generally a careful leader and the situation at Tolvajärvi worried him. Furthermore, the Finnish supply lines were stretching through difficult terrain and had reached their temporary limit.

As mentioned, the more southerly deployed VII Corps under Major General Hägglund had been given the task of capturing Sortavala. Between him and his goal was the Red Army's 168th Division under Colonel Andrey Bondarev (the same unit that had previously escaped by water from a *motti* on the northeast bank of Lake Ladoga).

Again the defence was very tough and the Soviet troops could only be forced to retreat slowly. Not until 24 July did the formation turn east and start to approach Sortavala. Meanwhile, a Soviet marine infantry brigade was landed on Lunkulansaari, an island off the northeast bank of Lake Ladoga 60km from Sortavala. Finnish troops recaptured the island two days later, but at the same time the Russians carried out a new landing operation on the neighbouring island, Mantsinsaari. The next day the Finns recaptured this island, too.

The Russians kept launching counterattacks in the area around Sortavala. Soon only the Finnish left flank was moving forward, and even that was a slow advance. Eventually, reinforcements had to be called in from II Corps, which was deployed on the Karelian Isthmus (see Appendix VIII). On 8

August the 2nd Division under Colonel Blick managed to cut off the Soviet escape route to the south and force the Russian troops out towards the bank of Lake Ladoga. Then Blick's division pushed the Russians into the arms of the 19th Division, arriving from the west, which split the enemy force into a string of *mottis*. While they were eliminated, the Finnish 7th Division encircled Sortavala from the north.

The 7th and the 19th Division (the nucleus of VII Corps) were on 13 August transferred to the newly launched I Corps. The rest of VII Corps (a cavalry brigade and two *Jäger* Brigades) were sent down along the east bank of Lake Ladoga to support the Finnish advance in this area.

Sortavala was finally captured by the Finnish 7th Division on 15 August after an attack lasting more than twenty-four hours. But once again Colonel Bondelev managed to gather most of his force and escape by water, this time in makeshift vessels.

With this, the Karelian Army had reached its temporary goal which, as mentioned earlier, was to drive a wedge into the Soviet forces on the north bank of Lake Ladoga and thus separate the Red Army units on the Karelian Isthmus from the units in Ladoga Karelia. Only five days after the fall of Sortavala the entire area along the north bank of the lake and a considerable area along the eastern bank were under Finnish control.

14th Division

The Finnish Army's 14th Division, which was deployed some 300km north of Sortavala and which operated as a separate unit, had orders to attack in the direction of Rugozero village (named after a nearby lake) some 100km inside Soviet territory. After capturing the town of Reboly, the Finns continued according to the plan but were stopped by a Soviet counterattack on 12 July.

For a week the situation was static at this point, after which the Finns attacked again and forced the enemy further east. Forest fires and mined terrain hampered the advance more and more, as the Soviet resistance started growing in strength again. It culminated in a fierce battle, during which the Finns managed to neutralise the Red Army's 337th Infantry Regiment. The Soviet losses were 900 dead and wounded, plus a huge amount of equipment.

The Soviet troops now continued their retreat, burning down the forest behind them as they fell back. The weather was extremely warm. New clashes took place, including a failed Finnish pincer movement. After that the Russians withdrew from the fighting and retreated further east.

Holger Hørsholt Hansen, a Danish journalist working for Associated Press as well as for the Copenhagen daily broadsheet *Politiken*, was in a group of international press reporters who visited the area after the fighting.

In many places we pass by battlefields where bitter combat has taken place. In vast areas all the trees have been shot to pieces. Wrecked aircraft – Russian and Finnish – tanks, cars, machine guns are scattered around. Russian steel helmets and empty cartridge cases are piled up along the roads. In several places we find empty Russian vodka bottles with 40 per cent printed on the label along with the price, 5 Roubles and 50 Kopeks.

In other places, where the Russian Army has obviously kept its field kitchens, there are piles of empty tin cans and bits of food. Everywhere there are big craters in the ground from detonated landmines and shells. The little bridges over brooks and streams have mostly been destroyed and then rebuilt. Wrecks of fishing boats are lying on the banks of the lakes. In one place we saw a completely smashed up American car, a Ford, and a Douglas aircraft. In several other places we found wrecked machine guns of American or British origin, signs of the Allied aid to the Soviet Union.[250]

On 7 August an attack by the Finnish 31st Regiment was stopped by soviet resistance at an unnamed swamp west of Lake Rugozero. The first company of the Finnish 10th Regiment (sent out to support the 31st Regiment) arrived at the battlefield from the north and was ordered by its commander Captain Laisto to move forward through the swamp without artillery support. As a result, the company was practically wiped out. In the war diary of the 14th Division, the losses are entered as forty-six wounded, sixty men 'sent back', the remaining forty to fifty men killed or mutilated.[251]

The fighting around Rugozero village started on 5 September and was marked by tough Soviet resistance. Six days later, two Finnish *Jäger* battalions managed to penetrate in between the buildings. After that, the attacks continued for a few days until the Finns were forced to realise that the Soviet position was too strong. Instead, they entrenched themselves and remained in their positions up until the final stages of the war.

Lieutenant Dmitrii Krutshikh, who participated in the Soviet defence of the village, later said in an interview:

On 4 July the Finns started their attack in the direction of Reboly against the 337th Regiment's troops. My battalion was dispatched to help them. At first we all retreated up to the Rugozero [lake] where we stopped the enemy. The most terrible fighting was in the Andron Mountain area. We repelled up to eleven attacks a day! The losses were substantial on both sides. There, during a hand-to-hand fight, I received an injury in my eyebrow from a bayonet.

Scene from the Finnish advance on Reboly. (SA-Kuva)

It happened that the Finns crossed a river near our flank. We had to stop them or they would set up a bridgehead. So we launched an attack. As we left our foxholes and ran towards the river, the distance between us and the Finns was about 400 meters. The Finns ran towards us, and everyone met in a bayonet struggle – the most terrible kind of combat!

The troops were scattered so that many small groups were fighting here and there. I noticed two Finns running towards a Soviet soldier. I fired a shot – and one of the Finns fell over. A moment later I heard something stirring behind me but I didn't pay it any attention until a rifle butt hit me in the back of my head. I fell over but my rifle was still in my hand. I glanced back – a Finnish soldier was about to stab me with the bayonet attached to his rifle. I managed to evade a direct thrust: his bayonet just glided past my head, as I fired into his stomach. For several minutes my eyes were filled with blood – I couldn't see anything.

We pushed them back and recaptured our old trenches.[252]

The Recapture of the Karelian Isthmus

Deployed along the border on the Karelian Isthmus, in the western sector, was the Finnish IV Corps under Lieutenant General Oesch. East of IV Corps was II Corps under Lieutenant General Laatikainen.

Until late July these troops had been deployed in defensive positions and had been involved in a few minor skirmishes while they waited for the Karelian Army to finish its operations in Ladoga Karelia. According to the plan, II Corps was then to cross the border in the eastern sector of the Karelian Isthmus and capture the terrain around Hiitola Village 75km southwest of Sortavala (Map 5). After that the corps' right flank was to march south to the bank of the Vuoksi River, cross the river and head on further south towards the 1939 border with the aim of driving a wedge between the Soviet forces.

Meanwhile, IV Corps was to attack in the direction of Viipuri. Any Russians escaping from the area were to be stopped and neutralised by the units from II Corps who had crossed the Vuoksi River.

On 31 July, II Corps received the order to launch its offensive, even though Sortavala had still not been captured. 2nd Division, which covered the corps' left flank, attacked the railway into Sortavala with strong artillery support but found the Soviet resistance extremely tough.

A little further west, at the centre of the formation, the 15th Division under Colonel Niilo Hersalo also ran into hard Soviet resistance. The problem was exacerbated because the three regiment commanders were so eager that they messed things up and the attack lost its focus. As a result, the situation became static, communication broke down, and in the midst of it all the Finns called down artillery fire on their own positions, causing outbreaks of panic in several units. A regiment of the reserve was sent forward to join the fight, but lost its way and reached the battleground too late. Meanwhile, Colonel Hersalo managed to move troops from the flanks into the centre and thus create a centre of gravity.[253] In consequence, the Finns managed to penetrate the Soviet line on 3 August and create a 4km wide opening.

II Corps' western flank was 40km wide and was covered by the 18th Division under Colonel Aaro Pajari. Its centre of gravity was its left flank, whose task was to support the 15th Division's assault on Hiitola. After a massive artillery bombardment the 18th Division moved forward and captured Ilmee Village on 4 August.

While these clashes took place, the 10th Division under Colonel Aarne Sihvo managed to slip through the terrain between the 15th and the 18th Divisions. Sihvo's men had previously been part of the reserve but were now given the task of stopping any Soviet troops who might try to escape from the fighting around Hiitola.

Meanwhile, the 2nd Division (covering the left flank of II Corps) had problems advancing due to Soviet resistance and confusion related to the siege at Sortavala. Only after some heavy fighting did the Finns manage to cut the railway and reach Lake Ladoga, where they arrived on 8 August. After that the divisional commander, Colonel Blick, was ordered to turn

Finnish troops march on Hiitola. (SA-Kuva)

northeast and join the fighting around Sortavala, as described previously.

The Finnish tactics during this part of the campaign were primarily to attack the Russians frontally and at the same time outflank them and cut them off from the rear. This was one of the basic tactical options for attack in the Finnish manuals. By tying the enemy down at the front and simultaneously attacking him in the flank or the rear, you cut him off from his supply and/or retreat lines. In fact, the frontal attack was merely intended to keep the main bulk of his troops busy so they could not be transferred elsewhere. However, where the Russians were trapped on the shore of either Lake Ladoga or the Gulf of Finland, it was assumed that a full encirclement was unnecessary. Still, as it turned out, the Soviet troops were often able to flee by water.

There was particularly tough fighting between the 15th Division (centre) and the Russians inside Hiitola. Not until 11 August did the Finns manage to capture the village, after which the remains of the Red Army's 142nd and 198th Divisions fled in the direction of Kilpolansaari, an island in the skerries of Lake Ladoga. Here the clashes between the two Soviet formations and the Finnish 15th Division continued over the following days.

As mentioned earlier, the Finnish 18th Division (who covered the right flank of II Corps) had captured Ilmee on 4 August. After that the division was ordered to turn southwest and continue in the direction of the Vuoksi River. The Finns fought their way through the terrain over a 25km wide front, until the eastern bank of the river was reached on 12 August. Two days later, after some more tough fighting and heavy losses, they reached the town of Antrea 25km from the 1940 border, and the industrial district of Enso, which was encircled but not captured until later when IV Corps commenced its advance.

On his own initiative, Colonel Pajari started preparing to cross the Vuoksi River on the evening of 16 August. The operation was carried out over the next twenty-four hours, after which Pajari received an order to do what he in fact had just done. Meeting no resistance, the Finns established a 1km wide bridgehead on the west bank of the Vuoksi River. The manoeuvre turned out to be of great advantage for the follow up operations in the area.

Since the 15th Division had forced the Red Army's 142nd and 198th Division out on to Kilpolansaari in the skerries of Lake Ladoga, troops from these formations could no longer flee south on the Karelian Isthmus. Hence, the Finnish 10th Division, whose mission had been to stop such fleeing troops, was released from this task and instead ordered to advance to the town of Käkisalmi on the west bank of Lake Ladoga. On the way, the division was held up by Soviet counterattacks, but Colonel Sihvo managed to reverse the situation and trap the Russians in a pocket. Before it could be closed, however, some of the Soviet force had been evacuated by boat.

After two more days of heavy fighting, the 10th Division captured the town of Kiviniemi and subsequently Käkisalmi, which was being ravaged by heavy fires. The division then continued south along the bank of Lake Ladoga to the mouth of the Vuoksi River at Taipale, where it arrived on 23 August. On the same day the two Soviet Divisions on Kilpolansaari were evacuated by water.

On 13 August the Finnish IV Corps under Lieutenant General Lennart Oesch had received orders to launch an attack from the corps' left flank. The aim was to force the Soviet troops in the area in the direction of Vuoksi River.

On 20 August the Finnish Light Brigade T, which belonged to IV Corps but was temporarily on loan to Pajari's 18th Division, attacked the Soviet positions 25km due east of Viipuri (the Light Brigade T included a tank platoon equipped with OT-130 flame-thrower tanks captured in the Winter War and possibly a platoon of armoured cars or amphibious tanks; hence it is in some sources referred to as the Light Tank Brigade T). Again the Russians put up tough resistance. The battle raged all night, until the Finnish brigade finally gained the upper hand in the morning.

The Soviet tactic, which so far had been to stand fast and hold out, was now replaced by fighting retreats. Hence, when the attack of the Finnish IV Corps started in earnest on 21 August, it almost took on the shape of a

Wounded Finnish soldier is aided by comrade. (SA-Kuva)

pursuit. The area through which the Finns were fighting their way was heavily mined and full of obstructions, but by sunset they found themselves 15km inside Soviet territory. Meanwhile, the remaining resistance at Enso had been defeated.

During the night, troops from the Finnish 8th Division discovered that the Russians were abandoning their positions east of Viipuri, and so the next morning the pursuit was resumed. In the evening the division's vanguard was just 20km from Viipuri, while the main force had almost reached the Gulf of Finland over a broad front.

The day had turned out less lucky for the left flank, which was 20km wide and covered by the 12th Division. The roads were heavily overcrowded, halting the attack. The 12th Division needed something to restore its momentum so Lieutenant General Oesch asked the high command to hand him back the Light Brigade T. His request was granted, but the transfer could not take place until the following day (23 August) at noon.

At this point another example occurred of the Finnish commanders' inclination to take personal initiatives. Generally, Mannerheim not only allowed such conduct, he also encouraged it. Most of the time the principle worked well, as when Colonel Pajari singlehandedly decided to cross the Vuoksi River. At other times there were less positive consequences.

In this instance, Pajari ordered the commander of the Light Brigade T, Colonel Matti Tiiainen, to attack and capture Viipuri (in the overall plan this task was assigned to IV Corps, to which the Light Brigade T was subordinated, which was perhaps why Pajari felt the brigade should make an attack on Viipuri).

In addition to the order from Pajari, Colonel Tiiainen had been instructed by the high command to return to II Corps the next day. The choice he had seemed to be easy enough, since the first order was somewhat contradictory to the overall plan, and the second order was issued by a higher-ranking source. Nevertheless, Tiiainen chose to carry out *both* orders by first defeating the Russians at Viipuri and then returning to II Corps.

That, however, was not to happen. After two days of heavy fighting around Viipuri, the Russians launched a counterattack during which Colonel Tiiainen was seriously wounded. He died two days later and was replaced by Lieutenant Colonel Valter Nordgren.

By now the 12th Division had become unstuck and so it continued its advance south along the Karelian Isthmus and on 23 August was just 10km from Viipuri. Here, however, it was met by a powerful Soviet counterattack aimed at its right flank. The Finns were forced back 10km but managed over the following two days to stabilise the situation. On 25 August the division's vanguard reached Kämärä Village, 15km southeast of Viipuri. At the same time other units reached the northern bank of Muolaanjärvi, a lake 10km further to the southeast. On the same evening the 4th Division, which had been fighting its way through the terrain southwest of the 12th Division, reached a point 10km north of Viipuri.

The next day the right flank of the Finnish 8th Division was shipped across the Viipuri Bay and landed 10km south of the town. At the same time, the division's left flank marched on the town from the northwest. The Finnish encirclement of Viipuri and the three Soviet divisions inside it was tightening. Desperate Soviet attempts at breaking out were repelled. But the Finnish IV Corps was so exhausted it failed to close the ring completely, and on 28 August the main part of the Soviet 115th and 123rd Divisions managed to slip out through a 2 to 3km wide opening in the Finnish lines.

Only the remnants of the two divisions, along with the entire 43rd Division, were now left inside the town. These units were soon to be either defeated or taken prisoner, many of them in the fighting over the Porlampi *motti* east of Viipuri, as we shall see shortly.

On 30 August the Finnish Army paraded in front of Viipuri's historic castle. By then the town was in a terrible state. The fighter pilot Eino Luukkanen relates a visit he made to his former hometown by car shortly after it had been recaptured:

> Once across the border to which we had retired after the Winter War the scene became most disagreeable, desolation and destruction everywhere one looked ...
>
> Although I had lived in Viipuri I could hardly recognise the city. The superb railway station designed by Eliel Saarinen and claimed to have been the most beautiful in the whole of northern Europe was now a pile of rubble, and few buildings stood unscathed ...
>
> We wandered around among the ruins, climbing piles of rubble and peering into the buildings that remained standing, and throughout our sojourn in the city we saw no more than a dozen other people. Feeling thoroughly miserable, we continued on through Viipuri until we

Finnish victory parade in the badly scarred town of Viipuri. (SA-Kuva)

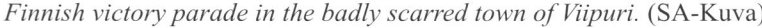

reached Sainio, where I had left much of my spare clothing and kit during the Winter War. Near the badly damaged hospital the horrible odour of burned human flesh assailed our nostrils, and we hastily turned away ...

Säiniä Railway Station and the Terijoki highway areas were jammed by the shattered remains of tanks, armoured cars, tracked vehicles and trucks, and it was with difficulty that we managed to edge our way through the tangled wreckage ... all that was left in this area, apart from the foundations of a large store, were corpses, the bloated carcasses of horses, heaps of ashes and mounds of debris.[254]

The Porlampi-*motti* was neutralised on 1 September. The Finnish war booty was enormous: 300 artillery pieces, 50 tanks, almost 700 trucks, 300 tractors and 4,500 horses. The number of prisoners exceeded 9,000. Among them was the commander of the 43rd Division, Major General Vladimir Kirpichnikov. The Finnish paramedic, Gunnar Bergström from the largely Swedish-speaking 24th Regiment, related how he was standing 1.5km southeast of Sommee railway station, enjoying the sunshine that had finally come out from behind the clouds after several days of rain, when some soldiers from another battalion approached, warning him that there were Russians in the forest next to the road.

> I immediately went into the forest and caught sight of two enemies lying there with rain ponchos pulled up over their heads. I pulled the poncho off one of them and saw to my amazement a living person looking up at me with staring eyes. He wore the insignia of a Major General and I immediately grabbed his hands and helped him stand up. I first took the general's 9mm Mauser pistol from him, then his thick map briefcase and finally his big canteen, which turned out to contain ¾ litre of vodka. Some of my comrades took care of the other officer, who was a lieutenant.[255]

The Danish newspaper reporter Holger Hørsholt Hansen saw the Porlampi *motti* shortly after the Soviet defeat:

> When I, along with a number of other foreign war correspondents, arrived at the battlefield, the Finnish troops were still occupied with the extermination of minor enemy groups who had slipped into the forest to continue the fighting from there. To arrive at such a theatre of war immediately after the fighting has ended – in this case it was the day after – is a terrible experience. Long before we reached the 6 square kilometre large area we were met by a choking stench. In

this *Motti of Hell* were not just individual soldiers, not tens or hundreds of them, but huge piles of mutilated and bloody corpses. Hundreds of dead horses added to the poisoning of the air. The sight was terrible and simply beyond description. Blown up bodies with intestines pouring out of big, gaping wounds, dead Russian and Finnish soldiers side by side in twisted positions, and terribly mutilated. The destruction was so complete it was hard to believe that this could take place in the year of our Lord 1941, in 'the century of culture and civilisation'. Brown, wrecked cars. The personal equipment of Russian and Finnish soldiers was lying in a mess on every square metre of ground along with cartridge cases and shell splinters. But the most terrible of all was the sight of the fallen soldiers, whose distorted faces spoke of the unbelievable pain they must have suffered. The bodies lay distended and black in the bright autumn sunshine, their arms reaching up to the sky in despair and empty eyes staring up through the tree tops towards the white clouds that sailed slowly across the firmament.[256]

The remaining operations on the Isthmus happened in quick succession. It was mostly what is described in military jargon as 'clean up missions'. The Finnish Army advanced on down the Karelian Isthmus, and by 2 September it had recaptured almost the entire area that had been ceded some eighteen months previously.

The overall military campaign had been a huge success for the Finnish military. Still, many things had not gone as well as expected. As this relatively rudimentary description has hopefully shown, the character of the fighting had been fundamentally different from that of the Winter War, much more than what can be ascribed to the weather conditions. The Finns were now the attackers, and the Russians were defending themselves. Though the Finnish Army was bigger now and far better equipped than during the Winter War, and though the Red Army was engaged over a broad front stretching all the way down through Eastern Europe, the Russians fought far more sturdily and effectively than in the previous conflict.

Some of the myths that had developed around the Finnish Army during the Winter War seemed to have gone to the heads of certain commanders, making them reckless. The Finnish high command came under criticism, too, particularly for having spread the troops too thinly on the southeast side of Viipuri. It was also pointed out that Colonel Tiiainen should have been stopped when he headed off with his brigade in the direction of Viipuri.

The Evacuation of Hanko
In the days after the outbreak of the war, the Finnish Army had encircled

the Soviet base at Hanko. There were artillery duels and skirmishes between patrols, but no real battles. The Finnish plan was to starve the Russians out of the base, even if they had to wait until the winter when the ice on the Gulf of Finland made it impossible to bring in supplies from Leningrad.

In the beginning, the Finnish force on the peninsula varied from 12,000 to 14,500 men, most of them belonging to the 17th Division. As it became clear that the Russians had no intention of attacking, Mannerheim transferred the division to the fighting north of Sortavala. Since then the Finnish force at Hanko really only consisted of the 55th Regiment (left behind from the 17th Division) some coastal defence groups and a Swedish volunteer battalion, which had been set up in August, and which also contained a group of Danes.

The Soviet force initially consisted of two infantry brigades and some engineer, railway, artillery and anti-aircraft units. Also there was an artillery battery of 305mm railway guns, for which they had constructed a railway line that ran between two artillery firing positions. Additionally, they had built an airfield from where they operated mainly fighter aircraft.

Since the Germans had overall control of the Baltic Sea and the Gulf of Finland, the main purpose of the Soviet presence at Hanko had disappeared, but it was thought in Leningrad that the Soviet troops on the peninsula tied

The Danish Lieutenant Jørgen Hagemann, killed during the fighting at Hanko in the summer of 1941. (SA-Kuva)

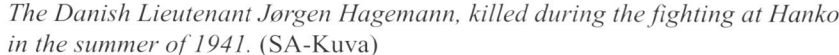

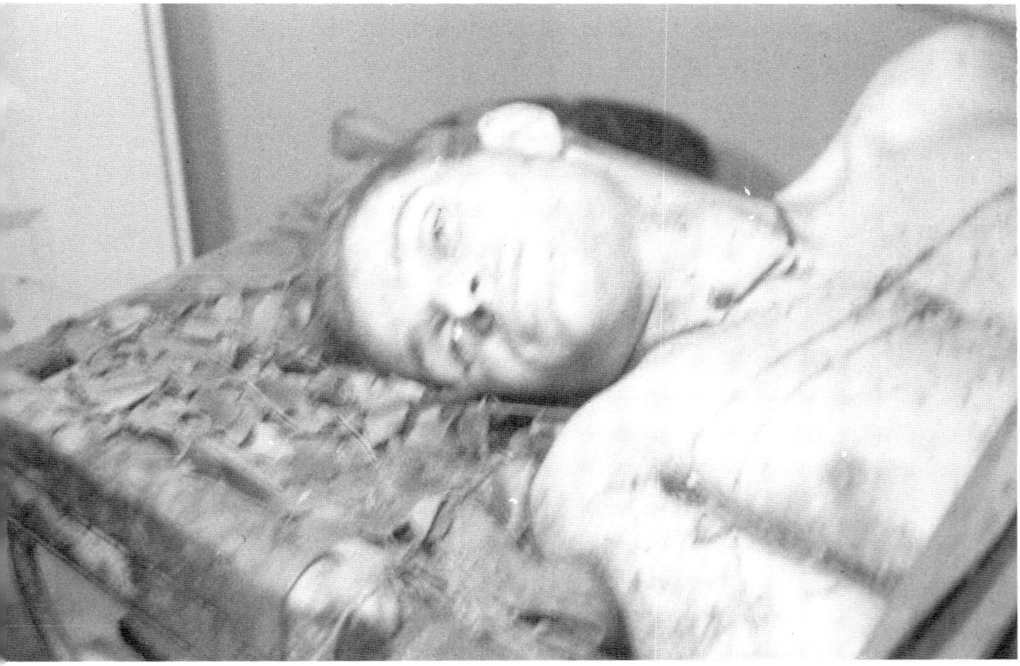

down a far bigger Finnish force than it actually did, so only a small evacuation was carried out during the autumn. However, the mining in the Gulf of Finland, combined with the threat from Finnish and German submarines, made it problematic to supply the base from Leningrad. Hence, from late October onwards the evacuation was stepped up considerably. It soon developed into a struggle against the clock, since the waters around Finland by now had started freezing up.

In the last convoy, which left Hanko on 3 December, was the big passenger ship *Josef Stalin*, whose fate is described in a document found in the Soviet archives:

> The ship participated in the evacuation of Hanko naval base and had on board 5,589 people. After it had passed Kronstadt as part of a convoy, three mines detonated and the ship was exposed to considerable damage (stern and storage room No 3). Afterwards, it was hit by a 12 inch shell when Finnish coast batteries fired at the convoy. The vessel began to sink. Despite the dangerous situation, minesweepers 205, 211, 215, 217 and five patrol boats managed to pull 1,740 people out of the water. After the water level had reached the deck, the ship stopped sinking, and it was escorted to Lohusalu on the Estonian coast where it ran aground. The survivors were taken prisoner [by German troops].[257]

The next day, the Finnish troops captured Hanko. The Swedish volunteer battalion had the honour of hoisting the flag on the partly burned down mayor's office. The few groups of Red Army soldiers who had been left behind soon surrendered. Also, there were 500 Estonian forced labourers in the camp. The majority later returned to their homeland, while the rest joined a regiment of Estonian volunteers in the Finnish Army.

Prior to the evacuation, the Russians had filled the harbour entrance with trucks, tractors, tanks, guns, locomotives and goods wagons.[258] In fact, huge amounts of materiel had been left behind all over the peninsula, but it was extremely dangerous for the Finnish and Swedish soldiers to remove it. The area was studded with mines, in total more than 50,000, and while clearing them the troops suffered losses in both dead and wounded.

The East Karelian Offensive

I Corps had primarily been set up with the purpose of capturing Sortavala. As soon as that had been achieved, the corps was reduced in size. The 2nd Division was again placed under II Corps and participated in the fighting on the Karelian Isthmus. The 7th and the 19th Division were returned to VII Corps and 'The Karelian Army', which was still commanded by Lieutenant

General Heinrichs, with Talvela and Hägglund as corps commanders and Engelbrecht's German division attached. Henrik O. Lunde writes: 'Up until this point, the Finns had basically recaptured territories taken from them during the Winter War. While their forces had crossed the pre-1940 border [= the 1939 border] in some places, particularly in Ladoga Karelia and the area west of Seg Lake [Segozero], those incursions into pre-1940 Soviet territories could be justified on military grounds as providing flank protection or as an attempt to obtain positions better suited for defence. This all changed with the commencement of what is commonly referred to as the East Karelian offensive, in September 1941.'[259]

Like many others, Lunde is of the opinion that the Finnish war effort now changed from being a justifiable recapturing of the territories ceded after the Winter War to becoming a campaign of conquest. We shall take a closer look at this argument later on.

What had happened was that the head of the Wehrmacht's high command, Field-Marshal Wilhelm Keitel, on 22 August had sent Mannerheim a message, partly to suggest how a joint Finnish-German siege of Leningrad could be carried out. Much to the surprise of the Germans, the Finnish reply was far from enthusiastic.

Mannerheim complained that the war was far too taxing on Finnish society, with 16 per cent of the population now carrying out work solely related to the war effort. Besides, the Soviet defences on Leningrad's

Finnish troops fighting in the village of Nurmoylitsy (Finnish name: Nurmoila) during the invasion of East Karelia.

Finnish tanks file past the commander of the army of Karelia, Lieutenant General Heinrichs, after the occupation of Petrozavodsk, now renamed in Finnish Äänislinna. (SA-Kuva)

northern outskirts were very strong, and the Finnish Army did not have sufficiently long-ranging artillery to carry out a siege of the kind suggested by the Germans. An invasion of East Karelia down to the River Svir remained on the Finnish agenda, but beyond that Mannerheim felt that increased Soviet resistance would make it extremely difficult to continue.[260]

The marshal did not have the final word in these matters, though, and the discussion had already been taken up in the cabinet. Unfortunately, the lack of sources once again makes it difficult to determine exactly who was of what opinion, but at least it is clear that a German victory was still taken for granted. As Vehviläinen puts it: 'In Finland, it was expected that Leningrad could fall any day.'[261] Hence, the Finnish leaders had some very good reasons to hold back in relation to Leningrad and let the Germans do the hard work. Such a policy would ease the pressure on Finland's own military forces and the resources of civilian society, and it would limit the damage to the country's reputation in the eyes of Great Britain and the USA. Participation in the planned German massacre of the entire population of Russia's second largest city would also damage Finland's relationship with its mighty neighbour for many generations to come. Furthermore, a Finnish participation of the kind the Germans requested would once and for all bury the already fragile myth that the country was waging a separate war.

The Germans were equally convinced that they could crush Leningrad alone, so the parties settled on a compromise. The Finns then advanced a short distance across the old border on the Karelian Isthmus until they were some 20km from Leningrad; but they were not meant to attack the city. Meanwhile, the Finnish offensive from Ladoga Karelia into East Karelia, across the 1939 border, started on 4 September 1941. The right flank of the offensive was aimed at reaching the Svir. In the centre the aim was to capture the capital of East Karelia, Petrozavodsk, on the west bank of Lake Onega. With regard to the left flank, the aim was to reach and capture the town of Medvezhyegorsk at the northern point of the similarly named lake.

The task of capturing the Olonets district (the southern part of East Karelia) was given to Major General Talvela. His corps had been reinforced by the newly formed Armoured Division under Colonel Ruben Lagus. The troops advanced quickly across the old border, and just three days later Talvela stood on the bank of the River Syvari (Svir). His men had by then advanced 70km in only three days (Map 4).

Still, the struggle had just begun. The fighting continued through the following month, until VI Corps finally gained control over the sector and could establish the so-called Svir Front.

The Finnish offensive was by then running out of steam, and the troops were becoming more and more insubordinate the further they were ordered to march into Russia. Still, Talvela felt the campaign should be continued

Finnish troops during combat at the River Svir. (SA-Kuva)

and so he asked Lieutenant General Heinrichs for permission to cross the Svir and set up a bridgehead on the south bank of the river. Permission was granted, but the first battalion that was ordered to cross the river refused to obey. The next battalion refused, too. Finally, on 6 October one unit crossed the river to the other side where it met with surprisingly weak resistance. Before long the Finns had set up a 100km wide and 20km deep bridgehead and had started to build defensive positions.

In the meantime other Finnish units had crossed the Svir, as well, but they met with strong resistance, particularly from the Soviet 144th Division, which had just arrived in the area. This Siberian elite unit penetrated the Finnish positions at several points in extremely bloody and chaotic combat. The situation was dragging out as winter was setting in, and it had become early December before a relative calm descended on the sector.

At this point Talvela's Corps was strongly reduced in size, and the surviving soldiers were completely exhausted after six months of constant fighting. Apart from the aforementioned episodes bordering on mutiny, there had been regular desertions and two soldiers had been executed, a form of punishment to which Talvela vehemently subscribed.

The operations into the area south of the River Svir have for many years been seen as mere attempts to secure the positions of the Finnish forces north of the river. However, research in more recent years has pointed in

Two Finnish soldiers, sentenced for severe disobedience or desertion, are executed by firing squad. (SA-Kuva)

another direction. A doctoral thesis from 2009 by Mikko Karjalainen at Helsinki University shows that plans existed for a continuation of the campaign further east, and judging from their presentation they were more than just theoretical projects. 'There is clear indication that the Finns would have attacked much further east had a German success made such an attack possible,' Karjalainen writes.[262] Hence, it seems reasonable to assume that the Finnish attacks in the area south of Svir had a scouting function in relation to the plans of carrying on the invasion in case of a German victory at Leningrad.

Somewhat further north, the centre formation of 'The Karelian Army' had meanwhile continued towards Petrozavodsk. The tactics employed consisted of exhausting flanking attacks through the wilderness instead of charging the enemy head on. But Soviet morale was high, and gradually the troops became better at finding ways to counteract the Finnish tactics. During five weeks of fighting, the Soviet 3rd Division managed several times to break out of traps, and the formation finally reached Petrozavodsk in good shape.[263]

The town was under siege from 30 September until 2 October, when it was captured by the Finns. As shown in a Finnish propaganda newsreel, the official name of the place was changed to Äänislinna and it was proclaimed as having now become a part of Greater Finland.

After the capture of Petrozavodsk, Heinrichs concentrated the activities of 'The Karelian Army' on its left flank, i.e. in the direction of Lake Onega and Lake Segozero. Despite tough Soviet resistance the area came under Finnish control on 8 December, as Soviet troops fled across the frozen estuaries at the northern end of Lake Onega.

Minelaying in the Baltic Sea
The commander-in-chief of the German *Kriegsmarine*, Grand Admiral Raeder, had from the start been against the invasion of the Soviet Union. He had even handed a report to Hitler, in which he advised against the campaign. His views, however, were ignored.

Hitler's plan was to push ahead as hard as possible from the very first day of the offensive, not just on land but also at sea. All Soviet vessels in the Baltic Sea had to be attacked, while German and Finnish submarines were to lie in wait outside the harbour entrances. The Gulf of Finland had to be very closely mined, but the mines were to be removed again after the Soviet Baltic Fleet had been destroyed, so the German iron ore imports from Sweden were not disturbed. Raeder had on 17 March signed a directive to meet these demands, and the Finnish naval commanders had subsequently been informed about the German plans.

Unlike the army, the Finnish fleet had not expanded particularly during the Interim Peace. Hence, it was decided to concentrate its efforts on minelaying and participation in the siege of the Soviet base at Hanko.

We have already looked at the first Finnish minelaying operations in the Gulf of Finland (p. 163). Whilst they were taking place, the naval command in the Gulf of Finland was ordered to lay out six barrages in Finnish territorial waters, starting on the night before 22 June.

The first phase of the German minelaying operation commenced a few hours later and was meant to prohibit a Soviet presence in the waters between the Soviet main bases in Liepāja (in western Estonia), Hanko, Tallinn and the Kotlin Island. Also, vast minefields were laid between Öland (off the southeast coast of Sweden) and the Lithuanian seaport of Klaipeda, and across the mouth of the Gulf of Finland. The minelaying carried out by the Finnish Navy took place from a point further east and stretched partly along the Estonian coast, partly across the gulf to the Finnish coast.

The Soviet Baltic Fleet also laid mine barriers by the mouth of the Gulf of Finland and later in the eastern waters of the gulf. Furthermore, many smaller minefields were laid in the entries to estuaries in the Finnish skerries.[264]

Soon the minelaying almost developed into a competition between the parties. The night before 23 June two Soviet vessels started laying 300 anchored mines and nearly twice as many anti-sweeping devices between Hanko and Osmussaari, an island 5km north of the Estonian coast. To protect the naval base in Tallinn another 500 mines were laid in a straight line starting from Naissaari, an island northwest of Estonia.

Initially these operations were carried out as discretely as possible, but after Finland had officially joined the war on 25 June the actions became more visible. On 26 June two newly acquired Finnish vessels laid 200 mines southeast of Hanko. The next day a similar number of mines were laid in the waters southeast of Osmussaari, and on the night before 30 June some 200 mines were laid in the waters off the Juminda peninsula on the north coast of Estonia.

The above have just been a few examples of the many minelaying activities that took place in the northeast waters of the Baltic Sea area by the start of Operation Barbarossa. Within two weeks Finland was practically cut off from the rest of the Baltic Sea.[265] By the mouth of the Gulf of Finland 5,200 mines were laid, while the waters around the Estonian islands were full of German magnetic mines.

One Finnish minelaying operation led to a particularly high number of Soviet losses during the evacuation from Tallinn on 27-30 August 1941. The Germans and the Finns had foreseen this event and had therefore since mid-July resumed the minelaying, which had otherwise been stopped temporarily.

The evacuation from Tallinn was carried out by 160 vessels which took on board 28,000 Soviet soldiers with 66,000 tons of materiel. On 28 August, as the convoy sailed through the closely mined waters off the coast of Juminda, it was also exposed to violent German air and artillery attacks. Sixty-six ships were sunk and many others damaged, while more than 12,000 people lost their lives.

As shown in the above, the Finnish-German naval operations in the Baltic Sea were closely coordinated and took place partly outside of Finnish territorial waters.

The Air War of 1941
The Finnish air force, like the navy, had not been expanded anywhere near as much as the army since the Winter War. Waging an aggressive war on a larger scale in 1941 generally included the use of bomber aircraft, but the Finns only had some twenty machines of that kind, mainly of the Bristol Blenheim type (a light bomber), plus eight Soviet planes they had captured during the Winter War. The number of fighter aircraft varies depending on which source you look at but seems to have been in the region of 150. Also, there were a few reconnaissance aircraft etc. Most of the aircraft were obsolete. Among the exceptions were some American Brewster Buffalo fighters. Since it was a highly inconsistent collection of machines there were communication problems, both between the aircraft and with the ground, as well as many other technical problems.

The Soviet air attack on Finland on 25 June has already been mentioned. The big differences in Finnish and Soviet losses during these clashes underlines a tendency that would continue throughout the Continuation War, and which had already been present in the Winter War: while the Finnish pilots made the best of their limited resources, the Russians had a colossal advantage materially which they failed to utilise.

'The Karelian Army' had at its disposal a total of thirty-four reconnaissance and seventy fighter aircraft. During the offensive into Ladoga Karelia the area was ravaged by huge forest fires, with smoke rising up to a height of 3km. As a result, the Finnish pilots in some cases attacked their own forces by mistake, so a ban was introduced against shooting at ground targets. The smoke made young pilots in particular lose their way; the older ones knew the area from the operations during the Winter War. At least it was less cold now inside the machines, but the temperatures could still go down to freezing, while on the ground it was the height of summer with temperatures up to 30 centigrade. Another problem was that the Italian Fiat planes in particular, of which there were a few, only had a very short range, which was badly suited to the wide landscapes in which the fighting took place.

210 Hitler's Nordic Ally?

Only a single Finnish squadron covered the fighting on the Karelian Isthmus. Here bombers would undoubtedly have been used if they had been available in sufficient numbers. But the few Finnish bomber squadrons were soon hit by serious losses, so strategic bombing was avoided and instead the planes were used for long distance reconnaissance tasks.

Though the loss of Finnish fighter aircraft was much less than the corresponding Soviet losses, the Finnish air force was simply too small to carry out even remotely efficient reconnaissance surveillance of the long front sectors and supply lines.

In total, the Finnish air force shot down 356 Soviet aircraft during 1941. Their own loss was eighty-four machines. The Finnish air force losses in personnel were seventy-five dead and thirteen wounded.[266]

II

Crossing the Border

*A free Karelia and a great Finland emerges before our
eyes from the mighty confusion of great historic events.*
CARL GUSTAF MANNERHEIM[267]

The Karelian Question
A wave of nationalism swept through Europe from the first half of the nineteenth century onwards, and with it followed a need for many people to define themselves as national entities. For this purpose, cultural, linguistic and geographical factors were often used.

It was a period where the power of the aristocracy was gradually being reduced, as democracy started gaining a foothold. Attached to this was the idea that, throughout history, those in power had been wheeling and dealing with the destinies of common people when wars were waged and borders drawn. In some regions this led to revolts and demands for secession and independence. In other places it was felt that people who naturally belonged together had been separated, so movements evolved that demanded a reuniting of such peoples into nations, as can be seen in, for instance, Scandinavism with its attempts to bond Denmark, Norway and Sweden more closely together.

Along with this emerged an interest in the art and culture of the common people. Folktales were collected by scholars of local traditions. The Brothers Grimm is a classic example. Hans Christian Andersen did not collect folktales but nevertheless based some of his stories on traditional, popular storylines and plots. Composers delved into folk music looking for the kind of ear-catching and enticing musical themes that no amount of studying at a conservatoire can teach anyone to write. There were no fixed frames; it was allowed to add one's own material and to fill out any holes. Authenticity meant less if only the result inspired the right feeling of national identity.

Around that time the Finnish Doctor Elias Lönnroth exercised his profession in Kajaani, an area in the eastern part of mid-Finland. From there he went on a string of field trips across the border into East Karelia to collect epic poems, for which there existed a particularly rich and dramatic tradition in this region. Because Finland since 1809 had been an autonomous duchy under the Russian Tsar, and East Karelia was a part of Russia, it was relatively easy to move back and forth across the border. With the inclusion of some personal creativity, Lönroth managed to piece together the *Kalevala*, an epic poem that has been described as a Finnish pendant to the *Iliad* and the *Nibelungenlied*. The *Kaleva* was first published in 1835 and in an extended version in 1849.

The work represented a popular artistic tradition that was dying out in Finland but had survived in East Karelia, and the publication heralded a strong wave of national consciousness in Finland. The Karelian population, who had previously been regarded as 'backwards', was now for the very same reason considered more 'genuinely Finnish' than people were in Finland itself. Well-to-do and learned individuals went on long journeys east of the border to experience the ancient lifestyle that had made it possible for this oral tradition to survive.

Over the years, Karelianism gradually developed and divided into two factions, a cultural and a political one. The latter incorporated the ambition of creating an empire of all the so-called Finno-Ugric tribes, of which there existed a considerable number around the Urals and the Volga River and further onwards in the direction of Siberia (hence the slogan of the most fanatic political Karelianists: 'Finland to the Urals'). A state of that kind was regarded by most Finns as utopian. Still, high-ranking scientists at Finnish universities showed an interest in researching these remotely related peoples.[268]

Linked to this wave of Finnish national consciousness was also the long-standing struggle against the privileged status of the Swedish language in Finnish society. It was common for patriotic Finns with Swedish names to change them to Finnish names. (For instance, Juho Kusti Paasikivi had been baptised Johan Gustaf Hellstén. Paavo Talvela's family name was originally Thorén, and so on. However, Swedish surnames were often not a sign of Swedish ancestry but could just have been adopted from a Swedish nobleman for whom a family member had once worked as a servant.)

The relatively open border between Finland and East Karelia meant that goods could be traded almost freely, and there were mixed marriages between people from either side. These contacts came naturally and needed no ideological or historical justification. If there were any cultural barriers, they were primarily of a religious nature. Finland was protestant, East Karelia was Russian Orthodox.

The outbreak of the Finnish Civil War in 1918 revived the interest in the Karelian and Greater Finland cause. Shortly after Mannerheim had been appointed commander-in-chief of the White Guard, he proclaimed on 23 February 1918 (in an order-of-the-day also known as *Mannerheim's First Sword Scabbard Proclamation*):

I will not sheath my sword before law and order reigns in the land, before all fortresses are in our hands, before Lenin's last soldier is driven not only from Finland, but from East Karelia as well.[269]

The Civil War was immediately followed by more-or-less state-subsidised military expeditions into East Karelia, referred to as the *Heimosodat* or 'Kinship Wars', with the purpose of encouraging the local population to revolt against the Russian Bolshevik rulers. Any successes, however, were very limited. The romantic feelings that people in Finland held towards the East Karelians were only reciprocated to a very small degree. What the East Karelians really wanted (in so far as they had the time and energy to pursue any wishes beyond what day-to-day survival demanded in these deserted and harsh northern regions) was independence from both Finland and Russia: to become a Karelian republic.

Likewise, none of the other so-called 'Fennic' people, except for the Estonians, seem to have had much notion of the kinship to which the Finnish nationalists were referring and whose members they had designated themselves to gather and lead. Furthermore, although the political Karelianists' were undoubtedly sincere in their worry over the poor state of their kinsmen in East Karelia,[270] it was a selective and patronising form of humanism that only included people of a certain 'race', and only if they subjected themselves to the ideology of their self-proclaimed liberator.

In this and several other areas the political Karelianism of the 1920s had parallels in Nazism, but a stronger relationship between the two movements was unlikely to occur. According to Nazi race theories, the Finno-Ugrian tribe was a mixed race with a non-Indo-European language,[271] and therefore the Finns could not be seen as real Aryans.[272] So the Karelianists were left to invent their own race theories, and in doing so they found support from scientists and other influential people (just as the Nazis did in Germany). These factors later became important for the Finnish administration of East Karelia, where academic research took place in a relationship tightly interwoven with expansionist and economic interests.[273]

Another similarity between political Karelianism and Nazism appeared in the way both movements used a patchy and partly self-invented mythological basis. In Nazism it was the notion of an Atlantis from where the Aryan race originally came (a partly distorted remake of the quasi-religious theories of the German-Russian occultist Helena Blavatsky). In Karelianism the legend concerned Karelia.

'Karelia is in many ways remote,' writes Outi Fingerroos, professor of Ethnology at Jyväskylä University. 'In fact, Karelia across the border is an imagined place: an abstract utopia, with which Finland … has obsessed itself from the late nineteenth century onwards.'[274]

The Greater Finland infatuation had its heyday in the decade after the Civil War, led by the student organisation *Akateeminen Karjala-Seura* (The Academic Karelia Society), often just referred to as the AKS. It was a very powerful organisation with many influential and long-standing members. While it would be wrong to call it a Fascist organisation, many of its members were sympathetic to right wing extremism, even to National Socialism.[275] Outi Fingerroos continues: 'AKS became a major ideological force among young Finnish university graduates.'[276] This exclusive academic society was from the mid-1930s onwards led by Vilho Helanen, a self-declared admirer of Adolf Hitler. Besides its general tendency to the right, the AKS had tight bonds to the Lapua movement and later on to the IKL.

During the Finnish-Russian border negotiations in 1920 in the Estonian town of Tartu, the Finns tried hard to unite Finland with the lands of East Karelia, but the Russians would not allow this. For them it was, as always, primarily a matter of securing Leningrad and the railway to Murmansk, but besides that they had their own ambitions in relation to East Karelia, inspired by the many former Finnish members of the Red Guard who had fled into the area and now lived there permanently. These people had read the *Kalevala*, too, and were romantically inclined towards the region, which they had earmarked as the primary base for a new Red revolt in Finland, followed by a unification of the two areas into one Socialist state.[277]

In the mid-1930s, however, many Finnish Communist expatriates became victims of Stalin's purges, which hit the Soviet peripheral regions particularly hard. Some 15,000 people of 'Fennic' origin are estimated to have perished for that reason, but in fact the number could be up towards 30,000.[278] In addition, many more were deported to other regions of the Soviet Union.

The main hero and martyr of the AKS was Hans Håkon Christian Sivén, better known by his nickname of 'Bobbi'. Sivén's enthusiasm for the establishing of a Greater Finland (*Suur-Suomi*) went so far that, in 1921, he shot himself dead in protest against the outcome of the border negotiations in Tartu. He was 21 years old. Mannerheim was present at his funeral and laid down a wreath. Every year on the anniversary of the Tartu Agreement, the AKS held a march to 'Bobbi' Sivén's grave in protest against the demarcation of the border.

The AKS initiation ceremony included kissing the flag of the society, into which was sown the bullet that had killed Sivén. Then the candidate would swear the fraternity oath:

> Under the flag of our society I swear, by all that is holy and dear to me, to sacrifice my work and my life for my motherland, to the

benefit of the national awakening in Finland, Karelia and Ingria [p. 258], Greater Finland. For as much as I truly believe in one great God, I also believe in a Greater Finland and its glorious future.[279]

In its most ambitious incarnation the dream of a vast Finnish nation stretched from the Gulf of Bothnia in the West (including bits of northern Sweden and Norway) to the Ural Mountains in the east and southwards to include Estonia in the Baltic States.

It would not be far wrong to say that the original Karelianism had been kidnapped and turned into a key political issue for the far right. This had a negative effect on its popular support up through the 1930s. Other factors played a part, too, for example that East Karelia experienced a vast immigration of Russians, not all of them voluntary immigrants (particularly in relation to the building of the White Sea Canal) and the consolidation of the Communist regime in the Soviet Union. It was simply no longer seen as realistic to embrace ambitions of a Greater Finland, and with that public support shrank, though the movement still had supporters even among Social Democrats.

It is unclear how much the Finnish-German military cooperation from the start was planned as a springboard for a Finnish invasion of East Karelia, but at least the issue presented itself along the way. President Ryti and his inner circle seem to have felt that Finland might as well profit from the situation as much as possible, since the decisive step was now taken. Hence, when the Continuation War broke out, political Karelianism received a fresh impetus.

Mannerheim's Second Sword Scabbard Proclamation
Like many other military commanders throughout history, Marshal Mannerheim had a certain partiality for writing grandiloquent orders-of-the-day. This particularly came to the fore in his proclamation issued on 10 July 1941, i.e. at the launch of the grand campaign of the 'Karelian Army' where he partly referred to the promise he had made on his appointment as commander-in-chief in 1918 (p. 213).[280]

When the draft for the proclamation had been received at the National Information Office (p. 176) on the previous day, the censorship department had immediately noticed certain phrases of a kind that would normally be omitted from official statements. Still, it was entirely out of the ordinary to delete anything from an order-of-the-day written by the commander-in-chief, so a couple of telephone calls were made, the first one to Defence Minister Walden and the second one to President Ryti. The proclamation was read aloud to each of them, after which they were asked for their opinion. Both men decided it was best not to intervene (although Ryti is said to have sounded worried), and so the order-of-the-day was issued without alterations.

Since Finland was still under heavy censorship, the proclamation did not at first cause any major discussions internally in the country. The Social Democrat press carefully expressed the view that the East Karelians should be allowed to choose their own future, while the Conservative newspapers were pleased with Mannerheim's declaration and, moreover, reminded their readers that the Finns had fellow tribesmen off in the areas surrounding Leningrad who were yearning for freedom, too.

Then followed a discussion about Finland's true war goals; but it was a subdued debate. Public opinion only started to get agitated when the Swedish press picked up on the matter, and from there criticism spread to Britain and the USA.

Mannerheim's Second Sword Scabbard Proclamation has since been the subject of much discussion in Finland. It has been said that it cannot be taken as an official expression of the Finnish war goals, since Mannerheim was not an elected politician and therefore could not speak on behalf of the Finnish state. That is formally true, of course, but it is also to neglect the status that the marshal truly had both at home and abroad, and which he should have been dutifully aware of. So at best the proclamation was thoughtless.

It has also been claimed that Mannerheim did not personally have ambitions for the creation of a Greater Finland but only wanted to motivate the soldiers with his fiery choice of words. That seems strange, too, since he must have been aware that a considerable part of the troops would not be motivated, but more likely worried over just what bellicose undertakings the 'masters' might have in store for them this time.

Mannerheim's private views are perhaps most clearly divulged in a letter he sent to his sister a week after the famous order-or-the-day had been issued. Here he openly declared that he hoped it would mirror his 'views on our war and its goal'.[281] However, the marshal has also claimed elsewhere that he was under pressure from 'hotspurs' in his immediate surroundings.

Problematic Invasion

Even if one accepts in principle that the occupation of East Karelia improved the defensive possibilities for the Finnish Army (which in itself is debatable), it has to be weighed up against the many problems the invasion also caused. Militarily, the Finns created logistical difficulties for themselves by stretching their supply lines to their limits, while shortening the enemy's supply lines. In other ways, too, there are limits to the practical benefits an army can achieve by invading foreign territories and using them as buffer zones. Besides, the Finns created a string of complications for themselves, partly on a diplomatic level, partly in administrative areas (to use a neutral expression to describe something that was really ethnic cleansing through the use of internment camps and projected transfers of non-'Fennic' peoples).

However, there were certain factors pushing the Finns in the other direction, too, particularly the need to remain on good terms with the Germans. Generally, the leaders in Berlin demanded very little from the Finns; they merely 'requested'. But there is little doubt that the Finnish leaders right from the start of their new relationship feared that too much reluctance or contrariness could land the country in an extremely difficult situation, so they tended to give the Germans too much rather than too little. In particular, there was the constant worry that Berlin might sever its foodstuffs and weapons exports to Finland. Vehviläinen writes: 'In October, the Finns announced to Germany that they needed 175,000 tons of grain to tide them over till the next harvest. Although the German authorities considered this estimate greatly exaggerated, the matter was settled at the highest level according to the Finns' wishes.'[282]

The 'highest level' mentioned here was none other than Adolf Hitler. When Finnish Foreign Minister Witting was in Berlin on 25 November 1941 to co-sign the so-called Anti-Comintern Pact, he met with the Führer who personally guaranteed that Finland would have its demands for cereal fulfilled. The promise was kept as far as was practically possible. Despite protests from his advisers, Hitler personally made sure that Finland received annual deliveries of 200,000 tons of grain, the equivalent of roughly half the country's own production. Finland was in other words not only dependent on Germany, but on the Führer's personal goodwill and generosity.

The diplomatic problems caused by the invasion of East Karelia were mainly in relation to Great Britain and the USA. London and Washington were sympathetic to the Finnish ambition of recapturing the ceded areas. But by invading real Soviet territory, the Finns were going too far, particularly since it jeopardised the Murmansk Railway and thus deliveries of Anglo-American aid to the Soviet Union.[283]

On 31 July British ships and aircraft had attacked Liinahamari on the coast of Petsamo. The attack was aimed at the German troops in the area and seems to have mainly been a display of support for Moscow. Nevertheless, the event signalled that the relationship between Finland and Great Britain was becoming very tense. The main reason was that Churchill needed the Soviet Union badly as his ally in the war against Germany and therefore had to yield to Soviet pressure in relation to Finland. However, the Finns were also under pressure from *their* belligerent partner. The

Germans felt that the many British diplomats in Finland were carrying out espionage (which indeed seems to have been the case), so two days after the British attack on Liinahamari, Helsinki severed its diplomatic relations with London.

The Finnish-American relationship was less stressed, and would remain so for most of the war. Most notably, the Americans never declared war on Finland. In August 1941 President Roosevelt received a message from Stalin, asking him to act as mediator so that separate peace negotiations could be set up between Moscow and the Finnish leaders. The Russians appeared willing to reduce their territorial demands, but the Finnish leaders ignored the approach. Even if they had wished to make peace at that time (which is unlikely since the Finnish Army was riding on a wave of success) it would undoubtedly have resulted in very serious repercussions from Germany.

Finland's relations with Great Britain and the USA were not the only ties that suffered because of the East Karelia invasion. The relationship with the Scandinavian countries was compromised, too. Even long before the war broke out, the left wing in Sweden had started looking at Finland with serious concerns, and these feelings were naturally amplified when the Finnish military crossed the 1939 border and marched into the Soviet Union. Because of the German occupation of Denmark and Norway the atmosphere in relation to Finland is harder to determine in these countries, but there are signs that the Danish sympathy for Finland had dropped considerably on the outbreak of the Continuation War. With the resistance against the German occupation being more pronounced in Norway, there is no reason to believe that the feelings towards Finland were less critical there.

Within Finland the invasion of East Karelia caused political friction, too, despite the heavy censorship. Vehviläinen writes that the resistance came 'mainly from among the Social Democrats and the Swedish-speaking sections of the population.' And he continues: 'In Tanner's opinion, Finnish conquests in the east would in the future turn out to be a dangerous encumbrance on Finnish relations with Russia, which when all was said and done would continue to be its neighbour.'[284]

Tanner furthermore predicted that staying within the 1939 border would serve Finland best during the final peace negotiations, in which the western powers would most likely participate.[285] In the end a compromise was reached: Tanner promised to stop criticising the invasion, and Ryti promised that Finland's war goals would remain undefined.[286] From then on, Finland's political course in relation to the East Karelia invasion was primarily Ryti's domain, while Mannerheim took care of the military issues, although there were incidents where their responsibilities overlapped.

With time, the negative results of the Finnish occupation of East Karelia became wide-ranging. The suffering that the invasion came to impose on the civilian Russian population, along with the Finnish treatment of Soviet war prisoners, constitute the darkest chapter in modern Nordic history and are probably the main factors behind the trauma which the Continuation War still represents to parts of the Finnish population. Still, it cannot be emphasized enough that the average Finn had no influence on the political decisions behind this and in fact had no idea what was truly going on in the occupied territories. As Fingerroos puts it: 'The Finns were not asked about their support for the abstract utopias of Greater Finland that were offered to them.'[287]

These issues will be looked at more closely as we go along. For the moment, it is enough to establish that the western sympathy which Finland lost by invading East Karelia could have been useful to the country during the final stages of the war. The same goes for the early post-war years, where a peace agreement was concluded and new borders were drawn up. It would certainly have made it more difficult for the Soviet Union to convince the world that Finland should be treated in the same way as the actual Axis nations. Indeed, it seems possible that Finland could have kept the 1939 border or at least Viipuri, had the occupation of East Karelia never occurred.

Still, it remains a question if the occupation could have been avoided. Though the relationship between Berlin and Helsinki looked harmonious on the surface, the Finns were in reality at the mercy of Nazi Germany. For example, shortly before the invasion of East Karelia, Berlin and Helsinki were discussing the arrangements for 15,000 tons of grain that the Finns were to receive.[288] If the Finns had refused to invade East Karelia, it might well have meant that Berlin would have cancelled such agreements, since the advance on the River Svir constituted an essential part of the shared planning (or at least the German perception of it).

The whole discussion, however, is rather academic, since the Finnish leaders apart from Tanner were not interested in avoiding this part of the campaign, in fact quite the contrary. Again, it might be that we are looking at a situation where the members of Ryti's inner circle were 'forced by circumstance to do something they actually wanted to do.'

Increased British and American Pressure

On 8 September, the day after Major General Talvela's troops had reached the River Svir, the German Army Group Nord (*Heeresgruppe Nord*) arrived at the southern shore of Lake Ladoga after having advanced through the Baltic States. It was the aim of this formation to capture Leningrad. The German and Finnish troops were now just 100km away from each other.

However, the parties never managed to force the Soviet troops out of the area between them.

The population in Leningrad still had access to Lake Ladoga and could get supplies in that way via the Soviet controlled area between the German and Finnish troops (Map 4). This gave an opening out to the rest of the world which under no circumstances was to be lost.

While the Soviet forces fought fiercely to prevent German and Finnish troops from reaching each other, Moscow tried to make the British and the Americans put pressure on Helsinki in time before the Finns reached the Murmansk Railway and then the White Sea. Meanwhile Alexandra Kollontai, who was still the Soviet ambassador in Stockholm, was ordered to make contact with Helsinki and try to bring the Finnish leaders to the negotiating table.

When the Finns ignored Kollontai's approaches, London sent its sharpest warning so far to Helsinki on 22 September. If Finland continued its invasion into 'purely Russian territory' the country would be treated as an 'open enemy' of Britain, not just in wartime, but also during peace negotiations.[289]

On 3 October it was the Americans who sharpened the tone. Foreign Secretary Cordell Hull called in the Finnish ambassador, Hjalmar J. Procopé, for a meeting to inform him about the American government's view on the situation. The conversation is summarised in a memorandum which Hull subsequently made public:

> I said that as heretofore stated by me to the minister [ambassador], I am glad to see Finland recover her lost territory ... therefore, the one question uppermost in the mind of my government with respect to Finland is whether Finland is going to be content to regain her lost territory and stop there, or whether she will undertake to go further, if she has not already done so, so that the logical effect of her course and action would be to project her on the side of Hitler into the general war between Germany and Russia and the other countries involved.[290]

When this warning also failed to halt the Finnish advance, the Americans, on 25 October, demanded unequivocally that the Finnish troops be pulled back behind the 1939 border if Finland wanted to remain a friend of the United States. This caused a sharp reaction from Ryti, who accused the USA of hypocrisy by proclaiming it was protecting peaceful countries and at the same time supporting the Soviet Union. Ryti also described Finland's 'separate war' as a purely defensive reaction to Soviet aggression, where it was necessary to occupy Russian bases used for attacks on Finland.

Despite this, Ryti told Mannerheim a few days later to stop the offensive at a point where it was most advantageous militarily. Mannerheim then gave the order to cease all offensive operations as soon as Medvezhyegorsk was captured. He also secretly gave Major General Siilasvuo the aforementioned order to stop the attack on Loukhi (p. 186). This meant in practice that the Finnish leaders abandoned the idea of permanently severing the railway connection between Murmansk and Belomorsk.

On 12 November the Americans finally received an answer from the Finnish leaders regarding Moscow's offer to start up peace negotiations. However, the reply was negative.

With that the initiative was handed back to Winston Churchill. Under pressure from Stalin he demanded that the Finnish Army pull out of East Karelia and stop all military operations from 3 December onwards. If this was ignored, Great Britain would declare war on Finland.

The message arrived in Helsinki on 28 November during a Finnish government meeting where Marshal Mannerheim was present. Väinö Tanner and Minister of Finance Mauno Pekkala, who belonged to the left wing of the Social Democrat Party, demanded that the military advance be stopped immediately and that a large amount of the men be sent home on leave. Tanner also wanted to give the British a guarantee that Finland would not advance any further. But Mannerheim insisted that it would be dangerous to stop before Medvezhyegorsk was captured. The result was a compromise: an unofficial message was sent to the western powers stating that the Finnish offensive would be stopped 'in the next few days'.[291]

The following day, Winston Churchill send a private message to Mannerheim:

> Surely your troops have advanced far enough … and could now halt and give leave. It is not necessary to make any public declaration, but simply leave off fighting and cease military operations, for which the severe winter affords every reason, and make a de facto exit from the war …
>
> It would be most painful to the many friends of your country in England if Finland found herself in the dock with the guilty and defeated Nazis.[292]

Mannerheim replied to Churchill on 2 December:

> … it is impossible for me to halt the military operations at present being carried out before the troops have reached the positions which in my opinion will provide us with the necessary security. It would be deplorable if these measures undertaken for the safety of Finland should bring my country into conflict with England … It was very

good of you to send me a personal message in these critical days, and I appreciate it fully.[293]

When Finland did no more in relation to the British telegrams, the British government declared war on the country on 6 December. Though it never came to any military confrontation, it is nevertheless one of the very few examples of a declared war between two democratic countries.

6 December was also the day when Finnish troops captured Medvezhyegorsk. With that, the Finnish offensive ended and despite German encouragement it was never resumed. It has been claimed that the Finns simply stopped because they had achieved all they wanted, but there is broad consensus among Finnish historians today that the invasion would have continued if it had been advantageous to the Finns.

What really stopped the Finnish Army was a string of factors put together, particularly the poor German performance on the Finnish Front, the increasing Soviet resistance, the British and American threats, and disciplinary problems among the troops. Meanwhile, the Japanese attack on Pearl Harbour had taken place and forced the United States actively into the war on the side of Russia and Great Britain. The Finns had to realise that the invasion of the Soviet Union would not be the swift 'Summer War' they had expected. Germany and its allies still held the initiative in what had now truly developed into a world war, but people close to Mannerheim had noticed that the marshal's faith in a German victory was dwindling rapidly.

By Christmas 1941 the Continuation War had lasted for more than five months and cost the lives of 25,500 Finnish soldiers, approximately the same number as during the Winter War. However, the number of wounded was much higher, around 75,000.

A Total War
The Finnish participation in Operation Barbarossa constituted a total war. 'Finland played a rather marginal role in the big war,' Henrik Meinander writes, 'but no other belligerent country mobilised so vast a percentage of its population for active service – not even Germany, which in 1943 bombastically proclaimed that it was now entering into a total war to secure its victory.'[294]

The military budgets were a monstrous burden on Finnish society. In 1944 they constituted 70 per cent of total public spending. Imports and exports were practically all under German control. The only exception was Finland's trade with Sweden, but the Swedish government was under pressure from the Allies, who tried to stop all trade to and from countries that were waging war on the side of Germany. In 1940 Sweden had supplied a quarter of Finland's imported goods. By 1944 the figure had dropped to 8 per cent.[295]

It goes without saying that a country in such a situation has to draw on all its resources. As a result, women, children and elderly people were left with a large part of the responsibility for keeping the wheels of society turning.

More than most other western countries, Finland had a tradition of women getting an education and working outside of the home. Still, nothing could have prepared the Finnish women for the work-related burden that the war placed on them. On top of that there was the psychological stress of having a husband and perhaps one or several sons at the front. Also, there were often elderly and weak family members to take care of.

The government tried to compensate for the lack of labour by introducing the so-called Work Responsibility Law, according to which citizens between fifteen and sixty-four years had to carry out work in the war industries, in agriculture or in forestry. Only women with children under six years were exempted.[296]

Furthermore, many women carried out voluntary work as members of women's organisations. Children often worked for volunteer organisations too, for instance as collectors of recyclable materials. In the bigger towns, boys from the higher school classes were trained to work as assistants in the anti-aircraft defences. A third of the Finnish population at the time were younger than 15 years and 10 per cent were under five years old.

A survey made in the spring of 1943 showed that 65 per cent of the workforce consisted of women.[297] In between they had to carry out their normal work as homemakers, which in a period before washing machines, supermarkets and kitchen machinery was no small task (it has been estimated that full-time homemakers in this era had an average working week of seventy hours).

The pressure that was placed on Finnish women had a substantial effect on the everyday life of their children, as could be seen in the health conditions among the many Finnish refugees that the Scandinavian countries received. These children were often undernourished, weak and infested with lice and fleas. One such evacuee, who was later adopted by his Danish foster family, said in an interview in 1996 with the Danish state radio:

> My mother had various jobs. For a while she worked in the kitchen at a restaurant and helped washing up and so on, and that was one of the places where my brother Kalle and I could go once in a while and have a little extra food in the war years of 1941-42. But I think I must have gone to bed hungry many times. My Danish parents told me that

when I came to Denmark I was very thin and skinny. As an 8 year old I was probably the size of a normal 4–5-year-old child.[298]

The same interviewee also described the differences between the lives that children had in Denmark and in Finland at the time:

Up in Finland we played war with wooden sticks and so on, pretending we sneaked up on the Russians and shot at them. But down here in Denmark we didn't play such games at all. We played rounders and football. I had brought a card game with me, Black Man or *Musta Pekka* as it is called in Finnish. There were four different family members from each country, and you had to collect those. There was a Finnish and a Swedish and a Danish family, and a German family with swastikas next to them, and also an English family. At one point I had cut out the English flags and glued them on to my school book and my pencil case. I did that to show I was on the side of the English, too, not on the German side, as you might think a Finnish child would be.[299]

In total some 80,000 children were evacuated from Finland during the Winter War, the Interim Peace and the Continuation War – the biggest evacuation ever of its kind. Most of them went to Sweden, others to Norway, and 4,000 arrived in Denmark where 10 per cent of them remained after the war. The children were mostly between 3 and 8 years old when they arrived. The majority came from poor families in industrial areas or border districts.[300]

Much has been said and written about the lives of the Finnish children in Sweden, where they experienced major cultural shocks and were often exposed to discrimination and bullying. However, all indications suggest that the ones who ended up in Denmark thrived and had a good life. The problems were mainly associated with the journey home. One of the Danish nurses who helped with both the arrival and the departure of the children, told Danish Radio:

The Finnish Lottas came and collected them. There were many foster mothers to whom I simply had to say: 'Now you *have* to leave. The little one has to understand it is time to go home now.'[301]

The Finnish families who had to carry the biggest burden were probably those who had small holdings, and where the father and maybe one or several grown-up sons were called up for military service. Most of the horses would normally also have been conscripted. To lighten the burden for the women, children and elderly family members, Soviet PoWs were sent out to work on the farms. The relationships between these prisoners and their host families seem in general to have worked out fine.

The political critique against the Finnish war effort grew during the conflict, but among the civilian population there was very little criticism. Most people firmly believed in the official portrayal of the war as a purely defensive struggle for independence, a war completely separated from the Nazi German terror campaign against humanity, a direct continuation of the Winter War and so on. It was the version of events that was the easiest to live with in an everyday existence under heavy pressure and marked by large personal sacrifices.

Perhaps the lack of criticism was also connected to the fact Finland's civilian losses were small compared to those of other belligerent countries. Approximately 1,900 civilians died in the Soviet air strikes (the number covers both the Winter War and the Continuation War), and some 200 inhabitants in the border areas in north-eastern Finland were murdered by invading Soviet partisans. These relatively small figures were due to the poor performance of the Red Air Force and the small number of bombing operations over Finnish territory. Another factor was the low density of the population in Finland, and also that by crossing the 1939 border the army had moved the fighting away from civilian Finnish territory.

The latter has often been used as an additional justification for the invasion of East Karelia. However, it might also be interpreted as if the Finnish leaders spared their own population from the cruelties of war by taking the fighting into an area which, ironically enough, they claimed that they had come to liberate. As such East Karelia almost seemed to have a 'dual nature' that could shift according to the view that best suited the Finnish leaders as circumstances changed. One moment it was an area where kinsmen were to be liberated from Bolshevik oppression, the next a military buffer zone whose destruction was of secondary importance, since the area was outside of 'Finland proper'.

This somewhat ambivalent Finnish view to East Karelia can be found in other contexts, too. During the early stages of the war, the region was cleansed of museum specimens and other cultural artefacts, which were taken away to be investigated at various academic institutions in Finland. The purpose was to prove the claimed historic and cultural connections between East Karelia and its new mother state. However, the investigations mostly came to the opposite conclusion. After that the relics mostly seem to have disappeared into private collections where they might even remain to this very day.[302]

Sexual Collaboration
In recent years, researchers have been investigating so-called sexual

collaboration between Finnish women (often young girls or women whose husbands were at the front or had fallen) and Soviet war prisoners who had been sent out to the farms to carry out forced labour. It is estimated that there were some 600 such relationships of which 200 led to pregnancies.[303] In one case the parties tried to marry but the attempt was rejected by the authorities.

The reactions of married men who came home from the front and discovered what had happened in their absence varied from killing the Russian (in one case killing the child as well) to fully accepting the situation and bringing up the child as if it were one's own.[304] There were also examples of relationships between Soviet PoWs and members of the Lotta Svärd organisation.

Sexual collaboration likewise occurred between Soviet female soldiers and male prison camp guards. In total, the Finnish Army took some 200 female Soviet PoWs (mainly nurses) during the Continuation War, of which the majority were placed in the Naarajärvi Camp. Here five child births took place (in one case the woman had already been pregnant when she was captured). All the children were handed over to the Soviet Union after the war.

From mid-1942 laws were introduced that prohibited civilians from fraternising with PoWs, an act which could be punished with up to six months in prison. The following year the maximum penalty was extended to four years imprisonment. The purpose was not just to stop the sexual collaboration, but also to keep the prisoners in a constant state of undernourishment, which made them easier to control.[305]

In East Karelia sexual fraternising between Finnish soldiers and the civilian population led to some 500 childbirths.[306] That is only the official figure, though, which excludes childbirths in internment camps and instances where the mother refused to give information about the child's father. Some researchers therefore believe that the number should really be as high as 900.[307] Rapes committed within the territory and sexual collaboration in the internment camps have only very recently become the object of research. It turns out that some women in the camps offered the guards sexual favours, mainly in return for bread. Rape cases outside the camps were in fact brought to court, at least on occasion, and pregnant women who were reluctant to reveal the name of the man they had been with, were interrogated elaborately in order to hold that person economically responsible for the child's upkeep.

Relationships between Finnish women and German military personnel before the outbreak of the Lapland War in the autumn of 1944 do not really constitute sexual collaboration, since Finland was not under German occupation. Nevertheless, the issue shall be briefly mentioned here.

In fact, relationships of that kind had existed ever since the arrival of the first German troop transports in the autumn of 1940. Initially, marriages between the parties were prohibited, but from 1943 onwards they could be allowed on special request if it could be proven to the Germans that the woman was of Aryan heritage. Since the Finns had gradually become accepted as such according to German race theories (which on the whole became more tolerant as Berlin grew increasingly dependent on foreign volunteers),[308] marriages took place, albeit only to a limited extent. Women of Sami heritage continued to be seen as *Untermenschen* (subhumans) and hence could not marry German soldiers.[309]

During the war, just under 1,000 children were born in Finland to fathers who were serving in the German military.[310]

III

PoW Camps and Internment Camps for Civilians

Then we were taken into a shed where there were long benches, and they put us on the bench and whipped us with rubber whips, 15 to 25 times each.
RAISA FILIPPOVA[311]

The Finnish Internment Camps in East Karelia
On 16 June 1941, more than a week before Finland officially joined the Germans in the war against the Soviet Union, the vice-chairman of the AKS (p. 214), Dr Reino Castrén, handed in a report to Finland's political leaders, explaining how he thought the future administration of East Karelia should be organised. Other AKS members and political Karelianists were involved in the work, too, among them Ragner Nordström (p. 174) and Reino Kuussaari, who had both already been given administrative tasks by Mannerheim.[312] On the whole, the marshal had a substantial and direct influence on the shaping of the project, including the assignment of personnel to a number of positions. Approximately half of the leading men were strongly engaged political Karelianists belonging to the extreme Right, which would leave its mark on the administration of the occupied territories.

The plan was to present the future invasion of East Karelia as a war of liberation, so during a meeting on 2 July 1941 in the mid-Finnish town of Kajaani, the Karelian Liberation Movement was launched. Also present at the meeting was the Nazi-inclined AKS leader Vilho Helanen. The newly formed movement was to be both ideologically and militarily based, with tasks and activities delegated by Mannerheim.

The first leader of the Finnish military regime in East Karelia was Colonel Väinö Aleksanteri Kotilainen, who had been one of the foremost political Karelianists and Finnish nationalists in the 1920s and since then had held the position of managing director for the huge paper and pulp concern Enzo Gutzeit Oy, where Nordström worked as his deputy. The main task of the administration was three-fold:

The inside of a Finnish internment camp for civilian Russians in Petrozavodsk, East Karelia, 1942. (SA-Kuva)

- East Karelia was to be brought up to a level of development on par with the rest of Finland so the area could form a solid 'bulwark against Russia'.
- The population had to be convinced that it would remain part of the new Greater Finland state.
- The area was to be ethnically cleansed of 'foreign elements', i.e. non-Finno-Ugric people.[313]

A considerable part of the activities were to be on the educational front, and the work commenced immediately, using specially written school books etc. New Finnish schools were opened from December 1941 onwards, and by the start of the following year compulsory school attendance was introduced. Likewise, the Finnish administration in the area did comprehensive work to improve the existing standards in health, which were lower than in 'Finland proper'. Despite these well-meaning initiatives, the area was both formally and in practise kept in a state of emergency and under military administration.

The welfare-related improvements were only applicable to people belonging to the Finno-Ugric tribes, referred to as 'nationals'. The 'non-national' inhabitants (nearly all of them Russians) constituted in 1941 approximately half of the remaining population of East Karelia, in total some 83,000 people. According to the Finnish plans, 'non-nationals' were to be arrested and put in internment camps.

Martti Haavio, one of the Finnish officials and AKS members who participated in driving these people out of their homes and into the Finnish camps, described on 21 September such a situation in a letter to his wife, Elsa. The episode took place near the River Svir, where some Russian villages had been abandoned so quickly that food and various possessions had been left behind in the houses.

> Our soldiers had already started looting. It was a tragedy, of course. But there is nothing you can do about it. It was tragic, too, seeing hundreds of Russians on their way to an concentration [internment] camp. But there is nothing we can do about it. Some of our men ... had started to feel sorry for them, but the general told me: 'We must get rid of men who feel compassion for them. This is all about the future of our own people.'[314]

In the beginning, the Finnish internment camps were isolated institutions. Later, a string of ghettos were set up in the towns of Petrozavodsk and Olonets. Furthermore, a camp was set up in Reboly for 'politically unreliable' people belonging to the 'nationals'.

In the autumn of 1941 about 27 per cent of the remaining East Karelian population had already been incarcerated in Finnish internment camps, in total 24,000 individuals. Lenin Makeyev from Petrozavodsk was one of the Russian East Karelians who spent his childhood in such a camp. In an interview made many years later he recalled:[315]

> My mother was nine months pregnant and in the village she gave birth to a pair of twin girls ... We were five families and, besides us from the village, Grandma and Granddad joined us. They put us in a room of 15 square metres ... We were spared no kind of sorrow.[316]

It has been claimed from the Finnish side that the purpose of the camps was mainly to protect the prisoners from the dangers of living close to the front. If so, it seems strange that only the Russian population had to be incarcerated. Another argument has been that it was necessary to prevent the civilian population from aiding Russian partisans who penetrated the area. Even if that is true, putting half of the population of such a large area in internment camps must be said to have been a very harsh measure of self-protection indeed. In any case, these factors can hardly have been more than side-issues, since the main plan from the start had been to transport the prisoners to German-occupied territories in Russia and settle them there, which in practise meant that they were to become slaves for the 'Germanic Master Race'. In return, Finno-Ugric people from Estonia and Ingria, in particular, were to be moved in the opposite direction and settled in Finland.

The Finns tried several times to make the Germans receive the Russian-Karelian prisoners while the war was still going on. The Germans approved of the idea, but said it would only be practically possible when the area south of Lake Ladoga had been cleared of Soviet troops, so communication could be established between the German and Finnish troops in the area. Since that never happened, the agreement simply petered out.[317]

In East Karelia practically all Russian men fit for military service had been called up, so the prisoners in the Finnish internment camps were nearly all children, women and elderly people. Nevertheless, they all had to carry out labour service. It was the same for the 'nationals' outside of the camps, but unlike the Russian prisoners they received wages for their work and had considerably better food rations.

Another former prisoner from Petrozavodsk, Alexander Vostryakovo, tells about his childhood in one of the Finnish camps:

> All that was left in our house was taken by the Finns. The house was torn down and the materials taken away to be used for building trenches and bunkers. The cattle they took, too.
>
> The camp area was surrounded by barbed wire. It was patrolled by guards, and on top of the towers along the fence there were sentries. We were sixteen people living in one room ... Many died; particularly in late 1941 and early 1942.[318]

As the quote indicates, there was a very serious foodstuffs crisis in the camps during 1941-42 and a high percentage of the prisoners died. The reason was partly the poor harvest in Finland, after which the Baltic Sea froze up so hard it was impossible for German merchant ships to get through. Even in Finland, conditions were so critical it occasionally bordered on a famine, particularly for people incarcerated in public institutions such as prisons and hospitals (i.e. those without access to the black market). Nonetheless, the death rate was much higher inside the camps in East Karelia than outside of them.

One of the first historians to look into this issue was Antti Laine, whose pioneering work took place in the early 1970s. He found that the death rate in the camps during 1942 was 13.5 per cent. At the same time, the mortality among the 'national' East Karelian population outside the camps was 2.6 per cent, while in Finland at large the mortality was only 1.31 per cent despite the on-going war. A survey made in 2007 by another Finnish historian, Lars Westerlund, puts the mortality in the camps at 18.2 per cent for the entire period they existed.[319]

The high death rate was not caused by hunger per se, but rather by severe malnourishment resulting in lethal constipation etc. Formally, it seems the prisoners received the minimum amount of food according to international rules, but the problem was that it was often mixed with elements of no real nutritional value, particularly bits of paper. Several witness statements reflect these conditions:

> The basic element of the food was, of course, flour. But it wasn't flour. It was pulverised white paper with flour added. You couldn't make bread or cakes from it, even if you tried. It turned into a grey pulp that stuck to your teeth and to the roof of your mouth. *(Viktor Volkov)*

> We collected moss, dried it, grounded it and made cakes from it. We made porridge out of sawdust from birch trees and we baked bread made of straw. Things like that can drain your body, and so entire families died. *(Anna Lukin, teacher at the school in Yandomozerskoy)*[320]

There seems to have been no conscious, pre-planned extermination strategy behind the high death rate in the camps. Instead, the overall picture points at gross neglect of incarcerated people caused and exacerbated by a more common problem, namely the general lack of foodstuffs. The common crises was allowed to cause the most suffering among those who were already the weakest, a group of people that were meant to be expelled as soon as possible by handing them over to the Nazis.

Another witness, Vladimir Mikhailov from Kharkov, told about the treatment of the prisoners:

> Most punishments were caused by people leaving the camp without permission. They were often children and teenagers who had been driven out into the town by hunger. They were put in a cold shack, beaten with rubber truncheons, sometimes they were even shot.[321]

Ultimately, Mannerheim was responsible for these conditions, since he was the highest military leader and East Karelia was under military administration. The excuse most often presented on behalf of the marshal is that for a long time he was not informed of the situation. When he finally was, he is supposed to have reacted promptly and ensured that the conditions in the camps were improved. A former child prisoner, Claudia Rogozin, from Petrozavodsk, recalled:

> Suddenly a tall military person with a moustache and a smart uniform steps into our room. I'd heard that the camp would be visited by Mannerheim, and I understood it was him. He shook hands with my brother and said in Russian: 'Hello.' Then he looked at us and said: 'What are you doing?' I replied that I had been given our family's flour ration and it had maggots in it ... Perhaps Mannerheim's visit improved life in the camp a bit. After that day we had better food and no more flour of that kind.[322]

It should be mentioned that this episode took place in 1943, when the Finns had started improving the conditions in the camps. The first advances in this respect had been introduced by the end of 1942 and are frequently seen in relation to the restoration of the foodstuffs situation. The conclusion has been that it had now finally become possible to give the prisoners decent food and so that was exactly what happened. Nevertheless, the improvements have also been seen in the light of the increasing possibility that the Germans might lose the war and that those who had been on their side would have their actions scrutinized in order to decide whether or not they should be put on trial for war crimes.

Since the autumn of 1941, the Finnish leaders had received reports of the Germans conduct towards the civilian population in the occupied areas of the Soviet Union.[323] Furthermore, it was around this time Churchill in a personal telegram to Mannerheim mentioned that the Finnish leaders were running the risk of ending up in front of a war crimes tribunal (p. 221). Hence, the members of Ryti's inner circle knew pretty well what the Allies had in mind for those who had aided and abetted the Nazis. Perhaps that was why the Finnish name for these camps in 1943 changed from 'concentration camps' to 'transit camps', and during the period from then until the end of the war conditions for the prisoners improved considerably. At one point they even started receiving small wages for their work. PhD and post-doctoral researcher Oula Silvennoinen sums up the situation as follows: '... as the war progressed and hopes of victory faded, interest in the decrees of international law grew. Practices deemed contrary to the letter or the spirit of the Hague and Geneva Conventions were quietly modified or dropped.'[324]

According to Russian sources, the number of prisoners who perished in the Finnish camps in East Karelia was far higher than has been suggested by the Finnish figures, in the region of 33 per cent. Still, Antti Laine maintains that the Finnish numbers are correct. 'The Finnish record-keeping of the population in the occupied territories was comprehensive and seemingly has no holes,' he writes. In his opinion the Russian numbers could be the result of a mix-up of statistics: 'You have to take into consideration that the entire civilian evacuation was gridlocked during the Finnish march on the River Svir ... At the same time the Red Army, and undoubtedly also parts of the civilian population, were hit by a supply crisis. We can partly see that from the condition the civilians were in, as described by the Finnish vanguard. Apparently, the record-keeping of these refugee groups was poor during this crucial stage.'

Laine then goes on to mention similar serious supply problems in relation to other evacuations, particularly in the Kandalaksha region, an area into which the majority of the Karelian population fled to escape the Finnish-German offensive: 'According to witness statements collected after the war there was hardly a single evacuated Russian family whose oldest or youngest members did not perish, particularly during the winter of 1942. This was perhaps the most serious result of the Finnish war effort after the invasion of East Karelia, a catastrophe the size of which has not been researched at all, and now it has probably become too late.'[325]

Camps for Soviet PoWs

In the Winter War, the Finns had taken 5,700 war prisoners. During the first six months of the Continuation War alone, they captured more than ten times that amount, approximately 65,000. The problems with incarcerating so many Russian soldiers resulted in 10,000 of them dying during the winter of 1941-42.

Large numbers of documents dealing with the running of these camps have disappeared. Only through laborious research has it been possible for Finnish historians in recent years to ascertain that the high mortality was not only caused by the general food supply crises in Finland at the time, which had previously been the established view. Instead, they refer to a whole string of factors, with the responsibility in several cases falling back on the overall military administration:

- The prisoner's huts were only built after the war had started and were only appropriate for summer use.
- The PoWs wore summer uniforms and were not equipped with warmer clothing by the Finnish authorities.

- The work demanded a bigger calorie intake than the prisoners were given.
- The food rations were small and consisted of foodstuffs that had been declared unsuitable for the Finnish Army.
- The guards were recruited among soldiers who were unsuitable for other kinds of service and who often had personal problems such as alcoholism and criminal records.
- Unlawful conduct against the prisoners would not be punished until after the war.
- The administration of the camps was inadequate and often left to the army.
- The camps were inspected by people who were sympathetic to the crude way in which they were run.
- Only a few of the camp doctors kept track of the prisoner's weights etc.
- There were not enough doctors and nurses.[326]

In regard to the first item on the list it should be mentioned that a few of the camps were attached to a civilian industry where the prisoners were used as forced labour. An example of this was the camp at Valkeakoski, which was owned by General Walden (p. 175), the Finnish Minister of Defence and one of the leading men in the Finnish paper and pulp industry. Walden had personally ordered the huts to be built as cheaply as possible.

The dead body of a Russian PoW in the Finnish Naarajärvi Camp. (SA-Kuva)

Though this was to have fatal consequences, he was never held responsible for his decisions. In fact, the story only became known to the Finnish public in 2011 during a TV documentary about the camps.[327]

It is, likewise, striking that a person such as Hans Kalm could be chosen as commandant of a PoW camp. Kalm was an Estonian officer who had formerly served in the Imperial Russian Army and later on in the White Guard during the Finnish Civil War (he also commanded a large unit of Finnish volunteers who fought in the Estonian War of Independence). He was a notorious war criminal, whose troops had carried out atrocious killings of prisoners, hospital patients and nurses in the Finnish Civil War (not to say that the other side was much better; in fact this terrible occurrence was allegedly an act of revenge for similar atrocities by the Red Guards). Furthermore, during the few weeks in 1918 when Kalm was commandant of the PoW camp in Lahtis, he was responsible for the killing of 500 prisoners, 170 of them female, including girls down to the age of 14.[328] Despite his horrendous past and his associations with Nazi circles, which were hardly unknown to the Finnish leaders, Kalm was in 1941 appointed commandant of War Prisoner Camp No 2 in Naarajärvi, the Finnish PoW camp with the highest death rate (though it should be mentioned that Kalm only briefly held this position).[329]

The historian Lars Westerlund writes about the disciplinary conditions in the Finnish PoW camps: 'C. 1,000 war prisoners, i.e. some 5 per cent of those who perished, were shot, primarily during attempts to escape.' Another historian, Antti Kujala, puts the number as high as 1,200. His assessment is also that the term *shot during attempted escape* was regularly used to mask illegal executions of prisoners. The reasons for these killings he sums up as fear, hatred, incompetence, alcoholism and straightforward sadism.[330]

Westerlund furthermore writes that 'probably several thousand PoWs were maltreated in one way or another. The camp commanders had the right to flog PoWs as punishment for offences, and indeed thousands of PoWs were publicly flogged.'[331]

The Finnish IV Corps in particular had a reputation for treating its war prisoners brutally. The corps commander, Lieutenant General Karl Lennart Oesch, was taken to court after the war and accused of war crimes. He was sentenced to twelve years imprisonment, but the verdict was subsequently reduced to three years. Kujala quotes the following from the Lieutenant General's instructions to his subordinates:

> Treatment of the prisoners has to be extremely strict. Any laxity is out of the question … Recalcitrant prisoners are to be executed on the spot to make an example for the others … One must bear in mind

that a Russki is always a Russki, and has to be treated and disciplined accordingly. Any mildness is out of the question, as the Russki is not accustomed to it and will consider it as a sign of weakness in his master … Recalcitrant prisoners and agitators (politruks) are to be done away without mercy. If executions are undertaken, such prisoners are to be marked in the documents as 'removed'.[332]

The prisoners' food and clothing also left a lot to be desired. According to Westerlund, Mannerheim was the culprit here: 'In reality, he was in his role as the Commander-in-Chief and Chairman of the SRK (Finnish Red Cross) ultimately responsible for the wide-spread, serious negligence in the provisioning of the Soviet PoWs.'[333]

Elsewhere Westerlund writes: 'Under Mannerheim's leadership the organisation was primarily meant to, in times of war, carry out basic tasks related to the health care of the Finnish combat units.'[334] And he concludes: 'Mannerheim chose to favour the military health care system at the expense of continued mass deaths among the Soviet PoWs.'[335]

Amongst the PoWs were some who belonged to Finno-Ugric peoples in the Soviet Union. To accommodate such prisoners, the Finnish authorities set up a special camp where the death rate was significantly lower, some 5 per cent or less, compared to a rate of 33.2 per cent for Russian PoWs, a figure higher than that of the notorious contemporary Japanese camps for Allied PoWs. Oula Silvennoinen writes: 'In Finnish eyes, Russians tended to represent the lowest rung on the national ladder, an ethnic group often seen as responsible for the Soviet system, with a racial bent towards Communism. Consequently, in terms of food, clothing and lodgings, their needs were the last to be taken care of.'[336]

When the conditions in the camps *were* improved, it was partly because a few international journalists drew attention to the problem, after which protests started to emerge. One was the aforementioned Danish news reporter Holger Hørsholt Hansen, who visited Finland in the winter of 1942 and was given access to various places, among them a PoW camp. Out of this experience came an essay that appeared in the Copenhagen daily newspaper *Politiken* on 7 March.

The essay caused a stir, and parts of it were even broadcast by Radio Moscow. Later on, Hørsholt Hansen wrote a whole book about his visit to Finland. It could not be published in Denmark due to the German occupation, so he had it translated and published in Sweden under the title *I krigets spår* (*In the Trail of the War*). Like Peter de Hemmer Gudme's book about the Winter War (albeit considerably more critically) it paints a unique and interesting outsider's view of the conditions on the Finnish Front. Of course, Hørsholt Hansen was not allowed to walk around freely, but was guided by military personnel. Nevertheless, he saw more than was intended and also managed to communicate it to others.

> Drab columns of emaciated, tattered Russian soldiers – still with terror in their eyes as a reminder of the terrible fighting they have been involved in … are marching across the open ground in the centre of the organisation camp somewhere in central Finland … What you see here are long rows of disillusioned, tired – dead tired – people, whose destiny it has been to form the pitiful remains of the much too quickly and insufficiently trained regiments on the Finnish Front …
>
> The most horrible sight that met me in the prison camp was the numerous invalids who, after having been taken care of at the hospitals, had arrived at the camp where they now lived in an isolated hut. They were sitting on wooden bunks, four on top of each other with less than 1 metre between them. Each invalid had a maximum of 1 square meter at his disposal, and the poor souls sat crouched up in this room nearly twenty-four hours a day. One was missing an arm, another a leg. A few were blind, and in the middle of the crowd I noticed a young man who had lost both his feet and whose stumpy legs were wrapped in old rags and paper …
>
> The distance between the bunks was so short that the prisoners were unable to sit up in a squatted position without hitting their heads against the bunk above them …
>
> There are many problems that have not been mentioned here. The camp food, hygiene and sickness are issues that deserve to be mentioned along with the workshops that have been set up for some of the prisoners.[337]

Finnish Soldiers in Soviet Captivity

The horrendous conditions in Soviet PoW camps during the Second World War are well documented elsewhere. Hence, this chapter concentrates on factors specifically related to Finnish War prisoners. The number of Finnish soldiers who were taken prisoner during the Continuation War was relatively small. The official Russian figure is 2,377 (of which 17 per cent perished in camps), while the Finnish figure is 3,402 (of which 40.1 per cent perished). In all likelihood the Finnish figures are correct, indicating that the conditions in the Soviet PoW camps were even worse than those in the equivalent Finnish camps.

The majority of the Finnish PoWs were incarcerated in the Cherepovets Camp some 350km southeast of Lake Ladoga. Others ended up as far away as the Siberian side of the Ural Mountains.

In his book *Suomalaiset Sotavangit Neuvostoliitossa 1941-44* (*Finnish*

War Prisoners in the Soviet Union 1941-44), the author Timo Malmi lets the Finnish former war prisoners have their say about the terrible living conditions they had to endure in the Soviet camps. One of the anonymous contributors speaks about the interrogations which followed his capture:

> I was held captured in a hole in the ground where it rained in all the time. I was interrogated and taken away for executions every other day. Though it was 20 centigrade below freezing, I was dressed only in summer clothes. I was interrogated repeatedly for some six months and then put in a camp.[338]

Typhoid, crabs, lice, diphtheria and dysentery were all a part of daily life in these horrendous places. Still, the prisoners preferred not to be admitted to hospital, since the conditions there were even worse.

As in the Finnish camps, hunger prevailed. The food was appalling and insufficient. The prisoners dug up plant roots or ate mushrooms instead. Another former PoW told Malmi:

> We would try to eat anything. We stamped on sparrows out in the parade ground. The guards tried to stop us, but hunger makes people go crazy.[339]

Stories describing these horrors can be found on nearly every page of this book, which also tells of how many of the prisoners, who later returned to Finland, ate themselves sick and in a few cases even died from it.

The prisoners were also exposed to tough political indoctrination. After they had been brainwashed in this manner, the intention was to exchange them for Soviet PoWs so that when they had returned home, they could conduct various kinds of fifth column activities. In some cases Finnish renegades were conducting the indoctrination. In another portrayal of the conditions for the Finnish PoWs, the former prisoner Arvi Nyman says:

> None of us took it seriously. We let it go over our heads. It was so idiotic it made no impression on normal people. We didn't even allow ourselves to be tempted by their promises of larger bread rations. The bastard could eat his own 'renegade bread' if he so desired.[340]

Because of the indoctrination they had been exposed to, many of the PoWs were looked upon with suspicion in Finland after the war, and some were still called in for interrogations by the security police as late as the early 1950s. Several felt so persecuted and frowned upon that they chose to immigrate, particularly to Sweden, and did not return to Finland until many years later.

Jews and Romas in Finland
The number of Jewish citizens in Finland around 1940 was very small; depending on which source you look at it swings between 1,500 and 2,300. Discrimination only took place on a small scale, but it did exist, for example, within the Lotta Svärd organisation. Some 300 Jews (again the number is uncertain) were called up to serve in the Finnish military. They were allowed to practice their religion freely and even had a small field synagogue near the front at the River Svir. There seems to have been no friction between these soldiers and the German military units who at times were camping nearby, and there were no German demands to hand them over. Likewise, there are no signs that the Jews in the Finnish Army felt they were in any kind of a dilemma.

The situation is different when we look at the Jewish refugees who had arrived in Finland in the late 1930s to avoid persecution in Austria or Germany. Apparently, there was an anti-Semitic element in the Finnish security police, VALPO, which decided to hand these refugees over to the Gestapo in the autumn of 1942. However, the motive might have been political rather than racist. In any case, the group of people who were handed over was very small, apparently just eight individuals.

In late July 1942 the head of the SS, Heinrich Himmler, arrived in Helsinki with the intention of persuading the Finnish politicians to hand over all of Finland's Jewish citizens. The Finnish leaders had been warned in advance and had agreed on a policy which, as so often before, was primarily aimed at delaying the procedures. They managed to do this so well that it saved Finland's Jews from extradition. According to himself, Prime Minister Rangell told Himmler: '*Wir haben keine Judenfrage*' ('We have no Jewish question').

In recent years, Finnish historians have also begun researching the circumstances surrounding the Soviet-Jewish war prisoners. It turns out there were approximately 500 of these, of which some 50 were handed over to the Germans. Nothing has been found to suggest that the handovers were based on racism. Like other ethnic minorities, the Jews were kept as an isolated group in the PoW camps. Approximately 100 of them died in the camps, which constitutes a death rate of roughly two thirds compared to that of the Russian prisoners.[341] The lower mortality was partly due to aid, which the prisoners received from the Jewish community in Finland. There seems to have been no discrimination towards Jewish-Soviet war prisoners from the Finnish side.

The terrible suffering of the Jewish people during the Nazi holocaust has for decades overshadowed the likewise tragic story of the European gypsies, now officially termed Romas. In Finland, too, the fate of the Romas during the Second World War has to a large degree been overlooked, though their numbers far exceeded that of the Jews. It is now estimated that around 6,500 Romas lived in Finland in 1939, and of those some 1,000 served in the Finnish Army during the war years. As with the Jews in general, no Romas were handed over to the Germans by the Finnish state, but plans did exist to round up those who were not serving in the army and incarcerate them in state-run internment camps.[342]

IV

Trench War

> *One has to remember that the men constantly emphasized that the war was 'a war of the masters' and that they themselves were totally indifferent to it. They put their attitudes towards the officers into one sentence: 'The masters are here only because they want to keep us in the most infernal conditions.'*
> KNUT PIPPING[343]

The War Stagnates

After the Finnish offensive halted in late 1941, the situation at the front turned into a trench war. From then on Finland's task as Germany's belligerent partner was mainly to tie up Soviet troops in the area between the River Svir and the Salla region, maintain the northern front in the siege of Leningrad and to secure the area along the Gulf of Finland.

'The Finnish brother-in-arms secured Germany's supremacy in the Baltic Sea,' Meinander writes, based on the German historian Bernd Wegner's assessments.[344] 'The six divisions of the Finnish Army tied up approximately the same amount of Soviet troops along the Finnish Front, which was close to the strategically important Leningrad and the east coast of the Baltic Sea.'[345]

Berlin had several times asked the Finns to participate more actively in the war, but Mannerheim turned down the idea every time, saying that his troops were too exhausted, that the Home Front was under too much pressure and that his supply lines were too long. For good reasons he did not mention the pressure that the western powers were putting him under, but it might in fact have been the most important factor.

It took some time before the Russians understood that the Finns really had no intention to continue their offensive towards Leningrad or to cut off the Murmansk Railroad permanently. Until then, they kept attacking the Finnish positions at several points, such as north of Petrozavodsk and along the River Svir. There was also some fighting over the island of Hogland in the middle of the Finnish Gulf. The Russians fought hard and intensely, and the struggle rolled back and forth, until the Finns finally managed to recapture the island early in the spring of 1942. But similar German attempts to capture a handful of smaller islands in the same waters failed, and further attacks were cancelled when the Russians made an attempted sortie from Leningrad, so German troops had to be transferred to the city from other parts of the region.

The Finnish infantry attacks on Hogland and a few other places were supported by fighter aircraft, but generally the Finnish air force still concentrated on carrying out reconnaissance and air combat operations. Soviet bombers were a rare sight, since they were mostly used in the struggle against the Germans further south. However, in November 1942 a single Russian bomber managed to cause more damage than many of the larger Soviet air attacks on Finnish towns. The victims were a group of people leaving a cinema in Helsinki; 50 were killed and 117 were wounded, 27 of them seriously.

As the situation at the front calmed down, it was decided to send large groups of the men home on leave. Since the summer of 1941 a third of Finland's male population had carried out some form of military service. A large number of farm horses had been conscripted, too. Women, children and elderly people alone could not gather in a harvest that even came close to the norm. Perhaps the colossal amount of troops used in the offensive stages of the war had been a dream scenario for the military elite, but it was a nightmare for the rest of Finnish society.

Now it was felt that enough was enough. Finland had done its share. The time had come to dig in and let the Germans take care of the rest. Some fighting was still initiated by the Finns during the next stage of the war, but it was mainly just local attacks to improve a position or force the enemy away from a strongpoint. Instead, sniper activity grew to become a serious factor. Patrol activity occurred also, often behind enemy lines, but they were normally carried out by special units (as we shall see in the next chapter). Every day had its losses on both sides, but the large-scale battles had become a thing of the past.

Instead, the problem on the Finnish side was simply how to pass the time. Card games became a passion that could lead to real tragedies when someone lost large amounts of money or even lost the family farm. The state offered other forms of entertainment: radio broadcasts, civilian education, patriotic and religious lectures etc. But most of the time seems to have been spent on woodwork and carpentry, to a point where some of the officers ended up living in veritable forest palaces with separate rooms, fine furniture, ornamented gable ends and banisters.

The widespread idleness also led to disciplinary problems, which many officers lacked the energy to address. It was later pointed out that building defence positions and maintaining the men's physical condition and military training was given a secondary role during the Trench Phase, so when the massive Soviet attack was suddenly launched in the summer of 1944, it gave the Finnish troops a shock from which it proved very hard to recover.

Patrol Activities
Both the Red Army and the Finnish Army carried out a substantial number of patrol operations during the Trench Phase. To this end the Finnish military headquarters used a special unit called Separate Battalion 4 (*Erillinen Pataljoona 4*). It comprised four roughly company-sized 'detachments' that were named after their leaders and each unit operated in a sector of the overall frontline. Furthermore, nearly all the divisions had their own special patrol unit.

The Soviet patrols were particularly active on the northern half of the front. The landscape north of Onega constituted the operational area of the 1st Partisan Brigade, which at times consisted as many as 1,000 troops, both men and women. In June 1941 the brigade undertook its biggest operation, the main goal of which was to carry out extensive sabotage behind the Finnish lines. Among the troops was a group of 'political workers' whose task was to encourage the local population to take up arms against the Finnish occupiers. It was quite normal for Soviet patrol operations to include a political aspect. The soldiers would hand out propaganda, try to start up a dialogue with the locals etc. This particular patrol lasted for a total of six months before it was spotted by Finnish troops in the area. The Finns then encircled the patrol, but its members managed to break out and flee back to their own lines.

Ever since the start of the war, the Soviet patrols had been a considerable nuisance to the Finnish III Corps in the Salla region. The northern front with its long, inadequately guarded sectors was well suited to patrol activity. The Soviet groups would occasionally penetrate so deeply behind the Finnish positions that they ended up on Finnish territory, where in some cases they murdered local civilians, including young children (p. 225).

The Russians also used armed paratrooper agents in the same way as the British intelligence organisation, the SOE, did in the German-occupied territories. Instead of Soviet uniforms they typically wore either civilian clothes or German or Finnish uniforms. Hence they were not seen as regular soldiers, but spies, and if they were caught – which they often were shortly after landing – they could be executed. During the Continuation War the Finnish authorities executed 447 spies of various kinds. One hundred and forty-one other captured spies were given lifelong prison sentences, while 161 perished for a variety of reasons (in skirmishes, during parachute jumps or at their own hand).[346]

The Finnish patrols could operate against targets up to 300km behind

Finnish soldier with child killed by Soviet partisans. (SA-Kuva)

enemy lines. This meant the patrol members had to be brought in and subsequently picked up by plane. One Finnish patrol, whose task was to observe the traffic on the Murmansk Railway Line, was flown to a point 250km behind the front where it set up an observation post in the wilderness. The patrol sent reports back to the military headquarters on a daily basis until it was time for it to return home. It then sabotaged a stretch of the railway[347] and headed off in the direction of the pickup point.[348]

Many other Finnish patrols managed to carry out their missions, too, but not all of them returned home intact. In fact, the home journey generally seems to have been the most problematic part of the operations, since by then the patrols had often been spotted by the enemy.

Finnish combat patrol moves out. (SA-Kuva)

The largest Finnish patrol consisted of two battalions whose task was to carry out comprehensive sabotage against Soviet supply and communication lines. The longest-lasting patrol took place in the summer of 1942 and was extended to fifty-six days due to supplies being dropped in the wrong places.

Hitler in Finland

On 4 June 1942 it was Mannerheim's seventy-fifth birthday. Adolf Hitler had decided to pay the marshal a visit which, for security reasons, was not announced until the very last moment.

Finland's importance to the German war effort was underlined by the elements of danger attached to the Führer's plane journey. In fact, things very nearly went wrong during the landing, when a wheel underneath a fuel tank caught fire. As the rescue crew arrived with their fire extinguishers, Hitler and President Ryti shook hands.

The meeting took place in the town of Immola, where Hitler was invited to lunch in the dining car of Mannerheim's special train. Hitler sat next to the centre aisle at a small table with Prime Minister Rangell on his left. Across from the Führer, Ryti was sitting with Mannerheim on his right. After lunch followed a conversation between the marshal and Adolf Hitler.

Part of this conversation, which was practically a monologue by Hitler, was recorded on tape by the Finnish intelligence services. Whether this happened by mistake or it was a deliberate act remains uncertain. In any case, the Germans discovered what was going on after eleven minutes and had the recording stopped. Amazingly, the Finns managed to avoid the recording being destroyed and the original is still today stored at the archive of the Finnish state radio. It has considerable historical value, since it is the only existing sound recording of Hitler during a private conversation.

The conversation between Hitler and Mannerheim consists mainly of the German Führer trying to iron out any creases there might have been in the relationship between Germany and Finland. He claims that during his meeting with Molotov in Berlin in November 1940 he personally saved Finland from a new Soviet invasion, and he tries hard to explain away the German underestimation of the Red Army's fighting power before Operation Barbarossa.

Hitler pays Mannerheim a visit on the marshal's seventy-fifth birthday, 4 June 1942. Mannerheim reciprocated later the same month by visiting the Fuhrer in East Prussia. The civilian conversing with Hitler is the Finnish President Ryti. (SA-Kuva)

It has generally been thought that Mannerheim at this meeting acted with badly disguised contempt for the German Führer. However, the German historian Michael Jonas, who has carefully analysed the Finnish-German relationship during the Second World War, is of a different opinion: 'Mannerheim responded warmly though without committing Finland further ... Being honoured by a birthday visit of such a surprising nature was certainly indicative of the esteem in which Berlin held its Finnish ally and even left Mannerheim not entirely unaffected.'[349]

The Submarine War in the Baltic Sea
The German imports of iron ore from Sweden continued to play an important role in the maintenance of the German war machine during 1942, so the Soviets decided to attack these maritime transports with submarines which could be sent out from Leningrad as soon as the ice on the Gulf of Finland started to melt. Such operations, however, had been anticipated by the Finnish and German side and precautions had been taken in the form of new mines being laid in the gulf, most importantly in a line starting from the northern coast of Hogland and stretching east along the south coast of Finland. The need to lay these mines had been the main reason for the Finnish conquest of the island earlier in the year (p. 242–243).

Still, some Soviet submarines found their way through the minefields and continued in the direction of the Åland Islands where they had some success in harassing the German convoys. Their own losses were considerable, though, particularly after the Finns launched a comprehensive submarine hunt in October. After losing twelve submarines, the Russians ceased operations in November around the same time as the waters started freezing over. By then they had sunk eighteen vessels, of which five were Swedish ships escorting the German transports. The Swedish losses caused some serious protests from Stockholm, but Moscow reacted coolly. Though Sweden was officially neutral, this was obviously a form of Swedish-German cooperation that benefitted the Nazi military.

Despite the five month long Soviet submarine offensive in the Baltic Sea, almost 5,000 German vessels managed to complete their transport of iron ore from Northern Sweden to Germany.

The Italian Motor Torpedo Boats on Lake Ladoga
By mid-September 1941 Leningrad was completely cut off on the land side. The Karelian Isthmus was under Finnish control down to a line just 20km from the northern suburbs of the city. The German frontline started on the Gulf of Finland, formed a semicircle around the southern districts of the city and continued north to Lake Ladoga. The only non-airborne transport route in and out of Leningrad now went across the southern part of the lake,

past the tip of a wedge that the Germans had driven into the Soviet forces in order to isolate Leningrad (Map 4).

Along this route, wounded people, children and others who needed to be taken out of Leningrad and had no important role to play in the defence of the city, could be brought out to safety, while crucial supplies could be transported in the opposite direction. The Russians called the route across the ice of Lake Ladoga *Doroga zjizni*, The Road of Life. The survival of Leningrad depended on it but there was a larger aspect, too. If the city fell, it would mean a big step forward for the German campaign of conquest so there were some very good reasons for the Allies to keep the difficult transport route across Lake Ladoga open. During the winter of 1941-42 they even constructed a railway line across the frozen lake.

The Germans were of course determined to sabotage the route in any way possible; on land, at sea or from the air. The Finnish government and supreme command were passive towards the transports, but certain parts of the officer corps had started considering if they could aid the Germans and put an end to Leningrad's persistent defence by taking independent initiatives. If so, it would have to be when Lake Ladoga became ice free in the spring of 1942. The problem was, however, that the Finnish fleet on the lake was very small, while the Soviet fleet was rather strong and included several gun boats etc. This all led to a curious intermezzo that serves as another example of the high degree of independence with which Finnish officers occasionally acted, often without even being reprimanded for it. It also underlines the special status that the Finnish Army held at the highest level in both Berlin and Rome.

On 2 April 1942 the chief of the artillery and infantry units covering the Finnish controlled parts of Lake Ladoga's shoreline handed a report to Major General Paavo Talvela, who was just about to go to Berlin once again where he was to act as Finnish military liaison to the OKW. The report recommended that the Finnish military start using offensive naval units on Lake Ladoga with a view to serving the transports going in and out of Leningrad. The use of large vessels was out of the question; it had to be a fleet of small, fast motor torpedo boats.

Talvela brought the report with him to Berlin, where he presented it without first having consulted with his superiors at home. Hitler personally took the report into consideration and gave it his blessing. Unfortunately, the Germans could not deliver the requested motor torpedo boats, but perhaps the Italians could? A telegram was sent to the Italian Navy, who, as it turned out, was willing to help. The plan was also presented to Mussolini, who found it interesting, and on 13 May the Finnish Navy's supreme command received a message from Berlin, stating that the German Führer had agreed to send Finland the requested vessels to strengthen the Finnish war effort on Lake Ladoga.³⁵⁰

Talvela had clearly led his superiors into a fait accompli, since there was no way they could turn down such an offer from both Hitler and Mussolini, and soon after the difficult transport of four Italian motor torpedo boats began from the Bay of Genoa to Lake Ladoga, a journey of 3,100km altogether. For practical reasons the transport could only take place over land, through the Brenner Pass and Innsbruck along narrow Alpine roads. As soon as the convoy entered the broad motorways of Nazi Germany, things became easier, and on 12 June the boats reached Finland. Later in the month six German minelaying vessels also arrived. The journey continued through canals and sluices, across land on a kind of summer sledges and then by railway, until the boats finally reached the town of Lahdenpohja on the northwest bank of Lake Ladoga. Here they were added to the Finnish fleet on the lake to form Naval Detachment K.³⁵¹

Supposedly, the Italian seamen with their smart speedboats made a certain impression on the local Finnish girls, but the unit's further story was rather anti-climactic. It carried out a few isolated attacks on Soviet patrol boats and barges, but it soon became clear that there was little it could achieve in a struggle against the superior Soviet fleet on the lake. However, the affair caused some international attention, and the presence of Italian and German naval vessels on Lake Ladoga under Finnish command did little to help the general attempts to separate Finland from the Axis powers.

Delving into the Finnish Army
The extra spare time that the Finnish soldiers had during the Trench Phase was spent in many different ways in addition to what has already been mentioned. Some of the men used the opportunity to get a civilian education, which was offered to them by the army. It was possible to serve an apprenticeship as painter, car mechanic or photographer. Academic education was also offered. In the spring of 1944, 279 Finnish soldiers passed the so-called 'Student Exam' (consisting of a broad set of subjects at secondary school level). Others spent their time on higher education. Doctoral dissertations were written in Mathematics, History and Theology.³⁵²

For some the time spent in the trenches became their first real encounter with literature, courtesy of the 'book boxes' that were regularly dispatched to the front. A corporal by the name of Väinö Linna became so taken with what he found in the boxes that he decided to become a writer himself. He started with notebooks which he filled with his and his comrade's experiences, as they fought their way through the terrain east of Lake Ladoga towards Petrozavodsk. Later, it would develop into one of the most prominent careers in modern Nordic literature, rewarded with the Nordic Council Literature Prize in 1963.

Linna's famous novel about the Continuation War, *Tuntematon sotilas*, was translated into English and published in 1957 under the title of *The Unknown Soldier*. A new translation with a slightly different title, *Unknown Soldiers*, was published in 2015. The novel was first filmed in 1954, while a remake of the film was made in 1985, directed by the renowned Finnish film director Rauni Mollberg.

Linna's depiction of life in the Finnish Army during the Continuation War is confirmed by another portrayal of the same circumstances given by one of his contemporaries, albeit in a fundamentally different type of text. He was Knut Pipping, son of a Sociology professor and himself a student of Sociology at Turku University. Like Linna, Knut Pipping had served as a corporal in a machine gun company during the war. Many years later he described how he had got the idea for his dissertation *Infantry Company as a Society*:

> I began this work in Pinduši[353] in the autumn of 1943 when I suffered from boredom caused by our small workload. I got the spark from my correspondence with my father … My companions gave me the material without being aware of it.'[354]

Piping's analyses of the sociological patterns within his immediate circle of acquaintances was subsequently published as a dissertation in Swedish in 1947. Since then this pioneering work of military sociology has been republished twice, first in Finnish in 1972 and later on in English in 2008.

Considering the efficiency of the Finnish Army during the Second World War, one could be led to believe that it consisted of highly motivated model soldiers. However, Linna and Pipping present a significantly different portrayal of the circumstances.

Pipping's revealing statement about the conscripted soldiers' general view of their officers forms the introduction to this chapter. The use of the term 'the masters', which also appears frequently in Linna's novel, suggests that the Civil War and the class hatred had by no means been forgotten in 1940s Finland, though some preferred to see it that way.[355] It had been shoved aside for a brief while during the Winter War, only to return at full force when the next war broke out.

Otherwise, Pipping's portrayal of the Finnish soldiers is not much different from what you would probably find in many other conscripted armies from democratic countries at that time. The men would swear and curse, complain and grumble, but in the end they did as they were told because that was simply the only way to survive. And above all: they were not first and foremost fighting for God, the motherland, their leaders or any political ideals. Each man fought for his primary group, and the enemy could be anyone who dared to threaten its wellbeing, whatever uniform he might be wearing.

Many Finnish officers dreamt of shaping their men into something much more militarily correct and disciplined. The privates could not see why they had to be bothered with what they perceived as irrelevant nonsense and forced to act in an unnatural way, saluting their superiors and addressing them in a formal manner. If the war was truly necessary for the survival of their country, there should be no need to make a fuss like that. Linna illustrates the issue in a highly ironic scene with the young Finnish officer, Kariluoto, whose dreams of staunch and Prussian-inspired elite troops crumble at the sight of a bunch of tatty Finnish reservists passing him on a country road.

> But no, there were no Storm Troops. There was nothing but a circus of scruffy wisecrackers, scrounging for food like a pack of homeless people. They were cursing and griping and wagging their tongues, desecrating every last sacred thing. They even had the gall to mock the noble and dignified manner in which the Marshal issued his Orders of the Day. They were almost like communists. They downed their emergency rations at the first pangs of hunger, and when they felt like singing, it was not 'Die Fahne hoch' but some rowdy rendition of 'Korhola Girls' that rang out from the ranks. And less inspiring, if more illustrative, were the names they gave themselves, such as 'the pack', 'the gang', 'the herd', 'the shit-shebang', 'the loony platoon' and 'the desperadoes'.[356]

Desertions and incidents of insubordination were certainly not unknown in the Finnish Army. During the Winter War, 1,054 cases of desertion were reported. Looking at the cold facts, the traditional image of the Finnish soldiers as steadfast defenders of their nation starts to crumble somewhat. From the early fighting at Kollaa comes a first-hand description made by an officer who had to threaten his men with his pistol to stop them from abandoning their positions. In the Continuation War there were often cases of insubordination, particularly around the time when the troops were ordered to cross the 1939 border and enter Soviet territory. The situation is portrayed in Linna's novel as follows, carried along by the author's typical blend of honesty and nuance:

> Towards the evening of the fifth day of the march they noticed that the road had started look less used. Soon after it had turned into a

mere wilderness track, and before them it appeared that a crude borderline had been cut through the woods.

– Chaps. It's the old border.

The event cheered up the mood a little. When Hietanen was in the middle of the opening he took a long stride and said:

– Right now. At this precise moment Mr Hietanen stepped into a foreign country.

– We are in Russia now, fellows, Salo said.

Lahtinen scowled angrily at the others as he staggered forward and said:

– We are indeed, yes. And this is as far as we have a right to go. From here on we are robbers on a raid, just so you know it.[357]

What in the above example manifests itself as a bit of grumbling among the men, actually expressed itself far more dramatically in some units. For instance, 200 men belonging to the 48th Regiment blankly refused to cross the old border on the Karelian Isthmus. Eighty-three of them later received prison sentences.[358]

While the situation surrounding the border crossing is generally given very little space in Finnish literature about the Continuation War, there is at least one MA thesis devoted to it, written by ex-army officer Harri Heinilä. His survey shows that among forty-five Finnish infantry regiments there were twenty-four registered expressions of opinions between the men in relation to the border crossing. In twenty of these cases the expressions were negative, while in eight cases they were positive (meaning that in four regiments there were both positive and negative expressions of opinion).

In the main group used in the survey 1,830 soldiers completely refused the order to march into East Karelia. To this number should be added some 500 men from other units, plus those who simply deserted. Most refusals occurred on the Karelian Isthmus, where at least every other regiment experienced mass refusals. Most cases were handled by the officers through conversations with the men, but in approximately 100 cases the matter ended before a military court where the accused individuals received sentences of six to ten years imprisonment. No death penalties were handed down.

Heinilä's research also deals with the social, political and geographical background of the soldiers involved. Those who refused to cross the border were generally people from the working classes and minor farm holdings, and most of them were Social Democrats or supporters of the agrarian party. Only a few were Communists, since supporters of the far left in most cases had already been removed from the front and some of them even put in prison. The majority of the protestors came from eastern and central Finland

and were privates or NCOs. There were no officers in the group. The tendency to refuse was particularly widespread among reservists and rarer among soldiers who were called up for the first time. A surprisingly large number of the refusals came from members of the Civil Guard.

Those who only made critical statements about the border crossing came from a similar background as the soldiers who plainly refused, but this group also contained officers and supporters of the political right.

Reservists generally thought and acted more independently than first-time conscripts and professional soldiers, while many of them were married and expressed worry over the welfare of their families. Furthermore, workers and Social Democrats were for ideological reasons often against waging a war of aggression, particularly when the fighting was taken into enemy territory. Another factor was solidarity with comrades who objected to the border crossing. Besides, there was widespread disappointment that the war seemed to be dragging out. Those who refused often expressed that they were tired, nervous, sick and scared. In many cases they belonged to regiments that on average had experienced tougher fighting and higher losses than the majority, which may be why there were more cases of insubordination on the Karelian Isthmus than in Ladoga Karelia and northern Finland.[359]

Between September and December 1941, after the old border had been crossed, the number of refusals rose in East Karelia, after which they fell again during the Trench Phase.[360]

As we shall see later on, the number of insubordination cases practically exploded during the Soviet offensive on the Karelian Isthmus in the summer of 1944. The total number of registered cases was higher than 10,000, but the real figure is impossible to assess, since the problem occurred constantly and at all levels, from privates up to majors. This was, however, by no means a unanimous protest, and only a very small number of cases included soldiers deserting to the enemy side. It was purely a situation generated by panic during a mass attempt to escape from an enemy attack of unfathomable dimensions.

The majority of these 'deserters' returned to their units after having recovered, but some ended up in a military court, which led to seventy-six death penalties being handed down before the end of September 1944. Of these convictions forty-six were carried out.[361] Additionally, there was an unknown number of instances where officers exercised their right to shoot soldiers on the spot for serious insubordination.

The most traumatic and least researched area of this issue seems to be the soldiers who suffered psychological breakdowns. However, in the late summer of 2013 a dissertation on the subject appeared, written by the historian Ville Kivimäki. It reveals that during the Continuation War 15,700

Finnish soldiers were removed from the front and subjected to psychiatric treatment (to this should be added an unknown number of cases where soldiers suffered breakdowns but received no treatment). During the Winter War the number of such cases was 2,500. This was not just an easy way to evade front duty, since Finnish Army psychiatrists were almost exclusively basing their methods of treatment on German military psychiatry as it had been performed during the First World War, meaning that the patients' problems were put down to personal faults, weak character, low intelligence or erratic temperament. In the mid-1990s there was finally a debate in Finland about whether compensation should be paid to psychologically injured veterans. However, the suggestion was met by resistance from both the war invalid organisations and doctors working for the office who handled these cases. During the entire decade, only 100 applications were accepted, of which several had formerly been rejected three or four times.[362]

V

The Volunteers

> *I met a Danish volunteer in Finland in 1941 (he was a lieutenant) and I had a feeling of something not quite right in his situation, since he in a sense was on the side of the Germans, but then the situation was more complicated for him than for a Swede.*
> PETER NISSER[363]

Nordic Brothers and Eastern Kinsmen
The Finnish experiences from the Winter War showed that the training and deployment of foreign volunteers was a slow and laborious process. To operate with such units was simply not worth the trouble. Besides, the Finnish Army was in 1941 big enough in itself, since it was now in a coalition with the German military (throughout the Continuation War the Germans kept 200,000 troops stationed in Lapland, while a varying number of units were deployed further south under Finnish commando).

But that was hardly the only reason why the number of Scandinavian volunteers was much smaller in 1941-44 than it had been in the Winter War. Even candidates who were willing to ignore the Finnish-German cooperation, or perhaps took it as an incitement, now had an alternative in the voluntary non-German units in the Waffen-SS.

This was particularly noticeable in Norway, where many of the SS volunteers claimed they primarily joined up to fight for Finland's cause. The Germans were aware of these feelings and made sure to exploit them as much as possible. The recruitment campaign for the Norwegian Legion (*SS-Freivilligen-Legion Norwegen*) was to a large extent built on promises that the volunteers would be sent to Finland to fight. The soldiers were even to wear badges featuring both a Norwegian and a Finnish flag. True to their style in such affairs, the SS soon broke these promises; but at least in the late summer of 1943 a Norwegian SS ski unit was set up and sent to the Finnish Front. Its name was SS Ski *Jäger* Battalion Norway (in Norwegian: *SS-Skijegerbataljon Norge*) and it was subordinated to the German 6th Mountain Division North. The battalion primarily carried out reconnaissance patrol operations in northern Karelia without being involved in any heavy fighting until the Soviet offensive at the height of summer in 1944.

It was a bit more complicated for Swedes to volunteer for service in the Waffen-SS. Nevertheless, the group of Swedish volunteers in the Finnish Army during the Continuation War was small compared to the size of the Swedish Volunteer Corps in the Winter War. A total of 1,694 Swedes performed some kind of military service in the Finnish Army. Some 800 were put in the Swedish Volunteer Battalion (*Svenska frivilligbataljonen*), which became part of the Finnish force at Hanko. In December 1941, after the Russians had abandoned the peninsula, the battalion was dissolved and most of its members were sent back to Sweden. However, the following month saw the launch of the Swedish Volunteer Company (*Svenska frivilligkompagniet*) where 400 Swedes and three Danes saw service over the next two and a half years. As time went by, the number of Swedish citizens in the unit was reduced to about fifty (sixty-two of the original volunteers had never returned from leave in Sweden), but the company was brought up to full size again by using Finno-Swedish conscripts.[364] Like most other units in the Finnish Army it lived a relatively quiet life during the Trench Phase until June 1944.

After *Operation Barbarossa* had started in the summer of 1941, there was in Denmark thoughts of setting up a new corps of Danish volunteers to join the Finnish Army. In particular a group of former volunteers from the Winter War showed an interest. The Social Democrat Party and the Radical Party were open to the idea, since they hoped it could soften the German pressure on Denmark and also prevent suspected plans to conscript Danish citizens into the German Army. However, the idea met with staunch resistance from National-Conservative circles, which blocked its further development.[365]

Another project, probably based on the same hidden agenda, dealt with the launch of a volunteer works corps. General With, who had been one of the driving forces behind the recruitment of Danish volunteers during the Winter War, was asked to head the new project. He rejected the idea vehemently, however, which signalled the end of the plan.

The idea of sending Danish volunteers to Finland was then taken up and continued more discretely through a society called Friends of Finland (*Finlands Venner*). The volunteers were primarily placed in Swedish units on the Hanko Front, particularly the 55th Regiment, where the Danes formed a platoon of fifty men. Two Danish privates and a lieutenant were killed in action in this sector, where the fighting was otherwise limited.

Around the same time, a few other Danish volunteers were sent east to the fighting in Karelia. They seem to have been former volunteers from the Winter War who had remained in Finland after the war had ended.

After the Soviet evacuation of Hanko, the Danish platoon in the 55th Regiment was dissolved, and like most of the Swedish personnel the Danes were dismissed and returned to their homeland, although a few were transferred to Finnish units in Karelia.

Early in 1942 the Friends of Finland society made a new attempt to set up a Danish volunteer unit, this time called the Danish Finland Legion (*Dansk Finlands-Legion*). Again, it proved impossible to gather more than some fifty volunteers. The Finnish supreme command placed them mainly in the Swedish speaking 13th Regiment on the Karelian Front, where the Trench Phase had now begun. But the unit had serious problems with discipline and leadership, and after three of its members had been killed and four wounded during a minor skirmish, the group was dissolved and the men distributed across various Finnish units in Karelia.

The total number of Danish volunteers in Finland during the Continuation War was slightly less than 200, of whom 35 were attached to the medical service. The entire group's losses were eleven dead and twenty-four wounded.[366] Unlike the Danes who served in the German Army during the Second World War, the volunteers in Finland were not prosecuted by the Danish authorities after the war.

By far the largest group of international volunteers in the Finnish Army during the Continuation War came from the Finnish-related population in Ingria, a name sometimes used for the area along the southern bank of the Gulf of Finland, including Estonia and the south-western Leningrad districts. Ingria has never been an independent state, but the area was given its name when it was under Swedish rule from 1617 to 1710, after which it was conquered by Russia. There was a considerable Finnish element in the region, linguistically and otherwise culturally, and the Russians were generally unpopular among these people. In the parts of Ingria that had been under Soviet control since the summer of 1940, some of the local population had been transferred to far-off regions, since Moscow considered them to be 'politically unreliable' (p. 165).

Ingria was included in the more ambitious plans for the creation of a Greater Finland. Among the Soviet PoWs that the Finns captured in the early phase of the Continuation War were soldiers from this area. They were given the opportunity to volunteer for service in the Finnish Army and promised Finnish citizenship if they did so. This category of volunteers would form a unit known as the Tribal Warrior Battalion. At its peak it comprised 1070 troops.

Another volunteer battalion, which in fact gradually expanded so much it became a full regiment (JR 200) in 1944, consisted primarily of Estonians who had fled across the Gulf of Finland to avoid German conscription in their homeland. The Germans were not pleased with this practise and considered these people deserters, but since they had chosen to become soldiers in a country that was cooperating militarily with Germany, the procedure was accepted.

Additionally, two Tribal Warrior Battalions (the Olonets Aunus Tribal Battalion and the Viena Tribal Battalion) were formed out of volunteers and conscripts of Karelian origin, who had lived in Finland before the war. Regular Finnish troops were used to bring the battalions to full strength.

Unknown Soldier
The Danish journalist Holger Hørsholt Hansen writes in his book *I krigets spår* (*In the Trail of the War*) about a Danish volunteer ('whose name for many obvious reasons I prefer not to mention') he met during his visit to Finland in 1942 and with whom he subsequently stayed in touch. The man had formerly been a volunteer in the Winter War. Hørsholt Hansen writes:

> The Danish volunteers in this war are – like probably most of the Swedes – not particularly popular. They are normally seen as bad soldiers, adventurers hoping to win a heroic name for themselves without too much effort. Still, it has to be said that after Germany occupied Denmark, the Danish volunteers have changed their views completely and are now uncomfortable with being soldiers in an army which – willingly or not – are fighting side by side with Denmark's oppressors. In Denmark they are quite simply seen as belonging in the same category as Danish Nazis and members of the Danish Legion in the SS fighting against Russia on more southern fronts.[367]

The same view of the situation can be found in a series of letters included in the book's final chapter, titled *Letters from the front*:

> I feel like a traitor against my own country when I am now forced to fight side by side with German soldiers. On the other hand I am afraid of committing double treason if I now betray Finland, where I have lived for so long.[368]

The following is a string of excerpts from the same letters,[369] which can also serve as more general examples of life on the Finnish Front during the Trench Phase.

First letter: From Hanko to the Eastern Front
I have now been rather a long time on the Eastern Front and I must say that the transfer from Hanko to here was like coming from

paradise and ending up in hell. The final part of the journey was the worst. I had to march 20km, and as you know all the roads here are completely cut up in the autumn and filled with mud that reaches up to your knees. We had three days of tough fighting before the Russians finally gave in. They attacked us in several waves, shouting hurrah. But it did them no good. We captured the town from which they had launched the attack and then we started cleaning up. It was a dangerous job. In nearly every shell hole and behind every house there where Russian soldiers hiding, and all you could do was throw hand grenades at them. Some of them were still moving about and pretending to be snipers, so walking around at night was pretty spooky. Can you remember how much I hated the snipers at Hanko? I am not a lot better myself now that I have managed to get hold of a fine new rifle, Model 1941, with a telescopic sight. It is Russian made and I have had several chances to experience how accurate it is. By and large, the Russians have good weapons – unfortunately.

Second letter: In the Wilderness
Between the Russians and us there is – or was – a village of some fifty houses. Two days ago we were five men who walked down to the village with bottles full of petrol and set fire to it. It was pitch black and the job took an hour, and all the time the Russians were shooting at us. But we made it and now we have a fine view ...

   This morning at three o'clock we were put on full alert. I was asleep when a submachine gun started firing nearby. We all jumped up immediately. A Russian patrol of twenty soldiers had penetrated our lines; they are undeniably good soldiers. Now they were moving in on us. Luckily, a Finnish corporal spotted the Russians in good time. He sent two privates he had brought with him down to alert the rest of us. Meanwhile, he hid behind a tree trunk and waited until the Russians was just 10 metres away from him. Then he opened fire. The Russians threw hand grenades at him, but strangely enough he survived. Then we arrived, and soon the battle was raging. In a glimpse I saw a Russian lying next to me behind a big stone. He was probably no more than 18 years old. Poor boy! God knows if I may one day be found like that by a Russian soldier? Will he call me a 'poor boy,' as well? I think it is possible, since we are human beings on both sides of the front, though we are killing each other.

   There is a big wilderness around here. We have problems getting enough food brought out to us. Though we treat the civilian Russian population with consideration, we sometimes have to kill one of their pigs or chickens in order to survive. But soon there will be nothing left to eat around these parts ...

I am lying here on the ground with a lousy battery torch writing you this letter, hoping that perhaps you can use it in some way or other.

Third letter: At the River Svir
After a few quiet days spent in a little village north of the River Svir, we were suddenly ordered to strike camp. It was a shame, since we had been quite cosy in that place. It was only recently we had captured it, and it was completely undisturbed when we got there. There were quite a few Russian families left; they had probably been taken by surprise with not enough time to flee. Most of them do that. It feels a bit strange that they flee from us. We thought they would be happy to be liberated. For the last few weeks we have been billeted in the Russian houses. For the first time in a long while we ate from real plates and drank fresh milk etc. The young people of the village would often come to visit us in the evening. There were some young girls who brought us much joy, and boys of up to fifteen or sixteen years. There were almost no grown men in the village. They were of course out in the forests shooting at us, the devils. The young ones who visited us sold us cigarettes and were very interested in listening to the radio we have. On several occasions we held little improvised parties that helped us keep up the spirit. But then we suddenly had to leave.

When we got to the other side of the Svir River, we expected to be granted a proper rest. We had heard that we would not be made to attack south of the river. Oh, well! The next morning at four o'clock the journey continued in the direction of Podporosje [Podporozhye, a town on the south bank of the Svir River 300km northeast of Leningrad]. The Finnish units ahead of us had been involved in some tough fighting, and everywhere along the roads there were signs of the struggle. Fallen Russian soldiers, dead horses, wrecked cars and war materiel lay strewn along the ditches. We are so used to these sights that they no longer bother us. Finally, we reached our destination where we were meant to relieve another regiment the next day.

Last week the Russians carried out several counterattacks, but they were all repelled. There is, however, still much patrol activity and new attacks can be expected at any moment. During the last few days it has started snowing quite a lot, and it has become easier for us to spot the Russian patrols. But it has also become easier for the Russians to detect us, and we have to be very alert. We are somewhere near the Murmansk Railway, against which we have carried out various kinds of attacks. So far, I have not personally participated in any of them, but that will probably come. According to rumours we have blown it up in several places.

Fourth letter: Civilian Russians
... When we approached the little village, we ran into a young woman who was weeping as she was pulling a cart. We thought she was trying to flee along with her belongings. She *was* fleeing but when we pulled the tarpaulin off the cart, we saw the corpse of a Russian man. He had been killed by a hand grenade. The woman broke down completely, weeping and sobbing hysterically. She said he was her husband, and she was taking his corpse along with her. Of course we could not allow her to continue, but I heard later that she had buried him in a nearby graveyard.

Another time we suddenly bumped into two women who came strolling out of the forest. They wept and told us they had fled from their homes, but now they had decided to go back. They said they had hidden their children in the forest and now they wanted to go and get them. We were rather suspicious, as they could well be spies, and the suspicion grew when they wanted to go back into the forest to collect their children. Some of us followed close behind them, though they were less than happy about it. It could have been an ambush, but all the same we dared not let them go on their own, since we had no idea how much they might have seen. But everything was fine. Inside the forest we found a bunch of kids, who followed us back. They looked a bit battered. They had lived in the forest for a whole week, and it was quite cold. If they had not been wearing their wadded clothes, which look funny but at least are warm, they would probably have frozen to death.

Fifth letter: Fighting over a Dug-out
Let me tell you a rather grim story. We had attacked a small underground *korsu* [dug-out] and encircled it. It was completely quiet inside it, so we had no particular worries about investigating it. Some of the chaps had started sneaking down into the dug-out when the man in front was hit by a bullet that killed him. We got angry and threw three or four hand grenades into the room. We heard some screaming and groaning, but then all went quiet again. We were certainly more cautious now, but also convinced that there could be no living creatures left in there. Oh, well! When we sneaked into the dug-out again, we hear another gunshot, although this time no one

was hit. A few more hand grenades and the path was clear. We continued downwards, rather nervously. The room was dimly lit. A woman who was lying in a corner suddenly started getting on her feet. She was furious, but also badly wounded. The revolver in her hand was pointing at us. Before she has time to pull the trigger on her weapon, two shots were fired simultaneously finishing her off. It is not that we enjoy shooting at members of the weaker sex, but in this case we had no choice. I shall never forget her eyes, shining in the dark like little dots. I have never seen such intense hatred.

Sixth letter: Pancakes
I had guard duty on New Year's Eve. We had been given a little extra food in the evening, and then the service commenced. When I came back from my guard duty, my comrades had made coffee and – would you believe – pancakes cooked on the hearth. Well, perhaps 'pancakes' was not quite the right word for it. They were distributed during dinner after they had been reheated. They were not exactly like Danish pancakes, but still – they tasted good.

Yes, I am still alive. I often think that it makes no difference what happens to me as long as I can avoid becoming an invalid.

I have to stop now. The next time I write to you, it will probably be from somewhere further north. I have asked to be transferred to Karhumäki [Medvezhyegorsk], so God knows how long I am to stay in this place.

Holger Hørsholt Hansen writes that the author of these letters was killed in action in October 1942.

VI

Peace Negotiations in Trouble

> *The outcome of the war was clear already then, and the military knew it. Peace could have been achieved. If Mannerheim, Ryti and the government had taken that view, the Finnish people would probably have accepted the agreement.*
> J.K. PAASIKIVI[370]

The Deterioration Phase
To make the Finnish-German relationship in 1941-44 easier to understand, the historian Lars Westerlund suggests it be divided into four phases:

- The *offensive phase* from the spring of 1941 until December the same year
- The *hesitating phase* from the end of 1941 until the end of 1942
- The *deterioration phase* from early 1943 until the summer of 1944
- The *hostile phase* from the armistice with the Soviet Union on 19 September 1944 until the end of April 1945[371]

We are now moving into the third phase of the relationship. The decisive event here took place far away from Finland, more precisely at Stalingrad, where the remaining Axis units surrendered in the days around 1 February 1943. The consequences could be felt immediately in Finland. At a meeting in Mannerheim's headquarters on 3 February, Ryti's inner circle decided to make an attempt to get Finland out of the war. The gravity of the situation was underlined by a secret survey, which showed that the Finnish people's belief in a German victory had been more than halved since September of the preceding year.

Ryti's presidential term was up on 1 March. Since the war made it impossible to hold an election, the new president was to be appointed by the same electoral college that had been chosen in 1937. The Agrarian Party chose Mannerheim as its candidate in the hope that he could get Finland out of the war. But when the marshal understood that Ryti was backed by a majority of the inner circle and the college, he withdrew his candidature, and so Ryti was almost unanimously elected. The news was received with satisfaction in Berlin. Both Hitler and Ribbentrop saw Ryti as Finland's most 'fanatical anti-Russian' and a suitable candidate for the position of the country's future Nazi puppet dictator.[372]

In fact, Ryti started his new presidential period by removing the members of the government who were primarily associated with the hitherto pro-German orientation. Rangell was replaced as prime minister by Edwin Linkomies from the liberal-conservative National Coalition Party. The Swedish historian Allan Sandström writes that the 48-year-old Linkomies in the past had 'been close to the IKL and was almost regarded as a black-blue right-winger', but that he had since then softened considerably, and in particular he subscribed to a peace-orientated line towards the Soviet Union, although he kept that to himself during his period as prime minister (at least according to his memoirs).[373]

The strongly pro-German Rolf Witting was replaced as foreign minister by Henrik Ramsay from the Swedish People's Party of Finland, which constituted the most peace-orientated block in the parliament. Ramsey was from an aristocratic Scottish heritage and had good connections to the Western Allies and to Stockholm. He was ten years older than Linkomies, but was nevertheless considered rather naïve in diplomatic affairs. This became a problem when the government shortly after Ramsay's appointment sent him to Berlin to probe the opinions of Hitler and von Ribbentrop.

At that time Helsinki had just received a new American offer to mediate between the Finnish and Soviet governments. The Finnish leaders were considering the proposal but were, of course, worried about how the Germans might react. Instead of approaching the issue carefully, Ramsay informed Ribbentrop directly. The German foreign minister replied curtly that if Finland tried to reach a separate peace with Moscow, Berlin would consider the country an enemy of the Third Reich. Or to put it in another way: the 200,000 strong German military presence in Lapland would turn into an occupation force and install a quisling as Finland's dictator (the candidate Berlin had in mind at this time was Major General Paavo Talvela, who in fact was made an offer by the Germans in 1944 but who rejected it; another candidate was the chairman of the AKS, Vilho Helanen).

Meanwhile, the peace opposition was gaining more and more ground, particularly among the Swedish-speaking minority in the *Eduskunta*. The tension grew throughout the summer, and on 4 August, thirty-three parliament members (including nineteen Finno-Swedes) delivered a declaration to Ryti, advocating strongly that negotiations with Moscow be initiated.

The request, however, was turned down due to fear of German reprisals. Prime Minister Linkomies later wrote about the government's approach to the situation:

The right time to sue for peace was when Germany could no longer prevent it and the terms were such that the Finnish people could accept them.[374]

Berlin had in the meantime started making plans for how it should react if Finland signed a separate peace with Moscow. These preparations became even more relevant with the abovementioned declaration by the peace opposition, which was supposed to have been kept secret but which was leaked to the public.

The strategy chosen by the Germans in relation to Finland was entirely different to the aggressive approach they had used recently against Italy and subsequently Hungary, when these two allies had tried to untangle themselves from their ties with Berlin. In the case of Finland, no offensive German action was to be employed. Instead, all German troops were merely to be pulled north to secure Petsamo. Later, plans were also made for an occupation of the Åland Islands and Hanko;[375] but it was still only limited interventions compared to the scenario that the Finnish leaders feared and on which they based their actions.

On 11 November 1943 the American, British and Soviet foreign ministers met in Moscow. After the conference, Molotov requested that the Allies demand unconditional surrender from Germany and its 'vassal states'.[376] The US Secretary of State, Cordell Hull, remarked that it was impossible for his country to make such a demand on Finland, since America had not declared war against that country.[377] Molotov seemed unaffected by this argument and stuck to his request, and in a subsequent Finnish language broadcast by Radio Moscow the Finns were told that if they wanted to make peace with the Allies, they would have to lay down their weapons and surrender unconditionally.[378] However, something appears to have happened behind the diplomatic curtains because later in the month the Americans communicated to the Finns that this piece of news was incorrect and *that Moscow in fact did not demand unconditional surrender from Finland, as it did from the Axis powers.*[379]

The Finnish leaders responded to this by sending a telegram to Moscow, in which they suggested that the 1939 border be used as a starting point for the negotiations. The Soviet leaders replied on 20 December that only the 1940 border was acceptable to them, but otherwise they were open to discussion. Meinander calls the Soviet telegram 'ominous', but it might be more correct to describe the Finnish expectations as rather naïve after they had occupied East Karelia and fought beside the Germans for more than two years.

The sequence of events is presented somewhat differently by the Danish historian Henrik Bertelsen in his essay 'Finland's vej til freden' ('Finland's Road to Peace'), which is partly based on the Swedish negotiator Erik

Boheman's memoirs.[380] Bertelsen writes that: 'Boheman's role as negotiator started for real when he was called in for a meeting with the Soviet ambassador to Sweden, Madame Kollontai, in her home after she had received an important message ... She was highly moved and pointed out that the message from Moscow said nothing about unconditional surrender. Kollontai asked Boheman to pass the message on to the Finnish leaders, whom she was unable to contact directly ... to Boheman's surprise, Kollontai added that she had the impression that Moscow preferred it if a Finnish request to leave the war was backed by Mannerheim, since otherwise there would be a lack of stability.'[381]

The Teheran Conference between Stalin, Churchill and Roosevelt took place between 28 November and 1 December 1943. Its main purpose was to coordinate the Allied war effort. The agreement was that the Western Allies should aim an offensive against German-occupied Europe from the west, Operation Overlord, starting with D-Day, a large scale landing of troops in Normandy. The Soviet Union was to launch Operation Bagration, a massive attack on the German and German-allied troops from the east.

Of course, Finland's situation only constituted a very small part of the issues dealt with at the conference, but at least the subject was touched upon. Moscow had long known that the Finns had no intention of continuing their offensive beyond the positions they had established two years previously. Still, there were four fundamental reasons why Finland needed to be forced out of the war.

- There was a potential danger of German attacks on Leningrad (with the rumoured new V-weapons) from Finnish-occupied territory.
- The threat against the Murmansk Railway had not been completely eliminated.
- The Finnish Army continued to tie down considerable Soviet forces that would be needed further south once Operation Bagration was launched.
- A Finnish capitulation would isolate the German Army in Lapland and make it easier for the Red Army to eliminate the force.

Stalin did not put forward these four arguments in Teheran, since they were self-evident. Instead he presented, on request from the two Western leaders, his overall demands in relation to Finland:[382]

- Re-establishment of the 1940 border, possibly with a Soviet takeover of Petsamo instead of Hanko. But where Hanko had been a lease arrangement, Petsamo was to be handed over permanently.
- Compensation for 50 per cent of the damages Finland had caused the Soviet Union. The exact amount was to be found through negotiation.

- An end to the Finnish-German cooperation and an expulsion of the Germans in Finland.
- A reorganisation of the Finnish Army.

Stalin also promised that the Soviet Union would not threaten Finnish independence, 'if Finland by its behaviour did not force Russia to do so'.[383] The only disagreement was over the size of the compensation Finland was to pay the Soviet Union. Churchill felt that Moscow's demand in this regard was unreasonable and impossible for Finland to fulfil. The issue, however, was postponed.

The planning and execution of the attempt to force Finland out of the war was to be carried out by the Soviet Union alone, and so in early December 1943 the Red Air Force's long distance bomber group was ordered to prepare for a large scale attack on Helsinki. The group spent six weeks on planning the operation and redeploying its units, and then began the wait for the weather conditions to improve.

An important telegram was dispatched from Helsinki to Moscow in early January 1944. The document has disappeared, but the two Finnish historians Osmo Apunen and Corinna Wolff, have put forward a believable theory on how it came about and what it contained. They write: 'The War Cabinet did not share Boheman's confidence in Kollontai's interpretation [of the latest telegram from Moscow]. It would be dangerous to send a peace delegation to Moscow, as the Germans would revenge themselves. A new negotiation initiative was made, in which the Finns demanded to keep a part of Finnish Karelia, more precisely Viipuri, Sortavala and Käkisalmi, as well as the financially important Enso factories.'[384]

The Finnish government was now under enormous pressure both internally and from the outside. Large groups among the right wing, the officer corps and the Karelians who had returned to their homes (or what was left of them) were against showing any leniency whatsoever towards the Soviet demands for a peace agreement based on the 1940 border. At the other end of the spectrum, the peace opposition was receiving substantial support from Stockholm. Meanwhile, the US sharpened its tone to a point where the Finnish leaders feared they might receive an American declaration of war in addition to the one they had already received from London. Furthermore, the constantly changing situation at the higher strategic level had to be taken into consideration.

A Soviet offensive began on 14 January on the Leningrad Front and broke the German blockade. As a result, the German Army was pushed 200km west. Mannerheim was deeply worried about the situation for the Finnish Army on the Isthmus, where large numbers of Soviet troops could now be deployed via Leningrad.

Finally, the Finnish government agreed that the time had come to once again send Paasikivi off to Moscow. Despite his many frustrating experiences on these missions, he accepted the task. First, however, he travelled to Stockholm on 9 February, officially to 'buy books'. In reality, Paasikivi's aim was to talk the situation through with Alexandra Kollontai.

Stranded Negotiations
The plans and preparations made by the Red Air Force for a bombardment of Helsinki had been completed in mid-January 1944, and since then the machines had been standing ready for take-off as soon the weather permitted. Altogether three bombing raids were carried out, all of them in the hours around midnight on the following dates in February: 6-7, 16-17 and 26-27. The targets were military, political and industrial centres. According to the orders, residential neighbourhoods were not to be bombed, but in practise this was impossible to avoid.

A massive air fleet was used, comprising 2,000 aircraft. Still, only 670 bombs hit their targets out of the 16-20,000 that were dropped. Both material and human losses were therefore relatively small: 146 dead and 358 wounded, while 6 per cent of the city's buildings were either damaged or ruined completely.

The lack of Soviet success in these attacks has puzzled historians. Contemporary bombing raids carried out by the Western Allies were considerably more efficient. According to Henrik Meinander, there were three main reasons for the Soviet failure: 'First, the total size of the Soviet attack measured in bomb tonnage and the number of dropped bombs was very limited compared to the Western Allies' raids on Germany . . . Second, the Soviet air force had nothing like the routine and professional knowledge about strategic bombing that the Western Allies had. Third, during the preceding months Helsinki had been equipped with ultramodern German anti-aircraft equipment that was used effectively and, along with well-functioning civilian protection systems and a resourceful fire brigade, contributed to keeping the human and materiel losses small.'[385]

Parts of this evaluation are supported by the following account from one of the Soviet pilots who participated in the bombardment:

> The enemy protected his large strategic targets with a barrage of anti-aircraft fire. In front of the bomber a wall of lethal fire rose up. Beneath and above us hundreds of projectiles of various calibres exploded, thousands of tracer bullets flew in all directions and beams of light traces swept across the sky. As we approached the target, we were attacked by enemy fighters, shooting at us with machine guns

and quick-firing guns. And somewhere in the dark there were barrage balloons. It wasn't easy to break through to the target.[386]

It seems the Russians were completely unaware of the feeble effect of these bombings. Instead, they assumed that Helsinki was lying in ruins after the attacks, which explains why the Red Air Force never bombed the city again (although they did bomb a string of other Finnish cities and towns, such as Kotka, Oulu and several localities in the Turku area). Still, part of the message behind the attacks had been understood: the people of Helsinki realised how lucky they had been and how bad things could become in the future, and for that reason the bombings increased the pressure on the politicians to make peace with Moscow.

After his meeting in Stockholm with Kollontai, Paasikivi packed his suitcase and embarked on a new journey to Moscow with a delegation of negotiators. This time he was assisted by Carl Enckell, yet another Finnish politician with his roots in the banking world; but Enckell had also previously been Finland's Minister for Foreign Affairs and for a long period of time the country's ambassador to Paris.

The negotiations began on 22 April, after which the delegation returned to Helsinki with the best compromise it had been able to achieve. But once again the Finnish government found the Soviet peace terms unacceptable. They felt that the deadline for the internment of the German troops in Finland (by the end of April) war unrealistically short, particularly since Moscow also demanded that the main part of the Finnish Army be demobilised. Likewise, it was said that the compensation demands were impossible to meet. But perhaps the main reason for this lack of compliance was that the Finnish leaders had recently come under renewed pressure from Berlin. The Germans had received information about the Finnish-Soviet negotiations, and so Hitler had secretly enforced an embargo on weapons and foodstuffs into Finland.

Paasikivi was appalled. Once more he felt that he had worked hard to achieve the best possible compromise with the Kremlin, and once more Helsinki acted stubbornly and irresponsibly in a way that would cost blood. He might also have felt let down by Mannerheim, who privately supported his views and also wished to make peace as soon as possible, but who refrained from making his views publicly known.

An internal political war now broke out in the *Eduskunta* between Ryti's inner circle and the peace opposition. It went so far that the Social Democrat Atos Wirtanen had to go underground and the peace opposition considered setting up a kind a government-in-exile in Stockholm. Such a course of action was halfway planned but had to be cancelled because of Paasikivi's opposition. Meanwhile, a new message from Moscow reached the peace opposition via Alexandra Kollontai (actually a repetition of what the Russians had already said the year before): it was the view of the Soviet leaders that Mannerheim should be more actively involved in the proceedings if a peace agreement were to be reached. The assessment in the Kremlin was that the marshal was interested.

In mid-May the Allies sharpened their tone towards the countries fighting alongside Germany. The longer these states kept dragging things out, the greater the possibility became that they would receive an unfavourable peace deal. But even after the allied landing in Normandy on 6 June, President Ryti felt that Finland's only salvation lay in a German victory, although he no longer regarded such a thing as probable. In a pro memoria he wrote on 1 June 1944 it says:

> The most likely outcome seems at the moment to be a victory for the Anglo-Bolshevik alliance. Finland has the choice between being either eliminated by Bolshevism or supporting the creation of 'Neuropa'. Finland can, of course, only support the latter alternative . . . A victory for the Axis powers will lead to German dominance over the smaller states of Europe and the end of the British Empire – a state of relative welfare for Continental Europe due to the exploitation of Russian and African natural resources. For Finland a British defeat will mean the loss of a good friend with whom we have many cultural ties. The adequate conditions in Fortress Europe with regard to raw materials, manpower etc. will make the Continent capable of withstanding a long siege, which can result in a compromise peace.[387]

VII

The Soviet Steamroller

> *My father was a soldier in the 30th Regiment (which was brought from East Karelia to Tali in June 1944) and he told me: 'We met crying soldiers, whose eyes were popping out of their heads. "No one can stand being out there," one of them said.'*[388]
> LEA TOIVOLA

Soviet Plans
Until mid-February 1944 Stalin felt that the Finns would most likely yield to his demands for a peace agreement. Therefore the Soviet planning for an offensive against the Finnish Army started relatively late. Another factor was Stalin's lack of confidence in the Allied Normandy landings. He thought it was best to wait and see how the situation developed before the Soviet Union threw itself into the agreed large scale offensive against Germany and its belligerent partners on the Eastern Front. In the meantime, the Red Army could concentrate its efforts on minor issues such as forcing Finland out of the war. The first real step in this direction was taken on 19 February where the Seventh Army at the River Svir was attached to the army group named 'The Karelian Front'.

'The Karelian Front' had been launched in August 1941 along with another army group called 'The Leningrad Front'. Both had risen from the ashes of 'The Northern Front', which had been split in two to form the basis of the new army groups.

In case of an attack on the Finnish and German forces, the two Soviet army groups were to divide the operational areas between them as follows: 'The Leningrad Front' was to carry out the operations on the Karelian Isthmus, while 'The Karelian Front' would cover the areas east of Ladoga and further north all the way up to the Barents Sea. The headquarters of the latter was to be established south of the River Svir on 1 March 1944 under the command of General Meretskov, who had led the decisive attacks on the Karelian Isthmus during the Winter War. His work started while the peace negotiations were still going on. Therefore his initial plans, which were worked out in March, were aimed at the German troops in Lapland, expecting a Finnish capitulation that would make the subsequent fighting purely a German-Soviet matter.

Despite these expectations, the Red Air Force carried out a string of reconnaissance operations over the Karelian Isthmus and photographed the area down to a height of 100 metres. The material was then analysed and used to decide the bombing targets in case of an offensive into the area.

As it gradually became clear that the peace negotiations would once again collapse, the plans were changed to encompass an attack on the Finnish Army. The final decision on this was made around 20 April. Instructions in regard to timing and the directions of the attacks were handed out two weeks later. The offensive on the Karelian Isthmus was to begin on 10 June and would be led by the commander of 'The Leningrad Front', General Govorov. The attack across the River Svir was to be launched 14 days later.

Professor Ohto Manninen writes that the minimal goal of the offensive must have been identical to the Soviet Supreme Command's declared goal for its operations of 1944, i.e. to force all enemy troops out of Soviet territory. And he adds: 'In Finland's case this meant that the Soviet Union could stop at the 1940 borders while saving face … The objective was to ensure the Red Navy free passage out of the Gulf of Finland and enable the Red Army to attack the German's flank in the north.'[389]

The more specific goals for the offensive on the Karelian Isthmus are harder to work out, but Manninen finds it reasonable to interpret them in accordance with the general view among Russian historians. It appears that the defeat of the Finnish forces on the Isthmus was to be achieved through an attack that started northwest of Leningrad, moved towards Viipuri and from there in a straight line towards the 1940 border. The border was to be crossed and the attack to be continued until the troops reached Kymijoki, a river that had constituted the Swedish-Russian border in the years after the Treaty of Åbo in 1743. According to the plan, the offensive was to be carried out in nine days.

The goal of the offensive in East Karelia was to a) split the Finnish main force north of the River Svir, b) capture the town of Petrozavodsk and the areas north and east of Lake Ladoga, c) cross the 1940 border north of the lake and d) capture the areas around the town of Ilomantsi. Manninen writes that 'the goal was not, at least in military documents, to incorporate Finland into the Soviet Union'.[390] Still, he feels there are signs that 'the Soviet leaders expected to bring Finland under control without any serious resistance, at least in the latter stages'.[391]

Other Finnish historians have interpreted the Soviet plan as an attempt to establish a new border along the Kymijoki. While that may be true, there is no certain proof of it, merely indications. In other words: the Soviet crossing of the 1940 border on the Karelian Isthmus *could* for that matter be justified in the same way as the Finnish occupation of East Karelia over the previous three years, i.e. as an attempt to set up better defence positions and create buffer zones. It is, however, true that for many years Russian historians regarded the Kymijoki as the 'natural border' between Finland and Russia.

The attack force on the Karelian Isthmus by the start of the offensive consisted of the Soviet Twenty-first and Twenty-third Armies (for a more detailed description see Appendix X). The size of the force was 270,000 men, 7,660 artillery pieces, 620 tanks and 1,500 aircraft.[392] But that was only at the launching of the attack; later on three more divisions along with extra artillery and tanks were added to the Twenty-third Army.[393] At its peak, the force comprised more than 450,000 men, 10,500 artillery pieces, 800 tanks and 1,600 aircraft.

The front on the Karelian Isthmus was 70km wide. In the main operational zone of the western sector, which was 12-15km wide, Govorov placed 200 artillery guns per kilometre. The quantitative advantage of the Soviet forces at the start of the offensive on the Karelian Isthmus was 4:1 for personnel, 5:1 for tanks, 6:1 for artillery and 15:1 for aircraft.[394]

The force used for the attack on the Finnish positions in East Karelia consisted of 184,000 men, 2,140 artillery pieces, 363 tanks and 700 aircraft. Here the front was 220km wide.[395] The troops belonged to the Seventh and Thirty-second Armies, which together comprised nine divisions, two engineer brigades, two tank brigades, three assault gun regiments and three tank battalions.[396]

The Finnish Position
During the past two and a half years, the Finnish troops had become used to the status quo at the front and they had almost reached the conclusion that the final phase of the war would bypass them. Not even the air attacks on Helsinki in February could change this optimism, which stretched all to way to the top of the military and political leadership. It seemed that the concept of waging a separate war was taken so seriously by the Finns themselves that they forgot how much they were relying on the German position in the Baltic States. However, the fact was that as soon as the siege of Leningrad was broken and the Germans were pushed back through Estonia, the Finnish defence would be seriously weakened. In that way Finland became highly dependent on the events on the so-called Narva Front in Estonia, not least because the aid from German could only be delivered as long as the Gulf of Finland was not under Soviet control.

The most critical sector of the Finnish Front was still the Karelian Isthmus because of the access it permitted to Helsinki and other communication centres. However, in the summer of 1944 the main part of the Finnish Army was still deployed in East Karelia, while only a quarter of it was positioned on the Isthmus. Apparently, Mannerheim's argument for this distribution of his troops was partly that East Karelia was an important buffer zone, partly that it could be used as a 'pawn' in negotiations with Moscow.

The Finnish Army had become lazy during the trench phase. Training had been lacking, discipline had steadily declined, work on the positions had been neglected in favour of sports competitions and other entertainment activities. It has been said that the most immediate consequence of the soviet offensive was a speedy Finnish change from gym clothes into uniforms.

The Finnish defence of the Karelian Isthmus was based on four defence lines (Map 5).

- Nearest Leningrad was the Main Line, which had been the frontline since 1941. It roughly paralleled the 1939 border at a short distance south of it. The weakest part of the line was its western sector.
- Behind the Main Line was a fall-back line that stretched from Vammelsuu village by the Gulf of Finland (60km northwest of Leningrad) across the entire Karelian Isthmus to Taipale village on the western bank of Lake Ladoga. This line was called the VT-Line.
- The second fall-back line, named the VKT-Line, started at Viipuri, stretched northeast to the island of Kuparsaari in the Vuoksi River, which it followed east also to end at Taipale.
- The Salpa Line (p. 121–122) was somewhat on the other side of the 1940 border. Its sector just east of the Isthmus stretched from the Gulf of Finland to Lake Saimaa. However, the line was so far west it cannot be said to have protected the Karelian Isthmus, rather it blocked access from the Isthmus into southern Finland.

According to the plans, all four defence lines should have been reinforced with concrete bunkers, but in the early summer of 1944 the work was still not finished. The VKT-line in particular was unprepared. On the drawing board it looked splendid, utilising all available terrain advantages, but work on it had only started after the New Year and only in the first sector nearest Viipuri.

The Salpa Line had been built during the Interim Peace and had since then been largely left untouched. It suffered furthermore from a lack of terrain advantages.

Likewise, the Finnish defence line north of the River Svir had not been improved to a degree where it could resist an attack of the kind that Moscow had in mind (for the Finnish order of battle see Appendix XI).

The Soviet Summer Offensive of 1944

As mentioned earlier, the first Finnish defence line on the Karelian Isthmus roughly followed the Rajajoki, i.e. the river which had constituted the 1939 border. However, both the extreme flanks of the position were on the north side of the river. This meant that the mouth of the river, where it ran into the Gulf of Finland at the town of Sestrorersk, was still under Soviet control, and here the Russians could lower the water level by opening a string of sluices.

To make it easier to cross the river during the coming attack, the sluices were opened overnight on 7 June, which brought the water level down to less than 1.5 metres and exposed several of the fords.

The following night, the Soviet Twenty-first Army moved its last few artillery units forward to their attack positions, and by dawn the next day all the Soviet guns deployed along the frontline released an extremely powerful barrage.

> It had been a clear and sunny day. Soon both the landscape and the sky were covered by a red cloud of dust. Trees fell to the ground.[397]

Meanwhile, the Soviet Thirteenth Air Army carried out an attack involving more than 1,000 aircraft as the infantry launched reconnaissance attacks against the Finnish positions. The fighting was particularly intense in the area nearest to the Gulf of Finland, although the Russians tried to disguise their centre of gravity by spreading the assault along the entire front.

This, however, was merely a preview of what was in store for the next day, when the offensive started at 5 am with particularly intense Soviet aircraft and artillery bombardments. The Finnish Front began to crumble, and the first desertions occurred along with outbreaks of panic.

> The feeling of panic was intense. I was paralysed … I was orderly to the company commander, but to be honest he was the first one to run away.[398]

Then the Soviet XXX Guard Corps, an elite unit, moved forward supported by tanks. Their centre of gravity was at Beeloostrov, a small town 4km from the Finnish border, which until 1939 had contained the last railway station on the Soviet side. The area was defended by the Finnish 10th Division, more precisely the 1st Regiment under Lieutenant Colonel Tauno Viljanen. But it was a hopeless task. The Soviet artillery concentration was so strong it exceeded anything that had previously taken place on the Eastern Front, including the fighting at Stalingrad. During the first couple of hours more than 200,000 shells were fired at the Finnish division in this sector, which was less than 20km wide.

Two deeply shocked, very young Finnish soldiers help each other escape from the Soviet artillery attack on the Karelian Isthmus. (SA-Kuva)

The effect was significant. The Finnish Front collapsed along the entire sector, and during the day the Russians penetrated 15km behind the line. Where the Finns managed to put up resistance, it was mostly carried out by small groups on their own initiative.

> I went over to my bunker to gather my group. There was no group any more ... Then I ran up the hill. Here I saw the last of our men who were retreating from the front. They were crying.[399]

The situation continued on the following day (11 June). The sight of Soviet tanks rolling unhindered towards the Finnish positions underlined the problem: the Finnish Army needed more effective anti-tank weapons. Although their anti-tank guns were better now than they had been during the Winter War, they were still primarily 37mm and 45mm weapons, which lacked the necessary stopping power when faced with the new, heavy Soviet tanks. There were also a few 75mm guns, but they were too few to make a difference, particularly since many of those the Finns did possess had been damaged during the attack two days previously.

What the Finns could use more than anything to stop the Soviet tanks was the new German weapon called the *Panzerfaust*, a disposable, short-distance mini anti-tank firearm that one man could carry and operate alone. A consignment of these weapons had already arrived in Finland from Germany, but they had not yet reached the front.

It was in this desperate situation that Mannerheim contacted the German liaison, General Erfurth, and through him requested support from Berlin. First and foremost he needed the Germans to lift their embargo on the ammunition that the Finns had ordered from them previously (p. 270). Even before the Germans had time to reply, Mannerheim had sent his next request. This was on the following day (12 June), and he was now asking the Germans for air support. It would be a big help for the Finnish Army, he pointed out, if the Luftwaffe could attack the Russians in the southern part of the Karelian Isthmus and disrupt their supply lines to the front. Furthermore, the marshal asked the Germans to lift the embargo they had put on a number of aircraft, assault guns and anti-aircraft guns, which Helsinki had previously ordered. For a start, Berlin promised to send ammunition and grain.

The German leaders had by now started to consider how the Soviet pressure on the Finnish positions could be used to strengthen the ties

Major General Pajari narrowly escapes a Soviet grenade during the fighting on the Karelian Isthmus in the Summer of 1944. (SA-Kuva)

between Helsinki and Berlin. Their main concern was for their own troops in Lapland. This 200,000 strong army would be seriously compromised if the Finnish defence in the south collapsed.

Over the 12 and 13 June the Red Army reached the VT-Line along its full length. Since the position was very strong in the middle, General Govorov decided to place his centre of gravity further southwest during the next attack, more precisely in the area around Kuuterselkä village, 50km southeast of Viipuri (Map 5). Meanwhile, the Twenty-third Army was directed towards the centre of the front to maintain the status quo in this area.

The Battle at Kuuterselkä started on 14 June at 7 am when the Soviet CIX Corps, supported by at least one tank brigade and naval units in the Gulf of Finland, launched an attack on the thinly manned Finnish positions. The Finnish defence was mainly carried out by the 53rd Regiment (of the 3rd Division). This formation was commanded by Aaro Pajari, who in October 1941 had been promoted to Major General. The battle rolled back and forth all day, until Pajari in the late afternoon threw in his reserves. Still, the Soviet pressure was relentless and eventually the Finns were forced to flee.

> Those who were fleeing from the positions all said the same: 'The Russians have broken through. We were ordered to flee, every man to himself.'
> Everything suggested that a breakthrough had really taken place and that our unit had been shattered and chased away from the VT-Line at Kuuterselkä.[400]

In later years, some historians have tried to revise the impression that a state of panic reigned among the Finnish troops during the first phase of the Soviet offensive. Reality is hard to deny, though, when you look at the plain facts. The number of registered desertions during June, July and August was 11,690, of which 6,821 cases took place in June alone.[401] Also, between 9 and 30 June some 29,000 soldiers either deserted or lost touch with their units for various reasons.[402]

When the situation was finally turned around, it was due to a number of factors, among them the arrival of reinforcements. A considerable number of troops had already been moved from East Karelia to the Karelian Isthmus, and the plan was that more should follow. Since this could easily lead to a chaotic situation in the leadership, Mannerheim appointed Lieutenant General Oesch as commander of all forces on the Isthmus. It was Oesch who, during the Winter War, had saved the Finnish Army from collapsing at the Viipuri Bay, making him an obvious choice for the new task. He immediately left his current command near Lake Onega and took up his new post on 15 June, while the Russians carried out new attacks on the VT-Line, penetrating it at several points.

Concurrent with the Battle at Kuuterselkä other Soviet attacks had taken place 20km to the northeast at Siiranmäki Village. Here the Finnish defence consisted of the 7th Regiment under Lieutenant Colonel Adolf Ehrnrooth. Siiranmäki was the first place where the Finns could use the new German anti-tank weapons, and the effect was considerable.

> The boxes were opened inside the post and with them came instructions in German. I had been an exchange student in Germany so I was quite good at German, and I started translating these instructions to the others. There was a smart private, who listened to my translation ... Afterwards he took a bundle of them under his arm, and shortly after I heard that he had destroyed six tanks after the little crash course I had given him.[403]

Despite the enormous Soviet pressure, the Finns held their positions, putting twenty-one Soviet tanks out of action. But it was not enough the save the VT-Line, and on 16 June the positions were abandoned on Mannerheim's order. The line at Siiranmäki was held until the evening. On the same day the marshal, despite German protests, also gave the order to pull the Finnish Army out of East Karelia.

On the Isthmus, the Finnish Army retreated to Viipuri and the VKT-Line over the following days, using delaying tactics. Mannerheim's plan was to win as much time as possible so more troops from East Karelia could be moved to the Isthmus. But the situation looked completely hopeless for the Finns. The VKT-Line was not even remotely finished, and during the days leading up to 20 June the Red Army deployed no less than 20 infantry divisions in front of it, reinforced with three artillery divisions, four tank brigades, at least four tank regiments and seven assault gun regiments.[404]

If the Finns threw in all their reserves, they would at best have ten divisions and four separate brigades to set against this massive Soviet force. On top of that their morale and energy were pushed to the limit after ten days of fighting in a constant hell of exploding shells, where sand and gravel rendered their weapons useless, as the ground beneath them was bouncing up and down like a trampoline, and shell splinters whistled through the air and exploded with deafening crashes, spreading death and destruction everywhere.

When the Soviet attack on Viipuri came on 20 June, the town was already practically evacuated without struggle. The Finnish 20th Infantry Brigade under Colonel Armas Kemppi had been given a hopeless task. Still, all was not lost. The Soviet attack had been so strongly focused on the city that the Finns were able to hold the VKT-Line further east, while they continued working on reinforcing the position and making it ready for use. Furthermore, the 10th and 17th Divisions managed to set up a strong defence line west of Viipuri. As in the final phase of the Winter War, the biggest danger was that the Russians would cross the Viipuri Bay, destroy the Finnish defences along the coast and continue towards Helsinki.

On the same day as Viipuri was captured, the Soviet Seventh Army started its offensive on the River Svir and forced the remaining Finnish units in the area back the same way they had arrived three years previously. The Greater Finland project was on its last legs. The only question now was how much longer the Finnish troops could keep themselves and each other going.

The Political Front
The attempts of the peace opposition to involve Mannerheim to a greater extent in a dialogue with Moscow finally paid off on 20 June, the same day that Viipuri was evacuated. The worrying military situation had reached a point where the marshal's legendary pessimism was on the brink of turning into panic. He decided that a new peace initiative must be launched and a new government installed. However, in the middle of the negotiations over the governmental reshuffle he changed his mind and chose instead to keep the current administration.

The next day Ryti's inner circle realised they no longer had a choice: a delegation had to be sent to Stockholm to visit Alexandra Kollontai and probe the possibilities for new negotiations with Moscow. Still, the façade had to be kept a little longer vis-à-vis Berlin since the Finnish Army was still lacking weapons.

During the night of 21 June the Finnish government received a telegram from Foreign Minister von Ribbentrop in Berlin, announcing his arrival in Helsinki the next day to meet President Ryti.

The course of the meeting is known from a description that Ryti later gave the German Ambassador Blücher. First the usual assurances that Germany would win the war despite its current predicament, since new, incredibly effective weapons had been developed and would soon be ready for use. Then a request that the Finns expel the American legation in Helsinki. Finally, the Germans demanded certain guarantees before Finland could receive further military aid. More precisely Ryti had to promise that Finland would not sign a separate peace agreement with the Soviet Union. As bait, von Ribbentrop produced a long list of weapons and units that Germany would sent to Finland if only the country remained on Germany's side in 'the struggle against Bolshevism'.

Meanwhile, American pressure had also increased. At about the same time as the meeting between Ryti and von Ribbentrop, the Finnish ambassador to Washington, Hjalmar Procopé, had to leave the US along with three high ranking members of his staff. Procopé had ignored several warnings to dampen his pro-German and anti-Russian announcements. From now on there were only two subordinate embassy officials left to represent Finland in the USA.

The worsened relationship with Washington was taken very seriously in Helsinki. So far the hope had been that America would support Finland's wishes to see the 1939 border re-established, perhaps even with parts of East Karelia added. As mentioned earlier the US had not declared war on Finland, and sympathy for the little Nordic country was pronounced among the American people.

22 June was also the day when the Finnish negotiation feelers reached Stockholm. Kollontai immediately passed the message on to the Kremlin and received a reply the next day. The Russians were willing to negotiate, but only if the Finns would abandon their usual delaying tactics along with their habit of sending negotiators without sufficient mandate to enter into agreements. In short, Moscow demanded that the Finns from the start declared themselves willing to capitulate.

The word is supposed to have sent a twinge of panic through the Finnish envoy, who was handed the message by Kollontai. She, always keen to get the dialogue off the ground, assured the envoy that it was probably not that bad. If nothing else it is possible to be *willing* to capitulate without actually doing so, she is reported as having said.

On the same day (23 June) the Foreign Policy Committee of the *Eduskunta* gathered to discuss the telegram from Moscow. The committee members, too, were highly suspicious of the Soviet demand that they capitulate. Ryti and Tanner suggested asking Moscow for a guarantee that the sovereignty of Finland would be respected. However, the rest of the committee presumed that the Russians would just beat around the bush, since Moscow was known for having other definitions of terms such as 'sovereignty' and 'democracy' than those used in the western world.

There exists, however, a different version of these events, according to which the Finnish leaders simply used the claimed linguistic entanglement as a means to drag out the negotiations, while behind the scenes they tried to reach an agreement with Berlin over more military support. The purpose was allegedly to strengthen the Finnish position on the battlefield as much as possible before entering into negotiations with Moscow. Such a procedure would be in accordance with traditional diplomatic conduct and for that reason alone it seems highly plausible.[405]

In any case the committee members decided to ignore the message from Moscow and instead they started discussing how to achieve the required support from Germany. They knew the two interconnected demands that the Germans were making: a) Finland had to give a political guarantee that it would not sign a separate peace agreement with the Soviet Union, and b) the country had to conclusively join the German war effort. The problem was that none of these demands had a chance of being passed by the *Eduskunta*. Mannerheim made a few suggestions on how the conundrum could be solved, but they were turned down by the majority of the committee. Instead, they decided that Ryti should offer Hitler a purely *personal* guarantee that there would be no separate peace between Helsinki and Moscow.

Some vague concessions were added to the proposal, which was handed to von Ribbentrop the next day. He was far from pleased and neither was the Führer back in Berlin. The Finns then exposed their German visitor to a diplomatic tug-of-war of the kind which they had developed into an art form during their years of negotiating with Moscow – a mixture of tough slowness and sullen silence.

It was too much for von Ribbentrop. In the end he went into a veritable fit of rage, which he took out on Ambassador Blücher, an aging government official of the old imperial school, for whom etiquette and eloquence were essential virtues.

The following day (25 June) the members of the Finnish Foreign Policy Committee were still discussing. Finally, they managed to put together a guarantee that was acceptable to the Germans, and which needed only to be signed by Ryti. But there was still a problem.

The crucial question was how Ryti alone could issue a presidential guarantee for something that demanded a parliamentary decision – in this case one which would undoubtedly be impossible to achieve. The loophole that the lawyers eventually found was a paragraph in the Finnish constitution, which said that questions about the country's status as a belligerent power could only be decided by mutual agreement between the president and the parliament. The rule was really aimed at the issuing of war declarations, but nothing said it could not be turned around and applied also to peace agreements. This meant that Ryti in effect had a veto in such matters, and hence he could give the Germans the requested guarantee by promising to turn down any proposal that might come up for a separate peace (Ryti's letter to Hitler can be found in Appendix XII).

Henrik Bertelsen writes: 'In the morning [of 26 June] the foreign minister of the Third Reich returned home to Berlin with a much needed political triumph in his pocket . . . Ribbentrop's blackmail had succeeded, but he had failed to see that Finland's democratic system had kept a back door open.'[406]

The Fighting at Tali and Ihantala

From Viipuri a railway line ran northeast, winding in and out between numerous small and bigger lakes, across bridges and isthmuses towards the town of Antrea. One of the first stops on the route was Tali. Its station was built in 1931, but the village did not have its own church. Instead, the locals frequented the church of another village, Ihantala, a few kilometres to the north (Map 6).

Today Tali is called Palsevo. Ihantala with its church has ceased to exist. It was levelled to the ground during the fighting that took place here in late June and early July 1944.

The German aid to Finland, which Mannerheim had requested on 12 and 13 June, had started arriving a few days later. It initially consisted of Detachment Kuhlmey (*Gefechtsverband Kuhlmey*), a unit of the Luftwaffe commanded by 'flying ace' Colonel Kurt Kuhlmey. The detachment comprised seventy aircraft, and unlike the material aid it arrived in time to make a difference to the fighting in the Tali-Ihantala area. During the following period it would carry out a total of almost 3,000 operations over the Karelian Isthmus. The detachment was on 21 June followed by half an assault gun battalion.

After the fall of Viipuri, the Red Army tried as planned to continue its offensive in the direction of the Kymijoki. But it was impossible for the Russians to get past Tienhaara Village west of Viipuri due to staunch Finnish resistance. On 22 June the worn-out Finnish troops at Tienhaara were replaced by a Swedish-speaking unit, the 61st Regiment, known as *Sextiettan* (the Swedish word for sixty-first), which is supposed to have included a small group of Danish volunteers. The regiment had strong artillery support and was also backed by Detachment Kuhlmey. Over the following twenty-four hours the situation developed into the Battle of Tienhaara, where *Sextiettan* repelled one attack after the other carried out by two divisions under the Red Army's CVIII Corps, which also had massive artillery support.

In the end, the Russians had to give up trying to break through the Finnish lines, and instead Field-Marshal Govorov chose to let the 21st Division move north to cross the Saimaa Canal and push further west from there. When that turned out to be impossible, too, because of tough Finnish resistance, he swung the formation east in the direction of Tali, where a large group of Finnish units had been pushed together. Here the terrain was relatively suitable for the use of tanks and generally looked as though it were made for major decisive clashes (for an overview of the Soviet, Finnish and German forces during the fighting around Tali and Ihantala see Appendix XIII and XIV).

However, before we look at the fighting itself, it should be mentioned that the very idea of seeing the combat in this area as one big isolated battle

– 'the Battle of Tali-Ihantala' – is of a newer date and has been criticised for being a Finnish neo-patriotic construction. It is indeed remarkable that the 'battle' does not occur in the Soviet accounts, nor is it mentioned by Earl F. Ziemke, the American military historian who elaborately researched the German northern theatre of operations in the Second World War. Even in Finland the fighting around these two Karelian villages was for many years merely seen as an integral part of a whole string of interconnected, very fierce clashes in the area between Viipuri and Vuoksi during the height of the summer of 1944.

Whether this is right or wrong, there is still no doubt that the Finnish-German resistance at Tali and Ihantala constituted an important part of the overall fighting to prevent the Red Army from crossing the 1940-border on the Karelian Isthmus and advancing on to Kymijoki, which would certainly not have been a desirable situation for either Finland or the rest of the Nordic countries. To mark out these events from the rest of the fighting in the area may constitute historical trickery, but then the same could be said for many other famous battles, particularly during this period, and at least it has meant that some significant events have been researched with a considerable accuracy that they would probably not otherwise have been granted.

The fighting, as it is outlined in the modern Finnish interpretation of the events, started on 25 June at 6:30 am with a Soviet artillery attack aimed at the Finnish right flank. Positioned here was the Finnish 3rd Brigade, also known as the Blue Brigade.

> It was as if the shells held their breath as they approached you. In such situations you have a tendency to check if there's another one

Soviet advance across the Karelian Isthmus, 1944.

coming. It was terrifying because you knew there would be another explosion in ten or twenty seconds, and after that there would be more shells.[407]

Ninety minutes later the thunder from the artillery waned, after which the Red Army's 314th and 158th Division attacked and forced the Finnish Blue Brigade onto the retreat. The Finns, however, soon took up new positions and repelled soviet attempts to push them further back.

Meanwhile, the Soviet main attack had started around Tali. Here too the artillery preparation had begun at 6:30 am, and after one and a half hours it was followed by an air attack. Then the Soviet infantry advanced. The third battalion of the Finnish 13th Regiment tried desperately to keep back the Soviet 45th Guard Division, but had to retreat with severe losses. Nevertheless, the Soviet advance was halted at 9 am, with only scattered groups carrying out reconnaissance attacks.

The reason for the pause was that Soviet units east of Leitimojärvi had advanced unexpectedly fast and scattered the Finnish forces near the lake, particularly the separate Battalion 28 and also the third battalion of the 28th Regiment, meaning that the Russians had to stop in order not to compromise communication between their advancing units.

In the meantime, the commander of the abovementioned third battalion, Major Tor-Oscar Erwe, had managed to collect a small group of his men half-way between Tali and Ihantala, where they repelled some of the Soviet reconnaissance attacks. After a while, however, the Finns were pushed north to Ihantala, where Erwe's battalion was assembled again.

By forcing the Finns out of the area east of Leitimojärvi, the Russians had created an opening in the Finnish line, which allowed them to move north around the lake and attack the first and second battalion of the Finnish 48th Regiment from the rear. Since all the Finnish units along the frontline were indispensible, parts of the reserve were thrown into the fighting to fill the hole. These counterattacks, however, were badly coordinated and consequently failed. Soon after it turned out that the Soviet attacks had created a long, sausage-shaped area that penetrated into the Finnish left flank northwest of Leitmojärvi. From this area the Russians could conduct tank operations and other forms of attacks. The Finns nicknamed the area the *Panssarimakkara*, meaning the 'Tank Sausage'. Inside it there were four Soviet infantry regiments, a tank brigade and several separate tank and assault gun regiments.

By noon, a communication error on the Finnish side allowed for twenty Soviet tanks to move freely up along the north-westerly road from Tali. At the first crossroads they reached, called Portinhoikka, the force divided. One group continued straight ahead, while the other turned right along the road going north to Ihantala. The first group soon ran into an improvised defensive position manned by Finnish pioneers, who destroyed two tanks. The other group was stopped just short of Ihantala, where a Finnish anti-tank gun team destroyed three of the Soviet tanks.

A subsequent Finnish counterattack aimed at the Portinhoikka Crossroads was repelled by a Russian force, which in the meantime had set up a solid defensive position. However, a new Finnish attack supported by tanks managed to drive the Russians away from the crossroads at 7 pm, although the Finnish Armoured Division was weakened after having suffered heavy losses since the beginning of the Soviet offensive.

> The place looked terrible … There were heaps of bodies. There were wrecked tanks with half-burned bodies hanging out. It was unbelievable.[408]

The two battalions of the Finnish 48th Regiment, who had previously been in danger of being attacked from the rear, had by now been forced out of their position west of Leitimojärvi.

After having captured the crossroads northwest of Tali, the Armoured Division continued its advance into the evening. Its third *Jäger* Battalion, with artillery support from 18th Division, nearly managed to get as far as the original positions of the 48th Regiment, when it was stopped by Soviet tanks at midnight.

26 June started on the Finnish side with a disagreement over the command relationships at the top of IV Corps. This would influence the situation for the rest of the day. Still, the third *Jäger* Battalion of the Armoured Division managed to break the Soviet resistance by dawn after which it continued in the direction of Tali. Around 2am the battalion had reached a point level with the positions of the 13th Regiment at the beginning of the fighting. Here eight Soviet tanks were either destroyed or captured by the Finns, but a Soviet counterattack forced the *Jäger* Battalion back to its starting point. Other Finnish tank units had to take up defensive positions, while others still kept counterattacking in an attempt to tie the noose around the 'Tank Sausage'. The attempt almost succeeded when the coordination between the Finnish units broke down, making it impossible to break the tough Soviet resistance.

By mid-afternoon the troops that had been scattered the day before were partly assembled into a combat group under Colonel Sven Björkman, who was also the commander of the Armoured Division's *Jäger* Brigade. He was ordered to move east around Leitimojärvi towards Tali and was given support from tanks, assault guns and anti-tank guns. However, the attack had only just begun when it had to be called off, since Soviet troops had started counterattacking in the direction of the Portinhoikka Crossroads. In the evening they captured part of the road to Ihantala, and in doing so isolated the Finnish units at the crossroads. The Finns managed to drive the Russians away, but other Soviet units occupied a different part of the road and in this case they managed to hold their positions.

By then the day was nearly over. Though it had brought some setbacks for the Finnish side, there had also been some progress, particularly related to the use of artillery and aircraft. However, the 18th Division was so worn out that its infantry units were moved to the rear for rest, while the division commander, Major General Paavo Paalu, was replaced by Colonel Otto Gustaf Snellman.

In the early hours of 27 June, the Armoured Division made another unsuccessful attempt to fully encircle the Soviet 'Tank Sausage'. Later in the day a Finnish-German attack on Leitimojärvi was launched to recapture the original positions. The attack started at 3 pm, but it soon ran into tough resistance and had to stop without any of its goals being reached. The fighting had by then been another serious drain on the already exhausted Finnish Armoured Division.

> On 27 June, when I was wounded, there were only 40 men left of each company as a result of the counterattack at Tali.[409]

Nevertheless, the Finns managed to clear the road going north to Ihantala. There were problems, though, since the losses were heavy, and at one point the German assault guns had to leave the battle. They had run out of ammunition, but since the Finns were not informed of this a rumour was circulating that the Germans were acting in a cowardly manner.

By sunset the attempts to encircle the 'Tank Sausage' had still not succeeded. Meanwhile, Finnish and German aircraft had carried out several attacks on a bridge that the Russians were constructing at Tali, and which was essential to their offensive. The attacks inflicted the intended destruction, but all damage to the bridge was promptly repaired by Soviet pioneers.

A new Finnish attack was launched on 28 June at a quarter past midnight, but it was almost immediately repelled and after four hours of intense fighting, the Finns had to retreat to the point where the attack had started.

In the early hours of the new day yet another Finnish attempt to fully isolate the 'Tank Sausage' failed, and for the rest of the day the Armoured Division was exposed to heavy Soviet artillery and air attacks. The unit was now very close to collapsing; in fact, the entire IV Corps was at the end of its resources.

At this point a new massive Soviet attack was launched, pushing the Finnish troops in front of it north so that by noon, the Russians were only

Finnish soldiers at Tali armed with a German Panzerfaust. In the background a destroyed Soviet tank. (SA-Kuva)

1km from Ihantala. This was the point at which the situation changed, as the Finnish 6th Division arrived on the battlefield. After several hours of fierce fighting the Finns managed to carry through a counterattack in the late afternoon and then stabilise their frontline. Still, the situation remained highly critical. The Russians had broken out of the 'Tank Sausage' and were threatening to isolate the Finnish 30th and 50th Regiments.

Shortly after midnight on 29 June, Lieutenant General Oesch and the commander of IV Corps, Lieutenant General Laatikainen, held a meeting to plan upcoming operations. They decided to end their counteroffensives in the direction of Tali and instead stabilise the defence at Ihantala. The Finnish frontline had to be straightened out and thus shortened, while exhausted units were to be sent to the rear and used as reserves. The two regiments in the southern sector had to carry out a fighting retreat. This was launched at noon, shortly after the new orders had been issued. Due to communication problems, however, some of the units were encircled during the retreat and had to fight their way out.

The Finnish forces east of the 'Tank Sausage' were exposed to heavy attacks throughout the day, and around 8 pm they were forced to pull back. This created a breach in the Finnish line east of Lake Ihantala; yet the Finns managed to mend it in time with reserves and support units from 4th Division, which was nearby.

Shortly after midnight the Finnish 50th Regiment along with the 30th Regiment and the Armoured *Jäger* Brigade (now down to less than one fifth of its original strength) finished their retreats covered by the 6th Regiment. After that the Armoured Division was taken out of the combat zone, while 6th Division started setting up a new defence line west of Lake Ihantala. The line was ready by mid-morning, at which time the 6th Regiment was also taken out of the fighting area. By midnight the situation appeared to be reasonably under control along the new Finnish defensive positions.

On 30 June the Finnish 12th Regiment pulled back from its vantage positions south of Ihantala Village, where it had been under heavy fire all morning. The unit established itself behind a new defence line, where it came under attack again in the evening. Here a Russian breakthrough with infantry and tanks was fought off with artillery and *Panzerfausts*, and the damage was repaired.

From the next day onwards, the fighting around Tali is considered to have ended. The clashes so far had been characterised by Soviet attacks and Finnish counterattacks; yet from now on the confrontations would primarily constitute a Finnish defence of the Ihantala area. The straightening out of the frontline had been a highly difficult and dangerous undertaking, on several occasions close to failing, but in the end the operation had succeeded. The Finns now found themselves in a position that was practically unfortified, but whose stony terrain in itself made for a natural fortification. Besides, the fighting during the preceding days had shown that the Finnish artillery had become extremely efficient. The same went for the new anti-tank weapons, which were perfectly suited to the kind of short distance combat that was typical of the warfare in the highly forested terrain on the Finnish Front.

The first Soviet attack on the new Finnish defence position was launched early in the morning of 1 July and was aimed at the Finnish 12th Regiment's second battalion inside of Ihantala village. However, the attack was repelled by the Finnish artillery. The next Soviet attack started around noon and was aimed at the same target. When that failed as well, the Russians tried instead to penetrate the Finnish line a few kilometres west of Ihantala at Vakkila Village. This time the target was first bombed from the air.

> The planes attacked us eight or ten at a time. First they flew in a circle and then they charged us one by one.[410]

The succeeding Soviet attack, carried out by infantry and tanks, was repelled by Finnish artillery and German fighter aircraft. In the evening a further three Soviet attacks (one aimed directly at Ihantala, one west of the village and one at the 12th Regiment's first battalion) were likewise fended off.

Despite constant Soviet artillery activity on 2 July, only two infantry attacks took place. The second one, however, was particularly fierce. Supported by tanks it started in the middle of the afternoon and managed to make a breach in the Finnish line; yet after the Finnish reserves had been thrown into the combat, the advancing Russians were driven back thanks to the precision of the Finnish artillery.

In the evening of the same day, Soviet aircraft attacked the airfield at Immola, which was used as a base by Detachment Kuhlmey. The attack destroyed thirty-three German aircraft, of which nine were subsequently beyond repair, and thus caused a serious weakening of the German air support to Finland.

On 3 July it was the Finnish-German side that initiated the fighting shortly after midnight, with a combined artillery and air attack. The Finnish intelligence services had intercepted a Soviet radio message about an upcoming large scale attack, and the plan was now to avert it before it had even started. As such the operation was successful; but instead the Soviet artillery, along with 200 bombers, started attacking the Finnish positions. The assault lasted for an hour, after which the Soviet tanks started rolling towards Ihantala. Again the Finnish artillery tried to fend them off, but the Russians forced the first battalion of the Finnish 12th Regiment to leave a strategically important, thinly forested hill named Pyöräkangas 1km west of Ihantala. After that the Soviet advance was kept in check while a Finnish counterattack was prepared. This was launched at 12:30pm and the hill was recaptured.

During the rest of the day, the Russians tried to launch several new attacks, but each time the Finnish artillery with almost uncanny precision managed to avert the threat before it became real. Only the flank of the Finnish 6th Division was reached by the Russians; but that was as far as they got.

After two minor Soviet infantry attacks had been fended off in the morning of 4 July, Finnish intelligence intercepted another of the enemy's messages. A large Soviet attack supported by tanks and planes was planned to start at 8 pm on the same day. In consequence, the Finnish artillery started a systematic shelling of the Soviet preparation areas. Two hours later it was reported by observers that the Russians were forming another attack force. Again the preparation areas were bombed so that this attack was averted, too.

There was only limited activity in the area on 5 July. The Finnish artillery repelled an attack on the 6th Division. The Russians captured part of the Pyöräkangas hill west of Ihantala but were forced off again by the second battalion of the Finnish 35th Regiment.

> The Russian concentration of fire, it was just enormous. I could never have imagined anything like that. It was just one long thunder clash.[411]

When the Soviet guns stopped firing, the infantry attacked supported by tanks, but again the advance was forced back by the Finnish artillery. The rest of the day was dominated by artillery duels, until a new Soviet infantry attack began, aimed at the Finnish 35th Regiment's first battalion. The Finns were forced to leave Pyöräkangas, but at midnight they launched a three-pronged counterattack with a force consisting of the first battalion of the 12th Regiment (from the west), the first battalion of the 35th Regiment's (from the north) and the separate Battalion 16 (from the east). Supported by fourteen artillery battalions the Finns recaptured Pyöräkangas on 7 July. Shortly after, their artillery repelled a new Soviet attempt to capture the area, and this scenario was repeated. Several other attempted Soviet attacks were forestalled by the Finnish artillery.

A Soviet attack on the right flank of the 6th Division was driven back on 8 July, and on the same day the Finnish artillery warded off an attack by the Russian 286th Division in the direction of Vakkila.

The fighting at Ihantala ended the next day, where the only form of activity was a few artillery attacks. The Soviet centre of gravity was then moved east in the direction of Vuosalmi.

Refugees for the Second Time

During the spring of 1944, 70 per cent of the Karelian refuges from the Winter War had returned to their original homesteads. At this time, however, the Finnish government realised that it might well be necessary to evacuate them again before long, and so preparations were made for receiving the anticipated wave of refugees.

The Soviet offensive on the Karelian Isthmus in June/July was so massive that not only the military but also the civilian situation – each exacerbating the other – approached chaos. Though the civilian evacuation initially took place with remarkably few losses, this came to an abrupt and tragic end on 20 June when fifty-five Soviet bombers carried out a massive attack on Elisenvaara Station near the northern bank of Lake Ladoga. Here four Finnish passenger trains stood as easy targets, packed with civilian refugees. The losses were 150 killed and 180 wounded. Less than twenty-four hours later the same kind of situation occurred at the railway station at Simola, where seventy people were killed.

But as the Finnish Army managed to stabilise the front and the refugees (about 340,000 in total) moved west, the panic wore off. The fleeing Karelians were temporarily housed in various locations around Finland, mostly in outbuildings and annexe buildings on farms.[412]

The Fighting by the Viipuri Bay

At the beginning of July, the Soviet offensive had developed in such a way that the attacks on Tali and Ihantala constituted the middle part of a three-pronged attack. The other two prongs were aimed at the Viipuri Bay and at Vuosalmi village on the east bank of the Vuoksi River.

The attacks on the Viipuri Bay had the same goal as the Soviet operations in the area during the Winter War, but where the bay at that time had been so hard frozen that it could carry the heavy Russian tanks, the Red Army now had to use amphibious vehicles and light vessels from the Baltic Fleet. The attack was carried out by two divisions of the Fifty-ninth Army under General Ivan Koronikov, while a third division was kept in reserve. The formations were heavily supported by artillery. The Finnish defence consisted of units from V Corps under Major General Antero Svensson and included from the start a coastal defence brigade, a coastal artillery regiment and an incomplete cavalry brigade. The Finns too were supported by naval units, and later on also by the German 122nd Division plus another coastal artillery regiment that was placed under Svensson's command.

The battle began on 30 June with a Soviet attempt to capture two minor islands in the bay. The Russians were driven back with heavy losses, but five days later they captured the somewhat bigger island of Uuraansaari.

On 4 July the Finnish Navy launched a counterattack with German support in an attempt to avert further Soviet attacks on the islands in the bay. The clashes continued during the following day and were mainly fought between motor torpedo boats with inland artillery support.

New Soviet attacks on 5 and 6 July, aimed at islands in the northern part of the bay, were repelled by the German infantry division. After that the Soviet initiatives declined and both sides went on the defensive.

The Battle of Vuosalmi

After the Soviet 21st Division had given up on penetrating the Finnish lines at Ihantala, it had turned east in the direction of Vuosalmi village, where heavy fighting had also taken place in the Winter War. Here the Soviet Twenty-third Army had for some time tried to force the Finnish 2nd Division away from the west bank of the Vuoksi River.

> The entire islet was 200m wide. Then there was a drop of 30m down to Vuoksi River, which was 400m wide. You really don't feel like fighting in such a place.[413]

Previously, on 4 July, the Red Army's XCVIII Corps had attacked the Finnish positions on the west bank of the Vuoksi. Over the following five days a violent battle raged, after which the Finns had to retreat across the river.

> We now had to get away from there. The Russians were already on the same side of the river as Vuosalmi. So we started swimming.[414]

The Soviet CXV Corps then crossed the river with all its three divisions, and over the next two days they established a bridgehead on the bank. On 11 July more heavy clashes took place, followed by smaller attacks and counterattacks.

> The tactic was simple. The first man jumped into the trench and started throwing hand grenades. After the grenades had exploded, a submachine gunner went ahead and continued the cleaning up.[415]

None of the clashes led to a definitive result, and here too the fighting ended with both parties going on the defensive.

The Russian Recapture of East Karelia
The situation for the Finns at the Svir Front was seriously weakened after so many units had been moved to the Karelian Isthmus. In consequence, they had to retreat from the north bank when the Soviet amphibious vehicles started to attack across the river on 20 June.

The Red Army recaptured Petrozavodsk without any major fighting. After that they started pursuing the Finnish troops as they moved west in the direction of the state border. The next two to three weeks consisted of a long fighting retreat for the Finns, until they stopped just short of the 1939 border at the so-called U-Line. Knowing that they were now again fighting for their country meant a boost to the morale.

> Everyone knew deep in their hearts that the time had come for a decisive battle. We couldn't afford to pull back any more.[416]

The U-line was now manned by the Finnish 8th, 5th and 7th Divisions, while the 15th Brigade was held in reserve. The defence of the position at Nietjärvi, a small lake 5km from the north-eastern bank of Lake Ladoga, was undertaken by the 2nd and 44th Regiments (both of the 5th Division). The 2nd Regiment covered the sector north of Nietjärvi, while the 44th Regiment manned the position between the southern shore of the lake and the bank of Lake Ladoga. After a series of reconnaissance attacks the Russians decided it was here, in the southern sector, that they wanted to launch their attack.

The battle at Nietjärvi started in the morning of 15 July with a Soviet artillery attack. Since the area was quite sandy, it was soon impossible to see more than a few metres in any direction and difficult to keep the weapons functioning.

> The most terrifying moment arrived when the artillery stopped and you awaited the infantry attack … Of course it's tragic for an 18-year-old boy to see headless bodies and such things.[417]

The Soviet infantry was supported by tanks and the attack led to the Finnish line being penetrated. Despite Finnish counterattacks the opening was expanded so that by sunset it was almost 500m wide. The fighting went on into the night, supported on both sides by aircraft.

Next day the battle continued, bringing more progress for the Russians, who captured Nietjärvi Village. Then, after an artillery preparation in the evening, the Finns tried to roll up the trenches that the Russians had previously captured from them. It developed into a series of close combat situations in which the Finns gained the upper hand. By sun-up the Russian positions had been captured, partly by the aid of a newly arrived flamethrower unit.

> A terrible close combat weapon. The trench, the corpses in it and the way they smelled in the summer heat was particularly disgusting.[418]

A subsequent Soviet attempt to recapture the position was fended off by the Finnish artillery.

Clashes continued to occur into August in the area north of Ladoga, particularly at the town of Ilomantsi. Here the fighting constituted the last real battle between Finnish and Soviet forces in the Second World War, and it was the only area where Soviet troops managed to force the Finns back behind the 1940 border. Between 21 June and 10 August a mixed group of Finnish Units, Group Raappana, managed to cut off, encircle and gradually destroy the Soviet 176th and 289th Divisions in a *motti* along a deserted and isolated forest road.

As such, the fighting between Finnish and Soviet forces during the Second World War ended in the early autumn of 1944 in the same way as they had started in December 1939; but minor confrontations continued to occur until a month later when an armistice was finally decided upon.

Armistice

After the signing of the Ryti-Ribbentrop Agreement, the Finnish leaders had eagerly awaited the arrival of the promised new weapons and foodstuffs from Germany. When they did not turn up in the expected amounts, Mannerheim started to become seriously suspicious that the Germans would ignore their part of the deal. On top of that came other worries such as the German plans to help Finnish right wing extremists carry out a state coup and install a quisling as national leader. Major General Talvela was offered

A young Finnish soldier shortly after the Battle of Ilomantsi, the last real battle of the Continuation War. (SA-Kuva)

the role but turned it down (apparently out of loyalty to Mannerheim), and it proved hard to find another even remotely usable candidate. The threat of a coup was further reduced on 28 June, when the last few Germans in southern Finland were shipped out from Hanko and sent south to join the heavy fighting at the town of Narva by Estonia's eastern border.

Meanwhile, the Peace Opposition revived its plan to set up a government-in-exile in Stockholm. But Moscow refused to back the scheme, and with that the initiative stalled for the second time. Instead, the Soviet leaders kept insisting that Mannerheim be brought into the picture. They wanted nothing to do with Tanner and Ryti. Paasikivi was acceptable to the Kremlin, but not to the leaders in Helsinki, who found him too soft and yielding.

The initiative to sue for peace this time had to come from the Finns themselves and so a peace feeler was dispatched via intricate diplomatic channels. It finally reached Alexandra Kollontai by the end of July and she immediately passed it on to Moscow. The Russians replied that they were willing to negotiate, but only if Finland had a new government.

Documents that have been found in the Soviet archives in recent years show that the Russians at this time were working on a set of very tough demands for a Finnish separate peace. It was required, for instance, that the border on the Karelian Isthmus be moved west into Finland to follow the Kymijoki. This would have increased the flood of Finnish refugees by a further 250,000 people. Also, it would practically have crushed Finnish economy, since a large part of the country's all-important paper industry was situated in the area that was to be handed over to the Soviet Union. However, these demands, which were set by Field-Marshal Voroshilov, were refused by Stalin.

Kimmo Rentola, one of the few historians who has analysed the final stage of the Continuation War in the light of the western democracies and their interest in keeping Finland independent, points to a string of factors that might work as an explanation for Stalin's relatively lenient policy towards Finland at this time. Rentola mentions that the war in Western Europe was approaching Paris and Brussels, and that many felt it would be over before Christmas. The Russians were involved in a multitude of projects with the Western Allies, such as the setting-up of allied occupation zones in Germany. The Warsaw Uprising (where the Polish resistance revolted against the Nazi occupiers and Stalin deliberately delayed sending in troops in support of the Poles) had already damaged relations between Moscow and the Western Allies, and Stalin must have foreseen that he would have to keep using harsh methods in Poland, which would further harm his relations with the West.

Rentola suggests the tense atmosphere meant that Stalin would have gained nothing by turning Finland into yet another area of conflict. He also takes it for granted that the Americans would have rejected Kymijoki as a new frontier, since Washington had decided once and for all that the 1940 border was to be kept. Finally, Rentola points out that the Finnish Army had shown it could not be defeated with the forces that were available to the Red Army in the border areas. This had, if nothing else, been made absolutely clear at the Battle of Ilomantsi.[419]

Ryti stepped down as president on 1 August, officially for health reasons, after which the presidential post was taken over by Mannerheim. Then began yet another reshuffle of the Finnish government. The ministers who had rejected the Soviet peace proposal in the spring and who since then had been behind the agreement with von Ribbentrop had to go. Only Walden continued, despite poor health, as Minister of Defence. Antti Hackzell became the new prime minister. He belonged to the liberal-conservative National Coalition Party and had previously been Finland's foreign minister, and for a while ambassador to Moscow.

On 17 August the German Field Marshal Keitel visited Mannerheim in his military headquarters in Mikkeli. During the meeting Mannerheim calmly declared that he hereby annulled the agreement between Ryti and von Ribbentrop. Equally coolly Keitel replied that such matters were outside of his domain. Mannerheim knew this, of course, but he assumed it was best to spread the news in this manner instead of presenting it directly to Berlin.

As expected the rumour spread quickly, and before long it became the issue of a conversation between the German ambassador to Helsinki, Blücher, and Carl Enckell, who had recently been appointed Finland's Minister for Foreign Affairs. Blücher claimed that Mannerheim, according to international judicial rules and common diplomatic practise, was obliged to carry on his predecessor's agreements, in this case the Ryti-Ribbentrop Agreement with its demand that Finland should remain an ally of Germany and was not allowed to sign a separate peace with the Soviet Union. Enckell tried to evade the issue and seemed rather indifferent to the ethical angles; perhaps he felt that a representative of the Nazi rulers in Berlin was the wrong person to lecture others on such issues.

A week later Mannerheim formally annulled the Ryti-Ribbentrop Agreement through Ambassador Kivimäki in Berlin. After that the time had come to re-establish the dialogue between Helsinki and Moscow in earnest. This was done through the Finnish Ambassador to Stockholm, Georg Gripenberg, who had a meeting with a Soviet representative, while Kollontai participated as interpreter. The representative emphasized how important it was that the Finns showed genuine willingness to find a solution and refrained from using delaying tactics.

On 28 August Helsinki received more specific instructions. The Russians demanded that Finland officially sever its ties with Berlin and order the German military to leave the country no later than 15 September. Should Berlin refuse to do so, the Finns would be committed to disarming the German troops in Lapland and placing them in PoW camps. The demands were co-signed by Great Britain. The US would be informed.

The Finnish leaders asked what exactly the consequences would be if the Germans had not left by the requested date and refused to let themselves be disarmed and incarcerated. Again, the question was sent to Moscow via Stockholm, but the reply was by and large just a repetition of the former message. The Finnish government then promised on 2 September to intern the German troops if necessary. In returned they demanded that the hostilities on the Finnish Front be stopped, preferably by the following day. After that the Finnish troops would pull back to the 1940 border within three days.

Later the same day the Finnish parliament was called in for an emergency meeting, where it was decided to accept the preliminary Soviet conditions and go to the negotiation table. A message to that extent was immediately sent to Moscow, while Berlin was told to remove all German troops from Finnish soil.

The Finnish people were informed of the new situation through a radio speech by Prime Minster Hackzell an hour before midnight. The Russians, however, disapproved of the speech since it contained nothing about the expulsion of the German troops in Finland. Once again the dialogue went via Stockholm and the disagreement was ironed out.

On 4 September at 7 am the guns on the Finnish side of the front went silent. For reasons that have never quite been clarified some Soviet artillery attacks continued through the next twenty-four hours, until they too stopped. With that the armistice had come into effect, but a permanent agreement still needed to be negotiated, and there were still 200,000 German troops in Lapland whose leaders in Berlin refused to realise that their time was running out.

A Finnish delegation led by Prime Minister Hackzell arrived in Moscow on 7 September, but it did not meet with the Soviet negotiators until five days later. There was a Romanian delegation with whom the Russians had to reach an agreement first. When the Finns finally got to the negotiation table, it was without their delegation leader. Shortly before the start of the meeting, Hackzell had suffered a stroke and lost his ability to speak. The Finns asked to have the meeting postponed, but this was refused. Walden then had to lead the delegation, while Molotov led the Soviet team. This situation lasted until 16 September, where Walden was replaced as delegation leader by Carl Enckell, who in the meantime had arrived by plane from Helsinki.

The Moscow Armistice was signed on 19 September 1944. By and large it reinstalled the 1940 border, although there were some changes. The Russians would now take over the Petsamo area and for fifty years they would rent Porkkala, a peninsula considerably closer to Helsinki than Hanko (this lease, however, was annulled in 1956).

With that the fighting was over between Finnish and Soviet troops during the part of the Second World War which the Finns call the Continuation War, and the Russians see as the northern flank in what they call the Great Patriotic War. The conflict had cost the Finnish Army 66,000 dead and missing in action, around 1,200 civilians perished, while 150,000 soldiers and civilians had been wounded.

The Soviet losses are, as with the Winter War, a hotly debated subject. However, the military historian Pasi Tuunainen in this instance again chooses to quote the figures listed in *Soviet Casualties and Combat Losses in the Twentieth Century*. According to this source the Soviet losses were 250,000 dead and missing, and 385,000 wounded. Furthermore, 190,000 are listed as 'sick'.[420]

PART FOUR

THE LAST WAR – AND THE PEACE

(1944–1945)

A Finnish soldier looks at the remains of Rovaniemi, the capital of Lapland, after the town had been levelled to the ground by the retreating Germans. (SA-Kuva)

I

The Lapland War

Finland undertakes to disarm the German land, naval and air armed forces which have remained in Finland since 15 September, 1944, and to hand over their personnel to the Allied (Soviet) High Command as prisoners of war, in which task the Soviet Government will assist the Finnish Army.
THE MOSCOW ARMISTICE, ARTICLE 2[421]

The End of a Brotherhood
The 20th Mountain Army, formerly the AOK, had on 8 September started to move west out of the Kestenga region (100km east of the Finnish border and halfway between Lake Ladoga and the Barents Sea). Since the troops were to leave Finland anyway, to participate in the fighting against the Western Allies who moved through Europe towards Berlin, there was really no reason for confrontations to occur between German and Finnish troops, particularly since the cooperation of the preceding years had taken place in a friendly atmosphere. The parties simply did not see each other as enemies, so during the first stages of the retreat, through Finnish Lapland, there were practically no clashes apart from a minor incident on 15 September, when a German three-man motorcycle patrol refused to surrender to a Finnish unit and as a result was gunned down by the Finns.

It was a different situation at the opposite end of the country, where a German force on the same day tried to capture Hogland. The invasion was repelled by the Finns and caused the Germans considerable losses.

To avoid further bloodshed, the parties on 18 September made an agreement in relation to the retreat, but the Germans wanted to take along as much equipment as possible, and the roads in the Lapland region were small and badly maintained so the retreat was dragging out. The agreement only managed to prevent further bloodshed until 28 September, when the first real battle of the Lapland War took place at Pudasjärvi 100km northeast of Oulu. By then the Germans had started blowing up bridges and depots along their retreat route, while the Finns were trying to stop them. Two days later the Finns attempted to encircle a German force in Pudasjärvi, but most of the Germans managed to escape. The few that remained blew up a depot and were then taken prisoner.

On the same day (30 September), the German 11th Regiment left Oulu by boat. After that the Kremlin started demanding a stronger Finnish effort. The problem was also that the Russians would not let the Finns use a force of more than 70,000 men, one third of the size of the German 20th Mountain Army, which was well armed, rested and had provisions enough to last them for a year.

On 1 October the Finnish 11th Regiment landed in Tornio, which threatened the German retreat from Rovaniemi. At the same time the Finnish Armoured Division moved in the direction of Pudasjärvi.

The next day the Germans launched an attack on Tornio. The ensuing battle lasted a full week and developed in a somewhat comic direction when several Finnish units bumped into the same well-equipped alcohol depot. After that the situation became static for almost a full day. Generally, the confusion was considerable and the morale was low. Nevertheless, the fighting was intermittently fierce, with heavy losses on both sides.

The battle ended with the Germans having to flee from the area. Meanwhile, Hitler had on 3 October given the final order for the 20th Mountain Army to leave Finland via Norway.

German Destruction

On 7 October, Finnish forces captured the town of Kemi 25km southeast of Tornio, while Soviet troops attacked the mining districts at Petsamo and forced the Germans to withdraw in the direction of Kirkenes in Norway (for a summary description of the Soviet Petsamo-Kirkenes offensive see Appendix XV). The latter was in fact much more worrying for the Germans than the Finnish pressure from the south.[422]

One week later the Germans set Rovaniemi on fire and burned it to the ground. On 14 October, when the Finns reached the vicinity, they found the area heavily mined. Meanwhile, much of the civilian population in Lapland had been evacuated to southern Finland and to Sweden.

The destructive activities of the German troops continued through the rest of the war and included blowing up railways, comprehensive minelaying and whole villages and towns being set on fire. Some German units seem to have acted more crudely than they were ordered to. The Finnish colonel and military historian Wolf Halsti, who was commander of the 11th Regiment, later wrote about the behaviour of the Germans in the Lapland War:

> In the direction of Rovaniemi it was ... blatantly clear that the Germans had used some kind of international SS gang to carry out

the destruction, with Dutchmen, Belgians and Croats involved, perhaps also Scandinavians. There were several reports to that extent, but no prisoners were taken. They had been using both cars and trains as means of transport. Alcohol played an important part in these people's lives. It is likely that the regular German troops tried to avoid unnecessary cruelty, at least to some extent.[423]

The actual clashes between German and Finnish troops now followed an almost set pattern. The Germans took up positions along a riverbank and the Finns tried to encircle them, but before the noose could be tied, the Germans had disappeared. They would then set up another ambush behind the next river.

Since the situation obviously demanded a stronger effort from the Finns, the government in Helsinki announced in late November that they intended to expand their force in the region. But Moscow rejected this and instead demanded that the Finnish Army be demobilised in accordance with the armistice. The demobilisation took effect from 1 November. Six days later the Finnish advance towards the Norwegian border was stopped at strong German defensive positions. The Finnish force was too small and inexperienced to carry out a sufficiently effective attack (from December onwards the army was reduced to 37,000 men and consisted primarily of recruits). Instead, the Finns simply waited for the Germans to pull back on their own accord.

On 12 December temporary alcohol prohibition was introduced in Finland due to problems with demobilised soldiers all over the country.

In the New Year, Mannerheim retired as commander-in-chief. He was deeply depressed and convinced that Finland's days as an independent state were numbered. Twelve days later Lieutenant General Heinrichs took over his post. Meanwhile, the German 2nd Mountain Division had pulled back from its positions at the River Lätäseno 300km north of Tornio/Haparanda and entered Swedish territory.

On 25 April two infantrymen were killed during the last skirmish in Finland in the Second World War. Three days later Lieutenant General Siilasvuo reported to Helsinki that the Finnish Army had concluded its task in Lapland.

The Finnish losses during the Lapland War amounted to 1,000 killed and missing in action, while 3,000 were wounded. The German numbers of men killed and missing roughly equated those of the Finns, while the number of wounded is reckoned to have been 2,000.[424]

II

The Post War Era

*How merciful we were toward Finland! We were smart not
to annex it. It would have been a festering wound. Not
because of Finland itself, but because that wound would
have afforded a pretext for anti-Soviet action.
People are very stubborn there, very stubborn. Even
a minority could have been dangerous there.*
V. M. MOLOTOV[425]

Court Cases
An Allied control commission with a strong Soviet bias arrived in Finland in late September 1944 to ensure that the country acted in accordance with the Moscow Armistice. This meant, according to Article 13 of the agreement, that Finland should prosecute its own war criminals. Shortly after the armistice had come into force, 1,400 individuals were put before military courts and accused of crimes committed against Soviet PoWs. Later on more cases followed.

By the end of 1946, a total of 723 individuals had been convicted of war crimes. Of these 107 were military officers, while 372 were NCOs and privates; the rest were civilians. The crimes included murders (42 cases) and homicide (342 cases). Nine of the accused were sentenced to life imprisonment, which was the strongest punishment.[426]

Mannerheim was not the only one who feared that Finland's independence was in jeopardy during the period after the armistice. Finnish officers started smuggling weapons out of army depots and hiding them around the country in secret caches. The purpose was to create a situation where underground resistance groups could be set up swiftly in case of a Soviet invasion or a revolt organised by local Communists. The scheme, however, was exposed in the spring of 1945. This led to a string of court cases, where almost 1,500 individuals were given short prison sentences. The story of course did nothing to repair the already tense relationship with Moscow.

By demand of Finnish Communists and the Allied Control Commission, the politicians who had been in power during the Continuation War were also put on trial. This became the so-called War-Responsibility Trials, which were launched in February 1946. The judges were Finnish, and the sentences were based on retroactive laws.

The convictions were as follows: Risto Ryti (ten years hard labour), J.W. Rangell (six years prison), Edwin Linkomies (five and a half years prison), Väinö Tanner (five and a half years prison), T.M. Kivimäki (five years prison), Henrik Ramsay (two and a half years prison, Antti Kukkonen (two years prison), Tyko Reinikka (two years prison).

Compared with the sentences generally given to political and military leaders in the actual Axis nations, the Finnish leaders were let off lightly. This was partly due to their success in covering up what had really been going on, particularly in the early stages of their cooperation with Nazi Germany, and partly because Finland had not followed a conscious ethnic extermination policy. Furthermore, the Western Allies still had a great deal of sympathy and understanding for the extremely squeezed situation Finland had been in during the Interim Peace. Also the separate war argument, although it was by and large a hoax, nevertheless had an element of truth to it that benefitted Finland's overall image.

In addition to all this, there appears to be little doubt that the Finnish military effort had inspired respect in the Soviet leaders, which may explain why no Finnish officers were charged at the War-Responsibility Trials. This included Mannerheim, who nonetheless until his death in 1951 lived in constant fear that something of the kind might happen to him (in fact, he always carried in his pocket a suicide pill). Perhaps that was why he spent his retirement moving between three countries that were known for their reluctance to hand over supposed war criminals to the Soviet Union, namely Sweden, Spain and Switzerland.

Other Finnish officers with reasons to worry, such as Lieutenant General Talvela, preferred year-long residencies in South America, but most of them gradually returned to Finland. A few settled permanently in the US and gained employment with the American military.

PoWs and Refugees

When the war between Finland and the Soviet Union ended in September 1944, there were 42,000 Soviet PoWs in Finnish camps. According to the armistice they were to be handed over to the Soviet Union. Among them were a few thousand who had collaborated with the Finns in various ways, and who after interrogations etc. were put in Soviet labour camps. Additionally, there were 2,500 German PoWs whom the Russians also demanded be handed over. These prisoners were placed in the Borovitshi Jegla camp in the Novgorod area, where the mortality rate in the winter of 1944-45 was particularly high.[427]

Soviet soldiers from an Ingrian background who had been captured by the Finns and had subsequently served in the Finnish Army's Separate Battalion 3 (the Tribal Warrior Battalion, p. 258) were also handed over to the Soviet Union. When the members of the unit during their transport towards the Soviet Union became aware of what was happening, they reacted by tearing medals and insignia off their uniforms, throwing them on the ground and spitting on them. Some managed to escape; the rest were persuaded to get back on board the train. However, the escapes continued and out of the original 650 men only 190 were left at the journey's end.

The Allied Control Commission demanded that the Finnish Army chase the refugees, and with time nearly all of them were caught, though in some cases it was not until several years later. In the Soviet Union they were generally sentenced to either ten or twenty years of imprisonment. Others were condemned to death. Executions were taking place as soon as the transports reached Viipuri.

Soldiers from the Separate Battalion 6, consisting of Ingrians who had fled to Finland to evade German military service, were likewise handed over to the Soviet Union and suffered a similarly miserable fate.[428] The voluntary regiment JR 200 (p. 258), consisting of Estonians, had been returned to their homeland in August 1944 to participate in the German attempt to stop the Soviet advance towards Berlin.

Beside the personnel in the kinsmen battalions there was in Finland 60,000 Ingrians with Soviet citizenship (p. 231). They had arrived in the country during 1943-44 as part of the planned population exchange and had been promised Finnish citizenship and permanent residency in the country. The Soviet Union demanded these people be handed over also in reference to Article 10 of the Moscow Armistice, although said article really only dealt with people who had been forcefully moved. The Russians promised the Ingrians that they could return to the districts of their old homes and that they would be given financial help to build a new life. Unsurprisingly, this appears not to have happened. Between 5,000 and 7,500 of the Ingrians had no faith in the Soviet promises and fled to Sweden to avoid being transported east.

Of the 3,400 Finns who had been taken as prisoners of war by the Red Army, some 2,000 were handed over to Finland after the war. Their subsequent fate has already been dealt with in this book (p. 238-240).

Reconstruction

In November 1944, Paasikivi had been appointed Finland's new prime minister, and he immediately formed a broad government with the participation of the newly legalised Communist Party. The way Paasikivi had been kept out of the political decision-making process during the war years now played to his advantage. He continued to be respected in Moscow, while at the same time no one in Finland could accuse him of left-wing sympathies. He was the obvious choice for the position as prime minister and held it for the next two years, after which he took over from Mannerheim as president.

As is often the case in countries that have lost a war, Finland managed to get back on its feet relatively quickly. The active phase of the Lapland War had been relatively short, and the demobilised soldiers generally returned to work sooner than expected. The refugees from Lapland returned to their home districts and started rebuilding their houses, while most of the Karelian refugees slowly learned to accept that they would in all likelihood never get their homes back (although it was attempted on several occasions, causing new hopes that once again ended in disappointment). The burden was lessened by the government's promise that the farming families would be given new land as compensation for what they had lost. Only some 2,800 refugees came from East Karelia.

The new situation in Finland led to significant changes in the political landscape. The IKL was prohibited along with other organisations deemed Fascistoid by Moscow, among them the Civil Guard and the Lotta Svärd organisation. As already mentioned, the Finnish Communist party was legalised after having been prohibited since 1930. In October 1944 the party became the leading faction in a left-wing coalition called the SKDL.

The first parliamentary elections in post-war Finland took place in March 1945. As in several other West European countries the result showed a marked rise in support for the radical faction of the left wing, who won 51 of the 200 parliamentary seats in the *Eduskunta*. The Communist Yrjö Leino became Minister of the Interior, which caused fears that the radical left wing faction would attempt a coup with Soviet support.

That, however, did not happen. The Russians had other things on their agenda. For the Soviet Union the war against Germany was not over until early May 1945. It was still at this point necessary for the Russians to keep fairly good relations with Great Britain and the USA, and for financial reasons it was best for them not to cause problems in their relationship with the Finns, from whom they were about to receive a considerable compensation amount in war damages.

The big peace conference held in the summer and early autumn of 1946 led in February of the following year to the so-called Paris Peace Treaties. Here Finland was placed in the same category as the actual Axis powers. The Finnish war compensations to the Soviet Union was set at 100 million dollars which, nominally, was half as much as the earlier Soviet demand. It turned out, however, that the amount was supposed to be calculated at pre-war value, so in fact it was no improvement. The Western Allies protested on Finland's behalf, but Moscow refused to budge.

The Paris Peace Treaties also granted membership of the UN to Finland and the participating Axis nations (Italy, Hungary, Bulgaria and Romania). However, the treaty only came into effect six months after it had been signed due to disagreements between Great Britain and the Soviet Union. After that, the Allied Control Commission in Finland packed up and left the country. With regard to the border drawing between Finland and Russia, the new agreements changed nothing from what had been settled at the armistice in September 1944.

The Finnish war compensation was to be paid in engineering industry products and raw materials from the country's huge paper and pulp industry. The compensation was to equate 2 per cent of Finland's GDP in the years up until and including 1952.

Early in 1948 an international crises emerged after a Communist seizure of power had taken place in Czechoslovakia with support from Moscow. In several West European countries there were rumours that they too were on the verge of becoming victims of Communist takeovers. Since the Finnish police was subordinated to the Ministry of the Interior, which was still under Communist leadership, there was a fear that an attempted coup might come from this angle, which made Paasikivi place the army on reinforced alert. The whole thing, however, turned out to be a storm in a teacup.

In the meantime Moscow had offered Helsinki a mutual assistance and friendship pact, which was also to include military aid. Now that Paasikivi had become Finland's president he could finally lead his negotiations with the Soviet Union to a result and he managed to make Moscow accept a number of fundamental changes to the agreement. Among them was the insertion of a clause saying that Soviet military aid to Finland could only occur with the consent of both countries.

This of course was an extremely important modification, but otherwise the agreement in many ways resembled pacts that other East European countries had already signed under heavy Soviet pressure, which again resembled the agreement that Helsinki had been offered in 1938 by Boris Yartsev. The underlying Russian agenda was the same, namely the protection of Leningrad.

As long as the Finns could convince the leaders in the Kremlin that their country was not a threat to the second largest city of the Soviet Union, Finland was allowed to remain in peace – and remain a Nordic country.

APPENDIX I

Structure of a typical Soviet infantry division during the Winter War

- The basic unit in the Red Army was the infantry division, which typically comprised 17,000 men. Each division consisted of 3 infantry regiments (called 'rifle regiments'), each comprising 4,000 men, plus artillery and support units.
- The regimental artillery consisted of 1 artillery regiment comprising 1,900 men, 36 guns of large calibre and a smaller number of howitzers. There was furthermore 1 howitzer regiment comprising 1,300 men and 36 howitzers.
- Attached to each division was 1 anti-tank battalion with 18 45mm anti-tank guns.
- In addition to the division's artillery regiment each 'rifle regiment' had its own regimental batteries consisting of 4 76mm guns and 1 anti-tank battery of 6 45mm anti-tank guns.
- Also attached to each division was 1 tank battalion, which could contain anything from 10 to 40 tanks. The tanks were Model T37, T-38 amphibious tanks or T-26 of various kinds.
- Finally, each division had 1 reconnaissance battalion with 1 attached cavalry squadron, 1 company of armoured personnel carriers, 1 motorcycle company and 2 loosely attached pioneer battalions.

Source
Irincheev: *War of the White Death*

APPENDIX II

The deployment and tasks of the Red Army at the start of the Winter War

- The *Seventh Army* was to penetrate the Finnish positions on the Karelian Isthmus and proceed to the area between Viipuri (inclusive) and the Vuoksi River. From there the army was to continue deeper into Finland in the direction of Lappeenranta, Lahti and Helsinki. The invasion was set to last three weeks. The marching speed would be 20km a day, the same as what was expected from a normal infantry division in peacetime.
- The *Eighth Army* was to attack north of Lake Ladoga. Its task was to reach the area between Sortavala and Joensuu and continue west towards the centre of Finland. The task included attacking the Finnish positions on the Karelian Isthmus from the rear.
- The task of the *Ninth Army* was to capture Kajaani in central Finland and continue to Oulu, thus cutting Finland in two horizontally.
- The operational area of the *Fourteenth Army* was the northernmost one. The task of the army was to capture Petsamo with support from the Red Navy, prevent a landing of Western troops on the Kola Peninsula and prevent an Allied offensive via Norway.

Sources
Manninen: *The Soviet Plans for the North Western Theatre of Operations in 1939-1944*
Irincheev: *War of the White Death*

APPENDIX III

Comparison between a typical Finnish and a typical Soviet infantry division at the outbreak of the Winter War

All figures below are rough generalisations based on a variety of sources, which explains certain inconsistencies. The purpose here is primarily to give an overall impression of the relative strengths between the two armies. (For more information on the Soviet divisions see Appendix I.)

- A typical Finnish infantry division consisted of 3 regiments comprising a total of 14,200 men – against 17,000 in the Red Army.
- Each Finnish infantry division also included 1 artillery regiment of 36 guns – the divisions of the Red Army each included (besides their individual regimental batteries of 4 76mm guns) 1 artillery regiment and 1 howitzer regiment, a total of 72 pieces.
- Two thirds of the Finnish artillery pieces were 3 inch guns from the times of Tsarist Russia, while the remaining one third consisted of heavy howitzers – all of it significantly inferior to the artillery pieces of the Red Army (see Appendix I).
- Each Finnish division also had 1 light unit consisting of 1 cavalry squadron, 1 bicycle company and 1 heavy machine gun company – together these units can be seen as a counterpart to the reconnaissance battalions of the Soviet divisions (see Appendix I).
- Finally, each Finnish division included 1 anti-tank company of 4 37mm guns (often non-existent) and 1 mortar company of 6 8mm mortars – the typical Russian division had at regimental level 6 45mm anti-tank guns and 4 mortar platoons with a total of 8 82mm mortars[429], and 1 attached anti-tank battalion with 18 anti-tank guns.
- The Finnish divisions had no tank units – the Russian divisions each had 1 attached tank battalion.

Sources
Irincheev: *War of the White Death*
Condon: *The Winter War – Russia Against Finland*
Isacson: *Ärans vinter*
Norris: *Infantry Weapons of the Second World War*

APPENDIX IV

Order of battle for the Finnish Army at the outbreak of the Winter War

- On the Karelian Isthmus was the 'Karelian Isthmus Army', consisting of II and III Corps.[430]
- II Corps under Lieutenant General Harald Öhquist covered the western sector. The corps consisted of 3 divisions and some attached separate units of cavalry and infantry battalions, several of them *Jäger* battalions.
- III Corps under Lieutenant General Erik Heinrichs covered the eastern sector. The corps consisted of 2 divisions plus 1 in reserve and 1 mixed group of reconnaissance units and field artillery.
- The front north of Lake Ladoga was covered by IV Corps under Major General Woldemar Hägglund. The corps contained 2 divisions, 2 separate battalions and 1 cyclist battalion, which constituted the reserve.
- The front further north followed approximately half of the entire border and was divided into three main sectors covered by separate battalions under the overall command of Major General Wiljo Tuompo.
- 1 division was held in reserve far behind the front at Oulu by the northern end of the Bay of Bothnia.

Source
Irincheev: *War of the White Death*
Condon: *The Winter War – Russia Against Finland*

APPENDIX V

Soviet and Finnish forces on the Karelian Isthmus on 1 February 1940

RED ARMY FORCES
- Seventh Army (western sector)
  12 infantry brigades, 7 army group artillery regiments, 4 corps artillery regiments, 2 extra heavy artillery battalions, 5 tank brigades, 1 machine gun brigade, 2 separate battalions, 10 aviation regiments
- Thirteenth Army (eastern sector)
  9 infantry divisions, 6 army group artillery regiments, 3 corps artillery divisions, 2 extra heavy artillery battalions, 1 tank brigade, 2 separate tank battalions, 5 aviation regiments, 1 cavalry regiment
- Reserve
  3 infantry divisions, 1 tank brigade, 1 cavalry corps

FINNISH FORCES
- II Corps (western sector)
  5 infantry divisions, 3 separate brigades
- III Corps (eastern sector)
  2 infantry divisions, 2 cavalry regiments
- Reserve
  21st Division

Source
http://winterwar.com

APPENDIX VI

Soviet and Finnish forces at the Viipuri Front on 1 March 1940

RED ARMY FORCES
- During February 1940 the Seventh Army had been reinforced so it now consisted of 13 divisions with various attached units. The divisional numbers were (listed as the formations were deployed from east to west): 43, 53, 86, 70, 113, 138, 24, 100, 123, 84, 51, 90 and 80.

FINNISH FORCES (from east to west)
- I Corps had been formed on 19 February from parts of II Corps, which had become so large it was causing operational problems. The corps consisted of the 1st and 2nd Division (formerly 11th Division) and covered the centre of the T-Line.
- The remaining part of II Corps was still commanded by Lieutenant General Harald Öhquist despite controversy between him and Mannerheim. The corps now consisted of 3 divisions that covered the sector nearest Viipuri.
  – 3rd Division: south and southeast of Viipuri
  – 5th Division: the north-eastern part of the town
  – 23rd Division[431]: stood further northeast up to a point near Tali where I Corps' positions began. (This division was hit particularly hard during the defence of the Viipuri area.)
- The Coast Group was activated on 1 March. It consisted of the 4th Division plus a large number of separate battalions and some poorly armed artillery batteries that had been assembled in haste. The commander was initially Major General Wallenius, who had recently arrived from Lapland with an infantry battalion that had been relieved by Swedish volunteers. Wallenius was on 3 March replaced by Lieutenant General Oesch.

The eastern flank, i.e. the remaining part of the sector that ended by the banks of Lake Ladoga, was covered by III Corps and not seen as participating in the defence of Viipuri.

Sources
http://winterwar.com
Condon: *The Winter War – Russia Against Finland*

APPENDIX VII

The Soviet General Staff's operational plan for an isolated attack on Finland, made in the autumn of 1940

MILITARY GOAL
- To penetrate deep into the centre of southern Finland from positions along the new border by the Karelian Isthmus and north of Lake Ladoga, occupy the territory and destroy the main part of the Finnish Army in the region.
- To cut off northern Finland by pushing through to the Gulf of Bothnia at Oulu and Kemi, partly by way of Suomussalmi, partly via Kemijärvi and Rovaniemi.
- To take control of Petsamo and take up position in the area.
- To attack and capture Helsinki from three directions: 1) along the south coast of Finland starting from the western bank of the Viipuri Bay, 2) from the north starting from the Viipuri area and moving west to Heinola and from there continue southwest, 3) from Hanko.

The campaign was to be carried out by troops from two military districts. The Leningrad Military District was to form 'The North-Western Front'; Arkhangelsk Military District was to form 'The Northern Front'.

'The Northern Front' would consist of four corps, a total of 15 infantry divisions, 1 artillery regiment and 23 aviation regiments. 'The North-Western Front' would consist of 29 infantry divisions, 2 armoured divisions, 1 motorised infantry division, 5 armoured brigades, 12 artillery regiments, 6 pontoon battalions, 7 pioneer battalions, 7 engineer battalions and 55 aviation regiments. The reserves of the supreme command would consist of 3 infantry divisions. Only 1 ski brigade would participate.

For the sake of comparison, the Red Army had by the start of the Winter War comprised some 20 divisions. Experience from this war had shown that it was probably a mistake to attack Finland in the winter. According to the order from Stavka, the detailed version of the above plan was to be finished by 15 January 1941. The Finnish military historian Ohto Manninen writes: 'Finland, at least, would have been in the danger zone in May 1941, if the Germans had turned their attention to the west or south.'[432] However, the finished version of the detailed plan appears never to have been handed in.

Source
Manninen: *The Soviet Plans for the North Western Theatre of Operations in 1939-1944*

APPENDIX VIII

Order of battle for the Soviet and Finnish forces along the border on 1 July 1941 (from south to north)

THE RED ARMY
- Twenty-third Army (4 divisions) under general Gerasimov covered the area across the Karelian Isthmus and along the north bank of Lake Ladoga to the town of Sortavala.
- Seventh Army (3 divisions along the front and 2 in reserve) covered the front between the north bank of Lake Ladoga up to a point roughly at level with Oulu.
- Fourteenth Army (4 divisions and 1 armoured division in reserve) covered the rest of the front up to the Barents Sea.

C-in-C of the abovementioned Soviet forces was Field-Marshal Kliment Voroshilov from the Leningrad Military District.

FINNISH FORCES
On the Karelian Isthmus
- IV Corps (Lieutenant General Oesch)
- II Corps (Lieutenant General Laatikainen)

North of Lake Ladoga: 'The Karelian Army' (Lieutenant General Heinrichs)
- VII Corps (Major General Hägglund)
- VI Corps (Major General Talvela) including the German 163rd Infantry Division
- Group Oinonen (Major General Oinonen)

Separate division
- 14th Division (Major General Raappana)

Under German command
- III Corps (Lieutenant General Siilasvuo, from September 1941 until March 1942 subordinated the Wehrmacht Army Norway)
- 6th Division (borrowed from III Corps, subordinated the German XXXVI Corps)

- Battalion Ivalo (Major Antti Pennanen, subordinated the Wehrmacht Mountain Corps Norway, a part of Army Norway)

Of the abovementioned Finnish corps the first two covered the front from the Gulf of Finland up to the north bank of Lake Ladoga, where the 'Karelian Army' took over to a point level with the north bank of Lake Onega. The next sector of the front was 150km wide and constituted the area of attack for the 14th Division. Further north III Corps bridged the Finnish forces in the south with the German forces covering the rest of the front up to the Barents Sea. The German XXXVI Corps, which was the main force of Army Norway, was deployed immediately north of the Finnish III Corps. The location and task of Battalion Ivalo is described in the main text (p. 184).

Source
Ekberg: *Finland i krig, bd. II*

APPENDIX IX

Mannerheim's Order of the Day 10 July 1941 (translated from Swedish, the language in which it was originally written)

During our War of Independence in 1918 I promised the people of Karelia on both sides of our eastern border not to sheath my sword until Finland and East Karelia are free. I swore this oath in the name of the Finnish peasant army, relying on its brave men and the selflessness of Finnish women.

For twenty-three years East Karelia has waited for the fulfilment of this promise; for more than a year the part of Karelia, which was torn away from us after our honourable Winter War, has lain barren in expectation of a new dawn.

Warriors of the era of our War of Independence, heroes of the Winter War, my brave soldiers! The day has cometh. Karelia arises, among your column marches its own battalions. A free Karelia and a great Finland emerges before our eyes from the mighty confusion of great historic events. May the providence that chains the destinies of nations not deny the Finnish Army to fulfil the promise I gave to the people of Karelia.

Soldiers! The ground upon which you now set foot is holy soil satiated by the blood and suffering of our tribesmen. Your victories shall grant Karelia its freedom, your deed shall grant Finland a great and joyous future.

Mannerheim.

Source
Sandström: *Fortsättningskriget 1941-44*

APPENDIX X

Order of battle for the Red Army before the offensive on the Karelian Isthmus, June 1944

Western sector (near the Gulf of Finland)
- Twenty-first Army (General Dmitrii Gusev) consisting of:
  – 6 divisions supported by twelve artillery brigades
  – 14 artillery regiments
  – 5 tank regiments
  – 3 assault gun regiments

Eastern sector (near Ladoga)
- Twenty-third Army (Lieutenant General Alexander I Cherepanov) consisting of:
  – 6 divisions supported by 1 artillery brigade
  – 3 artillery regiments
  – 1 tank regiment
  – 1 assault gun regiment

Support
- The Soviet Baltic Fleet, comprising:
  – 2 battleships
  – 2 cruisers
  – 4 mine sweepers
  – 3 gunboats
- Thirteenth Aviation Army (1,294 aircraft)

APPENDIX XI

Order of battle for the Finnish Army before the Soviet offensive in June 1944

On the Karelian Isthmus
Western sector (near the Gulf of Finland)
- IV Corps (Lieutenant General Taavetti Laatikainen)

Eastern Sector (near Lake Ladoga)
- III Corps (Lieutenant General Siilasvuo)

At the River Svir
- V Corps (Major General Johannes Svensson)
- VI Corps (Major General Anders Tapola)

East Karelia
- II Corps (Major General Einar Mäkinen)

At Rukajärvi
- 14th Division (Major General Erkki Raappana)

APPENDIX XII

President Ryti's letter to Adolf Hitler dated 26 June 1944

With reference to the negotiations which have been conducted with you I wish to express my satisfaction with Germany's promise to meet Finland's wishes with regard to military aid and immediately assist the Finnish troops by sending German reinforcements and war material to repel the Russian attack in Karelia. Furthermore, I have noticed the promise made in your government's name committing the German Reich to also in future provide Finland with all the support that is within Germany's realm of possibility with the aim to, along with Finland's armed forces, fight back the Russian offensive against Finland.

In relation to this I assure you that Finland is determined to continue, along with Germany, the war against the Soviet Union until the threat, which Finland is facing from the Soviet Union, is averted. Given the brother-in-arms aid granted by Germany to Finland in the current difficult situation I declare as President of the Republic of Finland that only with the full consent of the government of the German Reich shall I ever make peace with the Soviet Union and I will not allow any Finnish government appointed by me nor anyone else to take up negotiations on a truce or a peace agreement or negotiations that serve such purposes unless I have the full consent of the government of the German Reich.
(s.) Ryti

Source
Bertelsen: *Finlands vej til freden*

APPENDIX XIII

Soviet and Finnish order of battle on the Karelian Isthmus before the fighting at Tali and Ihantala

SOVIET TROOPS (General Leonid Govorov)
- Twenty-first Army (General Dmitrii Gusev)
  – constituted the main force meant to lead the attack on Tali, with XXX Guard Corps (Major General Nikolai Simonyak) in front supported by 3 tank brigades. The Army consisted of 4 corps totalling 14 divisions plus a large number of tank brigades and assault artillery regiments.
- Fifty-ninth Army (Lieutenant General Ivan Korovnikov)
  – had recently arrived from Estonia. The army covered the left flank and was also to be used for an attempt to cross the Viipuri Bay.
- Twenty-third Army (Lieutenant General Alexander Cherepanov)
  – was deployed by the western bank of Lake Ladoga and as such covered the right flank of the offensive.

FINNISH TROOPS (Lieutenant General Oesch)
- V Corps (Major General Antero Svensson)
  – had recently arrived from the Olonets area. The corps covered the defence of the west bank of the Viipuri Bay.
- IV Corps (Lieutenant General Taavetti Laatikainen)
  – covered the VKT-Line between Viipuri and the Vuoksi River.
- III Corps (Lieutenant General Hjalmar Siilasvuo)
  – covered the remaining of the position along the Vuoksi River to Lake Ladoga.

APPENDIX XIV

Finnish-German forces during the fighting at Tali and Ihantala

IV Corps (Lieutenant General Taavetti Laatikainen)
- 3rd Division (Lieutenant Colonel Lauri Hanterä)
- 4th Division (Major General Pietari Aleksanteri Autti)[433]
- 6th Division (Major General Einar Vihma)
- 11th Division (Major General Kaarlo Heiskanen) (arrived 27 June 1944)
- 18th Division (Major General Paavo Paalu until 26 June 1944, then Colonel Otto Snellman)

Supporting units
- 3rd Brigade (attached to 18th Division)
- The (Finnish) Armoured Division (Major General Ruben Lagus)
  – The Tank Brigade (Colonel Sven Björkman)
  – The *Jäger* Brigade (Colonel Albert Puroma)
- *Sturmgeschütz-Brigade 303* (Captain Fritz Scherer)
- Finnish Air Force Squadron 3 (Lieutenant Colonel E. Magnusson)
- Finnish Air Force Squadron 4 (Colonel O. Sarko)
- German Detachment Kuhlmey (Lieutenant Colonel Kurt Kuhlmey)

APPENDIX XV

The Soviet Petsamo-Kirkenes offensive in October 1944

In the autumn of 1944 the Soviet supreme command, Stavka, ordered General Meretskov to plan and execute an offensive against the 56,000 German troops belonging to XIX Mountain Corps who covered a defence line 70km northwest of Murmansk.

Meretskov formed his main attack force as two infantry corps, 1 'flying' formation about the same size as a corps and two encirclement units. The latter consisted of a) 2 marine infantry brigades and b) 2 light infantry corps, each consisting of 2 brigades. The total force numbered 96,000 men from army group 'The Karelian Front' and was supported by the navy group 'The Northern Fleet' under Admiral Arseniy Golovko. The formation included more than 110 tanks and assault guns, and 2,100 artillery pieces and mortars. Control over the air space completely belonged to the Red Air Force.

By early October, specially trained Soviet pioneer units carried out reconnaissance operations up to 50km behind the first line of the German positions. The battle started on 7 October 1944 with an artillery preparation during which the Russians fired 97,000 shells. This was followed by an infantry attack, whose main force penetrated the lines of the German 2nd Mountain Division. Meanwhile, one of the two light Soviet infantry corps carried out an exhaustive march through extremely difficult terrain and encircled the southern flank of the German position.

Late the same day a Soviet 3,000 strong marine infantry brigade was landed on the coast of the Barents Sea behind the German northern flank. On 10 October this force linked up with another marine infantry brigade. Furthermore, special units of marine infantry from 'The Northern Fleet' were landed on 12 October and then directed an attack on the German left flank. The German XIX Mountain Corps was thus pushed back at the front and threatened on both flanks. The corps retreated through Lapland and across the border into Norway. Meanwhile, soviet troops occupied Liinahamari on 15 October (some sources give a slightly different date here).

Three days later the first Soviet units crossed the Norwegian border by the German northern flank. This was followed by a crossing of the border further south on 23 October. Two days later the Red Army captured

Kirkenes, which had been badly bombed and scorched. The Soviet pursuit of the retiring German I Corps in the north continued until 30 October, when the Russians stopped by the River Tana. A part of their southern flank had by then swung south towards Ivalo Village where they stopped on 2 November.

The Soviet occupation of Northern Norway continued until October 1945.

Sources

Gebhardt: *The Petsamo-Kirkenes Operation – Soviet Breakthrough and Pursuit in the Arctic/October 1944*
Ziemke: *German Northern Theatre of Operations 1940-1945*

Notes

1 Khrushchev, p. 250
2 https://www.eduskunta.fi/FI/kansanedustajat/Sivut/910346.aspx
3 Jakobson, p. 60
4 Dyke, p. 4
5 *Ibid.*
6 Jakobson, p. 73
7 Khrushchev, p. 248
8 *Ibid.*, p. 225
9 Chuev, p. 9
10 Paasikivi 1958, p. 9
11 Jakobson, p. 107
12 Chuev, p. 10
13 Paasikivi 1958, p. 34
14 Vehviläinen, p. 35
15 'Memorandum of the Government of the USSR, handed in Moscow on October 14th, 1939, by MM. Stalin and Molotov to M. Paasikivi'. Source: *The development of Finnish-Soviet relations during the autumn 1939 in the light of official documents. Publication of the Ministry for Foreign Affairs of Finland. Doc. nr. 13.* Suomen Kirja, Helsinki 1940.
16 T. Polvinen: *J.K. Paasikivi – Valtiomiehen elämäntyö*, Vol. III, p. 32, cf. Vehviläinen, p. 38
17 Jakobson, p. 123
18 Paasikivi 1958, p. 60
19 Jakobson, p. 143
20 Paasikivi 1958, p. 81
21 Jakobson, p. 131
22 Jonas, p. 95
23 Meinander 2012, p. 66
24 Jonas, p. 95
25 Jakobson, p. 151
26 *Ibid.*, p. 150
27 *Ibid.*, p. 153
28 Chuev, p. 8
29 Khrushchev, p. 255
30 Chuev, p. 10
31 Cf. Paasikivi 1958, p. 50. Quoting from a discussion among Finland's political leaders in October 1939.
32 https://www.marxists.org/reference/archive/stalin/works/1939/02/23.htm
33 Nozdrachov, p. 4
34 *Ibid.*, p. 25–26
35 *Ibid.*, p. 11
36 Vehviläinen, p. 43
37 Irincheev, p. 6–7
38 http://www.finlex.fi/fi/laki/alkup/2007/20071443
39 Meinander 2010, p. 201

40 Gudme had been a *Fendrik* (junior officer) in the Wasa Grenadiers and participated in the Battle of Tampere. Source: Sørensen 2004, p. 151
41 Gudme 1921, p. 285
42 Welle-Strand, p. 525
43 Ahlbäck, p. 50
44 Jääskeläinen (no page numbers)
45 Ahlbäck, p. 89, 128
46 *Ibid.*, p. 128
47 Cf. Halsti, W.: Me – Venäjä ja muut (Helsingfors, Otava 1968); Ahlbäck, p. 162–169 with several references
48 http://www.mosinnagant.net/finland/thecivilguardoffinland.asp
49 Tuunainen, p. 141
50 Condon, p. 30
51 Vehiväinen, p. 53
52 *Ibid.*
53 Mann & Jörgensen, p. 7
54 Geust & Uitto, p. 9–14
55 Isacson, p. 42
56 The number varies according to how the term 'bunker' is defined
57 Tuunainen, p. 142
58 Ekman, p. 170
59 Irincheev, p. 7
60 Törmä, p. 6–10
61 Tuunainen, p. 144
62 The Finnish Jäger-units at this time were light infantry operating as bicycle infantry in the summer and ski units in winter. They had a certain elitist status, but were conscripted personnel and thus not directly comparable to the special units in more modern armies. However, during the Continuation War, Jaeger Battalions that served with Armoured Division became elite units.
63 Martti Hakala is the main character in the novel *The Winter War* by Antti Tuuri.
64 Roselius, p. 231
65 Irincheev, p. 11
66 *Ibid.*, p. 26
67 *Ibid.*, p. 27
68 Isacson, p. 77
69 Irincheev, p. 44–46. The wording has been slightly adjusted.
70 Condon, p. 75
71 Irincheev, p. 48. The wording has been slightly adjusted.
72 *Ibid.*, p. 58
73 *Ibid.*, p. 74–75
74 *Ibid.*, p. 29
75 Palolampi, p. 62
76 Irincheev, p. 97–99. The text has been slightly altered for linguistic reasons.
77 *Ibid.*, p. 101–102
78 Appendix to the war diary of the Finnish 13th Division, 31 December 1939 (Liite N:o 555 IV AK:n sotapäiväkirjaan 13. Divisioona, the Finnish National Archive).
79 Gudme 1941, p. 80
80 *Ibid.*, p. 79
81 Westerlund 2004, pp. 198–199
82 Ulrich, p. 96–97

83 *Ibid.*, p. 110
84 Juul, p. 54
85 Isacson, p. 65
86 Juul, p. 52
87 Pekkanen, p. 312
88 Junila, p. 195
89 I. Kemppainen: *Isänmaan uhrit – Sankarikuolema Suomessa toisen maailmansodan aikana* (Helsingfors 2006), p. 234–243, if. Junila, p. 197
90 http://teema.yle.fi/ohjelmat/juttuarkisto/pirjo-honkasalon-ja-pekka-lehdon-kainuu-39-on-tositarina-miehittajan-piirittam
91 Erkkilä, p. 169–184
92 *Helsingin Sanomat*, 6 September 2012
93 Junila, pp. 214–15
94 Jessen: *Finnebørn* (Danish radio montage, 1996)
95 Cf. Gudme 1941, p. 163
96 *Ibid.*, p. 161–162
97 Dyke, p. 103–104
98 Irincheev, p. 78
99 106 http://www.winterwar.karelia.ru/site/article/44
100 Jakobson, p. 214
101 Paasikivi's views are available in two somewhat different versions, partly his memories which are quoted in this book, partly his diary which was published later on. The diary has the advantage of containing his views as things were happening. The memoirs have the benefit of being written at a point when he had gained a larger overview, but they are probably also influenced by the times in which they were written, i.e. the 1950s when it was important for Finland to maintain a friendly relationship with the Soviet Union, and where Paasikivi was president. Hence one can say both for and against the use of either of the two publications as historical source material, but it should be mentioned that the diary in places has a more negative view of the Soviet leaders' willingness to find peaceful solutions.
102 Paasikivi 1958, p. 152
103 Cf. Meretskov, p. 112
104 Dyke, p.137
105 *Ibid.*, p. 136
106 'Notes on the Polish Campaign and the War with Finland in 1939–1940 written by the Participants. A Soviet army officer, M.I. Lukinov.' From the home page *I Remember – Soviet the Second World War Veteran Memoirs* (the very direct translation has here been modified into more natural English).
http://english.iremember.ru/artillerymen/7-mikhail-lukinov.html?q=%2Fartillerymen%2F7-mikhail-lukinov.html
107 Irincheev, p. 127–128 (the somewhat direct translation has here been modified slightly)
108 The Soviet sources often use the term 'the White Finns', as if the Finnish Army during the Second World War represented the same ideology as the White victors in the Finnish Civil War.
109 Irincheev., p. 131
110 *Ibid.*, p. 132
111 http://www.geocities.ws/finnmilpge/fmp_coast_infantry39_40.html
112 Irincheev, p. 178
113 *Ibid.*, p. 178–179

114 The Finnish Tank Company comprised thirteen tanks, but due to water in the petrol tank only seven of them participated in the attack.
115 Irincheev, p. 188–189
116 Finnish Jäger Sergent Vasama cf. Irencheev, p. 181
117 Roberts, p. 155
118 Vehviläinen, p. 67 with several references
119 Meinander 2012, pp. 66–67
120 Rentola 2002 (no page numbers)
121 Juul, p. 101
122 *Ibid.*, p. 102
123 *Ibid.*
124 Tuunainen, p. 172. The author quotes three well-reputed sources for these casualty figures, which include those who died shortly after the war for war related reasons.
125 http://www.winterwar.com/War%27sEnd/casualti.htm#nonc
126 Khrushchev, pp. 253–54
127 Tuunainen, p. 172
128 Lieutenant General Heinrichs on 14 June 1941 to Swedish Military Attaché Curt Kempf, cf. Jokipii 1978, p. 96
129 REPORT ON THE FOREIGN POLICY OF THE GOVERNMENT, Delivered by Comrade V.M. Molotov, Chairman of Council of People's Commissars and People's Commissar of Foreign Affairs, at Sitting of the Supreme Soviet of the USSR on March 29, 1940. http://www.histdoc.net/history/molotov.html
130 Kulkow, p. 10–12
131 Linna 1954, p. 2 (in latest English translation)
132 Krosby, p. 293
133 Meinander 2011, pp. 57–58
134 Jonas, p. 129
135 *Ibid.*, p. 102
136 Manninen 1988, p. 19
137 *Ibid.*, p. 20
138 Seppinen, I.: *Suomen ulkomaankaupan ehdot 1939–1944* (Helsingfors, FHS 1983), pp. 46–48 cf. Vehviläinen, p. 77
139 Jonas, p. 100 (with several references)
140 Kivimäki, p. 26–27
141 Jonas, p. 134
142 Manninen 1988, pp. 23–24
143 Krosby 1987, p. 297
144 Laine 1987, p. 715
145 Jernström, p. 40
146 Mikola & Juutilainen, p. 171
147 Johnson & Hermann, p. 46
148 Misionas & Taagepera, pp. 35–38
149 Vehviläinen, p. 82
150 Paasikivi 1959, p. 23
151 http://heninen.net/sopimus/1940_e.htm
152 Misiunas & Taagepera, p. 20–22
153 Paasikivi 1959, p. 80
154 Manninen 1988, p. 24
155 Jokipii 1987, p.36

156 Korhornen, p. 157
157 Mannerheim, p. 251–254
158 Manninen 1988, p. 27
159 Министерство Иностранных Дел Российской Федерации: Документы, Внешней Политики, 1940–22 Июня 1941, "Международные Отношения", Том Двадцать Третий, Книга Вторая (Москва 1998) [Document 491]
160 Ibid., Document 198
161 http://www.histdoc.net/history/NaSo1940-11-12.html
162 It says in the German memorandum: 'The Führer replied that, in the Secret Protocol, zones of influence and spheres of interest had been designated and distributed between Germany and Russia. In so far as it had been a question of actually taking possession, Germany had lived up to the agreements.'
163 Министерство Иностранных Дел Российской Федерации: Документы, Внешней Политики, 1940-22 Июня 1941, "Международные Отношения", Том Двадцать Третий, Книга Вторая (Москва 1998) [Dokument 511]
164 http://www.histdoc.net/history/NaSo1940-11-13.html
165 A particularly criticisable version can be found on a website run by The World Future Fund, where the already dubious English translation has been broken into paragraphs, each with its own interpretive heading added.
166 Chuev, p. 18
167 Halder, p. 25. General Halder was chief of the OKH General Staff from 1938 until September 1942
168 Jokipii 1978, p. 82; Kohonen, p. 159
169 Manninen 1988, p. 23
170 Министерство Иностранных Дел Российской Федерации, Документы: Внешней Политики, 1940-22 Июня 1941, Москва, "Международные Отношения", 1998, Том Двадцать Третий, Книга Вторая. [Document 505]
171 Manninen 2004, p. 62
172 http://bdsa.ru/index.php?option=com_content&task=view&id=1512&Itemid=30
173 Manninen 2004, p. 63
174 Ibid., p. 59
175 Halder, p. 71
176 Talvela, p. 254
177 Tarkka, p. 137
178 Lunde, p. 38
179 Cf. Jokipii 1978, p. 83. Vilhelm Assarsson was a Swedish diplomat who worked as an envoy in Moscow
180 http://www.mannerheim.fi/13_erity/e_muiste.htm
181 http://www.alternatewars.com/WW2/WW2_Documents/Fuhrer_Directives/FD_21a.htm
182 Lieutenant General Alfred Jodel, chief of the OKW general staff
183 H.P. Krosby, *Suomen valinta 1941* (Helsinki, Kirjayhtymä 1967), p. 317 cf. Jokipii 1979, p. 110
184 Engel, p. 93
185 Halder, p. 101
186 Mikola & Juutilainen, p. 170
187 *Die deutsche Wochenschau* 24 September 1941
188 Vehvilainen, p. 86
189 Manninen 1998, p. 30
190 Mikola & Juutilainen, p. 171
191 Jokipii 1978, p. 98

192 Egbert, p. 311 (the very direct original translation has been somewhat modified)
193 Ziemke, p. 129
194 Assarsson: *Stalinin varjossa* (1963), p. 63, cf. Jokipii 1978, p. 83–4
195 Meinander 2012, p. 71
196 Jernström, p. 41
197 Kemiläinen, p. 216
198 The Finnish National Archive, General Erforth's diary (copy) 14 June 1941, cf. Jokipii 1978, p. 95
199 Jokipii 1978, pp. 91, 112
200 Manninen 1988, p. 36
201 Egbert, p. 312–313
202 Ekman, p. 99–100
203 *Erfurth, an OKH Attache Abteilung, fuer GenStdH,, Op. Abt., 16.6.41, in Chefsachen Bd. 1941. H 27/43*, cf. Ziemke, p. 136
204 Risto Ryti's Diary p. 5, cf. Jokipii 1978, p. 93
205 Jägerskiöld, p. 52
206 Jokipii 1978, p. 96–102
207 Cf. Ziemke, p. 204 with several references
208 *Ibid.*
209 Ziemke, p. 136. More precisely, Heinrichs suggested that the Finnish attack be delayed two or three days after the start of Operation Silberfuchs. This was the common name for three operational plans that were really an extension of each other and individually carried the names of Renntier (based on the German plan of the same name from August 1940 when the plan had only covered an occupation of the Petsamo region), Platinfuchs and Polarfuchs. Since the launch of Operation Renntier was to coincide with the launch of Operation Barbarossa, it is correct to interpret Heinrich's query of 16 June as a request to delay the Finnish part of the invasion until a few days after the German main attack
210 Ekman, p. 106–107
211 Appel, p. 54–55
212 *Ibid.* 76–85
213 Antonnen (no page numbers)
214 Jonas, p. 122–113 with several references
215 Jokipii 1978, p. 108
216 Kinnunen & Kivimäki, p. 6
217 Ziemke, p. 134
218 Office of United States Chief of Council for Prosecution of Axis Criminality, p. 1089. The exact meaning of the term 'federated state' is uncertain. Hitler might have meant Neuropa, or he might have referred to *Reichskommissariat Ostland* as a federation.
219 Jokipii 1987, p. 313–314
220 *Ibid.*
221 Ziemke, p. 204
222 Jernström, p. 142
223 Lunde, p. 55
224 Meinander 2010, p. 214
225 Pimiä, p. 403–405
226 Manninen 1980, p. 201
227 *Ibid.*, p. 202–203
228 *Ibid.*, p. 72–73

229 Office of United States Chief of Council For Prosecution of Axis Criminality, p. 1089
230 Häikiö, p. 22–23
231 Manninen 1980, p. 206
232 Office of United States Chief of Council For Prosecution of Axis Criminality, p. 1089
233 Engel, p. 108
234 Ryti's diary, p. 5, cf. Jokipii 1978, p. 93
235 Jokipii 1978, p. 93
236 Turtola (no page numbers)
237 Manninen 1988, p. 22
238 Pipping 1976, p. 570 and 572
239 Linna 1954, pp. 6–7 (in latest English translation)
240 *Ibid.* 1954, p. 78
241 The figures are just a rough estimate. There is strong disagreement on the exact numbers
242 http://www.ihr.org/jhr/v19/v19n6p50_Hitler.html
243 Jonas, p. 117 with several references
244 Meinander 2012, p. 71
245 http://i033.radikal.ru/0803/e8/34e7d143cf6b.jpg
246 Rahko & Geust, p. 49
247 Bruun, p. 130
248 Vehviläinen, p. 93
249 Ziemke, p. 154
250 Horsholt Hansen 1943, p. 62
251 The war diary of the Finnish 14th Divisions 1941/42, p. 38 (*14. Divisioonan esikunta, Toimisto III, 17.6.1941 – 31.5.1942*, The Finnish National Archive)
252 http://english.iremember.ru/infantrymen/52-dmitrii-krutskikh.html (a few linguistic changes)
253 Brunila, p. 69
254 Luukkanen, p. 98–99
255 Walllenius, p. 105
256 Hansen 1943, p. 26–28
257 http://militera.lib.ru/h/mmf/02.html
258 Sandström, p. 58
259 Lunde, p. 172
260 Ziemke, p. 196–199
261 Vehviläinen, p. 94–95
262 https://helda.helsinki.fi/handle/10138/19520
263 Mann & Jörgensen, p. 78
264 http://kotisivut.fonet.fi/~aromaa/Navygallery/Mines/mines.htm
265 *Ibid.*
266 Bruun, p. 141
267 From Mannerheim's Order-of-the-Day to the Finnish Army 10 July 1941 (for the full version see Appendix IX)
268 Pimiä, p. 399
269 http://heninen.net/miekka/p-1918_e.htm (with small linguistic changes).
270 It should be noted that Holger Hørsholt Hansen in his book mentions that during his visit to the area in 1941–42 he found many signs of the opposite. The occasional poor living conditions, which he also observed, he felt had been caused by the ongoing war

271 Kemiläinen, p. 206
272 In fact, this idea goes back to French race theorists in the 1900s, who also claimed to have found a race-related connection between Prussians and the 'Mongol-related' Finns. In Germany the existence of such a connection was stubbornly denied
273 Pimiä, p. 403–419
274 Fingerroos, p. 499
275 Mäkinen, p. 282
276 Fingerroos, p. 248
277 Laine 2000, p. 7
278 Kostiainen (no page numbers)
279 Sode-Madsen, p. 229
280 The most controversial part of the order-of-the-day has already been used as introduction to this chapter. For the whole text see Appendix X
281 Jernström, p. 143
282 Vehviläinen, p. 101
283 The American-Soviet Lend-Lease Agreement was signed on 1 October 1941, but a so-called Pre Lend-Lease Agreement had already been in force since 22 June.
284 Vehviläinen, p. 93
285 Manninen 1980, p. 210–11
286 *Ibid.*, p. 212
287 Fingerroos, p. 500
288 Ziemke, p. 199
289 Vehviläinen, p. 98
290 http://www.ibiblio.org/pha/timeline/411003awp.html
291 Vehviläinen, p. 100
292 http://heninen.net/sopimus/kirjecm_e.htm
293 http://heninen.net/sopimus/kirjemc_e.htm
294 Meinander 2009, p. 112
295 *Ibid.*
296 Junila, p. 208
297 Brunila, p. 182
298 Jessen: *Finnebørn* (Danish Radio Montage 1996)
299 *Ibid.*
300 Junila, p. 219
301 Jessen: *Finnebørn* (Danish Radio Montage 1996)
302 Pimiä p. 395–431 and in a private correspondence with the author of this book
303 Westerlund 2011 Vol. II, pp. 105, 109
304 *Ibid.*, p. 117
305 *Ibid.*, p. 115
306 Koponen & Laine, p. 297
307 Kappula, p. 320–21
308 Kemiläinen, p. 216–217
309 Westerlund 2011 Vol. I, p. 178
310 *Ibid.*, p. 155
311 Former Russian child prisoner in Finnish concentrations camp http://pobeda.gov.karelia.ru/Veteran/memory.html
312 Laine 2007, p. 69
313 Laine 2007, p. 71–72; Manninen 1980, pp. 190–191
314 Eskola, p. 299
315 This and other similar witness statements featured in this chapter are taken from

the home page of the Karelian Republic, which in 2005 made a string of interviews with people who in their childhood had been incarcerated in Finnish internment camps.
316   http://pobeda.gov.karelia.ru/Veteran/memory.html
317   Antti Laine 2007, p. 71
318   http://pobeda.gov.karelia.ru/Veteran/memory.html
319   Westerlund 2008, p. 8
320   http://pobeda.gov.karelia.ru/Veteran/memory.html
321   *Ibid.*
322   *Ibid.*
323   Meinander 2012, p. 74
324   Silvennoinen, p. 394
325   Antti Laine 2007, p. 72–73
326   http://forum.axishistory.com/viewtopic.php?f=59&t=182358
327   V. Suhonen: *Jäämarssi* (TV Documentary, Yle TV2, 2 October 2011)
328   *Helsingin Sanomat* 20 May 2007
329   In 1944 Kalm fled to Sweden and then to the USA, fearing that he might be extradited to the Soviet Union and sentenced as a war criminal because of his administration of the Naarajärvi camp. Thirteen years later he returned to Finland where he lived as a free man until his death in 1981, some of the time working as a homeopath (until one of his diabetes patients died, after which he was banned from practicing).
330   Kujala: 'Illegal Killing' (in *Slavonic and East European Review*, Vol. 87, Nr. 3, 2009, p. 447), cf. Silvennoinen p. 378
331   Westerlund 2008, p. 9
332   Kujala: *Vankisurmat* (WSOY, Helsinki 2008, p. 171–172), cf. Silvennoinen p. 379
333   Westerlund 2008, p. 300
334   *Ibid.*, p. 301
335   *Ibid.*, p. 304
336   Silvennoinen, p. 379
337   Hansen 1942
338   Malmi, p. 26
339   *Ibid.*, p. 213
340   *Helsingin Sanomat*, 28 September 2001
341   Silvennoinen, p. 380
342   Panu Pulma: '*Romanit Suur-Suomen rakennustyössä*', presentation at the seminar *Romanien holokausti*, Helsingfors 8 April 2010, cf. Kinnunen & Jokisipilä, p. 475–476
343   Pipping 2008 (originally 1947), p. 128
344   Bernd Wegner: '*Das Kriegsende in Skandinavien*' in *Das Deutsche Reich und der Zweiten Weltkrieg, Vol. 8* (München 2007), p. 963–972, cf. Menander 2009, p. 34
345   Meinander 2009, p. 17
346   Haapanen, p. 452
347   Finnish sabotage operations against the Murmansk Railway took place quite often, but traffic between Murmansk and Moscow still continued via the so-called 'Belomorsk-Obozerskaya side track' (Ziemke, p. 288).
348   Brunila, p. 165
349   Jonas, p. 121–122
350   P.-O. Ekman, p. 233
351   *Ibid.*, p. 234

352 Sandström, p. 92
353 Pinduši (Ru: Rundishi, Fi: Pinduinen): Karelian name for a town/district immediately east of Medvezhyegorsk, by the northern point of Lake Onega. The area was occupied by the Finnish Army 1941–44.
354 Pipping 2008 (originally 1978), p. 46
355 Jääskeläinen (no page numbers)
356 Linna 1954, p. 122 (in the latest English translation)
357 *Ibid.*, p. 128
358 Seppälä, p. 153
359 Heinilä, p. 75–82
360 *Ibid.*, p. 84–85
361 E. Eräsaari, 1/1986, pp. 4–8 & 2/1986, p. 62–65
362 http://suomenkuvalehti.fi/jutut/kotimaa/suomi-vieritti-sotatraumat-sotilaiden-omaksi- syyksi-psyykkinen-haavoittuminen-oli-heikkoutta?ref=top
363 The Swedish author Peter Nisser (1919–1990) in a private letter to the author of this book dated 25 September 1988. Peter Nisser was a Swedish officer of the reserve who volunteered for Finnish war service in both the Winter War and the Continuation War.
364 Nilsson, p. 196
365 Nielsen 2002
366 *Ibid.*
367 Hansen, p. 51
368 *Ibid.*
369 Hansen, p. 51–60
370 Paasikivi 1985, p. 35
371 Westerlund 2008, p. 11–12
372 Jonas, p. 123
373 Sandström, p. 127
374 Edvin Linkomies: *I mit lands tjänst – Minnen från statsministertiden 1943–1944* (Stockholm 1974), p. 244, cf. Meinander 2009, p. 23
375 Meinander 2009, p. 18
376 *Ibid.*, p. 19
377 Vehviläinen, p. 127
378 Bertelsen, p. 524
379 Meinander 2009, p. 19
380 Erik Boheman: *På vakt – Kabinettssekreterare under andre värdskriget* (Stockholm, 1964)
381 Bertelsen, p. 525
382 United States, Department of State etc., p. 593
383 *Ibid.,* p. 590
384 Apunen & Wolff, p. 194
385 Meinander 2009, p. 50
386 *Ibid.*, 55
387 R.R. Kokoelma: *Jatkosotan aika promemoriat*, p. 4–6, cf. Bertelsen, p. 533 (with minor linguistic adjustments)
388 Lea Toivola in correspondence with the author of this book, 11 July 2013
389 Manninen 2004, p. 134
390 *Ibid.*
391 *Ibid.*, p. 135
392 Lunde, p. 272. The number of tanks is here corrected (from 1,600)

393 Manninen 2004, p. 137
394 Göran Westerlund: *Finland överlevde – Finlands krig 1939–45 i ord och bild* (Helsinki, Schilds Förlag 2007, p. 155), cf. Lunde, p. 272
395 Lunde, p. 272
396 Manninen 2004, p. 137
397 Anonymous Finnish soldier cf. Rintala 1967, p. 17
398 *Ibid.* p. 29 and pp. 32–33
399 *Ibid.*, 49
400 *Ibid.* p. 108
401 Eräsaari, January 1986, pp. 4–8 and February 1986, pp. 62–65
402 Meinander 2009, p. 184
403 Finnish veteran Carl Carlsson in video produced by T. Rysti
404 Ziemke, p. 284
405 It seems that Alexandra Kollontai subsequently informed her superiors in Moscow that there were linguistic problems between the parties. At least we know that Stalin on 26 June asked the American diplomat W. Averell Harriman to explain to the Finns that the Soviet Union had no intentions to take away their independence. This was officially backed by Moscow on 2 July in an article in *Pravda*, and in subsequent Soviet messages the word 'capitulate' did not appear.
406 Bertelsen, p. 553
407 Finnish veteran Säppo Härmälä in *The Miracle of Ihantala – The Battle of Tali-Ihantala Summer 1944*.
408 *Ibid.*
409 *Ibid.*
410 *Ibid.*
411 *Ibid.*
412 Meinander 2009, p. 126
413 Finnish Second Lieutenant Berndt Anthoni, *Suomen sodat – Kesän 1944 torjuntataistelut* (Kärkijoukkue Productions DVD).
414 *Ibid.*
415 Finnish lance corporal Pohtola, platoon leader, 27th Separate Anti-tank Company, *Suomen sodat – Kesän 1944 torjuntataistelut* (Kärkijoukkue Productions DVD).
416 Finnish Second Lieutenant Allan Virta, intelligence officer at 44th Regiment, *Suomen sodat – Kesän 1944 torjuntataistelut* (Kärkijoukkue Productions DVD).
417 Tor Wikström, Finnish private in 3rd Field Artillery Regiment, *Suomen sodat – Kesän 1944 torjuntataistelut* (Kärkijoukkue Productions DVD).
418 Finnish Second Lieutenant Allan Virta, intelligence officer at 44th Regiment, *Suomen sodat – Kesän 1944 torjuntataistelut* (Kärkijoukkue Productions DVD).
419 Rentola 2001, p. 60
420 Tuunainen, p. 172
421 http://heninen.net/sopimus/1944_e.htm
422 Tuunainen, p. 171
423 Halsti 1957, pp. 508–509
424 Tuunainen, p. 170
425 Chuev, p. 10
426 Westerlund, p. 16
427 *Ibid.*, p. 14
428 Nilsson, p. 202
429 The figure is from B. Irincheev's *War of the White Death* and seems grossly

underestimated. J. Norris writes in *Infantry Mortars of the Second World War* (pp. 17–18) that each rifle battalion was 'formed into three rifle companies and a support company equipped with machine guns and mortars. The 50mm mortars were allocated two per rifle company in a small mortar section under the company headquarters. These sections were eliminated by 1943. The rifle battalions' sixty-one man mortar company had three platoons with three 82mm mortars each. Each rifle regiment also possessed a seventy man mortar battery with two platoons. Each platoon had two sections of two 120mm mortars for a total of eight in the battery. In addition specialised mortar brigades were formed within divisions and equipped with at least 100 120mm mortars.'

430 This division was seriously lacking in equipment. At the start of the war it even had no rifles. Hence it was in effect a unit being trained and equipped rather than a reserve unit.

431 The 21st, 22nd and 23rd Division had been formed on 19 December 1939. There were no divisions numbered from 13 to 20.

432 Manninen 2004, p. 73

433 4th Division did not participate directly in the battle but handed over both artillery and infantry units to other formations that were involved in the combat.

PLACE NAMES

Names used in this book are marked with *

FINNISH	RUSSIAN	SWEDISH	OTHER
Ahvenanmaa		Åland	Åland Islands (English)*
Antrea*	Kamennogorsk	St Andree	
Enso*	Svetogorsk		
Hanko*		Hangö	
Helsinki*		Helsingfors	
Hiitola*	Khiytola		
Ilmee*	Ilm	Ilmes	
Ilomantsi*		Ilomants	
Itä-Karjala/Kauko-Karjala	Vostočnaja Karelija	Fjärrkarelen	East Karelia (English)*
Joroinen*		Jorois	
Kantalahti	Kandalaksha*		
Karhumäki	Medvezhyegorsk*		Karhumägi (Karelian)
Karjalankannas	Karelskij pereseek	Karelska näset	The Karelian Isthmus (English)*
Kiestinki	Kestenga*		
Kilpolansaari*	Kilpola		
Kitelä*	Kitelya		
Kiviniemi*	Losevo		
Koivisto* (town)	Primórsk		
Koivisto* (island)	Berëzovye ostrova	Björkö	
Kuparsaari*	Zhadanovsky		
Kuuterselkä*	Lebyazhye		
Kymijoki*	Kymi	Kymmene älv	
Käkisalmi*	Priozersk	Kexholm	
Kämärä*	Gavrilovo		
Lahdenpohja*	Lakhdenpokhya		
Laitimojärvi*	Ozero Leytimo-Yarvi		
Lasisaari*	Ostrov Steklyannyy		
Liinahamari*	Liinakhamari	Linhammar	
Louhi	Loukhi*		
Malmi*		Malm	
Mikkeli*		St Michel	
Muolaanjärvi*	Glubokoye		
Laatokka	Ladozjskoje ozero	Ladoga	Lake Ladoga (English)*
Nietjärvi*	Niyet-Yarvi		
Aunus	Olonets*		Anuksenlinnu (Karelian)
Oulu*		Uleåborg	
Petroskoi/Äänislinna	Petrozavodsk*	Onegaborg (obsl.)	
Petsamo* (village)	Pechenga		Petsjenga (Norwegian)
Petsamo* (area)	Péčengskij rajón		Petsjenga
Pinduinen	Pindushi*		Pinduši (Karelian)
Pori*		Björneborg	
Porlampi*	Sveklovichnoye		
Rajajoki/Siestarjoki	Sestroretsk*	Systerbäck	
Repola	Reboly*		Rebol'ä (Karelian)
Rukajärvi	Rugozero*		
Seesjärvi	Segozero*		
Siiranmäki*	Siyranmyaki		
Sortavala*	Sórtavala	Sordavala	
Sotjärvi*	Shotozero		
Suomi		Finland	Finland* (English)
Summa*	Soldatskoye		

Place Names

Suojärvi*	Suoyarvi (lake)		
Suvilahti*	Suoyarvi (village)		
Suursaari		Hogland	Hogland (English)*
Syväri	Svir	Svir	River Svir (English)*
Säinö* el. Yläsäinö	Tšerkasovo		
Säämäjärvi*	Syamozero		Seämärvi (Karelian)
Taipale*	Solovyovo		
Taipaleenjoki*	Burnaja		
Tampere*		Tammerfors	
Teikarinsaari*	Igrivyj		
Tenojoki		Tenaelven	Tena (Norwegian)
Tienhaara*	Seleznevo		
Tolvajärvi*	Tolvayarvi		
Tornio*		Torneå	
Tuppurasaari*	Vikhrevoy		
Turku*		Åbo	
Uhtua	Ukhta* (now Kaleva)		
Uikujärvi	Vygozero*		
Utti*		Uttis	
Uusikirkko*	Polyany	Nykyrka	
Vaasa*		Vasa	
Valkeasaari	Beloostrov*		
Vammelsuu*	Serovo		
Viipuri*	Vyborg	Viborg	
Vuoksi*	Vuoksa	Vuoksen	Vuokša (karelsk)
Ääninen	Onezjskoje ozero	Onega	Lake Onega* (English)

LITERATURE, AUDIO, VIDEO AND DVD

Ahlbäck, A.: *Soldiering and the making of Finnish manhood. Conscription and masculinity in interwar Finland, 1918–1939* (Doctoral Thesis, University of Turku 2010)
Anon (Finnish governmental publication): *Blå-vit bok om utvecklingen av relationer mellan Finland och Rådsunionen hösten 1939 i belysning av officiella dokument* (Stockholm, Kooperativa förbundets bokförlag 1940)
Anon: *Jatkosodan Katsaukset I / Continuation War newsreels I (1941–42)* (4-DVD, Finn Kino 2008)
Anon: *Jatkosodan Katsaukset II / Continuation War newsreels II (1942–44)* (4-DVD, Finn Kino 2008)
Anttonen, H.: '*Luftwaffe – Flying Units in Central and Southern Finland 1941–1944*' (http://www.oocities.org/finnmilpge/fmpg_lw_lfl1.html)
Appel, E.: *Med döden i hälarna. Högkvarterets fjärpatruller 1939–1945* (Esbo, Schildts Förlag Ab 2005)
Apunen, O./Wolff, C.: *Pettureita ja patriootteja. Taistelu Suomen ulko- ja puolustuspolitiikan suunnasta 1938–1948* (Helsinki, Suomalaisen Kirjallisuuden Seura 2009)
Bergquist, M.: 'Debatt om Finlands forsätningskrig' (in *Statsvidenskabeligt tidsskrift* vol. 84/ 3 1981, p. 162–167)
Bertelsen, H.: 'Finlands vej til freden' (in *Jyske Samlinger, Ny Række XVI* 1985–1987, p. 519–595)
Brunila, K.: 'Vinterkrigets konsekvenser', 'De politiska aspekterna', 'Hemmafronten', 'Landstridskrafterna' (in Ekberg bd. II)
Bruun, C.-E.: 'Luftstridskrafterna' and 'Luftstridskrafterna 1942–1943' (in Ekberg bd. II)
Chuev, F. & Molotov, V.M.: *Molotov Remembers – Inside Kremlin Politics* (Chicago, Ivan R. Dee Inc. 1993)
Clark, A.: *Barbarossa. The Russian-German Conflict 1941–1945* (New York, William Morrow 1966)
Condon, R.W.: *The Winter War – Russia against Finland.* (New York, Ballantine Books Inc. 1972)
Dyke, C. van: *The Soviet Invasion of Finland 1939–1940* (Oxon, Frank Cass Publishers 1997)
Edwards, R.: *White Death – Russia's War on Finland 1939–40* (London, Weidenfeld & Nicholson 2006)

Egbert, L.D.: *Trial of the Major War Criminals before the International Military Tribunal, Nuremberg, 14 November 1945 – 1 October 1946* Vol. VII (Nuremberg, AMS Press 1947)
Ekberg, H. (red.): *Finland i krig* Vol. I (Esbo, Schildts Förlag 2001)
Ekberg, H. (red.): *Finland i krig* Vol. II (Esbo, Schildts Förlag 2001)
Ekman, P.O.: 'Sjöstridskrafterna' (in Ekberg bd. I)
Ekman, P.O.: 'Sjöstridskrafterna' (in Ekberg bd. II)
Engel, G.: *Heeresadjutant bei Hitler, 1938–1943*. (Stuttgart, Deutsche Verlags-Anstalt 1974)
Enäjärvi-Haavio, E.: *Itään. Elsa Enäjärvi-Haavion ja Martti Haavion päiväkirjat ja kirjeet 1941–1942*. (Helsinki, WSOY 2002)
Erkkilä, V.: *Viimeinen aamu – Neuvostopartisaanien vaietut jäljet* (Helsinki, Otava 2011)
Eräsaari, E.: 'Raportti jatkosodan karkureista' (in *Kansa Taisteli* 1/1986, p. 4–8 og 2/1986, p. 62–65)
Eskola, E. (red.): *Elsa Enäjärvi-Haavion ja Martti Haavion päiväkirjat ja kirjeet 1941–1942* (Helsinki, Toimittanut 2002)
Faurby, I.: 'Hvorfor gå frivilligt i krig?' (ni *Kungl. Krigsvetenskapsakademiens Handlingar och Tidskrift* nr. 1/2010, p. 77–95)
Fingerroos, O.: 'Karelia Issue' (in Kinnunen/Kivimäki)
Gebhardt, J.: *The Petsamo-Kirkenes Operation – Soviet Breakthrough and Pursuit in the Arctic, October 1944* (Library of Congress, 1990)
Geust, C. & Uitto, A.: *Mannerheim-linja: Talvisodan legenda* (Helsinki, Ajatus kirjat 2006)
Gudme, P. de Hemmer: 'Krigerlivets Religion og Etik – Oplevelser fra Bolshevikkrigen' (in *Gads Danske Magasin*, maj-juni 1921, p. 285–296)
Gudme, P. de Hemmer: *Finlands Folk i Kamp* (Copenhagen, Gyldendal 1941)
Haapanen, A.: *Viholliset keskellämme – Desantit Suomessa 1939–1944* (Helsinki, Minerva Kustannus Oy Kustasnnus Oy 2012)
Halder, F.: *War Journal of Franz Halder Vol. V* ([United States]: A.G. EUCOM)
Halsti, W.H.: *Försvaret av Finland* (Stockholm, Norstedts Förlag 1940)
Halsti, W.H.: *Suomen sota 1939–1945, 3. osa, Ratkaisu 1944*, (Helsinki, Otava 1957)
Hansen, H.: 'Menneskeskæbner i fangelejre' (in *Politiken* 7 March 1942)
Hansen, H.: *I krigets spår – Ett ögonvittnes skildring av krig och stillestånd i Fjärrkarelen* (Stockholm, Tidens förlag 1943)
Heinilä, H.: 'Vanhan rajan ylitys jatkosodan hyökkäysvaiheessa 1941: Jalkaväkirykmenttien miesten suhtautuminen siihen' (in *Ajankohta – Poliittisen historian vuosikirja*, Helsinki 1997)

Howard, M.: *The Causes of War* (London, Maurice Temple Smith Ltd. 1983)
Huuska, V.: 'Rouva Boris Jartsev – Nainen jolla oli neljä nimeä ja värikäs elämä' http://veikkohuuska.blogit.fi/tag/boris-jartsev/
Irincheev, B.: *The War of the White Death – Finland Against the Soviet Union 1939–40* (Yorkshire, Pen & Sword Books Ltd. 2011)
Isacson, C.: *Ärans vinter – Finska vinterkriget 1939–40* (Stockholm, Norstedts Förlag 2007)
Jakobson, M.: *The Diplomacy of the Winter War – An account of the Russo-Finnish War 1939–40* (Cambridge, Mass Howard University Press 1961)
Jensen, D. m.fl.: 'Arbejderbladets vinterkrig' (Roskilde University, Bachelor projekt, Autumn 2011, Institute for Culture and Identity, History)
Jernström, K.: 'Inför ett nytt krig', 'De finländska krigsmålen' (in Ekberg bd. II)
Jessen, L: *Finnebørn* (Danish Broadcasting Corporation, 19.8.1996)
Johnson, H.: *Frozen Hell – Finland in the Winter War and Beyond* (Austin Texas, Gurps 2003)
Jokipii, M.: 'Finlands väg till fortsättningskriget' (in *Skandia, Tidsskrift for historisk forskning*, No. 1 1978 pp. 76–113)
Jokipii, M.: *Jatkosodan synty – Tutkimuksia Saksan ja Suomen sotilaallisesta yhteistyöstä 1940–41* (Helsingfors, Otava 1987)
Johnson, E. & Hermann, A.: 'Last Flight from Tallinn' (in *Foreign Service Journal*, May 2007, pp. 46–51)
Jonas, M.: 'The Politics of an Alliance' (in Kinnunen/Kivimäki p. 93–138)
Jones, M.: *Leningrad – State of Siege* (London, John Murray 2008)
Jowett, P. & Snodgrass, B.: *Finland at War 1939–45* (Oxford, Osprey Publishing 2006)
Junila, M.: 'Wars on the Home Front' (in Kinnunen/Kivimäki)
Juul, O.: *Den røde sne* (Copenhagen, Aschehoug Dansk Forlag 1952)
Jägerskiöld, S.: *Suomen marsalkka – Gustaf Mannerheim 1941–1944* (Helsinki, Otava 1981)
Jääskeläinen, S.: 'Political Taboos and National Trauma in Finland Caused by the Civil War 1918' (European University Viadrina, Faculty of Cultural Studies 1999)
Kan, A.: 'Storfurstendömet Finland 1809–1917 – Dess autonomi enligt den nutida finske historieskrivningen' (in *Historisk tidsskrift* 128:1 2008, pp. 3–27)
Karjalainen, M.: Ajatuksista operaatioiksi: Suomen armeijan hyökkäysoperaatioiden suunnittelu jatkosodassa https://helda.helsinki.fi/handle/10138/19520

Kauppala, P.: '"Children of Love" and their Mothers in Postwar East Karelia' (in Westerlund 2011 bd. II)
Kaspersen, L. & Loftager, J.: *Klassisk og moderne politisk teori* (Copenhagen, Gyldendal 2009)
Kemiläinen, A.: *Finns in the Shadow of the Aryans: Race Theories and Racism* (Finnish Literature Society 1998)
Khrushchev, N.: *Memoirs of Nikita – Commissar 1918–1945* (Penn State Press, 2004)
Kinnunen, T. & Kivimäki, V.: (red.): *Finland in World War II – History, Memory, Interpretations, History of Warfare Vol. 69* (Leiden, Boston, Brill 2012)
Kinnunen, T. & Jokisipilä, M.: 'Shifting Images of "Our Wars"' (in Kinnunen/Kivimäki)
Kjersgaard, E: *Besættelsen 1940–45, bd. I: Lysene slukkes* (Copenhagen, Politikens Forlag 1980)
Klinge, M. & Kolbe, L.: *Helsinki – Daughter of the Baltic* (Helsinki, Otava Publishing 1999)
Koponen, M. & Laine, A.: 'The Illegitimate Children of Finnish Soldiers in Occupied East Karelia, 1942–1944' (in Westerlund 2011 bd. II)
Korhonen, A: *Barbarossaplanen och Finland* (Stockholm, Natur och Kultur 1963)
Kostiainen, A: 'Genocide in East Karelia – Stalin's Terror and the Finns of East Karelia'
http://www.genealogia.fi/emi/art/article255e.htm#Alku
Krosby, H.: 'The Diplomacy of the Petsamo Question and Finnish-German Relations March-December 1940' (in *Scandia, Tidsskrift for historisk forskning* Vol. 31:2 1965 pp. 291–330)
Kärkijoukkue (produktionsselskab): *Suomen sodat – Kesän 1944 torjuntataistelut* (DVD, Kärkijoukkue Productions Oy 2004)
Kulkov, E.N. & Rzheshevsky, O.A.: *Stalin and the Soviet-Finnish War, 1939–1940* (London, F. Cass 2001)
Kärkijoukkue (production company): *Suomen soldat – Kesän 1944 Torjuntataistelut* (DVD, Kärkijoukkue Productions Oy 2004)
Laine, Antti: 'Suomi sodassa' (in Zetterberg)
Laine, A.: 'Between East and West – Karelia in a Regional Historical Perspective'
http://www.oslo2000.uio.no/program/papers/s9/s9-laine.pdf
Laine, A.: 'Lapsia piikkilangan takana eli historian monta totuutta' (in *Historiallisen Aikakauskirja*, Nr. 1/2007 pp. 67–77)
Lindman, Åke, *Tali-Ihantala 1944, Siellä Suomen kohtalo ratkeaa* (DVD, Åke Lindman Film Productions Oy 2007)
Linna, V.: *Unknown soldiers* (Novel, London, Penguin UK 2015, English

translation by Liesl Yamaguchi, original Finnish edition 1954)
Linna, V.: *Finlandia* (Novel, Copenhagen, Grafisk Forlag 1961)
Linna, V.: *Oprør* (Novel, Copenhagen, Grafisk Forlag 1962)
Linna, V.: *Sønner af et folk* (Novel, Copenhagen, Grafisk Forlag 1963)
Luukkanen, E.: *Fighter over Finland* (London, McDonald 1963)
Lunde, H.O.: *Finland's War of Choice – The Troubled German-Finnish Coalition in World War II* (Newbury, Casemate Publishers 2011)
Lundin, C.: *Finland in the Second World War* (Indiana University Press 1957)
Malmi, T.: *Suomalaiset sotavangit Neuvostoliitossa 1941–1944 – Miehet kertovat* (Jyväskylä, Atena 2001)
Mannerheim, C.G.E.: *Minnen* bd. II (Helsinki, Holger Schildts Förlag 1952)
Manninen, O.: *Suur-Suomen ääriviivat* (Helsingfors, Kirjayhtymä 1980)
Manninen, O.: 'Poliittinen kehitys talvisodasta heinäkuuhun 1941' (in *Jatkosodan historia* bd. I, Helsinki, WSOY 1988)
Manninen, O.: *The Soviet Plans for the North Western Theatre of Operations in 1939–1944* (Helsinki, National Defence College 2004)
Mann, C. & Jörgensen, C.: *Hitler's Arctic War – The German Campaigns in Norway, Finland and the USSR 1940–1945* (Hersham, Surrey, Ian Allen Publishing 2002)
Mariager, R. (ed.): *Danskere i krig* (Copenhagen, Gyldendal 2009)
Meinander, H.: *Finland 1944* (Helsinki, Södertröms, 2009)
Meinander, H.: *Finlands Historia – Linjer, strukturer, vändpunkter* (Helsinki, Söderströms 2010)
Meinander, H.: 'A Seperate Story?' (in Stenius, H., Österberg, M. & Östling, J. (ed.): *Nordic Narratives of the Second World War*, Lund, Nordic Academic Press, 2011)
Meinander, H.: 'Finland and the Great Powers in World War II' (in Kinnunen/Kivimäki 2012)
Meretskov, K.A.: *Serving the People* (Moscow, Progress Publishers 1971)
Mikola, K. & Juutilainen, A.: 'Suomen sotilaalliset ratkaisut alkuvuoden 1941 aikana' (in *Jatkosodan Historia* Vol. I, Helsinki, WSOY 1988)
Misiunas, J. & Taagepera, J.: *The Baltic States – Years of Dependence, 1940–1980* (London, C. Hurst & Company 1983)
Moore, C.: *The Soldier – A History of Courage, Sacrafice and Brotherhood* (London, Icon Books Ltd. 2009)
Mäkinen, I.: 'Fates of books and archives during the war between Finland and the Soviet Union 1939–40 and 1941–44' (in *Knygotyra* vol. 48, Vilnius 2007)
Nielsen, J.: 'For Finlands frihed og Danmarks ære' (in *Jyllands-Posten* 28 November 2002)
Nielsen, J. & Kirkebæk, M.: 'Med dødseskadronen i vinterkrig' (in

Mariager, pp 52–91)
Nielsen, N.: 'Demokrati og kulturel nationalisme i Norden i mellemkrigstiden – En realpolitisk højredrejning' (in *Historisk tidsskrift* 124:4 2004 p. 581–603)
Nilsson, O.: 'Stamfrändernas hårda öde' (in Ekberg bd. II)
Norris, J.: *Infantry Mortars of the Second World War* (Oxford, Osprey Publishing 2002)
Nozdrachov, O.: 'Application of the Soviet Theory of "Deep Operation" During The 1939 Soviet-Japanese Military Conflict In Mongolia' (a thesis presented to the Faculty of the U.S. Army, 1997) http://www.dtic.mil/cgi-bin/GetTRDoc?AD=ADA524118
Office of United States Chief of Council for Prosecution of Axis Criminality: *Nazi Conspiracy and Aggression Volume VII* (Washington, United States Government Printing Office 1946)
Paasikivi, J.: *Minnen I: 1939–1940* (Stockholm, Albert Bonniers Förlag 1958)
Paasikivi, J.: *Minnen II: Mellankrigstiden – Som Sändebud i Moskva* (Stockholm, Albert Bonniers Förlag 1959)
Paasikivi, J.: *Dagböcker 1944–56 bd. I: Vid Katastrofens rand* (Borgå, Askelin & Hägglund 1985)
Palolampi, E.: *Kollaa kestää – Kertomuksia Kollaanjoen rintamalta* (Porvoo, WSOY 1940)
Pekkanen T.: *Ajan kasvot – Muistoja ja tunnelmia sotavuosilta* (Helsinki, WSOY 1942)
Pimiä, T.: 'Greater Finland and Cultural Heritage' (in Kinnunen/Kivimäki)
Pipping, K.: 'Den finländske soldaten i litteraturen' (in *Finsk Tidskrift* 1947, p. 225–234)
Pipping, K.: 'Nytt ljus över fortsättningskriget' (in *Finsk Tidskrift* 1976, p. 559–581)
Pipping, K.: *Infantry Company as a Society* (Helsinki, National Defence University Department of Behavioural Sciences 2008)
Rahkola, E. & Geust, F.C.: *Vaiettu Elisenvaaran pommitus – Evakkohelvetti 20. kesäkuuta 1944* (Helsinki, Ajatus kirjat 2008)
Rentola, K.: 'Stalin, Mannerheim ja Suomen rauhanehdot 1944' (in *Historiallinen aikakauskirja*, 1/2001, p. 47–61)
Rentola, K.: "Residenttimme ilmoittaa." Tiedustelun vaikutus Stalinin päätöksiin talvisodassa' (*Suomen historiallisen seuran ja Historiallisen Yhdistyksen luentotilaisuudessa*, 7 October 2002) http://www.ennenjanyt.net/4-02/rentola.htm
Rintala, P.: *Soldaternas röster om genombrottet på Karelska Näset 1944* (Stockholm, Bonnier 1967)

Roberts, E.: *Freedom, Faction, Fame and Blood – British Soldiers of Conscience in Greece, Spain and Finland* (Sussex Academic Press 2009)
Roselius, A: *Isänmaallinen kevät – Vapaussotamyytin alkulähteillä* (Helsinki, Tammi 2013)
Rosenqvist, G.O.: *Från hårda år – Indtryck och upplevelser från Finland 1939–1944* (Uppsala, J.A. Lindblads Förlag 1946)
Rystad, G.: 'Porkkala – Hankö – Aaland: A contribution to the history of the Finnish-Russian cease-fire negotiations, September 1944' (in *Scandia, Tidsskrift för historisk forskning* Vol. 34:1 1968 pp. 1–23)
Rysti, T.: *The Miracle of Ihantala – The Battle of Tali-Ihantala Summer 1944*, (Video, AV Caesar Oi & Tykkimiehet Ry, YLE, 2001)
Sandström, S.: *Fortsättningskriget 1941–1944* (Örebro, Bokförlaget Libris 1991)
Seppälä, H.: *Suomi hyökkääjänä 1941* (Helsingfors, WSOY 1984)
Silvennoinen, O.: 'Limits of Accountability' (in Kinnunen/Kivimäki)
Simelius, S.: 'How aware was the Finnish press about the persecution of Jews during the years 1938–1942, and what was its approach to the Jewish Question in Finland?' http://www.aka.fi/Tiedostot/Tiedostot/Viksu/Satu%20Simeliuksen%20ty%C3%B6.pdf
Sode-Madsen, H.: 'Den finske Lappobevægelse 1929–1932' (in *Scandia, Tidsskrift för historisk forskning* vol. 36:2 1970, p. 203–248)
Suhonen, V.: *Jäämarssi* (Film documentary, Yle TV2, programme broadcast first time 2 October 2011)
Sørensen, S.: *Vinterkrigen i Finland 1939–40* (København, C.A. Reitzels Forlag 1990)
Sørensen, S.: 'Krigsdræbte danske deltagere i Finland 1918' (in Westerlund, 2004)
Talvela, P.: *Muistelmat 1 – Sotilaan elämä* (Helsinki, Kirjayhtymä 1976)
Tarkka, J. & Tiitta, A.: *Itsenäinen Suomi – 90 vuotta kansakunnan elämästä* (Helsinki, Otava 2007)
Trotter, W.R.: *Frozen Hell – The Russo-Finnish Winter War of 1939–40* (Chapel Hill, North Carolina, Algonquin Books 1991)
Tuomioja, E.: *Häivähdys punaista – Hella Wuolijoki ja hänen sisarensa Salme Pekkala vallankumouksen palveluksessa* (Helsingfors, Tammi 2006)
Turtola, M.: 'Ryti, Risto (1889–1956). President of Finland.' http://www.kansallisbiografia.fi/english/?id=630
Tuunainen, P.: 'The Finnish Army at War' (in Kinnunen/Kivimäki)
Tuuri, A.: *Vinterkrigen* (novel, Copenhagen, Hekla 1984)
Törmä, K.: *Läpi vesiperäisten niittyjen – Sotilaallinen maastotiedustelu Karjalan kannaksella 1918–1939* (Pro gradu, University of Jyväskylä 2000)

Ulrich, J.: *Døden har vinger – En dansk flyvers beretning om krigen i Finland* (Copenhagen, Schønberg 1941)
United States, Department of State, Historical Office, Bureau of Public Affairs: *The Conferences at Cairo and Tehran 1943* (Washington, United States Government Printing Office 1961)
Upton, A.: 'History and national identity – Some Finnish examples' (in *Studia Fennica Ethnologica* No. 6 1999, pp. 153–165)
Vehviläinen, O.: *Finland in the Second World War – Between Germany and Russia* (Chippenham, Wiltshire: Anthony Rowe Ltd 2002)
Vercamer, A.L.: 'Naval War in the Baltic Sea 1941–1945' http://www.feldgrau.com/baltsea.html
Vilhaväinen, J.: 'A History of the Finnish Civil Guard' http://www. mosinnagant.net/finland/thecivilguardoffinland.asp
Vuorenmaa, A. 'Den sovjetiska krigsmagten 1941' (in Ekberg bd. II)
Wallenius, K.O.: *Tjugofyran – Infanteriregement 24:s Historia i Kriget 1941–1944* (Helsingfors, Shildt 1974)
Welle-Strand, E.: 'Amatørkrigen i Finland' (i *Gads Danske Magasin,* pp. 515–537, 1918)
Westerlund, L. (red.): *Norden och krigen i Finland och baltikum 1918–19* (Helsingfors, Statsrådets kanslis publikationsserie 2004)
Westerlund, L.: *Sotavangit ja internoidut* (Helsinki, Finnish National Archives 2008)
Westerlund, L.: *Children of Foreign Soldiers in Finland 1940–1948 Vol. 1* (Helsinki, Finnish National Archives 2011)
Westerlund, L. (ed. and contributor): *Children of Foreign Soldiers in Finland 1940–1948 Vol. II* (Helsinki, Finnish National Archives 2011)
Ziemke, E.: *German Northern Theatre of Operations 1940–1945* (Washington D.C., Department of the Army Headquarters 1959)
Zetterberg, S. (red.): *Suomen historian pikkujättiläinen* (Helsinki, WSOY 1987)

Maps

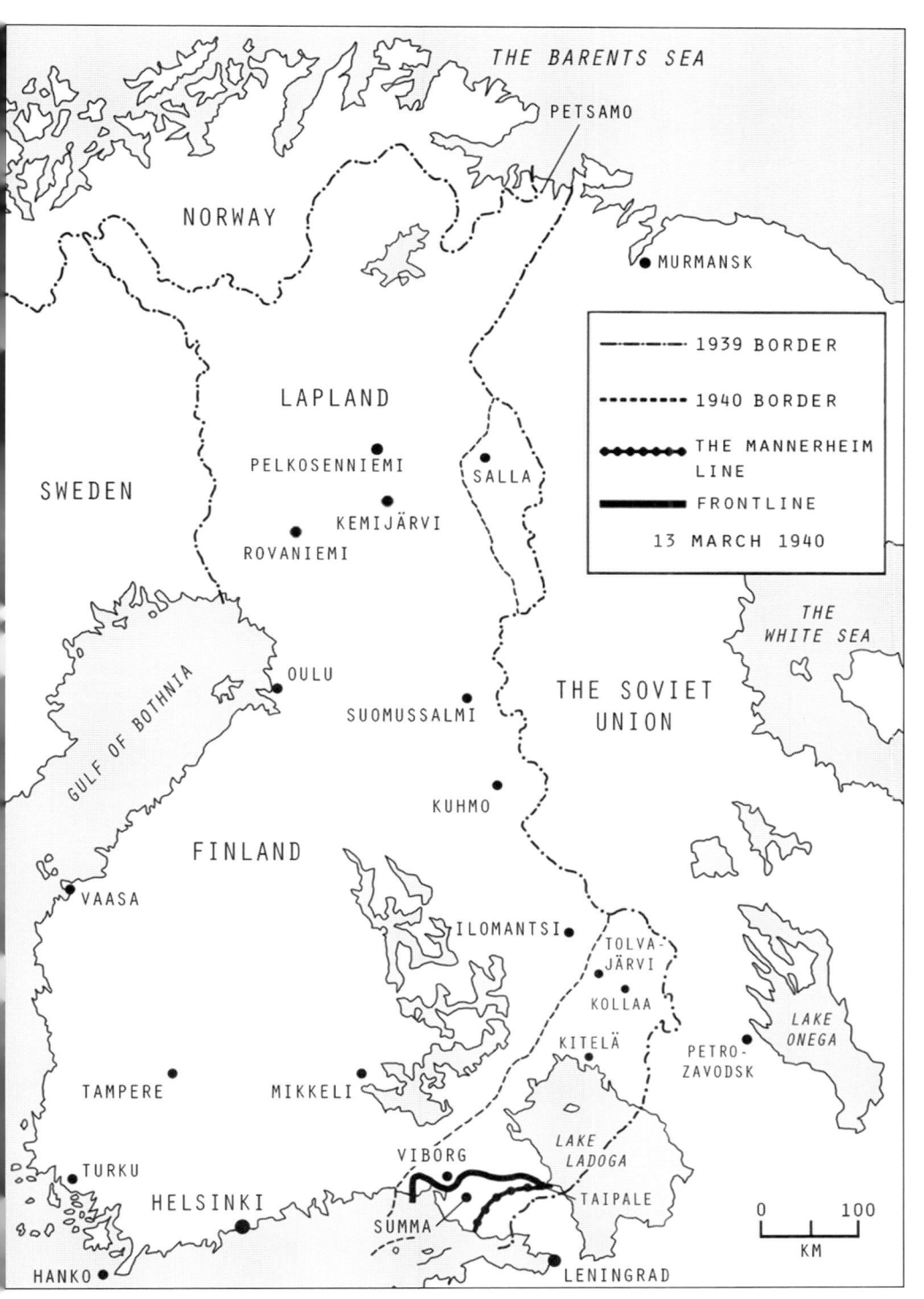

Map 1. Finland during the Winter War.

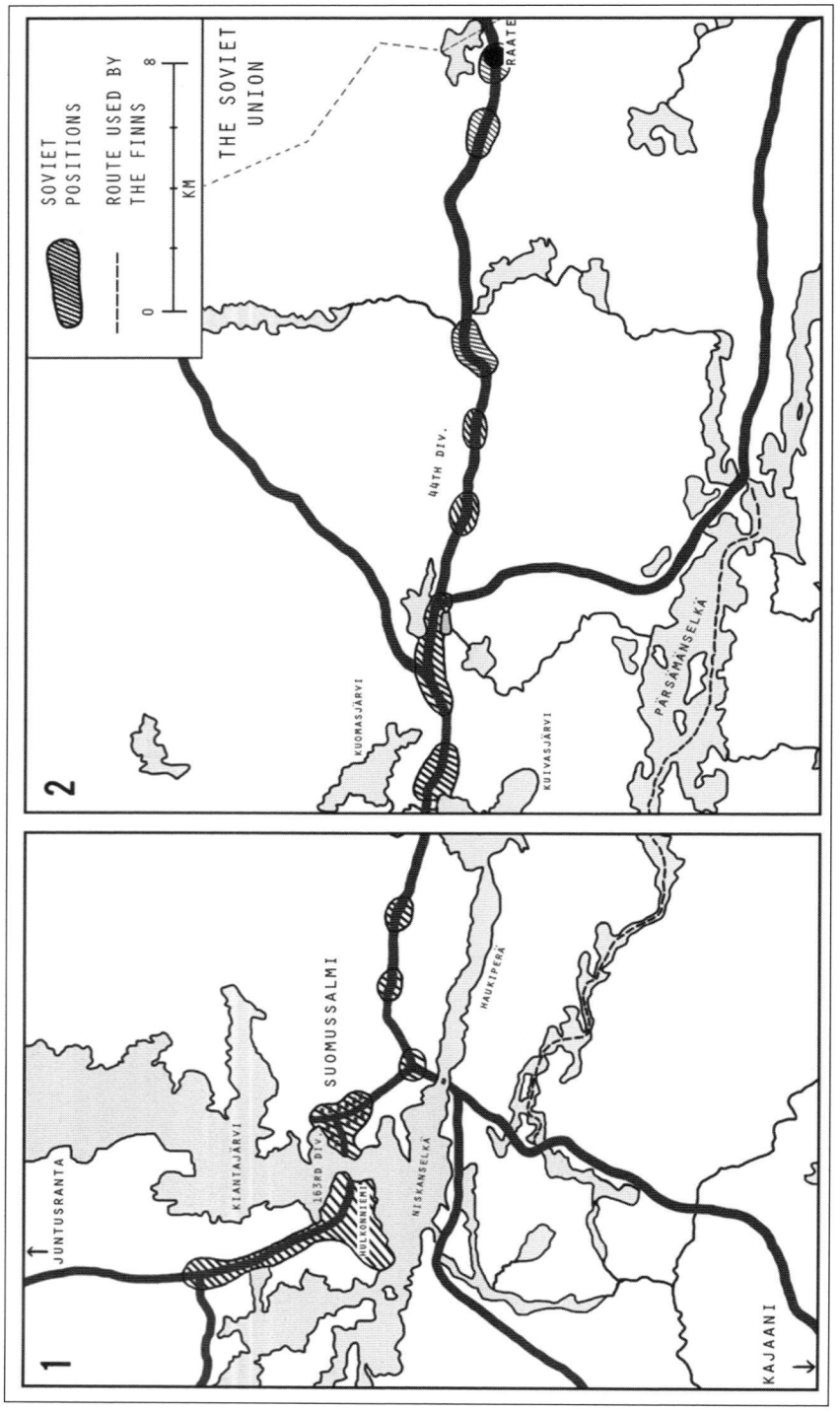

Map 2. (1) The Battle of Suomussalmi, December 1939. (2) The Battle of the Raate Road in early January 1940.

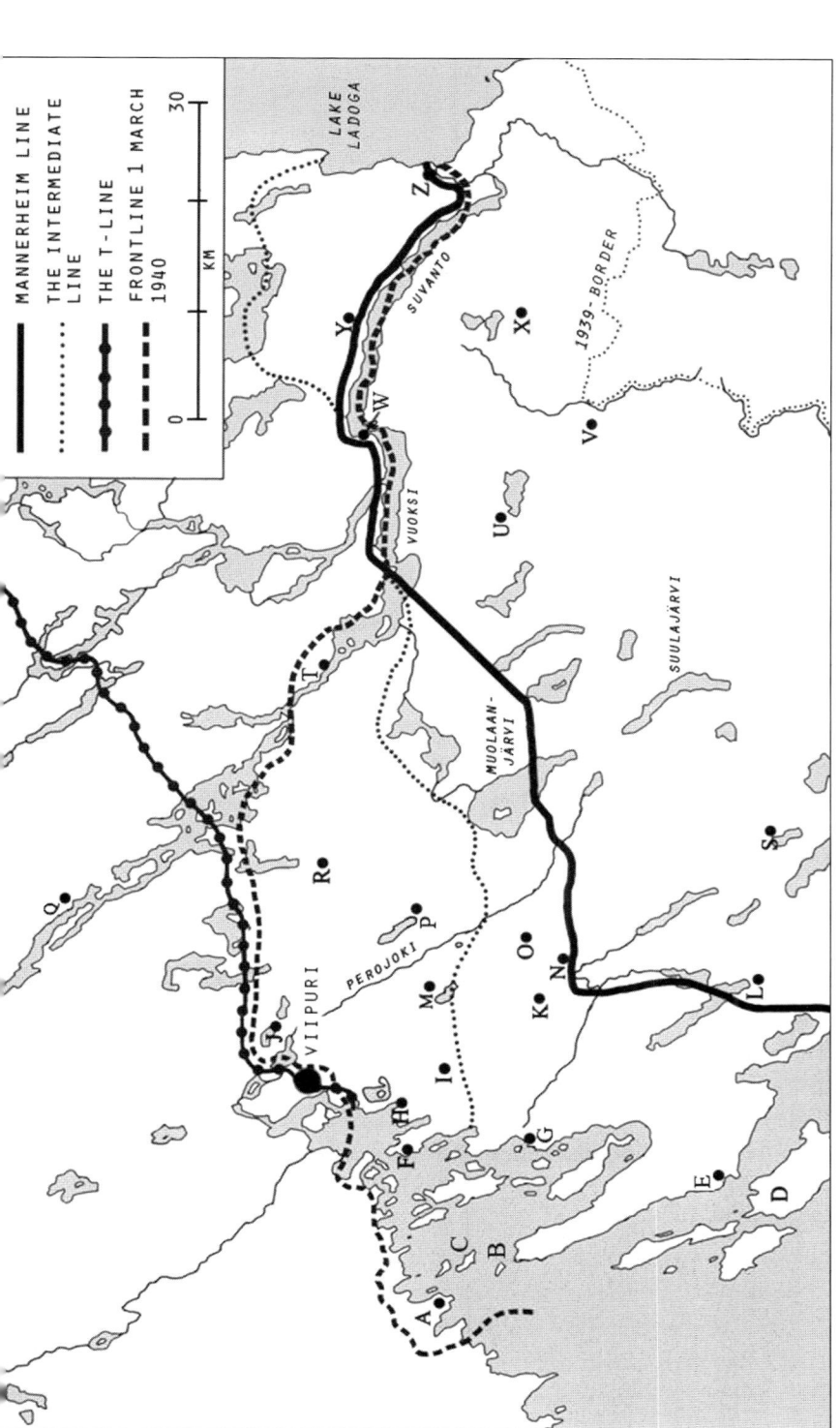

Map 3. The Karelian Isthmus during the Winter War with the most important place names:
A) Vilaniemi, B) Tuppurasaari, C) Teikarinsaari, D) Koivisto (island), E) Koivisto (fort), F) Lihaniemi, G) Johannes, H) Nuoraa, I) Ylä-Sommee, J) Tali, K) Suokama, L) Kuolemajärvi, M) Honkaniemi, N) Lähde, O) Kämärä (village), P) Kämärä (lake), Q) Antrea, R) Heinjoki, S) Uusikirkko, T) Vuosalmi, U) Valkjärvi, V) Lipola, W) Kiviniemi, X) Rautu, Y) Sakkola, Z) Taipala

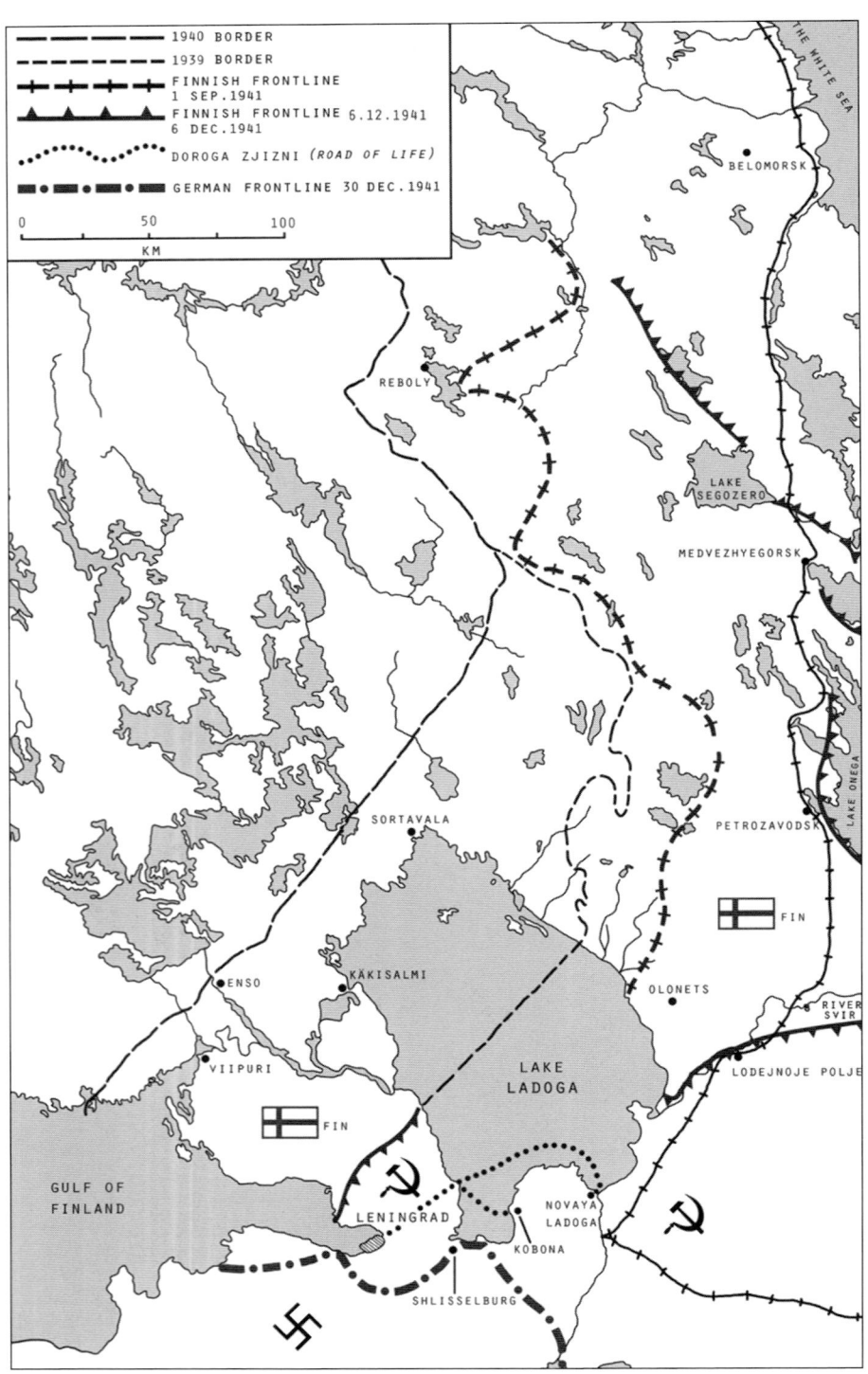

Map 4. The Continuation War 1941-1944. Borders, frontlines etc.

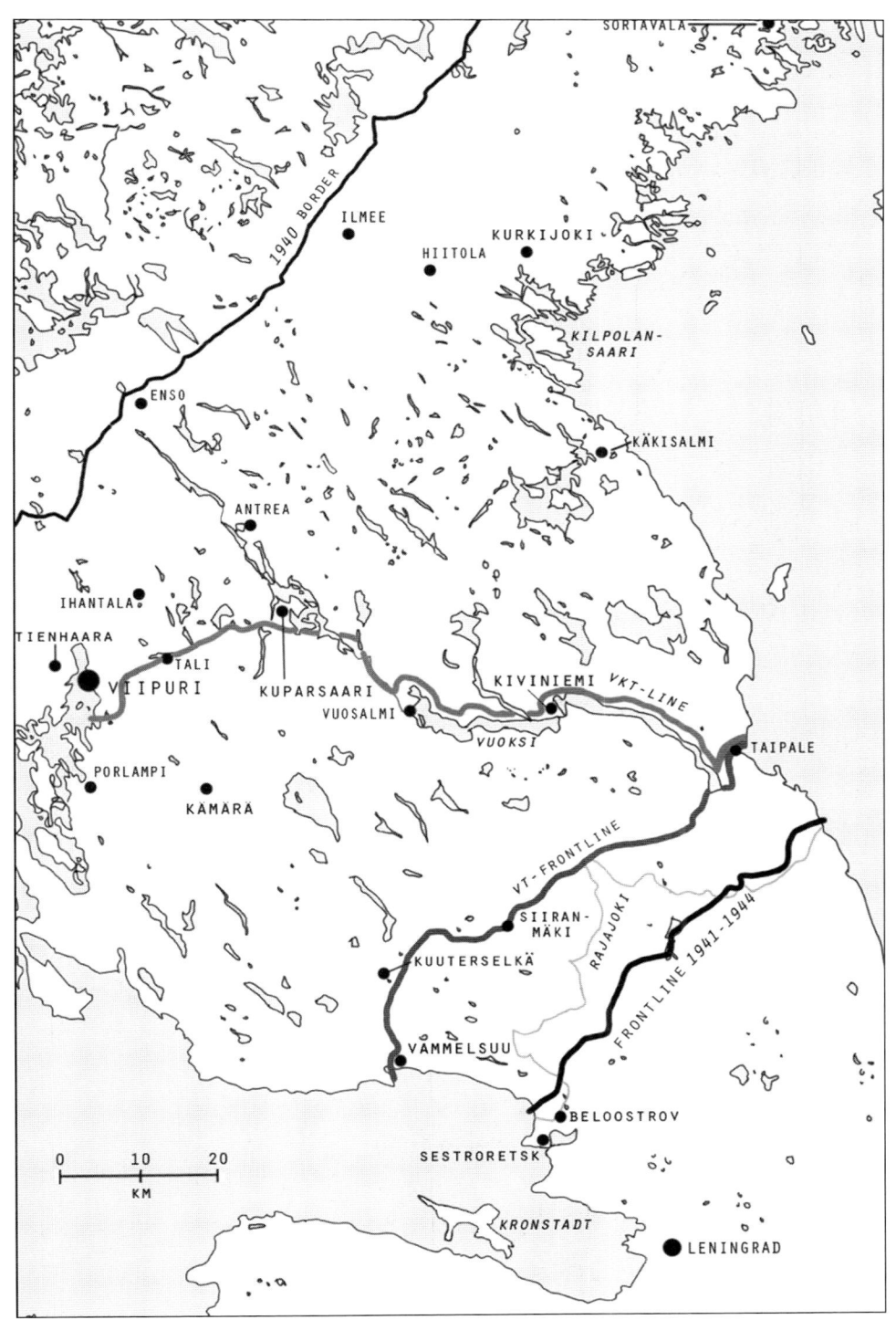

Map 5. The Karelian Isthmus during the Continuation War with the most important place names, defence lines etc.

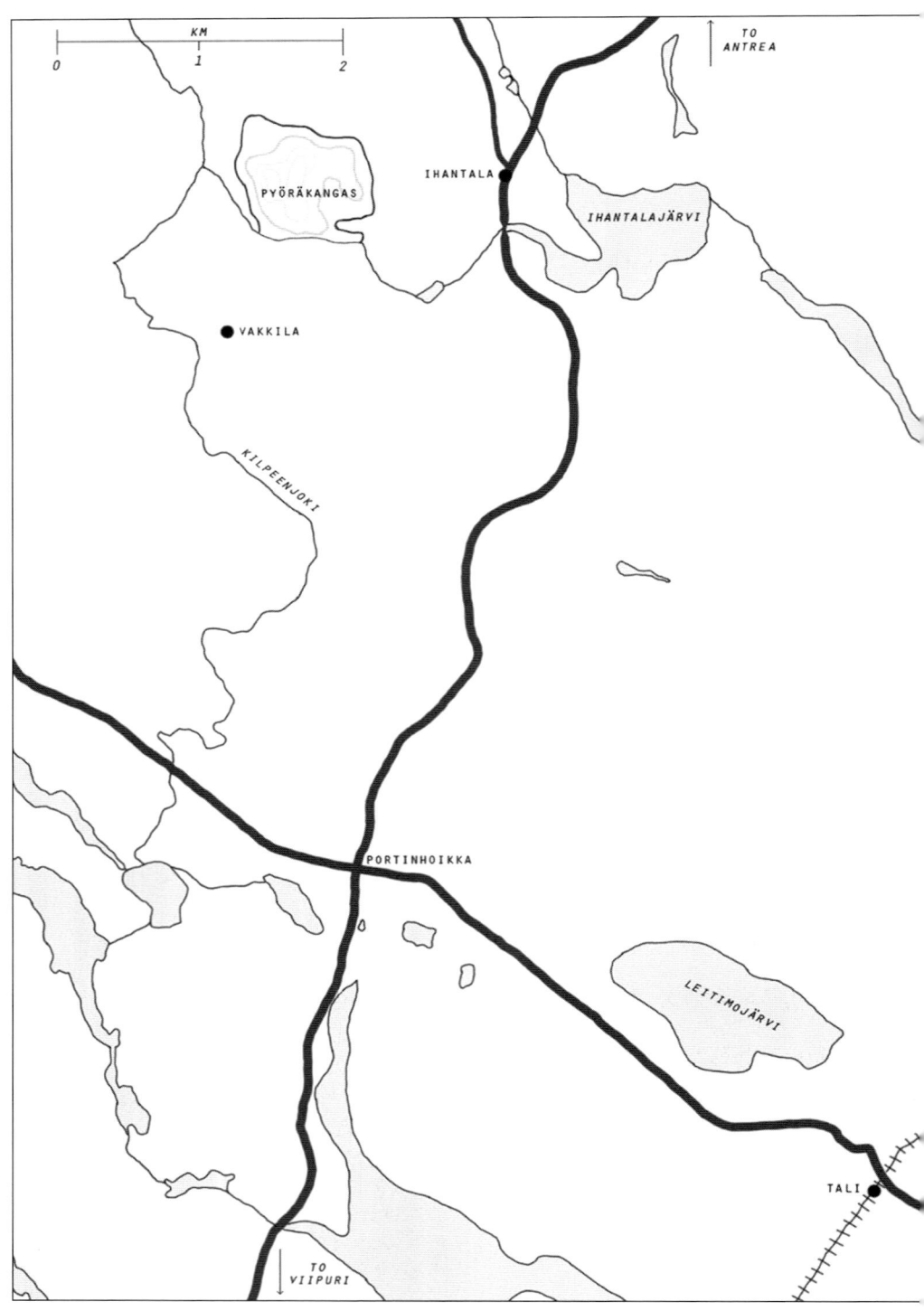

Map 6. The area around Tali and Ihantala northeast of Viipuri on the Karelian Isthmus.

Index

Airo, Aksel F., 154, 171
Alksnis, Yakov, 26
Apunen, Osmo, 268, 337, 342
Assarsson, Vilhelm, 103, 149, 156, 332-3
Auer, Väinö, 170
Autti, Pietari A., 325

Beliaev, Nikolai, 57
Bergstrom, Gunnar, 199
Björkman, Sven, 287, 325
Blavatsky, Helena, 213
Blick, Aarne, 187, 189, 190, 193
Blücher, Wilpert von, 90, 126, 182, 281, 283, 298
Boheman, Erik, 267-8, 380
Bondarev, Andrey, 189
Bormann, Martin, 172
Born, Ernst von, 131
Buschenhagen, Erich, 152-4, 160

Cajander, Aimo K., 5
Castrén, Reino, 228
Cherepanov, Alexander I., 321, 324

Dietl, Eduard, 135, 182, 184-5

Ehrnrooth, Adolf, 280
Enckell, Carl, 270, 298-9
Engel, Gerhard, 149, 151, 172, 332, 334, 343
Engelbrecht, Erwin, 188-9, 202
Erfurth, Waldemar, 158, 160, 163, 278, 333
Ericsson, M.G., 97

Erkko, Juho E., 4, 5, 7, 10, 12-15, 21-2
Erwe, Tor-Oskar, 286

Fagerholm, Karl-August, 131
Falkenhorst, Nikolaus von, 102, 155, 184
Feige, Hans, 184, 186
Filippova, Raisa, 228
Fingerroos, Outi, 213-14, 219, 335, 343

Gladyshev, Stepan T., 57
Golovko, Arseniy, 326
Göring, Hermann, 112, 135
Govorov, Leonid, 273-4, 279, 284, 324
Greiner, Helmuth, 151
Gripenberg, Georg A., 124, 161, 298
Gusev, Dmitrii, 324
Gudme, Peter de Hemmer, 29, 65, 67, 79, 114, 337, 329, 330, 343
Günther, Christian, 92, 103

Haavio, Elsa, 343
Haavio, Martti, 230, 343
Hackzell, Antti, 298-9
Hägglund, Woldemar, 54-5, 84, 187, 189, 202, 314, 318, 347
Halder, Franz, 141, 146-7, 151
Hansson, Per Albin, 70, 103, 125
Hanterä, Lauri, 325
Harriman, William A., 338
Heinilä, Harri, 253, 337, 343

Heiskanen, Kaarlo, 325
Hersalo, Niilo, 193
Himmler, Heinrich, 135, 240
Hitler, Adolf, xiii, xi, xii, 3, 4, 9, 90, 122, 127, 133-5, 137, 140-2, 144, 149, 151-2, 155, 167, 172-36, 175, 181, 185, 207, 214, 217, 220, 246-7, 249, 250, 265, 270, 283, 304, 323, 333, 346
Holsti, Rudolf, 3, 4
Hölter, Hermann, 150
Hynninen, Paavo, 156

Jaakkola, Jalmari, 171
Jakobson, Max, 14, 328, 330
Janarmo, K.W., 71,
Jodl, Alfred, 150, 154,
Jokipii, Mauno, 123, 149, 150, 153, 158-9, 161, 165, 168-9, 174, 331-4, 344
Jokisipilä, Markku, xiv, 342, 345
Jonas, M., xiv, 15, 16, 164, 248, 328, 331, 333-4, 336-7, 344
Julkunen, Matti, 65
Jutikkala, Eino, 170

Kallio, Kyösti, 41, 69, 136, 145
Kalm, Hans, 236, 336
Karjalainen, Mikko, 207, 344
Keitel, Wilhelm, 203, 298
Kemppainen, Ilona, 77, 330
Kemppi, Armas, 280
Keskinen, Lauri, 52
Khruschev, Nikita, 3, 7, 9, 20, 115, 328, 331, 345
Kirpichnikov, Vladimir V., 199
Kivimäki, Toivo, 112, 145, 156, 174, 298, 307
Kivimäki, Ville, xiv, 166, 254, 331, 333, 343-48
Kollontai, Alexandra, 91-2, 220, 267-271, 281-2, 297, 298, 338

Kondrashev, Grigorii F.K., 84-5
Kordelin, Alfred, 174
Korhonen, Arvi, 171, 375
Korovnikov, Ivan, 324
Koskimies, Eino, 187
Krutskikh, Dmitrii, 191
Kuhlmey, Kurt, 294, 291, 325
Kujala, Antti, 236, 336
Kukkonen, Antti, 307
Kuusinen, Otto, 27, 42
Kuussaari, Reino, 228

Laatikainen, Taavetti, 192, 289, 318, 322, 324-5
Laine, Antti, 232, 234, 331, 335-6, 345
Lagus, Ruben, 205, 325
Lehmus, Kalle, 176
Leino, Yrjö, 309
Linkomies, Edwin, 265, 307, 337
Linna, Väinö, 121, 177, 181, 250-2, 331, 334, 337, 346
Lönroth, Elias, 212
Lukinov, Mikhail, 95, 330
Luukkanen, Eino, 198, 334, 346

Magnusson, E., 325
Makeyev, Lenin, 230
Mäkinen, Einar, 322
Mäkinen, Ilkka, 335, 346
Malmi, Timo, 239, 336, 346
Mannerheim, Carl G.E., vi, x, xii, 6, 12, 13, 16-18, 20-2, 24, 30, 33-7, 41-8, 51-2, 54, 65, 75, 82-3, 91, 94-8, 101-103, 105, 110, 112, 119, 122, 124-5, 127, 134-6, 145, 147, 149, 153, 155, 156, 158-63, 167, 170, 172-4, 182-3, 185-87, 189, 197, 201, 203-04, 211-12, 214-16, 218, 220-2, 228, 233, 237, 242, 246-8, 264, 267-8, 270-1, 275, 278-81, 283-4, 295,

297-8, 305-07, 309, 316, 320, 331-2, 334, 343-4, 346-7
Manninen, Ohto, 127, 144, 159, 273, 312, 317, 331-5, 337-9, 346
Meinander, Henrik, 16, 29, 112, 156, 170, 222, 242, 266, 269, 328, 331, 333-8, 346
Meretskov, Kirill, 143, 272, 326, 330, 346
Mikhailov, Vladimir, 232
Mollberg, Rauni, 251
Molotov, Vjatjeslav, viii, 6-8, 10, 11-14, 16-22, 27, 35, 50, 74, 90, 93, 103, 112-13, 119-20, 126, 131, 137-145, 175, 247, 266, 299, 306, 328, 331, 342

Nielsen, Jan A., 337, 346-7
Nicholas II, 30
Niukkanen, Juho, 14, 41, 124
Nordgren, Valter, 197
Nordström, Ragnar, 174, 228
Norris, John, 339, 347
Nyman, Arvi, 239

Oesch, Lennart, 105, 192, 195-6, 236, 279, 289, 316, 138, 324
Öhquist, Harald, 37, 51-2, 98, 110, 314, 316
Oinonen, Woldemar, 187-8, 318
Orlov, Pavel, 155

Paalu, Paavo, 288, 325
Paasikivi, Juho K., 2, 10, 13-14, 17, 21-22, 24, 41, 91, 102, 112, 128, 130-1, 145, 153, 155-6, 175, 212, 264, 269-70, 297, 308, 310, 328, 330-1, 337, 347
Pajari, Aaro, 55, 193, 195,197, 278-9
Palolampi, Erkki, 53, 329, 347
Pekkala, Mauno, 221

Pennanen, Antti, 53,184, 319
Pimiä, Tenho, xiv, 333-5, 347
Pipping, Knut, 242, 251, 334, 336-7, 347
Procopé, Hjalmar, 220, 281
Puroma, Albert, 325

Quisling, Vidkun, 265, 295

Raappana, Erkki, 295, 318, 322
Ramsay, Henrik, 265, 307
Rangell, Johan W., 125, 145, 153, 159, 161, 174, 240, 246, 265, 307
Reinikka, Tyko, 307
Reitz, Wilhelm, 135
Rentola, Kimmo, 297-8, 331, 338, 347
Ribbentrop, Joachim von, 8, 16, 20, 74, 90, 134, 137-9, 143, 265, 281-3, 295, 298
Rogozin, Claudia, 233
Rybkin, Boris (alias Boris Yartsev), 3
Ryti, Risto, vi, 41, 102, 112, 118, 122, 124-5, 127, 131, 134-6, 145-6, 153, 158-9, 161, 163, 168, 170-1, 173-6, 215, 218-20, 233, 246-7, 264-5, 270-1, 281-3, 295, 297-8, 307, 323, 333-4, 348

Saarinen, Eliel, 198
Sandström, Allan, 265, 320, 334, 337, 348
Sarko, O., 325
Schalburg, Chr. F. von, 72
Scherer, Fritz, 325
Schnurre, Karl, 127
Schulenburg, Friedrich-Werner Graf von der, 142
Seidel, Hans-Georg von, 153
Semyonov, Vladimir S., 120

Shaposhnikov, Boris, 243
Shoenfeld, Arthur, 125
Sihvo, Aarne, 193, 195
Siilasvuo, Hjalmar, 60-3, 88, 135, 153, 159, 186, 221, 305, 318, 322, 324
Silvennoinen, Oula, 233, 237, 336, 348
Simonyak, Nikolai, 324
Sivén, Hans H.C. (alias Bobi), 214
Snellman, Otto G., 288, 325
Stalin, Josef, viii, 6, 8, 9, 11-14, 17-22, 24, 26-7, 93-4, 120, 137, 143-4, 155, 164, 175, 202, 214, 218, 221, 264, 267-8, 272, 276, 297, 328, 333, 338, 345, 347
Steinhardt, Laurence, 113
Suhonen, Ville, 336, 348
Sundman, Svante, 160
Svensson, Antero, 293, 322, 324
Svinhufvud, Pehr E., 145

Talvela, Paavo, 54-5, 131, 146-7, 150, 162, 174, 187, 189, 202, 205-06, 212, 219, 249, 259, 265, 295, 307, 318, 332, 348
Tanner, Väinö, 2, 3, 14, 17, 21-2, 24, 41, 90-2, 102-03, 113, 124-5, 131, 145-6, 159, 175, 218-19, 221, 282, 297, 307
Tapola, Kustaa, 154, 160, 322
Tarkka, Jukka, 332, 348
Tiiainen, Matti, 197, 200
Tiili, Kauko, 100
Timoshenko, Semyon, 83, 95, 143
Tukhachevsky, Mikhail, 25-6

Tuomioja, Erkki, 348
Tuompo, Viljo E., 314
Tuuri, Antti, 329, 348

Ulrich, Jörn J., 71-3, 329, 349

Vehvilainen, Olli, 128, 184, 204, 217-18, 328, 331-2, 334-5, 337, 349
Veltjens, Joseph, 135-6
Vihma, Einar, 325
Viljanen, Tauno, 276
Volkov, Viktor, 232
Voroshilov, Kliment J., 27, 83, 297, 318
Vostryakovo, Alexander, 231

Walden, Rudolf, 112, 124-5, 135, 156, 158-9, 161, 174-5, 215, 235, 298
Wallenius, Martti, 65, 68, 105, 316
Weissauer, Ludwig, 134
Westerlund, Lars, 69, 232, 236-7, 264, 329, 335-8, 345, 348-9
Wirtanen, Atos, 270
With, Erik, 257
Wolff, Corinna, 268, 337, 342
Wuolijoki, Hella, 91-2, 348

Yartsev, Boris (alias Boris Rybkin), 3-5, 7, 310, 359

Ziemke, Earl M., 169, 185, 285, 327, 333-6, 338, 349
Zotov, Ivan, 131, 155